EVERYDAY TRANSGRESSIONS

EVERYDAY TRANSGRESSIONS

DOMESTIC WORKERS' TRANSNATIONAL CHALLENGE TO INTERNATIONAL LABOR LAW

ADELLE BLACKETT

ILR PRESS

AN IMPRINT OF CORNELL UNIVERSITY PRESS

Ithaca and London

First published 2019 by Cornell University Press

Library of Congress Cataloging-in-Publication Data

Names: Blackett, Adelle, 1967– author.
    Title: Everyday transgressions : domestic workers'
transnational challenge to international labor law / Adelle
Blackett.
    Description: Ithaca [New York] : ILR Press, an imprint
of Cornell University Press, 2019. | Includes bibliographi-
cal references and index.
    Identifiers: LCCN 2018044260 (print) | LCCN
2018045317 (ebook) | ISBN 9781501715778 (pdf) |
ISBN 9781501715761 (epub/mobi) |ISBN 9781501736315
(cloth; alk. paper) | ISBN 9781501715754 (pbk.)
    Subjects: LCSH: Household employees—Legal status,
laws, etc. | Labor laws and legislation, International. |
Foreign workers—Legal status, laws, etc.
    Classification: LCC K1841.H68 (ebook) | LCC K1841.
H68 B53 2019 (print) | DDC 344.01—dc23
    LC record available at https://lccn.loc.gov/2018044260

For Mom,
With respect and gratitude

Contents

ACKNOWLEDGMENTS

This book is not the book I thought it would be ten years ago when I started the standard-setting process at the ILO. I acknowledge the many colleagues who welcomed and nourished my commitment to this topic from the start of my affiliation with the ILO in 1993—in particular, Anne Trebilcock, Shauna Olney, Zafar Shaheed, Edward Yemin, and Mary Hamouda. I thank Manuela Tomei for immediately recognizing the significance of the standard-setting process in 2008, and entrusting me with the drafting of the ILO's Law and Practice Report ("Report IV(1)"). I also thank Cleo Doumbia-Henry, who tutored me in the standard-setting process as soon as I was appointed. It was an honor to work with the many international labor officials who contributed in a myriad of important ways to the success of the ILO standard-setting process. Throughout the process, I interacted with representatives of a number of other international organizations and independent experts of the Office of the United Nations High Commissioner for Human Rights, including those affiliated with the Women in Informal Employment: Globalizing and Organizing (WIEGO) network and Human Rights Watch, who contributed significantly to the overall process.

I thank the Fondation du Barreau du Québec, which not only provided start-up funding for me to pursue comparative law research on citizenship at work for domestic workers, focusing on collective bargaining and compliance simplification mechanisms such as service checks in France, but also generously agreed that my own publications on this topic would be deferred so that I could contribute both time and the fruit of that research to the ILO in support of the standard-setting process.

Gregor Murray, director of the Interuniversity Research Centre on Globalization and Work (CRIMT), and his colleagues supported the International Seminar on Decent Work for Domestic Workers, funded by the Government of Canada as part of the International and Comparative Dialogue Celebrating the ILO at 90 and Preparing for Standard-Setting into the Future, on March 29, 2010. Selected papers presented at the conference were published in a special issue of the *Canadian Journal of Women and the Law* in 2011.

I was grateful for the precious research time afforded by the Social Science and Humanities Research Council's 2010 Bora Laskin National Fellowship in Human Rights Research, which enabled me to think through the relationship between human rights, legal pluralism, and relative power. The International Development Research Centre provided a small grant for research innovation, which enabled me to meet with social and institutional actors in South Africa, Côte d'Ivoire, and Kenya. Support to finalize the book has come from my appointment as Canada Research Chair in Transnational Labour Law and Development. In each of these contexts I worked with teams of researchers, and I wish to thank especially Evance Kalula from the University of Cape Town, Fairuz Mullagee and Darcy du Toit from the University of Western Cape, Assata Koné-Silué from Université Houphouët Boigny in Côte d'Ivoire, Lyn Ossome from the Makerere Institute of Social Research, and Dzodzi Tsikata from the University of Ghana in Legon. Interviewees in Côte d'Ivoire, France, Kenya, South Africa, and Switzerland were extremely generous with their time and insights. I am grateful to them all.

Many colleagues invited me to present portions of this work while it was in progress and offered comments or encouragement along the way. They include Gay McDougall (Office of the High Commissioner for Human Rights' Forum on Minority Issues, 2010); Judy Fudge, Shae McCrystal, and Kamala Sankaran (Oñati Institute for the Sociology of Law, 2010); Kim Rubenstein (University of Canberra, 2011); Ron McCallum (University of Sydney, 2011); John Howe (University of Melbourne, 2011); Evelyn Calugay and Fo Niemi (Filipino Women's Organization in Quebec, PINAY, and the Center for Research-Action on Race Relations, 2012); Valerie Oosterveld (Canadian Council on International Law, 2012); Chrysal Kenoukon (Université D'Abomey Calavi, 2013); Katherine Lahey and Bita Amani (Queen's University, Ontario, 2014); Julia López and Chelo Chacartegui (Pompeu Fabra University, 2014); Evance Kalula and Rochelle LeRoux (University of Cape Town, 2014); Darcy DuToit and Fairuz Mullagee (University of Western Cape, 2015); Peggie Smith and Angela Onwuachi-Willig (Lutie Lytle Workshop at Vanderbilt University, 2015); Elsa Gallerand and Martin Gallié (Université du Québec à Montréal, 2015); Kerry Rittich and Jennifer Nedelsky (University of Toronto, 2015); Pierre-Paul Van Gehuchten, Pascale Vielle, Marthe Nyssens, and Olivier de Schutter (Université de Louvain, 2015); Claire Thompson (International Development Research Centre, 2016); Lorena Poblete (Princeton University, 2016); Diamond Ashiagbor (University of London, 2016); and Marty Chen and WIEGO (Harvard University, 2017). Many other colleagues offered detailed comments on my work. They include Harry Arthurs, Eileen Boris, Michael Fischl, Guy Mundlak, Jim Pope, Peggie Smith, Anne Trebilcock, and Lea VanderVelde. The Labour Law Research Network and the annual meetings of the Law and Society Association have been prime sites for critical feedback throughout the writing of this book and encouragement to stick with the project. This book is stronger because I had these occasions to interact and exchange ideas with colleagues.

I am also grateful to my deans at the Faculty of Law at McGill University, who accommodated me in my role of providing academic expertise to the ILO on standard setting for decent work for domestic workers and my research for this book. My sabbatical in 2014–15 was a decisive time that enabled me to consolidate much of my writing, but it was the support of the Canada Research Chair in Transnational Labour Law and Development that made completion possible. Writing retreats at the Monastère des Augustines in Quebec City provided the space and calm necessary to bring this book to fruition. At McGill I also thank Catherine LeGrand, Colleen Sheppard, François Crépeau, Vrinda Narain, Alana Klein, and Tina Piper for their support.

I worked with tremendous teams of undergraduate and graduate student research assistants over the decade that this book was in progress, as well as during the standard setting. I live in fear of forgetting someone, as they were all formidable. Several are mentioned throughout this book and in other related publications. In alphabetical order, they include Michael Blashko, Amina Chaouni, Maude Choko, Sarah Goldbaum, Tatiana Gómez, Renz Grospe, Alika Hendricks, Katie Kaufman, Aurélie Lanctôt, Sydney Lang, Alice Mirlesse, Mae Nam, Marion Rebière, Marie-Alice Remarais, Cassandra Richards, and Marion Sandilands.

Fran Benson of the ILR Press imprint of Cornell University Press was an early believer in this book. Her support kept me focused not only on completing the book, but also on keeping it accessible. This book has also benefited from the editorial skills and insights of Erin Davis and the team at Westchester Publishing, as well as McGill law student Talia Ralph, who as a food industry journalist shares my passion for cookbooks.

I owe a debt of gratitude to my partner, Aristide Nononsi, and children, Jean-Richard and Baï Daisy, who have also spent a decade living with this book. Baï Daisy would sit beside me as I was drafting it, and draw pictures like the one reproduced below (figure 1). My family have all been gracious about it and have been making some of those recipes I have been writing about.

Finally, I am grateful to Evelyn Mondonedo Calugay and the committed community supporting domestic workers at PINAY in Montreal; Myrtle

FIGURE 1.   Portrait of the artist and her mother. Credit: Baï Daisy Nononsi.

Witbooi and the movement of domestic workers at the International Domestic Workers' Federation; and, of course, Muriel Blackett and Lucien Smith. Their courage and conviction on social justice for domestic workers sustains this work.

Montreal, January 5, 2018

EVERYDAY TRANSGRESSIONS

Introduction
Who Cares?

> So often we overlook the work and the significance of
> those who are not in professional jobs, of those who
> are not in the so-called big jobs. But let me say to you
> tonight, that whenever you are engaged in work that
> serves humanity and is for the building of humanity, it
> has dignity, and it has worth. One day our society must
> come to see this.
>
> —Rev. Dr. Martin Luther King Jr., *All Labor Has
> Dignity*, 171.

In late March 2008, I got an urgent call from the
United Nations' specialized agency on labor, the International Labour Organization (ILO). To the surprise of many observers, the ILO's Governing Body
had just adopted a resolution requiring it to prepare to negotiate a new international treaty on decent work for domestic workers.[1] The international official who would become the representative of the Secretary-General in the
standard-setting process and carry the heavy political agenda, Manuela Tomei,
asked me to serve as the ILO's lead expert.

There was a ton of work to do. As soon as my teaching term ended, I promised my children that I would be back soon and would bring them chocolate,
then boarded a plane to Geneva. It was not lost on me that most domestic
workers who leave their children behind to work for someone else cannot
promise to come home soon and bring chocolate.

As the people who care for others, domestic workers are accustomed to
not being really seen or heard. Historical accounts remind us of the link to
domestic slavery and colonial servitude and of the persisting vestiges found
in the so-called common sense of the status-based relationship of the master
and the servant.[2] Many poignant sociological accounts of domestic work in
postcolonial or postapartheid states emphasize domestic workers' invisibility,
even as they perform the hard and dirty work associated with social reproduction.[3] The political economy literature stresses the extent to which domestic

workers—often highly educated and with care responsibilities of their own—leave family and home to travel abroad to provide care.[4] These works capture the extent to which this traditionally feminized labor remains economically and socially undervalued.

No one captures this point better than domestic workers themselves. Fatima Elayoubi, a domestic worker of Moroccan heritage living in Paris, wrote her book *Prière à la Lune* (Prayer to the moon) while recovering from a nervous breakdown. She consciously chooses to speak for "all the Fatimas who work in the shadows, alone, far from their families."[5] Elayoubi reminds us of the art in her backbreaking work:

> Many people do not understand what is art. I have always worked looking for the elegance in what I do. Even when I iron a shirt . . . I want to feel inside of me an aesthetic harmony. I iron shirts; I dust. I clean the world to admire the beauty and the cleanliness. This art, to which I have applied myself nine hours each day all these years, no one sees it. When I come back, the next day, I commence to suffer yet again in my body, and in my soul. . . .
>
> I am a woman who uses her body as her work tool. Nothing else is left.[6]

The fact that the magnitude of this staggering transnational care work has only recently been quantified is one more reminder of its invisibility. When standard setting got off the ground, the ILO's educated guess, based on the limited statistical sources available, was that there were 51–100 million domestic workers.[7] The ILO has since refined its numbers, finding that there are "at least 67 million" men and women in domestic work; one in every twenty-five women workers worldwide is a domestic worker.[8] Yet rather than improve the working conditions of domestic workers, there is a long history of countries relying on migration schemes to meet demands for affordable labor.[9] Women migrant workers make up approximately 50 percent of all migrants,[10] and a significant majority of those women are or become domestic workers.[11]

Domestic workers' contribution to the global economy has also been undervalued. In the contemporary economy, there is a growing demand for privatized care, as governments in the global North retreat from providing various forms of social protection. It is primarily women from the global South who migrate so that they can send remittances to support their own families in the absence of social protection in their home countries. Some people speak of global care chains; sociologist Rhacel Parreñas refers instead to care resource extraction, noting that the sending countries of the global South provide subsidized, often well-educated workers to the global North, which further enables the global North to build its markets on the backs of migrants from the global South.[12]

Contemporary transborder movement by domestic workers is a remittance-based strategy associated with a neoliberal approach to economic development that is anchored in temporary migration.[13] Domestic workers support families and whole communities back in their home countries on worldwide remittances that exceeded $575 billion in 2016, according to the World Bank. Of that amount, developing countries received approximately $429 billion. The true size of remittances—which far exceed official development assistance amounts—is considered to be significantly larger, if informal practices are taken into account.[14] But what are the costs?

Practices vary widely, of course, but the direst consequences for the workers and their own families can be devastating. Take the case of a destitute domestic worker named Lila Aacharya, who left her home in rural Nepal to perform domestic work in Lebanon. Her family lost all contact with her, until she came home just months later in a body bag.[15] She had been subjected to unspeakable abuse, apparently at the hands of her employer. Domestic workers show tremendous agency as they make hard decisions to travel around the world to work to support their families. Yet they are rendered invisible in private households and left to the mercy of individual employers.

While Lila's is a story of extreme abuse, it is anything but exceptional. Feminist political economy literature in particular has long scrutinized the claim that remittance-based policies foster development, focusing attention on the costs to states, communities, households, and the workers themselves, while some of the leading ethnographic research on domestic work has chronicled the extent of the abuse.[16] Extreme abuse coexists with the everyday undervaluing of domestic work that results in low pay and low status. Yet care work, as so many leading advocates for domestic workers affirm, is also at its most fundamental level what makes us human.[17] Decent work for domestic workers had to reject any starting assumption that care should come at the cost of rendering domestic workers—including domestic workers' own care needs—invisible.

Putting the ILO to the Test

In the process of international standard setting, domestic workers demanded recognition.[18] The ILO was founded in 1919, as part of the peace treaty that ended World War I. In the wake of revolution in Russia, it offered a liberal alternative. The first words of the ILO Constitution state that "universal and lasting peace can be established only if it is based on social justice." In 1944, near the end of World War II, the ILO reaffirmed that principle in an annex to the ILO Constitution, the Declaration of Philadelphia, adding that "labour is not a commodity."[19] The ILO has largely sought to achieve social justice by adopting international labor conventions and working with its 187 member states to ratify and implement them.

During its long life, the ILO has adopted many international labor standards: 190 conventions and 204 recommendations on a range of working conditions.[20] Whether or not a member state ratifies a convention, it can use the convention to inspire its own laws. Many international labor standards deal with basic issues that many people now think of as normal in a labor code: having a weekly day of rest and annual vacations with pay; securing protections against forced labor, child labor, and discrimination at work; and having social security benefits. But some of the conventions have not been widely ratified. For many workers in standard, relatively well-paying jobs in Western Europe and countries like Canada, the United States, Australia, and New Zealand in the era after World War II, these kinds of features could be taken for granted, although some countries did not ratify a lot of ILO conventions. They just became part of the workplace norms—the law of the shop—in sectors that epitomized standard industrialized jobs, as in auto manufacturing.

Domestic workers, in contrast, have never been able to take decent working conditions for granted, so having domestic work as the only standard-setting item placed on the agenda for the 2010 International Labour Conference by the ILO's Governing Body in 2008 was a sign of the times. Many an item has remained on the ILO Governing Body's agenda for years, and the ILO's factory of international labor standards had virtually ground to a halt by the 1990s, as ratifications slowed and standard setting itself was called into question.[21] The specter of the ill-fated attempt to adopt a convention and recommendation on contract labor a decade earlier hung over international officials' heads, and no one wanted to see a repeat. The ILO secretariat still seemed haunted by the too-close-for-comfort adoption of the Home Work Convention, 1996 (No. 177).[22] Although home work is close to domestic work as both tend to be performed by women in a household, home work is really the part of the work in global production chains that happens in the workers' homes, sometimes with children in the family helping stitch clothes together or make other products for sale to intermediaries, who then sell them to companies at home or abroad. Home work was actually much closer to the failed contract labor discussions than to domestic work, but both easily came to mind once domestic work came under consideration.

The ILO had repeatedly adopted international labor standards since 1919 on one of the world's first global industries, staffed by 1.2 million seafarers: the overwhelmingly male maritime industry.[23] The ILO had managed to make spectacular innovations in this field, despite a more generalized slowdown on standard setting. The Maritime Labour Convention of 2006 was backed by a significant industry lobby and the powerful International Maritime Organization. It is experimentalist and bold, but much about the way it was developed and framed made it a happy exception.[24]

That takes me back to 2008 and the reason I found myself in Geneva, contributing to international standard setting on decent work for domestic workers. Although the ILO was founded to improve working conditions, this was a thoroughly ubiquitous category of workers who seemed to fall outside of that promise altogether. The ILO had shifted its focus in 1999 to emphasize "decent work for all," so it was no longer good enough to say that domestic workers were not the kind of workers the ILO was meant to foreground.[25] Instead, their work was understood as absolutely essential to the functioning of modern market economies in which both women and men were to be included.

Those hedging their bets would have said a standard-setting item on domestic workers could not be approved. As if more reasons were needed, they argued that common sense seemed to militate against a specific new standard. Were domestic workers even real workers? They worked outside of the productive economy, which was the ILO's historical focus. They worked in private homes, where labor law seemed naturally to give way to family norms. They were like members of the family, so how could you even define the term? Moreover, there was little research about them. At that time, many countries did not even know how many domestic workers were trying to earn a living within their own borders. Domestic workers' labor could barely be regulated, so few states had tried. There were also concerns that regulation might cause massive unemployment in this sector, and in any event, households could not comply with rigid rules. Besides, were domestic workers not only unorganized but also unorganizable?[26]

Central Actors in Their Own History

How many people, when they think of the Montgomery, Alabama, bus boycotts at the height of the US civil rights movement, think of the massive number of domestic workers who insisted on walking to work? They were not just following orders. As the historian Premilla Nadasen compellingly demonstrates, they acted at great cost and risk, insisting that their civil rights be respected. Domestic workers' massive participation in the civil rights movement has tight links to movements for their rights as domestic workers. Indeed, as Nadasen argues, "the struggle for domestic workers' rights brings . . . greater nuance to the meaning of black freedom and labor organizing."[27]

Domestic workers have been anything but passive onlookers in their own lives and history: they have repeatedly engaged in individual acts of resistance to exercise control over their working time. Around the world, domestic workers have tended to reject live-in work and have opted to live out whenever they have been able to do so.[28] These forms of resistance have been crucial in enabling domestic workers to carve out some limited autonomy in their highly personalized work relationships. Domestic workers have also acted collectively—for example, through media campaigns, lobbying efforts, hunger strikes, and calls for one-day work stoppages.[29] Their goal, as I discuss in chapter 1, has been clear: to change the unjust law of the household workplace. Similarly, domestic workers' dynamic participation was crucial at the ILO. Domestic workers' agency—even militancy—needed to be made clear, to prevent the myth of their passive acceptance of their lot from stalling standard setting on decent work for domestic workers any longer.

However, some people in the international labor community were steeped in a set of literatures that portrayed domestic workers as passive victims who were unable to organize, or as servants so wholly devoted to their employers' family that they lacked a working-class sensibility. Even Beatrice and Sidney Webb, the British Fabians at the heart of the development of modern industrial relations as a field of study, did not hold out much hope for organizing by domestic workers at the end of the nineteenth century. In fairness, the Webbs were probably more worried about women employers, who they thought were at domestic workers' mercy. They thought that these mistresses would be "forced to defend themselves by taking refuge" behind profit-making intermediaries—that is, employment agencies.[30] While their analysis of who actually holds power tends to take the women to be the sole or main employers of the domestic workers, and magnifies employer dependence to the point where the disproportionate risk of abuse experienced by domestic workers becomes invisible, they were onto something.

First, the Webbs captured the fact that power is multiple. Nadasen's ethnographic work with African American domestic workers allows her to address this point with nuance. She recognizes that the "personal relationship that made this job so capricious and unpredictable could also be a source of power for domestic workers."[31] Families might well come to see themselves as dependent on the domestic workers who care for them. They might forge emotional ties with and come to trust the domestic workers. As chapter 3 shows, some domestic workers were able to draw on those ties to negotiate better working conditions.[32] Nadasen also recognizes, as do the ethnographies foregrounded in chapter 3, that the negotiations are high risk when domestic workers' employment can be terminated so easily.[33] By interviewing domestic worker organizers, Nadasen is able to show the structural reasons why domestic workers have to negotiate individually. She also discusses the racialized exclusions of domestic work and agricultural labor—primarily African American occupations—from labor laws. Mainstream unions historically failed to build a movement that included domestic workers like the women who organized the National Domestic Workers Union of America.[34] Yet the domestic workers developed their own collective strategies, like producing model contracts and individually negotiating to refuse to do certain kinds of work. In other words, they transgressed and in the process reconfigured the law of the household workplace. They managed to build enough consciousness and capacity at one point to be able to get domestic workers in Chicago, one by one, to refuse to get down on their knees to scrub floors until the norm was changed and employers would stop asking them to do so. Overall, Nadasen's work supports the conviction of domestic workers worldwide that legal support and the support of workers' organizations—including mainstream trade unions—are important to make collective bargaining possible.

Second, the Webbs realized the significance of the agency relationship. Contemporary employers have turned to agencies, particularly in contexts of transnational labor migration. In many contexts, agencies may be seen to make the relationship more formal. They are intermediaries—surely they could make it easier to negotiate conditions of employment, standardize norms, and in the process make the workplace more egalitarian? Like much of the literature surveyed in chapter 3, the Webbs' analysis highlights domestic workers' recognition that agencies have historically protected employers.[35] Agencies are no substitute for collective organizing by domestic workers to defend their own rights. Some employment agencies in some places under some conditions might well be repurposed to play a major role in regulating the household workplace differently. While results vary, studies emphasize that agencies tend to make the workers' situation worse.[36] In addition, they might help sustain job segregation and wage differences based on race, as when Filipina domestic workers are hired to take care of children and earn more than others who do the same work while Ghanaian women are hired as cleaners.[37] Formalization, in other words, may not be the primary goal, because formalization without paying attention to the unjust law of the household workplace might simply make matters worse. To transgress is to set out to uproot and transform the unjust law of the household workplace, formally and informally.

By 2006, domestic workers had decided it was time to defend their rights internationally.[38] They knew they would have to push back against many of the stereotypes about them that had prevailed when the Webbs were writing, and that persisted. They knew they would have to chart their own path to get where they wanted to go, but they were off to a great start. Their militancy and organization might still have been invisible to many when the topic of regulating decent work for domestic workers came before the ILO's Governing Body, but they would not stay invisible for long.

What Had the ILO Done for Domestic Workers Lately?

It is not as if the ILO had never turned its attention to domestic workers: in fact, the subject of standard setting for domestic work had come up repeatedly at the ILO. As early as 1936, the International Labour Conference set about establishing a standard on holidays with pay. One decision to be made was whether domestic workers would be covered. Delegates to the International Labour Conference resolved to ask the Governing Body to consider putting the protection of domestic workers on the agenda for future sessions.[39] While the committee of delegates to the International Labour Conference negotiating the new standard took the time to include a flexibility clause into the comprehensive Holidays with Pay Convention, 1936 (No. 52) to allow ILO Members to articulate exemptions, only Belgium ultimately excluded domestic workers from the convention.[40]

In 1945, when the International Labour Conference turned its attention to child labor, domestic workers were mentioned specifically.[41] Again in 1948, the International Labour Conference adopted the Resolution Concerning Holidays with Pay for Domestic Servants, in which it noted that it is "the duty of the ILO to extend the benefits of international protection" to domestic workers.[42] In it, the International Labour Conference asked the Governing Body "to inscribe the question of holidays with pay for domestic servants on the Agenda of as early a future session of the conference as possible and to consider at the same time whether other conditions of domestic servants' employment could form the subject of international regulation."

In 1965, it adopted the Resolution Concerning the Conditions of Employment of Domestic Workers. It observed that there was an "urgent need" for standards "compatible with the self-respect and human dignity which are essential to social justice" for domestic workers.[43]

Several detailed studies had been published in the ILO's flagship journal, the *International Labour Review*—including one by the ILO itself—about its comprehensive survey in 1970 on the employment conditions of domestic workers in private households.[44] Well-regarded ethnographies published by leading scholars abounded, alongside compelling reports from highly respected human rights NGOs that often cited ILO publications.[45] The ILO had also commissioned contemporary working papers that had set out a rationale for standard setting a full decade earlier: "Specific regulation testifies to a level of recognition of the social importance of domestic work and attempts to value it. . . . [I]t forces those who pay for the work, those who regulate the work, and even those who do the work to think about it in a radically different manner. Through that dynamic process, specific and ultimately more accurate regulation has the potential to restore some respect and dignity to domestic work."[46]

The ILO's inability to set standards on domestic work was getting a little embarrassing. How was it that the ILO, which recognized that decent work applied to all workers, had not yet managed to agree on a convention for domestic workers?[47] How could some members still be calling for further study? Why did others want only a general discussion? And why did still others seem to want to focus on child labor or labor migration without grasping the urgency of including domestic work labor law more generally?

Biting the Bullet

The 2008 meeting of the Governing Body turned out to be quite a surprise, at least for some ILO observers. Domestic workers might have been missing from among the Governing Body's members who represented labor ministries, national employers' federations, and traditional trade unions. Yet domestic workers had done their homework. They constituted a global, well-organized, and dynamic social movement. And they had planned long and hard to enable the ILO to seize the moment.

Although regional organizations of domestic workers had sprung up in different parts of the world decades earlier, in 2006, over sixty representatives from the International Union of Food, Agricultural, Hotel, Restaurant, Catering, Tobacco and Allied Workers' Associations (IUF) met in Amsterdam. It was the first time that a global union federation had offered sustained support

FIGURE 2. Congratulations, Now Ratify. Credit: ILO.

to a group of female workers in the informal economy. A key focus of the meeting was to organize to make international labor standards on decent work for domestic workers a reality.[48]

The members of that global social movement felt that they had waited long enough. They wanted the ILO to act—now. Back at the ILO in Geneva, Sir Leroy Trotman, a leader of the ILO workers' group from Barbados, seized the stage to remind the Governing Body that decent work for domestic workers was the group's priority for 2010 and to make a compelling case for why the ILO Members must bite the bullet. The greatest good for the greatest number meant supporting standard setting on decent work for domestic workers. The tide had turned in favor of that standard setting, and the compelling accounts by a wide range of governmental members underscored that, while challenging, adopting the new standard would allow the ILO to make history.

A resolution to put a convention and recommendation before the International Labour Conference was adopted.[49] The ILO's permanent secretariat, the International Labour Office, needed to respond quickly. That is why, by May 2008, I was on official travel to the International Labour Office in Geneva, developing a work plan with the ILO's Social Protection unit's team and building a team of research assistants at McGill University to draft under rather urgent conditions *Report IV(1) on Decent Work for Domestic Workers*, also referred to as the *Law and Practice Report*. Amid report writing, questionnaire development, and late-night drafting sessions came the intense two-year negotiations process at the 99th and 100th sessions of the International Labour Conference. Throughout, there was committed involvement from key ILO officials and delegates, and intense, inspiring activism from domestic workers' social movements themselves. Joyously, and to the astonishment of many, the ILO made history when it adopted the new Domestic Workers Convention (No. 189) and Domestic Workers Recommendation (No. 201) on June 16, 2011.[50] Without missing a beat, domestic workers unfurled a banner that said, "Now ratify!" (figure 2).

Telling the Backstory of the Invisible Law of the Household Workplace

My book tells the backstory of this historic moment. You might think that would mean this book focuses on the story starting in 2008. However, I could not have written the *Law and Practice Report* had I not already developed a longer-term vision of domestic work and how to regulate it. That vision came in part from belonging to a family and community of women who had been domestic workers. This is at once a personal story, as I explain in the postface, and a story that belongs to communities throughout Africa and its diasporas in the United States and Canada and throughout the Caribbean and Europe. The story has roots in the long history of slavery but is particularly punctuated by the global institution that is the centuries-long transatlantic slave trade. It encompasses the colonial encounter in Africa, Asia, and the Americas. In other words, it is part of the transnational history of racialization. As sociolegal scholar Eve Darian-Smith observes, "Legal constructions of race, and the shifting practices of domestic racism, have always overflowed the boundaries of national jurisdictions and been constitutively shaped."[51] This story cannot be told without explaining those dynamics.

The claim I make in this book is simple but far-reaching: the common sense way in which the domestic work relationship is understood and regulated is part of a global legacy of subordination and servitude that operates in particular places and in particular ways on particular women's bodies. I refer to it as the asymmetrical, unequal, and largely invisible law of the household workplace. That is, nothing about the relationship was made to allow us to see just how unjust it is. We are meant to take it as a given that we are not supposed to see domestic workers' needs, desires, or aspirations. The relationship involves domestic workers, but their role is to get everything done—the cooking, the cleaning, and other so-called menial work that includes so much of the child care and even the emotional labor that it seems invisible.[52]

The law of the household workplace does not require the state to enact legislation or a court to decide a case. In this sense, the law of the household workplace is to be understood in sociolegal terms. In the words of transnational law scholars Gregory Shaffer and Terrence Halliday, law establishes "generalized normative expectations understood and used by actors within a particular context for purposes of constraining and facilitating particular behaviors."[53] In other words, focusing on the law of the household workplace is a way to recognize that the domestic work relationship has, over time and in particular places, generated its own law.

To understand this relationship and make it visible is already to transgress the law of the household workplace. This book tells the story of those everyday transgressions, by domestic workers themselves. We are often taught that to transgress law is wrong. But domestic workers embody a long tradition of resistance that refuses to confuse laws that exact servitude with social justice.[54] A big part of the standard setting on decent work for domestic workers was working against invisibility and the unjust law of the household workplace. The standard-setting process deliberately set out to root out intersectional subordination faced by Black and other racialized women, a necessary precondition to make the law governing the household workplace equitable.[55] Change was possible because the pluralist law of the household workplace that normalizes and governs the domestic work relationship had been observed up close and carefully, especially by domestic workers and those who took the time to study them.[56] The insights were achieved through a multiple consciousness method that focused on seeing realities that outsiders with greater societal privilege might miss and making careful, strategic decisions about how to use that knowledge of multiple overlapping worlds of law known as interlegality to work for justice.[57]

Chapter 1 takes us through the standard-setting process at the ILO to show how a transnational legal order on decent work for domestic workers was established. The chapter focuses on the actors and serves as a reminder that domestic workers were not going to let the ILO—however well-meaning— render them invisible either. The chapter chronicles the shifts in framing that allowed an alternative, transgressive transnational legal order on decent work for domestic workers to emerge. No international standard alone could establish a transnational legal order. In this chapter, I emphasize the militancy of the domestic workers' social movements, the ILO preparatory work that happened at times in parallel, and the interactions between the parties in building a community of learning out of which the transgressive transnational legal order could emerge.

Shaffer and Halliday frame the notion of transnational legal ordering as "a collection of formalized legal norms and associated organizations and actors that authoritatively order the understanding and practice of law across national jurisdictions."[58] They pay attention to how transnational legal orders are established, conveyed, and in some cases institutionalized, as well as to the relationship between preexisting national norms and whatever is being created transnationally. They show that legal organizations or networks that transcend the nation-state, as is the case in the domestic workers' social movements, play a major role throughout the process of establishing a transnational legal order.

This book builds on Shaffer and Halliday's framework to sharpen the focus on acknowledging and dislodging asymmetrical power. Transnational labor law is a prime field to use in explaining what an alternative, transgressive, or counterhegemonic transnational legal order looks like. When regulating decent work for domestic workers, it was simply not enough to accept the naturalized, asymmetrical law of the household workplace that then existed. It was necessary to make that law visible to dislodge it, so that a transgressive transnational legal order could emerge. Framing mattered: it turned out to be strategically helpful to understand domestic workers' access to labor rights as a human rights concern. Chapter 1 focuses on how the change happened. It is a meditation on the depth of the challenge that the ILO faced in imagining alternatives to the legacy of subordination and servitude that faced domestic workers. I confess that to this day, despite the tremendous amount that has been accomplished, I fear that the depth of the challenge may still be underestimated. There is a terrible risk that those regulating domestic work will continue the spatial perpetuation of subordination and servitude through rather than despite labor law reform initiatives in the wake of the new international standards.

This lingering concern was crystallized for me when I saw how quickly the International Labour Conference moved from the transgressive transnational legal order constructed through Convention No. 189 and Recommendation No. 201 of 2011 to a rather flattened vision of how to formalize the informal economy that included domestic workers in the Transition from the Formal to the Informal Economy Recommendation, 2014 (No. 204). As I discuss in chapter 2, informality is not synonymous with a lack of order.[59] Structural subordination on the basis of the intersectional positionality of racialized women in domestic work adheres to a very particular "system of meaning"[60] that makes it seem natural for historically subordinated groups to continue to perform domestic work in the growing tertiary or service economy. I argue that to address this point, it is necessary to understand the norms that render the workers ubiquitous and yet invisible. In other words, it is necessary to understand and make visible the law of the household workplace and its roots in older logics of subordination and servitude.

The ability to transform the domestic work relationship extends beyond law, of course. But it is too easy to say that. Law is one of the most important structuring and institutional ways of knowing. This book seeks to take seriously the risks and the challenges within law. Domestic workers require an alternative—an emancipatory labor law, transnationally constructed through a thick understanding of the law's role in perpetuating subordination and servitude and resolutely focused on uprooting it.

Chapter 3 therefore seeks to explain the problematic perpetuation of subordination and servitude. It foregrounds seven leading ethnographies that span the period after 1979 that is associated with globalization. The insights from those ethnographies—and countless others—were pivotal to me as I wrote the ILO's *Law and Practice Report*.[61] Although they often had only a small number of interviewees, they were rich in their textured analysis of the nature of domestic workers' invisibility. I study these ethnographies comparatively, to frame the contemporary law of the household workplace. In the process, chapter 3 exposes the invisible and inequitable law of the household workplace. That law is laden with assumptions, stereotypes, and expectations about the domestic work relationship that might relate to domestic workers' self-awareness as workers; their expected working time, levels and nature of pay (including so-called gifts), and living conditions; or the way their employment was terminated. They all reveal taken-for-granted understandings and expectations of domestic work that suggest that a particular law was at play, and that it was not necessarily the law upheld or applied by the courts.

Domestic workers' resistance is an integral part of the story that is told through the studies in chapter 3. The chapter explains how domestic workers worked both with and against the law (even protective state laws) to make sure that they could take control of their working conditions and fight for change. As I noted above, the law of the household workplace has become naturalized and seems strikingly fixed across time and space. This led me to want to think more about how to historicize that law. Lawyers tend to turn to cases to find the law. I discuss some particularly compelling ones, but the focus on cases draws on an understanding of the law that comes from a common sense about the state. It can compound domestic workers' invisibility by obscuring the prospect that the law of the household workplace could come from alternative, less settled sources that emerge from or reflect the interplay between places—not just courts, but also kitchens. If you were a British housekeeper in colonial India, where would you turn to find the law? You might likely turn to other British housekeepers, and do so, literally, in their kitchens. Might you even turn to text?

The quest led me to a surprising place. Let me come clean: I delighted in what I found. Chapter 4 suggests you might have turned to cookbooks, which in the eighteenth through the early twentieth centuries often included codes or manuals on the rights and duties of domestic workers. Some similar texts could also be found in the manuals on domestic economy that began to appear. Chapter 4 identifies four key sources from 1846–1902, written by employers, and finds explicit references to the law of the household workplace. These cookbooks were widely circulated and used. Many served a particular purpose: they ensured that domestic workers were at once altogether present and yet invisible. They resonate with the law of the household workplace seen in chapter 3, and they became part of the forgotten backstory after the *Law and Practice Report* was completed.

Domestic workers also used the cookbook genre. For example, former domestic slaves wrote cookbooks with their own interpretation of the law of the household workplace. Those cookbooks became public and were invariably mediated expressions of self. This book canvasses four books, from 1825–1866. Through them, I began to sense how domestic workers who were faced with evident constraints found ways to transgress the law of the household workplace that I will interchangeably refer to in this book as asymmetrical, unequal, or simply unjust. They were very much about, but not only about, the recipes; they told necessary, alternative stories so that alternative realities could be widely shared and cooked up.[62] The cookbooks prepared by domestic workers gave me new insight into postcolonial public intellectual C. L. R. James's analysis of direct democracy, *Every Cook Can Govern*.[63]

Chapter 5 returns to the International Labour Conference to trace and evaluate the shift in understanding that emerged through the deliberations and is reflected in the approved texts of the Domestic Workers Convention and the Domestic Workers Recommendation. The chapter focuses on some of the thorniest topics: working hours and wages, migration, and employment agencies. It discusses the mechanics of building and settling the transnational legal order on decent work for domestic workers. It does not shy away from the indeterminate character of some of the necessary multiple consciousness moves.

Chapter 6 moves past the International Labour Conference to tell the story of how this transgressive transnational legal order is being diffused and settled. It looks at four studies of countries—two from the global South and two from the global North, two that have ratified the Domestic Workers Convention (South Africa, Switzerland) and two that have not (Côte d'Ivoire, France). The transnational legal order is transgressive in the extent to which the diffusion of decent work for domestic workers has been multidirectional. By studying the innovations that were taking place in ILO member countries, it became possible to conduct the preparatory work for the new transnational legal order. The momentum of the international standard-setting process has led to more innovation, both while the process was going on and since the adoption of the Domestic Workers Convention and the Domestic Workers Recommendation. The transnational legal order transgresses traditional understandings of legal transplantation that imagine law reform to migrate from the global North to the global South. Influential countries of the global South have shaped the direction of the diffusion of decent work for domestic workers and continue to add texture to the pivotal, but infinitely challenging, topic of domestic workers' collective autonomy.

I conclude this book by acknowledging that much work remains to be done. As labor law scholar Lizzie Barmes presciently observes, "It is an error to neglect the multiple ways that law embeds and extends existing hierarchies, even those it appears to challenge."[64] And as the concluding chapter recalls, we must take seriously the risk that the new transnational legal order contributes to embedding and extending the hierarchies, particularly in the context of migration. That inescapable fact does not take away from one of the most significant accomplishments, which happened to be foreseen in the *Law and Practice Report*: the Domestic Workers Convention and the Domestic Workers Recommendation enable the ILO to enhance transnational cooperation on decent work for domestic workers. By working with constituents to share comparative information and experience and foster learning from good practices in the regulation of domestic work,[65] the ILO is moving from standard setting to the unsettling of the law of the household workplace, and the diffusion and implementation of a new transnational legal order. However, and perhaps paradoxically, this shift allows the ILO and domestic workers' social movements to move beyond the human rights framing to offer a deeper critique, including of the profound limit to decent work that characterizes the current approach to temporary migration. Domestic workers presented an equality-based claim for inclusion at a moment when labor law itself was widely perceived to be in crisis.[66] Regulating decent work for domestic workers at its heart calls for labor to be regulated as if the most marginalized workers matter. Their marginalization has to be unsettled and they must be brought to the center of transnational labor law's concern. Otherwise, the asymmetrical law of the household workplace will persist.[67] On the eve of the ILO's centenary, I conclude this book by making the case for thinking transnationally, by centering an acknowledgment of the structural inequality of global migration, of the market-enabling nature of care work, and of the imperative of international solidarity. Thinking transnationally is a way to pry open space and to be reminded of how domestic workers' inclusion ultimately enlarges the scope of labor law for us all.

CHAPTER 1

Establishing a Transgressive Transnational Legal Order

> If they don't give you a seat at the table, bring a folding chair.
>
> —Shirley Chisholm, quoted in Vanessa Williams, "'Unbought and Unbossed'"

On the historic night of November 4, 2008, when Senator Barack Obama was elected president of the United States, I made a conscious decision to miss the celebrations. Instead, I put my joy and hope for change into a transnational justice initiative. After months of research, I confined myself to a hotel room for a week in an intensive effort to finish writing the bulk of the International Labour Office's *Report IV:1 on Decent Work for Domestic Workers* (referred to as the *Law and Practice Report*) on decent work for domestic workers.[1]

Uppermost in my own mind throughout was the conviction that domestic workers had to remain central actors in the process, and they did. They mobilized and organized in support of the implementation of the Domestic Workers Convention and the Domestic Workers Recommendation, were involved in negotiating the terms, and have since ensured that the convention is ratified and both instruments are implemented. A complex dynamic has been set into motion, one that reflects the interplay between a new social movement from below and an old international organization uncertain about transnational change but certain that social justice must be front and center. I believe that negotiating decent work for domestic workers changed the International Labour Organization (ILO) and has helped increase certainty that international labor law has a transnational future.

Laying the Groundwork for New Labor Standards

The document that became the ILO's *Law and Practice Report*, including the detailed questionnaire, needed to make the case that decent work for domestic workers was feasible, now. The report had to explain the past but also convince constituents that it was possible to break with that past. It needed to show how domestic workers were denied rights but also make the case that they had rights that needed to be recognized specifically and in context. It had to be technically sound, and it had to persuade. The questionnaire asked ILO members what specific provisions they would be prepared to accept in a convention and recommendation, in part on the basis of what they had learned and what had resonated with their experiences in the *Law and Practice Report*.

The first matter of business was to clarify any misconceptions about the ILO. It was necessary for the *Law and Practice Report* to be crystal clear about the fact that domestic workers were not starting from ground zero in terms of international labor standard setting. The report wound up emphasizing a pivotal starting principle: unless one of the hundreds of existing conventions or recommendations of a general nature expressly excluded domestic workers, those workers are included in each international instrument's scope and are supposed to enjoy its protections.[2] Domestic workers were covered under most international labor standards, including those that the ILO considered to be fundamental: those dealing with freedom of association and equality, the prohibition of forced labor and child labor.[3] The ILO's supervisory bodies, including the Committee of Experts on the Application of Conventions and Recommendations and the Freedom of Association Committee, had for decades interpreted international labor standards to make sure domestic workers' rights were not overlooked. The supervisory bodies emphasized that domestic workers should have the freedom of association, and the Committee of Experts called for equal pay for work of equal value to valorize the skill involved in domestic work, condemned very specific conditions of racialized slavery in domestic work and forced labor conditions in migrant domestic work, and underscored the fact that domestic work was a prevalent (and often the worst) form of child labor.[4]

The *Law and Practice Report* documented a familiar international treaty-making practice: ILO members often spent a lot of time negotiating flexibility devices such as exception clauses into international labor conventions.[5] Yet there was a paradox: "Although ILO members have expended considerable efforts in the drafting of flexibility clauses, few have resorted to them in practice."[6] It was clear that even governments that might exclude domestic workers from the scope of their legislation were seeking guidance on how to do things differently. New international labor standards were a way to start.

Traditionally, domestic work was considered to be something other than work. The *Law and Practice Report* emphasized that the specificity of domestic work—the fact that it takes place in households, is care work central to our humanity, and is vital to enabling and sustaining work outside of the household—made it all the more important but still did not make it something other than work. The report particularly acknowledged the taken-for-granted skill and effort that goes into carrying out domestic work, to make it visible as work.

I started to frame the specific regulation of domestic work with a deliberate juxtaposition: "work like any other" and "work like no other."[7] The juxtaposition of these two ideas was widely cited and debated in the academic community, as some scholars sought to choose one or the other.[8] My position has consistently been that both are necessary. It is not enough to say that domestic work is work like any other and delete the words in an international labor convention or a national law that lists domestic workers among the exclusions. I argued that "the challenge here is to move beyond the formal—but largely invisible—inclusion of domestic workers in labor legislation and toward the specific regulation of their employment and their real visibility."[9]

History helped some people to see this point. Domestic work is primarily done by women, as it is gendered. But who were the specific women and men who did domestic work in other people's households? Asking that question brought difficult, unsettling histories to the fore, especially histories of slavery and colonialism.[10] Their legacies still affect who does the work: racialized or Indigenous people were expected to do it, on the basis of some supposedly innate predisposition to domestic servitude. I kept reinforcing the point that to make any real change, it was important to focus on the specific ways in which domestic workers faced not just typical employer control, but vestiges of servitude in the work that they did. It was important to see this, name it, and find a way to change it. The "it" was a form of law that I called the law of the household workplace. That law kept domestic workers in positions of exploitation and actual exclusion, even when they were technically included in labor laws and ratified international labor conventions.[11] The *Law and Practice Report* concluded that "mere tinkering with informal rules in formal legislation is not enough. . . . A complementary mix of carrots and sticks—capacity building for domestic workers, implementation incentives for employers and robust enforcement by governments—is needed" to achieve decent work for domestic workers.[12]

It helped a great deal that through the *Law and Practice Report*, it was possible to point to the many examples of creative experimentation related to domestic work that were under way worldwide. The ILO could support the case that "well-crafted regulatory mechanisms with a suitable enforcement machinery make an important difference in the everyday lives of domestic workers—and they convey the message that domestic workers are indeed workers who deserve both rights and respect."[13] One researcher has subsequently referred to the report as an "exhaustive" document on the specificity of domestic work in the contemporary economy, which included a detailed survey of national and international law that "set the stage for discussions on international standards." She added that "the comprehensive nature of this report aided governments in responding to the closing questionnaire."[14] The questionnaire apparently received a higher response rate than any such document in the previous fifteen years, which may have been why it played such a large role in the committee's discussions.

Who Was in the Room? Reinvigorating the International Labour Conference

With a copy of the *Law and Practice Report* and the draft conclusions in delegates' hands, the 99th International Labour Conference (ILC) Committee on Decent Work for Domestic Workers began its work. Geneva's flora was in full bloom in June 2010, but one of the most peaceful places on earth was also filled with urgency. Domestic workers had come from around the world, united in their pursuit of a long overdue act of social justice: international recognition as workers.

The committee met not in the gray concrete building that houses the ILO, but rather in the monumental Palais des Nations of the United Nations (UN). The room was packed, and because so many domestic workers were present, it was not filled just with the usual suspects. Even the way the space was organized spoke volumes: In addition to the front podium, where the representative of the secretary-general of the International Labour Conference (that is, the director-general of the International Labour Office), the chairperson, and the experts and technical staff members were seated, and the middle ground floor, where the interpreters sat, there were three large areas for the ILO's tripartite constituents. Government officials from countries as diverse as the United States, Uruguay, and the United Arab Emirates occupied the large space in the middle of the meeting room, loosely arranged in alphabetical order according to their country's name, flanked by representatives of the main

Figure 3. The Committee on Decent Work for Domestic Workers. Credit: ILO.

employers' federations on the right. On the left was the workers' delegation. Some domestic workers were scattered among the habitual attendees of the workers' group, who had worked hard to build as representative a group as possible. Just behind the workers and farther off to the side were all other people considered to be observers—which included most domestic workers (figure 3).

The international organization predates the UN system—it was initially part of the League of Nations, founded as part of the Treaty of Versailles in 1919. The ILO's tripartism means that nonstate actors make international law, which sets it apart from other treaty-based international organizations.[15] The negotiation process for the Domestic Workers Convention and the Domestic Workers Recommendation with domestic workers present in the room offered an unparalleled opportunity to address some of the criticism of the ILO's tripartite structure and begin to imagine reinvigorated deliberation on the ILO's future.[16]

Domestic Workers' Labor Rights as Human Rights: Shifting the Frame

Creating the proposed Domestic Workers Convention and Domestic Workers Recommendation was a tall order, and the challenges involved could easily have scared away the faint of heart. Yet the claim in the proposed international labor standards was, at its heart, a simple claim, and it resonated with domestic workers' social movements as well as those who took the time to understand why this work was so important. Groups like the National Domestic Workers Alliance lost no opportunity to underscore the fundamental humanity of care work as well as its economic importance in the home as the part of the "central dignity and humanity of caring for others."[17] Domestic workers had a substantive equality right to be meaningfully included in labor law.

I wanted the ILO's standard-setting process to be part of a rethinking of labor law's boundaries. The biggest challenge was to ensure that domestic workers have the right to be included in labor law.[18] This was significant because the Domestic Workers Convention and the Domestic Workers Recommendation were not intended to be symbolic instruments or even an abstract charter of rights. They were detailed and comprehensive. They were meant to give broad meaning to the notion of decent work that the ILO had been championing since 1999. Under the convention and recommendation, decent work would come to include decent working conditions and much more.

It would come to mean recognizing domestic workers' rights to equality and the freedom of association and providing protection against forced labor and child labor. It would come to include access to social protection such as maternity leave, occupational safety and health, and social security protections—even though there is some recognition of the need to improve some protections progressively. But there was still more in the documents. A premium was placed on making sure that mechanisms for inspection and dispute resolution were available. Decent work would also mean that special attention was needed to the nature and terms of contemporary labor migration, at the very least to rein in exploitative practices.

Deliberation through Definition: How Standards Solidify

After exchanging congratulatory words in their introductory statements, delegates got down to business. Soon they were deliberating over the definition of "domestic work" in article 1. They poured over potential carve outs for "babysitters" and even "au pairs," despite the care taken in the *Law and Practice Report* to reverse the common perception that au pairs are not subject to serious workplace abuse.[19] North-South concerns about informal care arrangements intersected when the delegate from Namibia, speaking on behalf of the Africa group, raised a question about babysitting.[20] Committee members could sense that this was one of the first decisive moments, testing whether the committee's secretariat could inspire confidence, and whether the committee members could work together to reach consensus. They reached out for help from the secretariat to understand how specific language such as "on a regular basis" had come to be understood in international labor law.

The committee took a scheduled break, during which I did some research and drafting. The representative of the secretary-general read the statement aloud when everyone returned:

The representative of the Secretary-General explained that the term "on a regular basis" was not used in international labour Conventions or Recommendations to qualify any occupational category currently covered by such standards. A similar issue had emerged in the *Home Work Convention, 1996 (No. 177)*, and had been addressed by including in the definition of home work, in Article 1(b): "persons with employee status do not become homeworkers within the meaning of this Convention simply by occasionally performing their work as employees at home, rather than at their usual workplaces."[21]

Committee members reflected and asked to convene a small, special tripartite working party. Its members met well into the night. During the following plenary session, they submitted a new draft text that enabled the committee to use a broad and inclusive definition of "domestic work," while crafting an internal limit rather than an optional flexibility clause. The discussion became the basis of article 1 of the Domestic Workers Convention:

For the purpose of this Convention:

(a) the term *domestic work* means work performed in or for a household or households;

(b) the term *domestic worker* means any person engaged in domestic work within an employment relationship;

(c) a person who performs domestic work only occasionally or sporadically and not on an occupational basis is not a domestic worker.

Reaching that consensus was so significant that the committee refused to touch it the following year. Some of the participants in that committee remained key actors throughout the two years of deliberation. The fact that it has been one of the most criticized parts of the convention afterward confirms the view of many people that it was imperfect. For example, it retains the language of an employment relationship for domestic workers, and it introduces a loophole in coverage. No similar working party was formed to deliberate separately from the whole—and away from the watchful eye of the workers' group as a whole—into the future. But the working party had illustrated that the ILO's deliberative community could work together. The spirit of consensus developed through that working party carried the constituents through the often rocky two-year process.

Standard Setting When the Household Is a Workplace

The *Law and Practice Report* was widely referred to by delegates during the committee meeetings. One of the most important elements of the standard-setting process was that it challenged the assumption that the location of the work prevented it from being regulated. According to the *Law and Practice Report*: "There is no fundamental distinction between work in the home and work beyond it, and no simple definition of public-private, home-workplace and employer-employee. Caring for children and the disabled or elderly persons in the home or in a public institution is all part of the same regulatory spectrum, wherein a range of migration and other policies shape both the supply of and the demand for care services."[22]

Domestic workers had been saying this for a long time. Take Carolyn Reed, a leading domestic workers' organizer at the National Committee on Household Employment in the United States in the 1970s, who highlighted the problem eloquently when she said that "the trouble is, people regard their homes as their empires. I say that you have no more right to exploit me in your home than you do to exploit me in your office."[23] And if the household was a workplace, and if domestic workers were workers, then regulating domestic work had to be looked at through a labor law frame. Delegates kept bumping up against that challenge throughout the deliberations.

Labor inspection has tended to be a primary casualty of the resistance to seeing the household as somebody else's workplace. Even though the ILO's Labour Inspection Convention, 1947 (No. 81) and the Protocol of 1995 to the Labour Inspection Convention should cover domestic workers, privacy and inviolability of the home came up as barriers during the deliberations.[24] The *Law and Practice Report* addressed this question carefully: "Respect for privacy, though important, need not result in an absolute bar on inspection visits. As observed by the [ILO's Committee of Experts], the consent of the employer or occupant of a household, or prior authorization by a judicial authority, ensure respect for the principle of privacy, while balancing this with workplace rights."[25]

The report cited cases and innovative practices around the world that allow for labor inspection in individual households, even in countries where the constitution provides for the inviolability of the home. Uruguay figured prominently, because it permits labor inspection where there is a presumed violation of labor and social security laws, and because it had formed a specialized section in charge of monitoring provisions for domestic work. Its laws include strict limits on nighttime inspections and required judicial authorization for daytime inspections.[26]

Representatives of governments, employers, and workers debated this question at length during the ILC. The government representative from Hungary, on behalf of the European Union member states, sought by amendment to introduce the notion of respect for privacy in the provision on dispute resolution, a motion that was immediately supported by the employers' group. The workers' group and several government representatives opposed it. The government representative from South Africa, speaking on behalf of the Africa group, rejected the amendment, explaining that "it did not examine the whole context of the issue of privacy. One could not deny that households had a right to privacy, but government certainly had the right to enforce labour legislation. A balance between these two rights was necessary, but the amendment failed to provide that balance."[27]

When the vice chair of the employers' group, Paul Mackay from New Zealand, cited article 12 of the *Universal Declaration of Human Rights*, the vice chair of the workers' group, Halimah Yacob—who has since become the President of Singapore—retorted that "labour inspection did not amount to arbitrary intrusion into private homes."[28] She followed up with arguments and examples of country practice offered in the *Law and Practice Report*.

It was time for informal discussions, a practice that delegates became increasingly at ease with once they had developed mutual trust and collectively resolved to make history. By the second year, there was an obvious momentum and a sense of excitement in the air—but the committee did not start out that way. In the case of labor inspection, Mackay presented a subamendment that the delegates adopted (article 17(2) and (3) of the current convention). This had not been easy, but it had preserved the use of labor inspection. By the end of the deliberations in June, no one seemed to bat an eye when paragraph 21(1)(b) of the recommendation allowed preplacement inspection visits of households where domestic workers would live and work.

The Long, Winding Road That Leads to "Aha" Moments

The labor inspection question was one of the first of several of what I refer to as "aha" moments during the committee's sessions. The specific regulation approach (work like no other, work like any other) to the international standard setting has produced a new twist in the debate about "labor rights as human rights."[29] Some experts on international labor law have been skeptical about using human rights language in labor law. They have worried in particular that human rights claims tend to be individualized and may move us away from the decidedly collective, social justice orientation of labor law.[30] Those critiques are important. However, in the case of domestic workers who have been outside of mainstream labor law for so long, even at the ILO, the human rights claim resonated differently. Their goal was to be included, equitably, within the core framework that international labor law provides. They were seeking both individual and collective aspects of labor law. In other words, by claiming a right to be included in labor law, they were demanding social justice.

Applying the lens of labor rights as human rights affected how the ILC delegates approached the standard-setting process. They repeatedly considered how domestic work is traditionally carried out. They contrasted that with recognized workplace norms generally applicable to most other categories of workers and with work relationships comparable to, but less marginalized than, domestic work. Then they considered how existing norms could be adapted to domestic work to arrive at a standard for decent work. It was remarkable to observe the many "aha" moments throughout the committee's work, when it became apparent that delegates were starting to see why a shift away from the inequitable, exclusionary way of understanding domestic work and toward a substantive equality based approach to inclusion was necessary.

Sometimes those "aha" moments came surprisingly quickly, as when minimum wages—historically quite a controversial topic seen to be closely linked to employment—were accepted with very little discussion.[31] However, other "aha" moments took longer to achieve. This was the case with the payment of part of domestic workers' salary "in kind." For domestic workers, this could be a bag of rice, old clothes, discarded household items, or room and board. Article 12(2) of the Domestic Workers Convention ultimately stated, "National laws, regulations, collective agreements or arbitration awards may provide for the payment of a limited proportion of the remuneration of domestic workers in the form of payments in kind that are not less favourable than those generally applicable to other categories of workers, provided that measures are taken to ensure that such payments in kind are agreed to by the worker, are for the personal use and benefit of the worker, and that the monetary value attributed to them is fair and reasonable."[32]

During the 2010 discussions, the employers' group introduced an amendment that would have rendered the provision on payment in kind so flexible as to leave it to national laws and regulations.[33] In other words, the international standard would no longer have required a change to the national laws and practices that guaranteed domestic workers' inequality. A lengthy discussion ensued, in which it became clear that the delegates were operating on the basis of very different assumptions about what should rightfully be considered payment in kind. If they were using a logic that reinforced the unjust law of the home workplace, then old clothes or similar goods given by an employer could be considered payment in kind. By challenging that starting point, some delegates were able to illustrate why they could not accept another proposed amendment, which would have added the words "with due regard to the specific circumstances of domestic work" to the provision. There again, they argued that there should be no license for an inferior method of payment between domestic workers and other wage earners. Some delegates made it clear that they were using specificity to make domestic work visible. They were not invoking it to avoid changing inequitable practices or to maintain an exploitative status quo.[34] The distinction was clear, and the amendments were withdrawn.

Domestic Workers Try to Take a Seat at the Table

The global movement of domestic workers has led to the diffusion of an alternative understanding of how the domestic work relationship is to be understood and regulated. At the ILO, domestic workers embraced the preparatory work that articulated their claim to the human right to be included as workers. The social movement left an indelible imprint on the ILO's work, not only on the substance of the new convention and recommendation but also on the standard-setting process itself. Tripartite social dialogue played a central role and took on a new meaning. The ILO's process became much more contextualized and concrete.[35] There was nothing abstract about the earnest domestic workers sitting in the room, forcing the delegates to see them.

All those in the committee room recognized sooner or later the challenges and limits of their own representativeness on the subject. Several participants and observers could not stop themselves from noting that employers of domestic workers were in each of the delegations and indeed among the international officials who had brought the issues forward. However, in the official delegations, domestic workers were few and far between.

Still, the committee was filled with actors new to international law, many of them racialized or Indigenous, determined, dynamic, and often charismatic women (and some men). They represented local associations from places as disparate as the Philippines, Colombia, Hong Kong, the United Kingdom, South Africa, Spain, Trinidad and Tobago, Canada, and the United States—and they came prepared.

A group of domestic workers' representatives had used the ILC in 2009 as an opportunity to learn about ILO processes and procedures. Several organizations like the research, activist and policy network Women in Informal Employment: Globalizing and Organizing (WIEGO) based at Harvard University; the International Union of Food, Agricultural, Hotel, Restaurant, Catering, Tobacco and Allied Workers' Associations (IUF), a global union federation; and the Global Labour Institute had given them access to delegates. The International Domestic Workers' Network was launched during that 2009 conference and became the International Domestic Workers' Federation soon after the adoption of the Domestic Workers Convention and the

Domestic Workers Recommendation. Domestic workers formed a steering committee, being careful to ensure that elected leaders of their organizations were at the center, supported by nonvoting technical advisers and some NGO participants. As Karin Pape, a WIEGO adviser, reports, the domestic worker representatives "made clear that they appreciate any technical support . . . but that the political decision-making lies with them."[36]

Domestic workers who were not officially part of a trade union represented at the ILC were not entitled to speak.[37] However, the International Domestic Workers' Network (IDWN) took a lead role, supported by WIEGO.[38] IDWN brought together domestic workers from a wide swath of national and regional domestic workers' associations, including the Committee on Asian Women and the Latin American and Caribbean Confederation of Household Workers, which had lobbied for years to change the landscape for domestic workers in their regions and had successfully spearheaded domestic law reform, particularly throughout Latin America.[39] They worked alongside the International Trade Union Confederation and key members of the International Union Federations, including the food and allied workers' global union, the International Union of Food, Agricultural, Hotel, Restaurant, Catering, Tobacco and Allied Workers' Associations.[40] Their members were interspersed among the workers' group and the observers' section of the committee room.

The chairperson and vice chairs of the workers' and employers' groups had agreed that some representatives of domestic workers could have limited speaking rights at the outset of each year's discussion.[41] The representatives used that time compellingly to insist that issues that they considered critical, including access to education, be addressed in the final convention or recommendation.[42] The representative of the Migrant Forum in Asia stressed the "importance of involving domestic workers themselves centrally and critically in the process of formulating the instrument, so as not to reinforce their nonrecognition and marginalization."[43]

However, these efforts did not translate into domestic workers miraculously gaining speaking rights throughout the negotiations. Some felt instead that they were officially silenced. They were made to feel their transgression when the chairperson of the 2010 session, Lourdes Trasmonte of the Philippines, was instructed to tell domestic workers and their allies that they could not applaud after statements supporting their rights, or otherwise express approval or disapproval audibly during the session. Myrtle Witbooi—at the time, General Secretary of the South African Domestic Service and Allied Workers Union, part of the Congress of South African Trade Unions (COSATU), and chair of the International Domestic Workers Network—took the floor of the plenary of the International Labour Conference on June 16th and graciously thanked the ILO "for the opportunity to participate in this Conference. Allowing this participation has made visible the work of millions of domestic workers. So please forgive us if, at times, we allow ourselves to get carried away by the excitement of this historic moment when the voices of domestic workers are heard for the first time at the international level." She added, poignantly, that "We have been waiting 63 years for this to happen, and we cannot lose this opportunity."[44]

Domestic workers did find many other ways to make their presence strongly felt. Early in the first year of the committee meetings, I watched from the podium as a team of Brazilian domestic workers surrounded the governmental representatives of their country, apparently impressing upon them the urgency to speak up in support of a workers' motion. I watched representatives of Human Rights Watch, a US-based transnational NGO that had been at the forefront of documenting domestic workers' abuse, take employers' representatives aside at a break and offer alternative language to help end a stalemate. The workers and their advocates were part of a social movement that sought to have human rights meaningfully included in the corpus of labor law. The workers' group's position was put forward by Yacob, who became a minister of state soon after the committee was over and then Singapore's president. Yacob's mother had been a domestic worker, and her intimate understanding of the nature of the shift that was under way was evident in her skillful, determined, and principled navigation of the commmittee. Her statements intersected with those of a core group of key governmental representatives—notably from South Africa; Australia; the United States; and, for much of the 2010 session, Brazil—who were consistently at the forefront of the debates. They regularly intervened to shift the narrative and keep the focus on the nature of the transition that was being put forward with each "aha" moment.

Throughout the conference, individual domestic workers participated in the workers' group meetings, lobbied their governmental representatives, and interacted with local Swiss media to ensure that their stories were told. A local newspaper, *Le Temps*, ran a series of interviews during the June 2011 ILC featuring domestic workers from around the world. In one telling interview, a domestic worker from Benin, Fataou Raimi, rejected the frequent designation of male domestic workers in West Africa as "boys," demanding respect for the dignity of his work and proclaiming his pride. The cook in an individual household with the "air of a diplomat" also presided over the Union of Hotel and Household Employees, who considered it a responsibility to come to Geneva to defend the rights of the ubiquitous categories of domestic workers in Benin.[45]

It is impossible for me to forget the steadfast presence of the domestic workers of African, Asian, and Indigenous descent who followed the deliberations intently, from beginning through to the wee hours of the night. They could teach the delegates a thing or two about long working hours. Most importantly, the domestic workers in the room held everyone else accountable—standard setting was not an abstract exercise for them, but rather a concrete manifestation of their demands to be visible and to be recognized, respected and work in dignity.

The Employers' Group in a Community of Learning

The provisional records of the committee meetings show a remarkable shift between 2010 and 2011 in how the standard-setting process was perceived. Perhaps no shift was more perceptible than that of the employers' group. Employers' representatives did not hide the fact that they faced a steep learning curve. The 2010 Employer Vice-Chairperson, Kamran Rahman of Bangladesh, was candid about this in his opening statement when the ILC's ninety-ninth session:

> The regulation of domestic work was an unusual area of involvement for the Employers' group, and would not directly affect the private sector companies that were its members. There were nonetheless risks involved in developing a standard for domestic work, and the creation of inappropriate legislation could have potentially deleterious economic effects. . . . Too much regulation might reduce employment in this sector, given that people employed domestic workers for the convenience that they brought. Employers of domestic workers often lacked the legal expertise to comply with rigid rules set by international labour standards. . . . Discrimination faced by domestic workers, in particular migrants, was a pressing issue. However, some discrimination might at times be considered acceptable, for example where families preferred specific characteristics in a domestic worker who provided care for their children.[46]

Rahman emphasized the divergence in state practices and argued that exclusions from coverage in international labor conventions could be justified. The overall point was clear: "a Convention should be reserved for unchanging principles on which broad tripartite consensus existed, and would be unsuitable for domestic work; the differences . . . were too great for an overarching, unbending standard."[47] Instead, the employers' group quickly introduced, then withdrew, an amendment seeking to convert the process into a general discussion. It then introduced an amendment seeking to create a nonbinding recommendation, which was put to a vote and rejected by 92,820 votes to 67,158.[48]

The employers' group was at the center of another memorably tense moment that seemed to come out of nowhere: employers wanted to know whether the committee recognized employers' freedom of association. Rahman proposed an amendment to what is now paragraph 2 of the Domestic Workers Recommendation. The employers wanted to add "and employer" to a provision that sought to provide specific guidance to constituents on how to ensure that a group that had historically not been able to enjoy the freedom of association and the right to bargain collectively might do so. The workers objected, as did some government representatives, and the employers called for a vote, which they appeared to lose in a show of hands. Rahman exclaimed that denying the freedom of association to employers would be a first for the ILO and demanded a recorded vote. Objections were raised and tensions rose; even the ILO's provisional record uses words like "astonishment" to describe the delegates' reactions.[49] For the ILO, this was a potentially quite serious moment, and some of the key political actors could be seen moving around the room, trying to manage the situation. It would not have been unreasonable if some people had feared that the employers might simply walk out and abandon the negotiations.

Instead, the recorded vote was taken, and most delegates abstained—preventing a quorum from being reached on the employers' motion without actually having a vote that denied employers their inclusion in a provision on the freedom of association. Several government representatives made a point of clarifying that the vote was not about employers' freedom of association at all. Then Yacob, for the workers' group, implored the committee members to get back to work, reminding them that "there were more than 100 million domestic workers worldwide who needed protection."[50] Discussions continued, even occasioning several moments of levity alongside the hard work.

However, employers did not hide their frustration at the end of the 2010 session. When the conclusions proposed in a plenary session by the Committee on Domestic Workers were adopted, several employers criticized the quality of the June 2010 discussions. The US employer representative was at pains to remark that NGOs had become a fourth dimension in what should have been tripartite discussions.[51] But by June 2011, the perceived interests of employers had evolved. It is not clear whether this was because the representative structure was different. The employers had replaced their previous spokesperson, who had been part of the pivotal drafting committee meeting.

There was another, less immediately perceptible difference: the delegation included at least one representative from a major domestic employers' association. Just having an employers' organization for domestic workers is rare, but in addition the French Union of Individual Employers (known by its French acronym SPE, for Syndicat des Particuliers Employeurs) is affiliated with both a major employers' federation in France, the Movement of French Enterprises (known by its French acronym, MEDEF, for Mouvement des Entreprises de France) and the International Organization of Employers. Its members include some of the major transnational agencies involved in placing migrant domestic workers. The SPE had a clear sense of why the discussions at the ILO were important and, in particular, why they would have a major impact on the so-called tertiary economy that is service provision in the household, which was being developed in France.

Employers no longer argued that a convention on decent work for domestic workers was irrelevant to them, and negotiations remained serious and intense. But neither did employers seem overly concerned about expressing their perceived interests. They seemed to understand that the international standard setting was about something bigger than them. The ILO had been around since 1919, but as its centenary approached, it was clear that an ubiquitous group of workers had been sorely neglected. The ILO had shifted its focus in 1999 to emphasize "decent work for all," so it was no longer good enough to say that these workers were not the kind the ILO was meant to foreground. Instead, domestic work was understood to be absolutely essential to the functioning of modern market economies in which both women and men were included. The "aha" moments seemed less periodic and, collectively, more like the guiding principle of the discussions in 2011. Throughout those discussions, employers' representatives paid close attention to the particular features relevant to regulating the domestic work relationship, including its migration dimensions. Human Rights Watch in particular played a pivotal role in the discussion of the regulation of agencies, working especially with employers to help dispel perceptions that these actors might appropriately be given a regulatory role in the international labor standard setting. The vice-chairperson of the employers' group took special pains to thank Human Rights Watch in his closing remarks "for helping open the eyes of the Employers' group to the plight of domestic workers." He added that "the Committee's discussions were a fine example of global tripartite negotiation" and that, while the employers' group had initially been in favor of a recommendation alone, it had accepted the choice of the majority to have a convention too, and that the group was not only "proud to be part of that process" but was also willing to "stand ready to support, lobby and push for implementation of the Convention at national level."[52]

Understanding domestic workers' rights as human rights had a real impact on how the Domestic Workers Convention and the Domestic Workers Recommendation were negotiated. Employers even withdrew a proposed technical two-part amendment that would have prevented the new convention from entering into force under the usual rules requiring two ratifications. Drawing on the fact that the consolidated Maritime Labour Convention of 2006 had drawn up a heavier formula for ratification, the vice-chair of the employers' group sought to change the rules for regular conventions to eighteen ratifications before the convention could enter into force.[53]

The amendment was proposed at the eleventh hour in the negotiations and could have had a significant impact on the life of the convention and recommendation that had just been negotiated. The legal adviser spoke to a point of order about whether the committee could even make such a decision (it could). Many members voted against adjourning the discussion and expressed their substantive objections right away. The workers' group and several government representatives challenged the assumption that the Maritime Labour Convention was a valid precedent and doubted that a committee on decent work for domestic workers was the best place to address these concerns.[54] In any event, the employers had made their point (which had little to do with domestic workers or the Domestic Workers Convention), reinforced by the representative of France on behalf of the European Union: the matter of ratification and denunciation should be addressed by the ILO, but not on the backs of a historically marginalized group claiming inclusion in the standard-setting process.

It was late, and victory seemed nigh for those seeking a new convention and recommendation. The employers' group threw its significant support behind the the adoption of the historic convention and recommendation. There was singing and dancing in the committee room. Domestic workers were seen and heard.

CHAPTER 2

What's Informality Got to Do with It?

On Invisibility

> For where there is no law, [there is] no transgression.
> —Romans 4:15

"This judgment arises from my disquiet." So begins a 2014 decision of the High Court of Pretoria by Judge Makgoka, who found that it was undignified, demeaning, and in violation of section 10 of the South African Constitution for sheriffs to address defendants by referring to them simply as "Bongiwe, a domestic helper," or "The Domestic Faith," or "Eliza, domestic worker." The judge continued: "There is no mention of their marital status or surnames. One thing is clear, though: all of them are indigenous African women. . . . As a nation, we emerge from a disgraceful and painful past. . . . The contents of the returns of service in these matters are reminiscent of that era, and conjure up deeply painful memories for the majority of the citizens of our country. . . . The mindset discernable . . . has no place in an open and democratic society premised on the foundational values of human dignity and respect . . . irrespective of . . . race or social standing."[1]

Judge Makgoka's decision refers to the everyday indignities that continue to surround domestic work twenty years after the end of apartheid in South Africa. And it goes beyond, to expose the laden, racialized history of domestic servitude, which leaves domestic workers' actual identities invisible even when they are formally and personally served by law. Makgoka does not call domestic work itself undignified, but he does highlight the depth of the disrespect faced by domestic workers.

It would be easy to view South Africa as an outlier, given its history of apartheid.[2] Yet it is precisely because South Africa has had to deal with the fact that so many African women are domestic workers a generation after the end of apartheid that it is ahead of the game in naming the practices that contribute to domestic workers' invisibility, even when they are ubiquitous. Judge Makgoka's decision is a strong example of that. His challenge is important for decent work for domestic workers in many other parts of the world. It is central to the main question of this chapter on labor market informality: when we use the label of informality, are we getting closer to naming and redressing historical forms of societal marginalization, exclusion, inequality, and invisibility?

The question is not simply about legal form. Lawyers might rightly say that domestic workers, because they have a relationship of subordination to an easily identified employer, are covered by an employment contract, whether it is written or (as is usually the case) oral. Because they have a contract, domestic workers are part of the formal economy. So why do we worry about them?

Legal formalism built on legal fiction can easily prevent us from seeing what formalization should mean. To address this problem, leading proponents of formalizing the informal economy in the global South have focused on whether domestic workers have social protection. Markers of formalization become, in addition to minimum wage protections, access to basic health care, retirement, or a guaranteed universal basic income adopted in a few countries around the world to guarantee regular, unconditional cash transfers across a person's life cycle.[3] These critically important markers of formalization place attention on the state and its responsibility to those who work outside of classic employment relationships in which an individual employer can readily be found. This is also where so much of the labor law literature emerging from the global North has turned its attention, as it grapples with a proliferation of forms of precarious work. So-called atypical work in postindustrial market economies has become typical, and solutions that extend the traditional normative core of employment relationships beyond the standard employment relationship are seen as increasingly necessary.[4] Domestic workers—who have among the lowest incomes in the world—stand to benefit from all of these initiatives.[5]

Focusing on domestic work from a legal perspective helps us see what we might be missing when we move too swiftly away from the work relationship and the legal normativity that flows through it. In formalizing informality, we may jump too quickly to the question of social protection, without sufficiently contemplating legal relationships. Attention is needed to the other sources of law—beyond the state—in a manner that considers relative relational power and structural inequality.

My contention in this book is that law has a role to play in the structural change from a historically laden social status to one of workplace citizenship. Some observers hailed the new standards developed by the International Labour Conference committee on decent work for domestic workers as part of the formalization of the informal economy. I would like to suggest that we should be looking more closely at the assumptions behind that framing, and at the kind of shift that was set in motion when a transnational legal order on decent work for domestic workers was adopted. My research in Côte d'Ivoire and South Africa frames this shift. The choice to speak through African examples is deliberate, as a key point in this book is that core insights on informality and how to regulate decent work for domestic workers have and continue to come from the global South.[6] In this book I focus on the privileged insights into regulation that come from acknowledging this transgression from more familiar stories of legal transplantation, and from taking history and geography—space and time—seriously.[7] This book is an exercise in paying close attention.

Domestic Workers Were Paradigmatic Employees Who Claimed Citizenship

The ink had barely dried on the Domestic Workers Convention and the Domestic Workers Recommendation when preparations got under way at the International Labour Organization (ILO) to adopt a different international labor standard on labor market informality, at the request of the ILO's employers' group. In June 2015, the ILO constituency adopted the nonbinding Transition from the Informal to the Formal Economy Recommendation, 2015 (No. 204), which includes domestic workers.

Informality is neither a new phenomenon nor a new concept, and it has been considered one of the ILO's "most distinctive contributions to development thinking."[8] It has been given a broad legal definition in the Transition from the Informal to the Formal Economy Recommendation, which moved away from the language of "informal employment"—terminology that the former ILO legal adviser Anne Trebilcock refers to as oxymoronic from a strictly legal perspective, but that has gained traction statistically and holds potential to break the hold of narrow contractarian notions without losing work relationships—although the more, well, *informal* language of "informal jobs" remains.[9]

I felt uneasy about this move, in part because it reflects shifting juridical understandings of the domestic work relationship over time. This unease may be illustrated by the story of a man I met in December 2013 on a research trip to

Abidjan, Côte d'Ivoire. Côte d'Ivoire was just emerging from over a decade of significant civil strife, and many institutions needed to be rethought and rebuilt. The man in question, Kone Tadjaga, was the secretary-general of the National Union of Domestic Employees of Côte d'Ivoire (known by its French acronym SYNEMCI, for Syndicat national des employés de maison de Côte d'Ivoire).

The word "employees," which appears in the union's title, should be emphasized. SYNEMCI is not one of the new unions created in different parts of the world during the significant mobilizing and advocacy that has both led to and accompanied the ILO's historic adoption of the Domestic Workers Convention and the Domestic Workers Recommendation. Rather, this union has been around for a while, as has been its leader. As an elder, Tadjaga would be regarded with respect in any case, but his self-respect came also from his occupational status. He informed me that he had been a domestic worker during the time of the union's founding, in the colonial era. At that time, to be a domestic worker was to belong to a new category of employees, those who fought for and claimed their status, in the historian Frederick Cooper's terms, as a "modern industrial working man."[10]

This leader witnessed the union's fight to end forced labor and then to transform itself into a full-fledged political party and claim political independence. Once the workers recognized that they could obtain some level of workplace citizenship, the move to political citizenship was hardly far behind.[11]

Metropolitan France's response to the claims in its West and Central African colonies was the 1952 Overseas Labor Code. France introduced a model of labor governance that paralleled in significant ways the governance of labor-management relations in France, including a broad swath of the governance institutions and a vision of the relationship between workers and employers as if it were universally relevant. The code was welcomed by the same citizens who sought recognition of their status as workers and was interpreted to include domestic servants. They were colonial migrant workers who had left subsistence agriculture in rural regions to join the ranks of modern urban employees governed by colonial capitalist laws. Yet the Overseas Labor Code, which by virtue of state law was of universal application, barely touched the economy now referred to as informal, "separating waged workers from people engaged in other forms of economic relationships"—that is, everyone else.[12] But the formal economy came at once to be aspirational and perceived as normal—that is, the way a modern labor market should be. Moreover, in 1952, under colonial rule, it was also a form of *commandement*, a technique of domination.[13] Despite minor modifications after independence, the Overseas Labor Code's framework largely remained in place and was ardently defended by unions of workers in the formal economy.

Development, Productive Employment, and Informality's Invisibility

The logic that prevailed in so many states during their late colonial or early independence periods was that the formal economy would develop through increased production. Of course, several schools of thought emerged to challenge modernization theory, recognizing the global North's role in causing underdevelopment in the global South.[14] This chapter offers only the barest of sketches. States in the global South experimented with significantly different approaches to development, including producing locally while exporting as much as possible through a range of import substitution policies. Some privatized, some nationalized, and many went back and forth between approaches.[15] Many newly independent states called for the international community to embrace a New International Economic Order that would change the status quo and enable them to "share on an equal footing in the blessings" of industrial democracies.[16] They relied on a broader range of international economic institutions to seek to develop an embedded liberalism framework to redistribute the gains of production among their citizenry through a variety of social welfare schemes, as in the global North.[17] But building a welfare state was rarely a realistic option economically for many of these states.[18] Decolonization claims became flattened once development came to be understood essentially as something that must occur at the level of the nation-state.[19]

The strategies did share one feature: formal employment remained front and center in the vision of development.[20] It is therefore not surprising that traditional approaches to labor law remained front and center, too. Developing countries sought technical cooperation and assistance to build labor law systems largely like those in the global North. They too sought to promote the objective of "full, productive, and freely-chosen employment," to use the language of the ILO's Employment Policy Convention, 1964 (No. 122). They spent little time trying to characterize actual work relationships, not to mention the workplace norms that governed them. It is little wonder, then, that when the informal economy was analyzed by researchers in the 1970s the language of "informal sector" is often attributed to the British anthropologist Keith Hart, whose research on urban Ghana was published in 1973. However, a team of Kenyan researchers from the Institute for Development Studies at the University of Nairobi published a 600-page International Labour Office report in 1972 on the informal sector—there was an intellectual battle over how to frame it.[21] The dominant framework was employment in the productive, formal economy. One option was to flatten the informal economy into a version of the traditional sector, the one newly independent states sought to move away from. But there was a problem: the researchers from the Institute for Development Studies emphasized that the overwhelming majority of work was in the informal economy.

Furthermore, the researchers suggested that the informal economy was actually economically efficient and could produce profit despite low wages and a dearth of technology, capital, and links with the formal economy. The authors of the 1972 report emphasized the "pervasive importance of the link between formal and informal activities," which are "not confined to employment on the periphery of the main towns, to particular occupations or even to economic activities. Rather, informal activities are the way of doing things."[22] This seemed to fly in the face of a vision of formal and informal sectors as part of a dualism—parallel tracks, rather than a spectrum of employment.

The icing on the cake is that the report's authors did not even seem to have a pejorative view about informality, although the title of the report focused on increasing "productive" employment. But they were alive to its invisibility, noting that "informal-sector activities are largely ignored, rarely supported, often regulated and sometimes actively discouraged by the Government."[23] So what happened?

Paul Bangasser suggests that this early, textured work that looked closely at relationships was flattened out in the ILO's World Employment Programme.[24] The approach was the one that seemed safe. It sought to help people suffering from informality rather than to learn from those who might be benefiting from it or consider the reasons for informality in the first place. In hindsight, though, it might be said that solutions to informality were made to fit the dominant development discourse and be minimally disruptive of the directional thrust of broader global employment policies upon which the story of labor law in industrialized market economies has been written. The deeper challenge of informality to conceptions of the formal economy was not—and arguably still has not been—acknowledged, even as the ILO set out to engage with gendered forms of informal economy work, such as industrial homework.[25] In the process, we may have lost sight of the work relationships.

Domestic Workers Are No Longer Paradigmatic, Although They Are Ubiquitous

It is true for Côte d'Ivoire and many other countries throughout Africa, Asia, the Middle East, Latin America, and the Caribbean: domestic workers are omnipresent. The economic capital of Côte d'Ivoire, Abidjan, is home to a million domestic workers. Almost every household—not only those of expatriates earning international salaries, but a wide range of households across some very modest income levels—has a domestic worker.[26] But if domestic workers are ubiquitous, they are no longer paradigmatic, in that domestic work no longer provides a normatively controlling idea about the way work should be organized. The labor law model of productive employment like that in the global North saw paid domestic work as a relic of the past. Like informality generally, it would disappear.

The Côte d'Ivoire Union of Domestic Employees in the contemporary landscape is a bare shell of the union it was at the country's independence from France in 1960. For one thing, membership in the contemporary context is considerably lower than it was then. The elderly male trade unionist I met seemed almost wistful about the other reason: in his day, the workers were predominantly male internal migrants. Now internal migration remains an important factor, but the workers are overwhelmingly young women.

But domestic work has not disappeared.[27] On the contrary, domestic work is on the rise throughout postindustrial economies too, as they also experience growth in informalization and precarious work. Informality is also on the rise in the global South, due to structural adjustment policies that touched groups like civil servants or employees in formerly nationalized firms who had moved into post-independence formal economy work.[28] In Côte d'Ivoire, as in most nations of the global South at varying degrees of development, labor market informality remains the norm. Domestic workers' invisibility is part of that norm. In other words, it is part of the law that governs the relationship.

While the dualist approach to labor market informality has largely been discredited, the erroneous presumption that labor market informality would essentially disappear has had a particularly constraining impact on mainstream labor lawyers, both nationally and at the ILO.[29]

Why Informality? Reflections on the Transition from the Informal to the Formal Economy Recommendation

Martha Chen and her colleagues at the Women in Informal Employment: Globalizing and Organizing network have pioneered close and careful research on specific aspects of the informal economy and are calling for precise measurements of workers nobody previously paid attention to. Chen and colleagues also pay close attention to how to deliver a range of social protection measures to those groups.[30] This is a crucial dimension of making domestic work visible. Their work makes domestic work count, and had a significant impact on the ability to make the case for standard setting at the ILO.

What if the problem is that—in a landscape in which informality and the employment relationship overlap—the label of informality from a legal perspective tells us very little about the appropriateness and adaptability of mechanisms meant to bring social justice to the world of work? What if informality simply becomes another label by which to fetishize a particular way of discussing formalization without calling it into question; that is, one that fails to call into question what we really mean to capture with the promotion of growth through certain kinds of laws and legal institutions? What if workers in the United States, as in Côte d'Ivoire—whether they are characterized as formal or the informal economy workers—no longer expect to receive health insurance or retirement pensions, and shoulder social risk alone?

Although some commentators have expressed concern that the Transition from the Informal to the Formal Economy Recommendation is light on labor standards, that to me would not necessarily be the main problem if an alternative vision of comprehensively (or, at least, carefully) regulating excluded categories of subaltern labor were to flow through it.[31] I think it is more informative to pay attention to what takes the place of standards.[32]

Beyond Customary Law

Trebilcock had proposed as early as 2004 that a situated methodology for assessing informality should be adopted, one that would focus on the realities involved, assess the specific international labor standards that might be applied and their utility in the real world, and consider the scope already available for their flexible application—relying implicitly on the insight that participation by those most concerned (through social dialogue) would provide both guidance and legitimacy.[33]

In my opinion, this calls for a critical legal pluralist framework, and I say this recognizing that there can be as many pluralisms as there are pluralists.[34] Although some pluralists use the language of customary law, which acknowledges the existence of alternative normative orders, I shy away from that language. Customary law, particularly in postcolonial settings, has been a troubled one, rooted in the relegation of those alternatives to a racial hierarchy of norms that made them subordinate to the law of general application.[35] The spaces that customary law held open for colonized peoples were circumscribed as "suited to their state of evolution," racializing representations of the law of the other.[36] These laws were relegated to particular spheres of application like family law or else largely treated as suspect or illiberal. Even in Europe, "what we know as custom was much more present in the lives of ordinary folk, but this was not conceptualized as binding obligation. It was rather simply a way of life."[37]

Understanding Invisibility in the Law of the Household Workplace

My framework approaches what has been referred to by Eve Darian-Smith as a "global" sociolegal perspective.[38] That is, I believe that the state should not simply be taken for granted as the only site for law. I look closely at local or substate levels like the household workplace. I seek to capture the dynamic interaction between multiple governance levels, including the international level where standard setting takes place. Darian-Smith suggests that this kind of trajectory is atypical for law and society scholars. I suggest, however, that the trajectory traced in this book should be a deeply familiar part of the story of labor law, which rests on a founding narrative that acknowledges the sociolegal notion of the law of the shop. Labor law sources are acknowledged to be plural, and the specificity of regulation emerges from the workplace—often taken to mean the industrial shop floor.[39] Social actors in labor law in many parts of the world are not merely one component among many in the legal process. Rather, they are labor law's center of gravity.[40]

Most of the work on the law of the shop focuses on unionized environments, but it is crucial to remember that the law of the shop does not exist only when workers have a representative who is able to bargain on their behalf and reach agreement with management. In the absence of the countervailing force of unions, or when unions have not specifically negotiated with management about a subject, managers manage alone.[41] The main point is that there is more alternative law within the workplace—whether that workplace is a factory or a farm, a hospital or a household—and it applies in ways that make it so that the state cannot, will not, or need not intervene. I am concerned therefore with identifying the living law of the workplace that may not be found in formal legal documents like collective agreements, labor codes, constitutions, or international labor standards.[42]

The alternative law, be it the law of the shop or the law of the household workplace, may be unequal and may inscribe subordination on the bodies of the workers. One need not look far for an example in domestic work. Consider two domestic workers interviewed at SYNEMCI. They slept together in a closet where luggage was stored, and they had to keep the closet door open to have enough space to lie down. In their words, the space was "not made for them."[43] The law of the household workplace may govern domestic workers, but it too was not made for domestic workers.

Even though this approach may sound familiar to labor lawyers, the insight has largely gotten lost in transplantation, in the pretense of the state's monopoly on law.[44] There are predictable cycles in the literature decrying the ineffectiveness of labor law in many developing countries. But the presumed universal coverage of formal state law, within the framework of Westphalian sovereignty, may be the true fiction. Some labor codes in fact only apply to a very small percentage of workers in the formal economy—sometimes less than 10 percent of the working population. Some law and society scholarship emphasizes the fact that there is a gap between the law on the books and the law on the ground. My approach goes beyond that. It challenges an idea that is central to transnational thinking about law, which—as the transnational legal theorist Peer Zumbansen emphasizes—is really a way to say that as long as the state alone is entrusted with establishing the law, only it can formalize law, and everything else is considered informal.[45] But what are we to do about the norms that exist in informality and the law of the household workplace? What if informality is normatively controlling?

I suggest that we need to start with a framework that pays attention to sites of alternative law that are actor-centered and that transverse the local and the global. The leading sociolegal theorist Boaventura de Sousa Santos refers to this as "interlegality," which he emphasizes is indeterminate.[46] Must domestic workers live by the law of the household where they work? Domestic workers resist or transgress aspects of the largely inequitable, alternative law of the household workplace that has emerged and changed over time and across space. Domestic workers transgress by insisting that the household is for them a workplace, to be governed by workplace laws.

I also invite readers to pay attention to the systems of meaning, including race, that have inscribed and ordered the asymmetrical law of the household workplace.[47] The legal anthropologist Sally Falk Moore is frequently and appropriately cited because she recognizes that state law is embedded in other forms of normativity. State law is semiautonomous.[48] It interacts with other social fields in an ongoing process.[49] Some interactions can be "so patterned or repetitive that they can perpetuate a social condition just as effectively as the calculated maintenance of an explicit set of rules."[50] Falk Moore's work helps explain how the law of the household workplace has become normalized, and as a result domestic workers' needs and justice claims as workers have become invisible.

Nothing in this discussion of the law of the household workplace is meant to suggest that domestic workers are merely passive victims who submit to their employers' dictates. Recognizing workers' agency is a core insight in labor law, and part of its specificity. Labor lawyers should not be surprised that domestic workers might even resist attempts by the state to infantilize them as vulnerable workers who need the government to step in to protect them.[51] Labor law is a constant struggle to balance protection and agency.[52] Many pluralists—including transnational legal pluralists—want to decenter the state and are wary of statism as a form of emancipation.[53] Still others want to preserve a role for the state in a world that is acknowledged to have many sites of law, some wielding disproportionate power. Notably, the sociolegal scholar Jean-Guy Belley wants to leave open spaces for alternative ways of thinking about political legitimacy and legal order, but he also wants to focus on the state's responsibility to achieve social justice without pretending that the state has a monopoly on doing that.[54]

These insights complement the approach to the development of a transnational legal order on decent work for domestic workers that is at the center of this book. They acknowledge that relative power matters. They do not dwell on hierarchies of law but instead look to discursive communities' understanding that they can change how power is held.[55] The basic point of this chapter, however, is that it is necessary to move beyond merely labeling domestic work as informal and to pay attention to and understand the pluralist law of the household workplace. It is necessary to understand the law in the household when that household becomes a workplace, even if that workplace is halfway around the world from the worker's own home. Understanding is a first step to identifying what must and can be changed, keeping it in motion and unsettling it.

CHAPTER 3

Subordination or Servitude in the Law of the Household Workplace

Decent Work for Domestic Workers

> Today as in the past, domestic workers are racialized people who largely come from former colonies. Their situation permits us to see, sometimes tragically, that racism, colonialism and servitude have not disappeared, even if they have taken on different forms. Feminists must address these questions.
>
> —Angela Davis, "Les combats d'Angela Davis," *Le Monde*, Paris, January 15, 2016

"Are You Eve?"

The historic downtown church was packed "with family, friends, and lawyers," joked a prominent entrepreneur and philanthropist who was paying tribute to a community stalwart and a distinguished founding partner of a law firm. I slipped into one of the few empty pews at the back, moments before the service for one of my former professors started, and participated in the moving service. As the congregation rose to leave, I watched my progressive young dean move effortlessly out of the church. He was surrounded by dignitaries.

And then it happened. Two women whom I have no recollection of ever having met seemed intent on gaining my attention. One asked, almost tenderly, "Are you Eve? I had been hoping to see our helper again." She asked again, staring at me searchingly. Under the silent gaze of a mortified graduate student who seemed more familiar with these fine old families than I was, I looked this woman squarely in the eyes. And then, after I was sure she had had the chance to really see me, I walked away.

Many postcolonial and critical race scholars have compellingly explored the significance of the crushing colonial alienation and objectification of misidentification in the Fanonian moment in *Black Skin, White Masks*. The psychiatrist and postcolonial theorist Frantz Fanon describes a time when a little white girl pointed at him and turned to her mother, stating, "Look, a Negro . . . I'm afraid."[1]

Author and former domestic worker Fatima Elayoubi recounts her own moment of objectification in the troubling experience of taking the bus with her eleven-year-old daughter, sitting next to an elegantly dressed woman who Elayoubi quickly sensed was troubled by her presence. When Elayoubi got up, her daughter became enraged. Her daughter indignantly affirmed both that Elayoubi needed the seat and that she was worthy of it—she had paid for her bus pass, too. Elayoubi publicly, and in French, acknowledges her daughter's anger—that is, Elayoubi speaks back, calling on her daughter to analyze her *ressentiment*, to see who was at fault. Elayoubi unambiguously concludes that the fault is on the side of the other woman, but her process of getting to that point is intriguing. She positions herself as "between the two colours, neither white nor black":[2] her analysis is deeply rooted in her identity as a working-class, North African immigrant woman in France and is at once a reflective and defiant response to the objectifying gaze. Speaking of herself in the third person, Elayoubi adds:

> You see, Fatima is 50 years old. She is clean. She dresses in French clothing, but not from Boulevard Haussmann. She shops at the weekly markets. . . . Her perfume comes from Monoprix. She is not refined but neither does she act ill at ease when someone else sits next to her. . . .
>
> This woman and many others like her needed Fatima when she was well. Fatima was her right hand. She cannot go to work without a Fatima, build her future, her family, earn money, buy perfume, beautiful clothing, without a Fatima. . . .
>
> When Fatima returns to her own home, after her work, another day begins. Everything waits for her: the cleaning, the cooking, the children. One day, Fatima can no longer stand.
>
> Do not be angry. Because where a parent is hurt, there is an angry child. Be proud of all the Fatimas who clean the houses of the women who work.[3]

Black feminist scholar bell hooks and critical race scholar Shireen Razack both focus on the experience of the subordinating encounter for racialized women.[4] Hooks challenges the assumption that intimate relationships, or even expressed desires for them, "eradicate the politics of racial domination as they are made manifest in personal interaction."[5] To understand Elayoubi's experience on the bus, and even my own experience in that church, it is necessary to be able to see how easily racialized invisibility coexists with and ultimately ascribes a filter through caste, in the presumed but ultimately spatially constrained and invariably fraught intimacy that epitomizes the domestic work relationship. You do not know or even see me, or my world. But you think you know my place in your world.[6] Elayoubi not only makes herself seen; she is heard, and, in particular, heard by her daughter. She acknowledges that the conditions under which she has done the work have literally broken her body, but insists on the dignity of her work. She calls for that dignity to be recognized in very concrete terms, including through the right to social protection that she was ultimately able to claim when she suffered a breakdown. Elayoubi's transgression of boundaries is an act of freedom.[7]

Shireen Ally, author of one of the seven leading ethnographic studies foregrounded in this chapter, starts her study of the approximately one million domestic workers in South Africa who have been stereotyped as "Eve" with the narrative of Hazel Sondlo, "a woman whose life story typifies the problem" central to Ally's analysis. Sondlo states plainly: "I was like a slave to that family. I was their black slave."[8] She describes the long hours and disrespectful treatment that she endured both before apartheid's demise and since the birth of the South African democratic state. Yet this same worker is not despondent about the legislative change in a context of broader political change: "This thing of democracy. . . . Now, I have rights. Rights like all other workers."[9] Ally's analysis includes this affirmation but does not stop at it. Instead, Ally questions what difference rights have made for domestic workers in South Africa.

Postapartheid South Africa made significant strides to legislate decent work for domestic workers, but persisting—even deepening—inequality is obvious.[10] Domestic workers live with stark disparity on a daily basis, as they move between their own impoverished households to the relative comfort of their employers' homes.[11] Labor and employment lawyers may talk about subordination and may recognize employers' and employees' obligations. But this domestic worker forces us to think about what work the gift plays in contexts of profound inequality, cementing obligations between domestic workers and their employers along the slippery spectrum reflected in subordination and servitude. As another domestic worker poignantly asked Ally, "how can you ever leave someone who buys you a house?"[12]

The international standard setting at the International Labour Organization (ILO) was based on the premise that domestic workers can claim inclusion in a contemporary framework of labor law that has historically been denied to them. However, there is a paradoxical flip side of the inclusion claim in the historicized law that governs them before and beyond the international standard setting: the law of the household workplace. By focusing on the law of that workplace, I contend that the domestic work relationship brings into sharp focus the extent that status has remained a critical component of contemporary labor law. To look at domestic workers' invisibility is to see the interaction of contract and status.

Consider the depth of the challenge that the ILO faced when it set out to imagine transnational alternatives. The pluralist law beyond the state in the domestic work relationship is powerful enough to have a tight grip on that relationship even in the presence of state law, national or international. The law of the household workplace is seen through the ethnographies discussed in this chapter as a basis for understanding the persistence of ritualized servitude in domestic work. State-based law is rarely intended to root out the inequality in the relationship; rather, it is more likely to perpetuate it. While the law of the household workplace might become a site of interaction and contestation, it certainly cannot be challenged without being understood.

In the international standard-setting process, I was focused on constructing a transnational law that avoided naturalizing and reinscribing inequitable relationships. I thought it perilous to purport to offer regulatory prescriptions without historicizing and contextualizing the work and the work relationship. This entailed taking seriously "the operations of power—with the real and symbolic effects of subordination and subjectification" that are inscribed on the historically marked, racialized bodies of domestic workers.[13]

I begin this chapter with an historical interrogation of subordination in labor law and in opposition to the history and legacy of slavery. I then analyze seven of the leading ethnographies conducted over the period generally associated with contemporary globalization, published before the ILO standard setting was completed.[14] They helped me understand legal transformation as including but extending both beyond state-centered law reform and across multiple governance levels. The multiple levels are woven together, sometimes loosely and sometimes tightly.[15] In labor law, the national and the transnational are simply not severable from local workplaces.[16] Regulating decent work for domestic work, including regulations by domestic workers themselves, is illustrative.

Subordination in Labor Law and the Persistence of Servitude

An all-too-familiar labor law narrative presents a clean historical transition from the master-servant relationship to the contemporary employment relationship. In the better texts, the untidy fact of the historical existence of slave relationships makes a de rigueur appearance, before dropping altogether out of the main transition to the core concern—the working class. Yet what are we to make of the remarkably prevalent use, in contemporary ethnographic studies on the domestic work relationship, of the language of employer and employee alongside the language of master or mistress and servant, or even slave? How do we explain the recurrence of the laden notions of status that are uneasily close to intersecting, othered identities, alongside the notion of the contract? Even the standard employment law language of subordination is used interchangeably with that of servitude and slavery in many of the studies, suggesting a structural, identity-based notion of inequality rather than the ubiquitous yet diffuse term that distinguishes labor and employment relationships from commercial contracts.

I refuse to cater to readers' comfort by tidying up the concepts or sweeping some under the rug to present the clean, familiar story yet again. I do not dichotomize free and unfree labor, leaving the reader with neat legal definitions for each and lining up the boxes in a tidy row.[17] The uneasy lack of order tells us something about the weight of the past on the present in domestic work governance. I insist on the need to live with the messiness of the domestic work relationship, and I do so by looking closely at the everyday law of the household workplace. This chapter therefore acknowledges the emerging historical literature that challenges dichotomies between enslaved and free labor in the history of the emergence of capitalism. Similarly, I reject stark characterizations of the metaphorical labor market as rigidly demarcated from reproductive household labor.[18] There are many layers to the complex coexistence of free and enslaved labor, and they persist today, paradoxically embodied in the domestic workers who are racialized and otherwise othered and rendered invisible.

The argument is heavily influenced—like the work of many critical labor law scholars—by James Atleson's pioneering critical work on the underlying values and assumptions of labor law in the US context. Atleson explains that "the alleged move from status to contract obscures the very special kind of contract that emerged," one that gives employers unilateral power to direct the workforce and determine the pace of work; requires loyalty and submission; and legitimates employer discretion, even as it lessens it through collective bargaining.[19] Yet scholars like Atleson, Judy Fudge, and Eric Tucker tend to agree in their analyses with Simon Deakin and Frank Wilkinson's comment on the UK context that "the legacy of the master and servant code was the assimilation by the common law of a hierarchical, disciplinary model of service."[20] Although Deakin and Wilkinson trace an evolution in the contracts of employment of "higher status" employees, they acknowledge that in particular context, the "imposition of a restrictive disciplinary code" on some categories of workers (in the nineteenth century, most industrial and agricultural workers) challenges any realistic prospect of considering that a "developed" theory of the contractual employment relationship existed.[21]

The notion of subordination originates from the household-based law of master and servant and, as Lea VanderVelde argues, from the law of master and slave.[22] To comment on rights and duties in "private economic relations," Sir William Blackstone identified those that he considered to be "great": that of husband and wife, "founded in nature, but modified by civil society"; that of parent and child, "which is consequential to that of marriage"; that of guardian and ward, "which is a kind of artificial parentage"; and—the relationship that he lists first—that of master and servant.[23]

For Blackstone, the relationship of master and servant is "founded in convenience, whereby a man is directed to call in the assistance of others."[24] Blackstone identifies several forms of these others, including apprentices; laborers hired by the day or week and who do not live *intra maenia* (that is, within the household) as part of the family; and a species of servants, "if they may be so called, being rather in a superior, a ministerial, capacity," like stewards, factors, and bailiffs. Blackstone also lists menial servants, so called precisely because they are *intra maenia*, while taking care to include gardeners who might live in a separate house without paying rent and even have "several inferior gardeners under him"[25] but excluding some others like secretaries, tutors, and governesses.[26] Citing case law on governesses, Blackstone reasons that a governess's position in society, station in the family, and "manner in which such person is usually treated in society" place her in a different position compared to domestic servants.[27]

Although Blackstone characterizes the employment relationship as arising out of a contract, that contract of hiring means that the master acquires property in the services of his domestics, purchased by giving them wages: "The reason and foundation, upon which all this doctrine is built, seem to be the property that every man has in the service of his domestics; acquired by the contract of hiring, and purchased by giving them wages."[28]

"Labour is the poor man's property," Blackstone asserts, and he is often quoted because he affirmed further that "pure and proper slavery does not, nay cannot, subsist in England, such I mean as gives an absolute and unlimited power to the master, over the life and fortune of the slave."[29] This is interesting for two reasons. First, the master-slave relationship is understood in relation to the master-servant relationship. Second, the framing makes it possible to engage with the existence of slavery, while preserving the contractual framing by focusing on relationships between persons, things, and actions.[30] As Orlando Patterson argues, however, to understand slavery through property is to miss the myriad ways in which property ownership characterized a number of status-based relationships, including marriage.[31] This follows Blackstone's discussion of the various relationships to persons and, as VanderVelde has emphasized, each of the relationships chronicled by Blackstone is a relationship of subordination.[32]

Although initially harshly critiqued in England, the impact of Blackstone's *Commentaries* on the development of law beyond England—in particular, in much of the colonial world—can hardly be overstated.[33] At least since publication of the *Commentaries*, courts and legal commentators have also expended extensive energy attempting to distinguish employment relationships from commercial relationships, using seemingly endless variants on, or expansive tests for, subordination. With domestic work, however, the subordination literally jumps off the page. The easily recognizable subordination in domestic work yields a further challenge for the dichotomization of subordination and slavery or servitude.[34]

Challenging the Legal Origins of Labor Law

Historical examples from eighteenth-century England make it possible to say something about the tendency to read the master-servant relationship as sharply separated from slavery. The leading British historian Carolyn Steedman recognizes that the occupation of paid domestic workers has sometimes been considered a status, even though at the time of her study, most white women or men would have been servants at one point in their lives. In her pivotal work, she draws upon English case law and doctrinal sources, which she found reinforced the early views expressed in religious tracts that the master was like a father to whom obedience and subordination were owed. But the language of contract—"agreement and retainer"—soon appears in the manner in which the relationship is understood.[35]

Steedman challenges Blackstone's use of the term "status," which is also found in many modern studies on domestic work. Yet remarkably, Steedman then turns both outward to studies of colonial Latin American countries (Peru and Brazil) and inward to the existence of slavery in Britain, all contemporaneous to her study of the eighteenth-century master and servant relationship. She offers these are counterexamples, places where performing domestic work might well be considered a status—in part because of the "absence of legal regulation."[36] In her reading of contemporaneous literature from both Brazil and Peru, she notes in particular the fact that "the system was strongly inflected by the experience of slavery and racial categorisation."[37]

In her discussion of Brazil, Steedman does not distinguish between the free women and the slaves who undertook similar work. Yet for eighteenth-century

England, she most assuredly does make the distinction, and sharply. She contends that the institution of slavery, and thus the role of the slave-servant, was framed as being of the past: the relationship became a basis for comparison, a way to illustrate the "self-possession and legal rights" of those in a "modern social order coming into being." But slave-servants were still present, just invisible: "they had no legal existence, and there was no name to call them." As Steedman powerfully states, "not being persons, of any kind or degree, slaves did not substitute for or enact any part of the owner's capacity. Rather, they were labour embodied: labour itself."[38]

Steedman's study is rightly recognized as offering a pivotal, largely gender-based corrective focusing on service work to E. P. Thompson's classic account of the *Making of the English Working Class*.[39] Yet remarkably, scholars who take the position that "we can look to the places eighteenth-century domestic workers chose to speak rather than to our assumptions about their silence and suffering" may unwillingly reinscribe the silence—the othered everydayness—of the African slave.[40]

Steedman discusses at great and fascinating length the case of one woman of African descent, Charlotte Howe, who was enslaved in the United States and arrived as a slave on British soil in 1782. This was well after Lord Mansfield's famous 1772 *Somerset* decision, which prevented a master from removing his slave from England against the slave's will. When Howe brought a case under the Poor Laws, Lord Mansfield decided that even though she had earned wages in her master's employ, she had never been hired. Consequently, she could not be a servant. It did not matter that Blackstone had written in his *Commentaries* that a slave becomes free on arrival in England. The decision was praised by contemporaneous commentators as respecting a hierarchy of norms that favored statute and contractual form over customary practice, and firmly reinscribing the boundaries of enslaved work. Howe was rendered invisible by the legal characterization and silent in the absence of a voice in a transcript.[41] We know nothing about how Howe lived her domestic work relationship, but we know she is taken to embody the enslaved: labor itself.[42]

Under the emerging employment contract, workers were paid wages and sold their labor power in the shadow of the law. In contrast, the institution of unfree labor (chattel slavery) meant that as property, the slave earned no wages, or at least that the wages were not his or her own—the labor was status-based servitude.[43] The subaltern slave-servant, paradigmatic in so many parts of the world where the British Empire and other colonial powers once reached, is thus rendered invisible to the law.

Historians of capital and slavery in the northern United States who challenge this invisibility allow a clearer picture to emerge of the relationship between slavery and employment. Seth Rockman in particular captures the coexistence of a broad spectrum of free and enslaved labor. Joanne Pope Melish documents the coexistence of employment and enslavement in the same person in eighteenth-century New England. What is more, Pope Melish highlights the racist ideology that persisted after the enactment of freedom in New England: "whites' eighteenth-century observation that servitude made slaves servile hardened into their nineteenth-century conviction that all people of color were inherently servile—freed slaves, perhaps, but free people never."[44] The legal conflation of race with status under slavery remained embodied, and Black, after abolition. To purport to study the law—or the absence of state regulation—without looking more closely at what law exists is to leave this conflation of race and status in place.

Seeing the Inequitable Law of the Household Workplace through Ethnographic Studies

Ethnographic literature sheds light on how domestic workers live at intersections of forms of inequality. By keeping the subject invisible, it is possible to legislate about, for, and upon her, but not with her. Yet at the core of labor law's specificity is its claim to see each worker and to care enough about her capabilities and agency to transform conditions and allow her to exercise collective autonomy. Labor lawyers who seek to understand and regulate atypical work relationships, or the generic category of labor market informality, must engage with this existing ethnographic work as a critical source of pluralist law. The domestic work relationship emerges from labor law's peripheries to claim inclusion and offers a pivotal starting point for reimaging an emancipatory labor law. That reimagination has to involve challenging invisibility. In this chapter I rely upon and, to some extent, subvert the typical way that many historical and current textbooks on employment law are framed. Implicitly, I challenge the presumptive starting points for a particular idea of industrial era labor regulation.[45] The ethnographies allow this to be done.

In the Shadow of the Contract: Postcolonial Racialized Histories of Servitude

Domestic workers have often been explicitly excluded from the legal framework applicable to other workers. Contemporary literature has tended to assume that the background rules governing the domestic employment relationship are the same ones available to the entrepreneurs in Stuart Macaulay's celebrated study of presumptively arms-length, formally equal business entrepreneurs who negotiated their interactional contracts in the shadow of state law.[46]

Historically, however, domestic workers have engaged from a very different place, despite the use of the language of contract to describe their relationship: the place where subordination meets servitude, in the household workplace. In a role rather like the one that criminal law and the penal enforcement of vagrancy laws played in master and servant regimes, state law continues to prevent domestic workers from exercising mobility and autonomy. Borders within and between states are policed in ways that reinforce racialization and recreate the postcolonial performance of place.[47] State law has bluntly structured domestic workers' mobility, most obviously through the enforcement of pass laws in apartheid South Africa, but also through the policing of undocumented workers in certain neighborhoods in various European countries. State law has also regulated domestic workers' mobility through its selective absences. For example, Christine Chin analyzes how the Malaysian state heavily policed migrant domestic workers' access to public spaces but refused to legislate their conditions of employment. The effect was to transfer the responsibility for determining work relations and boundaries to employers and foreign domestic workers.[48] The asymmetry in the relationship cements them to the place where subordination meets servitude; concretely, the state's regulatory choices compound the difficulty for domestic workers to escape abusive workplaces, not to mention to demand decent work.

There is also more law in the shadows than state law. Law emerges from the history of domestic work, inscribed with permanent marker on the bodies of racialized, postcolonial subjects. Who does the work, and under what regulatory conditions, becomes part of the fabric of the law of the household workplace that is sewn together.

Ally, for one, challenges both the perceived naturalness and willingness of African women's migration into domestic work in South Africa and any suggestion that the state was absent from this development. Ally recalls that in the settler colony in South Africa, particularly in the Cape region, it was Africans who were required to serve as slaves, and slaves who served as domestics.[49] In the early twentieth century, the colonial government sought to promote and structure the employment of native women in domestic work. This active colonial role challenges any assumption that the state was somehow absent from the organization of the sector along particular racialized and gendered lines. After the abolition of slavery and the use of a spate of European immigrants in domestic work, African women returned to domestic work through a process of urbanization under what the South African Native

Affairs Commission called "the apartheid architecture of citizenship" that prevented alternative forms of economic activity for women and that had more urgent need for the initial male domestic servants (houseboys) in the mines.[50]

Initial attempts to use the law to compel African women to enter domestic service were met with militant protests.[51] But a range of legislative measures—from the Masters and Servants Act of 1889 to the Vagrancy Act of 1879—produced a supply of domestic workers.[52] Public employment agencies throughout the apartheid era controlled influx into the sector so that it was predominantly occupied by African women.[53] Knowing this history, it is not surprising that domestic workers were active leaders of the anti-apartheid struggle. After apartheid, the South African state needed to address the conditions under which South African domestic workers labored. Largely protective labor standards regulation ensued in "one of the most extensive and expansive efforts anywhere in the world to recognize paid domestic work as a form of employment."[54] This reform is discussed in some detail in chapter 6.

Chin paints a similarly complex portrait of the colonial and postcolonial history of domestic service in Malaysia, chronicling the waves of migration from Chinese and Indian immigrant males to Malay women and Chinese and Indian immigrant women and Indonesian and Filipina temporary migrant domestic workers. Certainly, Chin is attentive to the modes of organization of domestic work and domestic workers' resistance. She also addresses the "gender-class-ethnic nexus" in the postcolonial Malaysian state, which made it untenable for modernization policy to be seen as encouraging Malay women to move into low-paying, low-status work.[55] After all, they—rather than the Chinese minority—were supposed to be the beneficiary of the policy. Practice turned into formal state policies that favored the recruitment of Indonesian and Filipina domestic workers. The state carefully determined who could employ foreign domestic workers, on the basis of income, family status (a marriage certificate was required), and religion. As Chin argues, "foreign female domestic workers would become boundary-markers for and of the expanding Malaysian middle classes . . . evidence that development had benefitted Malaysians."[56]

Jacqueline Andall's study of Black immigrant women in Italy from the "early period" of the 1970s through to a period of transformation and change in the 1980s and 1990s traces the law and policy reform on domestic work in Italy. Andall dates the move toward protective inclusion of domestic workers in labor law to the post-1969 period, when article 2060 of the Italian Civil Code of 1942 no longer excluded domestic workers from its scope.[57] Mainstream trade unions got involved to negotiate collective agreements for domestic workers. Andall emphasizes the originality of the new regulatory framework, but she pays attention to the context in which Black women were understood to have no options beyond domestic or sex work.[58]

Judith Rollins starts her book by surveying domestic work in a range of regions around the world before focusing on the historical legacy of slavery in the United States. Rollins underscores the migration of African Americans from the US South to the North and observes that African American women constituted 28.8 percent of domestic workers during the nineteenth century but 45.8 percent by 1920—when white women were able to work in factories instead.[59] A key insight emanating from her analysis is that "while an employer-employee relationship is by definition unequal, the mistress-servant relationship—with its centuries of conventions of behavior, its historical association with slavery throughout the world, its unusual retention of feudal characteristics, and the tradition of the servant being not only of a lower class but also female, rural, and of a despised ethnic group—provides an extreme and 'pure' example of a relationship of domination in close quarters."[60]

The two other ethnographies that focused on the United States trace complementary histories. Pierrette Hondagneu-Sotelo's *Doméstica: Immigrant Workers Cleaning and Caring in the Shadows of Affluence* attributes the expansion of paid domestic work to the growth in income inequality in the United States since the early 1970s, in what is commonly referred to as the advent of the new economy—in particular, "global cities."[61] While college-educated two-income professional couples could pay for care, blue-collar workers were increasingly pushed out of downgraded manufacturing positions. In other words, and drawing on the insights of Saskia Sassen, she argues that "globalization's high-end jobs breed low-paying jobs."[62] Recalling that Los Angeles was Mexican territory until 1848, Hondagneu-Sotelo traces the impact of the Bracero Program from 1942 to 1964, which authorized five million Mexican men to work in agriculture in the United States. The men were not permitted to reunite legally with their families until the early 1970s. Hondagneu-Sotelo also attributes the macroeconomic crisis in Mexico along with structural changes in both the US and Mexican economies to growing "transnational informational social networks" that led Mexican women to take jobs in factories, hotels, and private homes.[63] Although Central American migrants who were fleeing civil war account for much of the modern migration pattern to Los Angeles, Hondagneu-Sotelo states that one of the most "stunning findings is that wherever Central American women have gone in the United States . . . they predominate in private domestic jobs."[64] Her work captures the increased homogenization over time of domestic work on the basis of race, nationality, and immigration status.[65]

Mary Romero's short historiography continues Hondagneu-Sotelo's discussion and allows for regional differences.[66] Her account is noteworthy because it categorically refuses to portray domestic service as "a (gradually disappearing) vestige of feudalism."[67] Instead, Romero resolutely privileges an analysis of domestic work under capitalism—a racial capitalism that she maps onto other historical patterns of subjugation, including slavery. She points in particular to the "obligation of care" that might have existed under feudalism, but which she argues does not exist under capitalism for the "mistress" in her relationship with her domestic servant.[68] Those private law rules that seem to reside in the background yet remain available to guide the negotiations and performance of the domestic work contract comprise what I am calling the law of the household workplace.

Daiva Stasiulis and Abigail Bakan's account is more contemporary, although the authors succinctly trace the history of regulatory shifts in migrant domestic work regulation in Canada. Their work captures the significance of racialized stereotyping to the development of migrant domestic work in Canada. The authors trace the roots of that stereotyping in debased images of the Black slave and servant that led to racialized and gendered portrayals of domestic workers "out of conditions of slavery, colonialism and an increasingly international market."[69] Domestic work was seen as the natural calling of Black women.[70]

Stasiulis and Bakan factor underdevelopment and structural adjustment policies into their discussion of the gendered migrations of women from the West Indies and the Philippines. Those policies have not only led to a relegation of unpaid work to women considered to be "shock absorbers" for market mechanisms that are presumed to be efficient.[71] The women also migrate in search of higher wages in a world of stark wage inequality.

A pivotal insight from the leading sociologist, Rhacel Parreñas, emphasizes that few of the migrants from the Philippines whom she interviewed had been unemployed before migrating, and few were in the informal economy. Parreñas discusses the genesis of the language of the care chain to describe the international division of reproductive labor in domestic work, but laments the elimination of the political-economic foundations of reproductive labor inequalities across transnational spaces.[72] She offers the language of care resource extraction: internationally mandated structural adjustment policies applied in many parts of the developing world in the 1980s and 1990s, including in the Philippines, exhausted any prospect of state-provided domestic care resources. The Philippines adopted an active debt financing process, serviced through the remittances from people who emigrated to find work elsewhere.[73]

Finally, Stasiulis and Bakan focus on the role of the state, showing how Canada institutionalized the threat of abuse faced by domestic workers through its 1992 Live-In Caregiver Program that was more restrictive than previous domestic worker programs. They highlight the fact that the Canadian government could instead have provided a framework to prevent abuse. Two features of the regulatory program in place when they studied it accentuate the point: there was a live-in requirement, and domestic workers became temporary residents rather than permanent residents (which was the case under the 1955 domestic worker program with people from the Caribbean). Stasiulis and Bakan's work underscores the significance of remittances for the prevalence of foreign women's migration to perform domestic work. For the authors, the regulatory framework serves a gatekeeping function that is supported by private placement agencies.[74] They also capture the paradox faced by nursing professionals from the Philippines who come to Canada as domestic workers, only to be unable to practice nursing once they achieved permanent residency status and despite demand for the labor. The authors refer to this as the perpetuation of racialized exclusions.[75]

In their framing of the regulatory context in historical perspective, each of these ethnographic accounts emphasizes the relationships between custom and ideology and between human agency and the persistence of historical legacies in contemporary institutional arrangements. Rollins implores us, in looking at the domestic work relationship, to recognize the "delicate conceptual balance we are forced to maintain if we are to at once see the people as they are and discern the social patterns they reflect and perpetuate."[76]

Interrogating Invisibility: What Work Is This, and Who Does It?

One of the first sources of invisibility tackled in the ILO's *Law and Practice Report* was the characterization of domestic work as work. The ethnographic analyses were part and parcel of the framing that led to a broad and inclusive definition of domestic work in the Domestic Workers Convention. Hondagneu-Sotelo's study led her to affirm that "paid domestic work is distinctive not in being the worst job of all but in being regarded as something other than employment. Its peculiar status is revealed in many occupational practices."[77] Consistent with this view, job descriptions in these ethnographic studies varied significantly and were rarely formalized. Domestic workers might cook, clean, take care of children, accompany seniors, or support people with disabilities. They might live with their employers or elsewhere. What remained constant was the intricate web through which the work was contracted. In her study of domestic workers in Los Angeles, Hondagneu-Sotelo captures poignantly the "parallel universe of women doing paid domestic work; it remains invisible, out of the sight and consciousness of employers, until the moment when it is tapped. Then, the network linkages act like dye to make visible the points of connection that socially and spatially link women of different groups."[78]

Hondagneu-Sotelo's work provides a particularly detailed account of the factors employers consider as they entrust their children, elderly family members, or home to a domestic worker. The author explores why personal referrals may be preferred to agencies in the search for trustworthy workers. She notes the particular emphasis that employers place on the personality of their workers.[79] In addition to her work, studies in a range of contexts, including those that involve interregional migration, underscore the more pronounced role that more or less structured agencies might play in connecting domestic workers with employers.[80] Niche networks based on national origin and ethnic ties, but operating across social class, and broader interpersonal connections and referrals tend to be intertwined in recruiting and placement.[81]

Stasiulis and Bakan emphasize the endemic character of racial stereotyping in the matching process, particularly when placement agencies are used.[82] The constant in this stage of contract formation is its structuring role—or, in Stasiulis and Bakan's terms, the agencies' gatekeeping function. Information about the domestic worker's personality and reliability, but also about pay and working conditions, serves to set and maintain a norm. In Hondagneu-Sotelo's words, "employer referrals . . . do more than help provide cleaning services: the employers are sharing information that is vital to structuring the job, as the hiring decisions of individuals are informed by what their friends tell them about their own domestic arrangements."[83]

Familiar frames for analyzing domestic work are identified to explain this difference: the location where the work is undertaken, often leading to kinship analogies; the fact that it is care work and the associations that are made between the person who provides it and the wife and mother in the family; and the personalized, even idiosyncratic nature of care work. This is all captured by Arlie Russell Hochschild as emotional labor.[84] For Hondagneu-Sotelo, "the problem of paid domestic work not being accepted as employment is compounded by the subordination by race and immigrant status of the women who do the job."[85]

The range of studies underscores one crucial point: who does the work matters.[86] Shellee Colen and Roger Sanjek stress the social message that is sent when "certain kinds of people do household work, and others do not"—there is an ideological reproduction of inequality.[87] W. E. B. Du Bois recognized this over a century ago, when he concluded that Black domestic workers were a "despised race in a despised calling."[88] In Rollins's study, for example, the majority of women were from the US South, and all but one of the domestic workers she interviewed had mothers who had also been domestic workers.[89] In her study of Filipina domestic workers in Rome and Los Angeles, Parreñas underscores how racialization may become a way for domestic workers to negotiate their loss of status by "claiming and embracing their racial differentiation from Latinas and blacks and highlighting their specific distinction as the 'educated domestics.'"[90] Across studies, the employer is identified either as Mrs. So and So or with another name conferring (often familial) social status, such as the use of "Mum" or "Auntie." Invariably, employers call the domestic worker by her first name. Plainly put, "the low status of caring work and the low status of care workers are mutually reinforced."[91]

Andall's interviews with informants in the Italian trade union—(known by the Italian acronym ACLI-COLF, Associazioni Cristiane Lavoratori Italiani or Italian Christian Workers Association-Family Collaborators)—offer further insight into who does the work and its impact on the meaning of subordination in contemporary domestic work relationships. In its attempt to adopt a more inclusive conceptual approach to migrant domestic work, the union acknowledged migrant workers' "weaker position" as compared to Italian domestic workers: the migrants earned lower pay and worked longer hours for more irregular work. The union also asserted that the employers of migrant domestic workers "appeared to have reverted to an outmoded formulation of the employer/employee relationship." The ACLI-COLF invoked the "almost total subjection" of domestic workers to their employers or employment agencies, concluding that this constituted "servitude."[92]

Boundariless Time

A key dimension of the standard setting on decent work for domestic workers surrounded time. There was nothing surprising about this focus, given that one of labor law's goals has been to standardize working time, and the ILO's first convention was the Hours of Work (Industry) Convention, 1919 (No. 1). The ILO aspired to ensure space for workers' autonomy, leisure, and rest.[93] Given the eroding industrial model, the challenges involved in making working time flexible and determining the space of the workplace are important in the contemporary context.[94]

Each of the ethnographies discussed reflects the broader social science literature: working time in domestic work is assumed to be boundariless. The assumption of general availability that prevails in domestic work is also reflected in the repeatedly reported difficulty associated with the standardization of working time. This may be particularly true for live-in domestic workers, although the ethnographies dispel the perception that using hourly paid live-out work leads to wage justice. Domestic work is treated as the subject of constant redefinition, and even recognizing the need for break time and rest periods is uncommon.[95] It raises the question of what is bought and sold in the domestic work relationship.

The issue of control over working time is understood to be in constant negotiation, particularly in Ally's work. In her response to this presumption of the protective, democratic state, Ally highlights repeated, unsettling micronegotiations between domestic workers and their employers. Through them, domestic workers in post-apartheid South Africa act—perhaps in surprising ways—upon the remarkable emergence of a relatively comprehensive set of employment standards for domestic workers. The shadow of state law becomes part of the frame that unsettles the law of the household workplace, and domestic workers are integral to that unsettling.

Chin's study addresses the construction of working conditions somewhat summarily, and in the broader context of employers' understanding of abuse as something different—like extreme physical or sexual assault. Chin reports that "many employers' refusal to provide rest days, adequate sleeping accommodations, structured work hours, and so forth, was justified instead from the perspective of protecting their servants from criminal influences, or that servants were lazy and stupid. Every employer believed that she had been 'taken advantage of' at one point or another by domestic servants."[96]

Andall captures other aspects of employers' control over domestic workers' time, even in domestic work relationships that were generally characterized by the worker as positive. For example, Antonia, a live-in domestic worker, was required by her employer to return to the employer's household by midnight on her days off. Andall quotes Antonia as follows: "Either I take no notice or else it really gets on my nerves because I don't see why I can't come home when I want. I'm 38 years old and have a 21-year-old son but you always remain a child here."[97] Andall's study provides a nuanced, critical look at the changes that take place when a collective agreement is negotiated. On working time, she stresses the significance of two changes. The first is the institutionalization of days of rest on two particular days: Sundays and Thursdays. For domestic workers who at best were traditionally allowed time off on Sundays, the addition of Thursdays was seen as progressive.

The second is that maximum working hours are progressively reduced. The first national collective agreement stipulated sixty-six hours a week, which gives an idea of how long they must have been prior to the regulation. The hours were further reduced to sixty in 1978, fifty-eight in 1984, fifty-six in 1988, and fifty-five in 1992.[98] Under the 2013 national collective agreement, which was signed after the adoption of the Domestic Workers Convention (ratified by Italy), the normal weekly working hour maximum is set at fifty-four hours, with a maximum of ten hours per day.[99]

Unjust Wages

The issue of wages was one of the areas on which members of the International Labour Conference Committee showed they had learned the most, as we saw in chapter 1. The payment of agreed wages for work or for a worker's availability for work is a crucial employer obligation, at the heart of recognizing the relationship as contractual.[100] It is worth recalling, though, that the institution of slavery could also sustain the payment of wages, alongside the "blurred boundaries between categories of labor, assuring the interchangeability of different workers along a continuum of slaves-for-life to transient day laborers—with term slaves, rented slaves, self-hiring slaves, indentured servants, redemptioners, apprentices, prisoners, children, and paupers occupying the space in between."[101]

A remarkably consistent feature in the law of the household workplace in a variety of contexts worldwide is that pay levels tend to be standardized around a going rate established in large measure through informal exchanges of information between employers.[102] This tends to be the case even when a generally applicable minimum wage should apply to (or does not expressly exclude) domestic workers. The ethnographic studies converge on the substandard pay received by domestic workers, which is often below minimum wage[103] and for long, boundariless hours—despite the inability to sweat workers as in a piece-rate factory setting.[104] This is the case whether the households are wealthy or of moderate income.[105] Moreover, providing room and board is typically seen as the basis for a deduction from wages, despite the perpetual availability for employers that live-in work is understood to create.

Several studies tackled the common rationalization that low wages in domestic work reflected domestic workers' own lack of attachment to money: they were naturally caring. The rationale that they were like one of the family was never far away. Some of the employers interviewed by Rollins mentioned that they had never even really thought about the fact that domestic workers' wages are low.[106] The relationship between pay and time is further explored by Hondagneu-Sotelo, who identifies a "general assumption that those who work more days will tolerate a lower hourly pay."[107]

Romero further underscores that there are virtually no structured pay raises for domestic workers. Raises are rarely ever offered, and have little correlation to employee fidelity and job performance over time; instead, the ethnographic studies report that raises tend to be granted only when domestic workers threaten to use their power to quit. Yet the withholding of wages for damage allegedly caused by the domestic worker—whether or not there has been any negligence—is a commonly reported phenomenon.[108] Under the law of the household workplace alone, overtime pay is routinely ignored, and vacation, health insurance, paid sick leave, paid maternity leave, and retirement pensions are all extremely uncommon or individually negotiated through the operation of a form of employer largesse.

Rollins's work captures the particularly strenuous nature of domestic work paid by the hour. Often this involves housecleaning. Several of the domestic workers Rollins interviewed felt that they were expected to complete too much work in the allotted time, or for the number of hours for which they were paid. Rollins adds that from the domestic work she undertook for the study, she "realized that [employers] being overdemanding was the norm" and learned to "pace [herself] more wisely."[109] During her day jobs, Rollins took standard morning and afternoon breaks, which she considers to have been "entirely out of the ordinary for this occupation." Although she reports having been glared at by an employer, the employer ultimately said nothing. As Rollins observes on the basis of her interviews with some domestic workers and even a few employers, employers liked to see domestics working or expressed displeasure at inactivity.[110]

A consistent theme in the foregrounded studies is that there is a wage hierarchy in domestic work linked to race or nationality. In Rollins's study, domestic workers reported that white domestic workers were paid more than Blacks.[111] Hondagneu-Sotelo notes a prevalent employer preference for Latinas, which operated in two ways. Some employers adamantly refused to hire Black women—mostly immigrants from Belize or Brazil—to work in their home. Latinas were also preferred to white domestic workers, as the former were othered in terms of language and race or ethnicity and so would be unlikely to have intersecting social circles with their employers; discretion could therefore be guaranteed.[112] In a study of the Netherlands, Sarah van Walsum similarly documents discrimination in pay against women from African countries, in favor of women from the Philippines.[113] Chin reveals that Filipina and Indonesian domestic workers were officially allowed to receive markedly different wages.[114] Religion was used as a basis on which to determine that lower-cost, Muslim Indonesians could only work for Muslim Malays. This resulted in a market for undocumented Indonesian migrant workers.[115]

Hidden in Plain Sight: Living in the Employers' Households

Andall offers a detailed portrait of the constraints on one live-in domestic worker's time during the early 1970s, prior to the trade union response. I have chosen to quote it at length:

> Lemlem['s] . . . employer was a housewife whose husband was a lawyer. They frequently entertained and on those occasions Lemlem would not finish working until 2 a.m. She was granted her two-hour rest period in the afternoon in accordance with the collectively bargained national contract. However, it is important to highlight that her two-hour daily rest period had to take place within the confines of the employers' home. In effect, this meant that she was virtually imprisoned in the home for extensive periods of time. Lemlem's free time on a Thursday afternoon and Sunday afternoon would be from 4 p.m. to 9 p.m. or 10 p.m. . . . Not only were the hours long, but her employers' primary interest in her labour meant that they attempted mentally, if not practically, to restrict other aspects of her identity. Her female employer did not want her to have a boyfriend and frequently told her that she should not get married. Thus even if Lemlem had finished all her work on a particular evening and asked to go out, the response would frequently be: "At this time? It's too late." . . . Lemlem stated: "I was always scared to ask permission. If I go out today, then tomorrow I really have to work hard." . . . when Lemlem started to work for this family she stated that she cried continually. She worked for this family for nine years, and despite their constant criticism of her ability to work: "you can't do anything, you're always making mistakes," when she eventually left them to work for two families on an hourly paid basis, they pleaded with her to stay.[116]

There is remarkable consistency across the ethnographic literature: whenever they can, domestic workers seek to live out. There is a strong link in the contemporary literature between labor migration—be it structured through migration programs, organized through recruitment agencies, or fostered by niche networks of relatives and friends (all three modes are intertwined)—and live-in relationships. Although live-in domestic work has been considered archaic and was predicted to all but disappear as societies became more egalitarian, there has been a stunning resurgence of it. Some people attribute this to the rise of the dual-income career family, whose employment is not easily mapped onto 9-to-5 arrangements. This is not the whole story, however. It is part of a story of expectations of perpetual availability: the domestic worker is expected to subordinate her life to those of the people for whom she works. In this sense, her work is boundariless.

Hondagneu-Sotelo states categorically that "most women are repelled by live-in jobs. The lack of privacy, the mandated separation from family and friends, the round-the-clock hours, the food issues, the low pay, and especially the constant loneliness prompt most Latina immigrants to seek other job arrangements."[117] She cites examples of live-in workers, like Margarita Guttiérez, who are required to sleep in the same room as the children for whom they care, and who "literally have no space and no time they can claim as their own."[118]

Hondagneu-Sotelo's work in particular captures the everyday indignities related to food in live-in, "room and board" arrangements, citing a range of examples of boundary-defining behaviors that emphasized domestic workers' exclusion. These included inadequate food, food items that were off limits to the domestic worker, or separate eating arrangements.[119] She also cites women who even held back from eating despite hunger, as they felt "subtle pressure to remain unobtrusive, humble and self-effacing."[120] Compared to the boundarilessness of live-in work, the hours of live-out jobs in Hondagneu-Sotelo's study were comparatively well circumscribed.[121]

Based as it is on entrenched power hierarchies, the live-in domestic work relationship is "archaic and oppressive," Andall argues, in that it "restrict[s] female migrants to a narrow labour function," negating their own family lives in the service of others.[122] Andall's work underscores the extent to which migrant women from Africa reluctantly meet a demand for live-in work that Italian workers are unwilling to do. Those who sought to transition to live-out work faced increased competition from Italian domestic workers, which made the migrant women's incomes more precarious. Domestic workers resign themselves to the work. In the Italian context, Andall establishes the absence of other alternatives for Black women. The phenomenon is also captured in the pragmatic statements of one of her interviewees, Antonia: "You have to resign yourself to domestic work, they are not going to give you a job in a factory or even to do cleaning in hospitals or nursing. Domestic work is, however, clean and honest work. Italian women do not want to do it so they cannot say that we're stealing work from them. You've got absolutely no chance of getting office work."[123]

Andall's analysis demonstrates that employer control over the space is "intrinsically connected to the question of migrant women's autonomy."[124] Domestic workers who live in consistently stressed the taxing nature of the work, the sense of "being on call for virtually 24 hours a day."[125] She cited two distinct examples: Tanha, who seemed to have enough autonomy to be able to invite Andall to her employers' apartment (when they were out) and offer her coffee; and Elsa, who came to an interview on the traditional day off for domestic workers, accompanied by her employer (he introduced himself as a magistrate). Andall also cites Elena, who found stable employment with an employer who treated her correctly but who still cherished the "dream" of "get[ting] a little house and liv[ing] by myself."[126] And Andall cites several other migrant domestic workers whose employers confined, or attempted to confine, them to the house. Undocumented domestic workers were particularly at risk of this kind of exploitation, given their fear of expulsion not only from the household but also from Italy.[127] Furthermore, she observed that those who had networks of friends who were living independently were sometimes able to leave an abusive live-in employment relationship.

Their extremely limited autonomy means that live-in domestic workers may face insurmountable hurdles to having a family life. Andall paints a particularly revealing portrait of women who decided to become mothers— rather than accidentally falling pregnant, as is commonly assumed to be the case—as an act of self-affirmation. She describes the particular difficulties faced by female migrants employed as live-in domestic workers in the context of maternity. Despite the legal framework and the collective agreements, some women were forced to leave their jobs during pregnancy or accept positions that required them to resume paid employment as a domestic only a few weeks after giving birth.[128] While her informants suggested that live-in domestic workers from the Philippines may tend to send their Italian-born children back to the Philippines to be cared for, women from war-torn countries like Eritrea or Somalia kept their children in Italy and were forced to rely on informal care arrangements or even Catholic-run residential homes for the long-term care of their children.[129]

Chin considered how living space is organized to be part of what she calls the purchase of spatial deference by employers. If domestic workers in Malaysia have separate rooms rather than storage rooms with no ventilation or corridors outside kitchens, the workers would be on a lower floor than their employers, with little expectation of privacy; employers would enter their rooms without knocking. Employers determine a domestic worker's availability—when they must be present to serve, and when they can go to bed.[130] The room becomes their only space, but they are expected to retreat to it as soon as, though only for as long as, they are no longer needed to serve. Chin chronicled workers' physical confinement in the home or room.

Tellingly, in another context in which the state (Canada) mandated live-in work, Stasiulis and Bakan suggest that employers did not actually demand this, despite state policy. The authors documented a variety of negotiated arrangements adopted by domestic workers in their employment relationship despite the strictures of the law and its potential impact on the workers' attaining permanent residency status, to mitigate partially the live-in requirement. They add, however, that "it is the interests of employer/citizens rather than those of employee/non-citizens that are considered as central to the policy."[131]

Who's Responsible? Employer-Provided Social Security

One of the dimensions of the standard setting where there was the most limited guidance in national laws concerned social protection, particularly employer-provided social security programs. Romero recalls the feudal obligation of care resting on the master for servants under his charge, arguing that no such obligation exists under capitalism.[132] Erna Magnus shows that historically in a range of jurisdictions in Europe, the law of the household workplace—conventionally, she refers to "custom and usage"—governed employers' responsibility to care for domestic workers in countries such as Great Britain, France, and Sweden, while some of the old master and servant laws and the civil codes of Germany and Switzerland explicitly recognized the employers' liability.[133] In some cases, employers were required to provide medical care during a domestic worker's sickness and sometimes were explicitly prohibited from removing the sick worker from the employer's household if doing so might aggravate her condition. For Magnus, this liability was a counterbalance for "the employer's right to make practically unrestricted demands on his servants' labour."[134]

However, an important transition occurred between the special liabilities that were prescribed either under special laws applicable to domestic workers or laws of general application to the development of social insurance systems. In their account of the development of the employment relationship, Deakin and Wilkinson consider the development of the modern welfare state to be pivotal in the crystallization of the employment relationship. Nascent social security programs that initially made employers liable for workplace injuries and diseases and that evolved into generalized programs covering health care, unemployment insurance, and retirement pensions through the state (all through the model of the national citizen male breadwinner) required employment relationships to be stable and regular. According to Deakin and Wilkinson, in a model that emerged in the period after World War II, "the welfare state extended its influence alongside increasing vertical integration of production and the emergence of the public sector as a significant employer."[135]

Domestic workers—often migrants and usually female—performing care work in private households tended to fall outside of this paradigm.

Only in Andall's study of Italy, where national collective agreements have been negotiated since 1974, is there documented access to maternity and sickness benefits through insurance payments by the employer.[136] In the case of illness, employment guarantees based on length of service are increasingly common. But Andall stresses the difficulty faced by domestic workers when employers refuse to make the appropriate financial contributions. The collective agreements have modified working conditions, and there had been a lot of optimistic expectation on the part of the ACLI-COLF that dramatic improvements would follow. However, they have been limited.[137] A particularly stark example is maternity benefits. Based on her interviews with one informant from another trade union, Andall reports that domestic workers are simply fired when they become pregnant, despite the available legal protection. Andall's informants suggested that while trade unions could get involved, if the relationship has broken down it will not be possible to reconstruct it.[138] This hints at the kinds of challenges that domestic workers can face if they seek any form of reinstatement.

Andall mentioned that noncompliance with social security legislation was "rampant."[139] She also indicated that a significant minority of the domestic workers she interviewed were registered for social security entitlements by their employer, and two of the employers she interviewed also indicated that they had taken out coverage for their domestic workers. Although some employers seemed not to know that there was social security coverage for domestic workers, Rollins also interviewed an employer who claimed that the workers systematically refused to be covered, preferring to receive cash without deductions. Rollins also considered that for the employers, the disregard was due not only to the added financial contribution but also to the added paperwork. But one employer's reasons stand out: "We rationalized it. Nobody did it; why should you be a dope and add to your burdens?"[140] Those who complied reasoned both in terms of the importance of following the law and the potential tax benefit of being able to claim child-care deductions. Hondagneu-Sotelo—writing shortly after the Zoe Baird scandal, during which President Bill Clinton's nominee for attorney general was found to have employed two undocumented migrants from Peru as a nanny and chauffeur for her children—reported that domestic employer respondents who were in positions that might entail comparable public scrutiny might well have adjusted their behavior to comply.[141]

The Emotional Labor of the Postcolonial Performance: Invisibility and Gifts

Invisibility surfaces in the postcolonial performance. By that I mean to capture the emotional labor involved in making oneself "invisible," with no needs and not requiring care, so as to be fully available for the needs of the employer or the household.[142] There are other ways of framing this, beyond being available for and present at work, with discretion and loyalty as the most immediately recognizable in contemporary employment law. But they are implied obligations of the domestic work relationship. Most of the ethnographies underscore the idiosyncratic nature of this aspect of taking care of others.[143]

Romero characterizes the establishment of an informal labor contract as negotiated between women in the domestic work relationship: "To a large degree, women employers govern the type of employee-employer relationship that is established. Under the influence of community norms and values, middle-class women employers negotiate an informal labor contract with working class women in the privacy of their own homes. The hardships, isolation and degradation experienced by women household workers are thus directly controlled by women employers. There is an enormous latitude in the contract."[144]

Domestic workers' isolation is often taken to be a defining characteristic of their work. They tend to toil alone in an individual employer's household, away from the camaraderie and solidarity that might develop in the quintessential industrial workplace and some parts of the broader service sector. Regulatory consequences are often based on this starting point. Romero also accentuates the expectation, characteristic of US employers hiring Mexican domestic workers in the 1950s and 1960s, "to purchase broadly defined labor power rather than specific labor services."[145] She adds that this is similar to mistresses at the turn of the century in the United States and underscores the prevalence of those expectations in more contemporary sources.[146] The tasks are intimate and subject to the risk of remarkably high degrees of supervision and the constant navigation of a one-on-one relationship.

The general expectation of available labor power is accompanied by an expectation of servitude. A visible representation of this is the domestic workers' uniform, representing an unequivocal demarcation between the family and the domestic other. For example, Romero reports that "white uniforms are used to distinguish the maid from families and friends, particularly when employers fear that others might mistake the reason for her presence."[147] As Romero argues, deference is purchased.

Romero's work offers a critically important reminder that domestic workers' isolation should be understood in "response to the norms and values surrounding domestic service."[148] It is precisely these expectations of behavior along the lines of class, gender, race, age, and immigration status that shape and entrench the law of the household workplace. The boundarilessness and subservience attached to the work—couched as it may be in maternalism but also, unmistakeably, in the vestiges of the master-servant relationship to which servitude was central[149]—is resolutely recast in light of the needs of the current era of global capitalism. With it comes the stigma that is attached to domestic work, characterized by Romero as a "perceived occupational hazard."[150] To be "rebuffed and ignored and [feel] that she became visible only when an order was given": this is how a domestic worker can feel isolated in a household full of people.[151] Throughout her work, Romero stresses that it is not the domestic work that is intrinsically demeaning; rather, it is the way the relationship—in particular, domestic workers' place in it—is structured.

Confirmation of the employer's status is not always accomplished by the physical presence of women of color or the use of white uniforms; it frequently requires daily practices of deferential behavior that continually affirm and enhance the domestic's inferiority. One classic, heavily racialized example amply documented in the relationship between white employers and Black workers in the United States and South Africa, and prevalent in a number of other postcolonial or racialized migratory contexts, is the use of the word "girl" to refer to adult women engaged in paid domestic work.[152] Variations on the same theme include referring to the domestic worker by her first name while the employers are addressed by their last name.

A related but distinct dimension of the postcolonial performance of deference is dealing with what Romero and subsequently Hondagneu-Sotelo capture in the act of so-called gift giving by the employer to the domestic worker.[153] Those gifts are most often items such as old clothes and other similar offerings that might humiliate the recipient. All underscore the shadow work inherent in domestic work. The domestic worker cannot say that she is insulted by the most prevalent gifts from the employer, used clothing. In Romero's words, "She must labor to disguise her true feelings."[154] The challenge permeates the employment relationship. Romero discusses the manner in which "hiring a domestic was likely to be presented within the context of charity and good works; it was considered a matter of helping 'these Mexican women' rather than recognized as a work issue."[155] The job itself, it would seem, is a gift that is to be received by the domestic worker with gratitude.

But Ally offers a different example, that of buying a domestic worker a small house in South Africa.[156] In all of these examples, employers are seen to give their domestic workers presents to make them feel an obligation to their employers.[157] Like Chin, Romero does not hesitate to call upon the language of obligation to capture this feature of the relationship, which is resolutely in the employer's interest.[158]

Invisibility Challenged: Not One of the Family

Across the ethnographic studies, employers consistently use the frame of "like one of the family," with the emphasis on the word "like." Most ethnographic analyses dismiss this terminology as opportunistic. Even if we were to take the family metaphor seriously, drawing on the history of the household economy, I would argue that rather than dislodging obligation, it asks: what kind of obligation? Even if we were to concede the subordination inherent in a patriarchal family's relationships, the domestic worker is not the spouse or the daughter. Her status in the family remains that of the other who is expected to deal with all of the physical and emotional labor and thus is visible when needed, but whose needs remain invisible. Romero captures the intensity of the status through domestic workers' own framing: they describe being treated as a "nonperson" or like a piece of furniture, rather than someone deserving of respect.[159] In other words, a further, critical part of the emotional work in domestic work is the obligation to be omnipresent but simultaneously invisible unless called, entirely loyal and trustworthy but knowing one's place. Romero addresses spatial deference in the US context as follows: "Even though few homes today are built with servant's entrances, women of color report numerous practices used to separate their presence from the employer and her family. They move around the house, ignored as if they were invisible, their existence acknowledged only when their services are required."[160]

Chin argues that employers purchase deference. Agencies instructed foreign domestic workers not to maintain eye contact with their employers and to speak only when spoken to. The norm is legitimized: "foreign domestic workers do not deserve to be spoken to or treated with respect."[161] Stasiulis and Bakan capture a dialectic of intimacy and distance, in which even responsibilities like grocery shopping are discouraged because they encourage precisely that which is discouraged: autonomy and physical distance from the household, as well as the domestic worker's mature discretion.[162] I would insist on acknowledging the dialectic from the point of view of someone whose role is to serve others. Romero's critique is particularly trenchant, as she underscores the dilemma—problematized even in historiographical, revisionist accounts of the feudal or master-slave relationship—of unidirectional obligations of care.[163] The asymmetrical law of the household workplace means that domestic workers care, but their own care needs are rendered invisible.

What remains clear is that some workers face intense requirements of loyalty, which is recognized to constitute a core part of their employment relationship. They are historicized others both within and beyond the household workplace. Rollins stresses the extent to which one of her interviewees—an employer who had grown up with and been partially raised by domestic workers in his household—spoke of his childhood self as one of the domestic workers' "employers." He added that one domestic worker could have been a surrogate mother for him, but when Rollins asked why she had not been, he responded that "to be frank, I think it was because she was a maid and therefore had a certain stigma attached to her—which I understood even then, in some primitive way. And I understood that she was from a different social [class]. And of course, she was black and that had to do with it."[164] For Rollins, this statement underscored the ways in which ideologies of race and class are transmitted within the domestic work relationship.

While I agree with Romero that the domestic work relationship must be understood through the prism of capitalism, I argue that its status did not disappear under capitalism but instead has been reinscribed in a capitalist relationship that depends upon workers' knowing their subordinate place. It is necessary to understand racial capitalism.[165] Consider the following quote from an African American domestic worker cited in Romero's book, named Ms. Pratt: "I don't think you can feel like one of the family . . . I don't expect her [the employer] to say do something without pay."[166]

This quote is important. Some domestic workers form genuinely close relationships with employers who may well act out of care and compassion rather than opportunistic maternalism. However, Pratt keeps the focus on her own reasons for selling her labor power, and for her intention, or aspiration, to remain in an employment relationship. It is overlaid with the status relationship and accompanied by domestic workers' knowledge of the deep sense of injustice of the law governing their work.[167]

Domestic workers know and affirm the dignity of their work and do so as a form of resistance that is understood by the foregrounded authors as action rooted in the consciousness of a shared struggle.[168] They know and affirm the legitimacy of aspiring to be treated as workers like any other. They also know—perhaps better than most ordinary and even other atypical workers—how permeable the boundaries are between servitude and subordination, normalized time and boundarilessness, and employers' emotional coercion and employees' free choice. They know how to challenge their invisibility. Good treatment by employers means not only respecting explicit contractual obligations but also treating workers as human beings—what one might refer to as an implicit obligation to respect their human dignity.

Resistance, Ressentiment, and Collective Action

Despite tremendous hurdles, domestic workers worldwide have been "willing to act collectively wherever possible to bring about structural change and combat exploitative working conditions and discrimination."[169] The foregrounded ethnographic accounts do not focus on traditional collective action in the labor context, emphasizing instead the boundarilessness of domestic workers' working time and live-in working conditions that undermine the scope for autonomy. The fact that some domestic workers fear that unionization will lead to their being dismissed by their employers[170] may indicate their internalization of the law of the household workplace. Moreover, Stasiulis and Bakan foreground the gatekeeping mechanisms in place at the level of both the Canadian state and private domestic placement agencies that progressively favored Filipina applicants instead of West Indian women given their "past history of organized resistance to oppressive conditions" under earlier domestic worker programs.[171] The authors interviewed placement agency representatives who continued to kindle that fear, even suggesting that domestic worker support groups were "giving the Filipino nannies a bad name" because of their militancy.[172]

Yet the studies do not stop at explaining the profound limits on domestic workers' autonomy. They also capture domestic workers' responses, and in a manner that challenges the frequently stated assumption that domestic workers somehow lack class consciousness. In their focus on negotiating citizenship, Stasiulis and Bakan stress domestic workers' practice of dissent and courage to present a different portrait of domestic workers and their associations. Indeed, some have challenged injustice through targeted court cases and through public campaigns in support of structural change.[173]

Rollins theorizes ressentiment, a notion emanating from analyses of the master-slave dialectic as analyzed by Nietzsche, Hegel, and Fanon.[174] For domestic workers, like Fatima Elayoubi on that bus, quoted at the beginning of this chapter, ressentiment is a "long-term, seething, deep-rooted negative feeling" about the asymmetry in the law of the home workplace.[175] The ressentiment is rooted in their refusal to internalize their inferior status, their belief in the injustice of the norms that govern their "treatment and position," and crucially "their rejection of the legitimacy of their subordination."[176] While a debate has proliferated in the literature about how to understand these strategies, whether they are largely masks protecting against psychological harm or forms of deep resistance alongside more overt actions explicitly designed to restructure the employment relationship, they are all ways to contest the legitimacy of the pluralist norm that governs the household workplace.

As Ally insists, those contestations are not viewed as individualized acts of resistance. Rather, as underscored by Bonnie Thornton Dill, a leading scholar of intersectionality, the individual acts can have "collective consequences for the overall organization of domestic labor as an occupation."[177] In other words, as Ally puts it, they are practices of power "best designated as a *work culture*" specific to the household workplace but that should be understood in relation to other forms of worker resistance and the construction of collective action.[178] Even under the live-in relationship prevalent during apartheid in South Africa, domestic workers were not "passive accoutrements to the wills and imperatives of political orders and employers."[179] Ally ably illustrates the ways in which domestic workers attempted to negotiate their working time with employers and continue to do so under a new order in which many choose to live out. Moreover, Ally's work challenges the assumption that live-out work necessarily increases autonomy, given the relentless family demands on South African domestic workers. Taking this reasoning further, Parreñas insists that the domestic workers' actions are rooted in "the collective consciousness of a shared struggle."[180] They differ only in terms of the tools needed to mediate and ultimately disrupt the relationship.

African migrant workers in Rome frequently changed jobs, both to resist abusive employment practices and to seek out employers who would be inclined to help them acquire or retain legal status.[181] Temporary insecurity was considered better than continuous exploitation. Andall's study of domestic workers in Italy also cites different forms of resistance, like sneaking out at night to go to a club and returning before the employers awaken, explained by one domestic worker, Antonia, as follows: "Every now and again you just have to do this, otherwise you would be really unhappy."[182]

Drawing on her "off stage conversations with domestic workers at 'informal assemblages' such as churches, shopping malls, and discotheques," Chin emphasizes the ways in which Filipina and Indonesian domestic workers resist Malaysian middle-class employers' construction of their identity.[183] While also drawing on the notion of ressentiment and Rollins's analysis, Chin highlights the specific ways in which domestic workers reject their dehumanization. This includes refusing their categorization as slaves. It might be through references to families, such as asking, "Am I not also human with a mother and a father?" Chin suggests that this form of pleading might be privileged by Indonesian migrants working with Malay employers, who consider themselves to be of the same ethnocultural group. Or it might be a Filipina migrant domestic worker who negotiates monthly rest time by playing into ethnic or national stereotypes about migrant domestic workers, feigning ignorance, and refusing to use sanitary napkins during her menstrual cycle. Dropping dishes to indicate a need for rest and fasting during religious holidays as a protest against abusive treatment are all part of the pattern of informal resistance related in Chin's narrative. Ultimately, exercising the exit option by running away, despite the risks, is seen as a form of resistance—even in a context in which foreign domestic workers are stereotyped as sexually immoral and frequently engaged in prostitution.[184] Although Chin frames foreign domestic workers as political actors, nothing about her analysis of everyday resistance suggests that she finds the actions to be particularly effective in dislodging the deeply asymmetrical law of the household workplace.

Parreñas's work emphasizes the spaces of collective action and solidarity claimed by Filipina migrant domestic workers, even when that means being visible in public squares on the one day a week that they have off from work. Her work also captures how those same domestic workers "control the script" in the household, to "manipulate . . . deference and maternalism as an act of immediate struggle."[185] Even when they are bombarded with rules from their employers, Parreñas argues, migrant Filipina domestic workers are simultaneously able to feel "attachment for and detachment from their employers," and in the process, to act through their subordinate positioning to subvert employers' authority.[186] It is not only employers who use emotion, in other words, to yield compliance. By normalizing the deference demanded by employers, domestic workers may "manipulate its normalization" because even small deviations from the script become immediately perceptible and elicit guilt, and even a willingness to please the worker who is usually so seemingly happy.[187] But as Parreñas insists, this form of resistance can only be used sparingly in the face of asymmetrical employer power, including on termination of the employment relationship.[188]

Termination of Employment: Who Is in Control?

Employment at will may be a doctrine particular to the United States, but every legal jurisdiction represented in the ethnographic studies understood the domestic work relationship as subject to immediate termination by the employer.[189] The ethnographic accounts are replete with stories of how the domestic work relationship just ends. For example, in Andall's study, one documented domestic worker from Cape Verde returned from a vacation to find that she had been permanently replaced by another domestic worker.[190] Rollins reports a case in which a live-in domestic worker was fired because she brought a man into her room. The employer told Rollins, "My husband didn't like that. So we had to fire her."[191] Until recently in most contexts, there have rarely been labor inspectors, court cases, or the payment of unemployment insurance premiums or social benefits like retirement pensions.[192]

Contemporary South Africa, however, is a partial exception. I was therefore somewhat surprised that Ally's study paid little attention to the significance of that country's Commission for Conciliation, Mediation and Arbitration, which provides a mechanism for a range of workers, including domestic workers, to have their disputes (mostly about the termination of employment) heard fairly expeditiously. This dimension is explored in chapter 6.

Everyday Transgressions

Labor law scholarship has a long tradition of foregrounding the law of the shop, or the intricate web of rules that invariably emerge to govern every workplace, as the pluralist law of the industrial workplace. The law of the shop may be the unilateral exercise of management power in the nonunionized workplace or the mediated and negotiated space of collective autonomy in the unionized workplace. Collective labor relations laws in particular sought to build on "the acceptance by parties of assumptions which are entirely alien to an era of individual bargaining" and, by extension, to the master-servant relationship.[193] However, subordination and servitude have persisted. I have tried to understand the regulatory logic, or code, that surrounds the household workplace in the domestic work relationship. In Kitty Calavita's words, "it is not just that historical global inequalities have produced post-colonial subjects who today provide cheap labor to first-world powers; those inequalities, and those post-colonial subjects, are reproduced from within."[194]

The law of the household workplace in historical and contemporary contexts reminds us that so-called labor market informality is not the absence of law, but rather the presence of the past in the prevalent but invisible norms and rules that govern the actors in this work relationship. It tells us about constructions from within and the underlying values and assumptions that continue to apply—to greater or lesser degrees—in labor law. The uneasy coexistence between status and contract is exploded in the relationship that carries so many vestiges of the past, written onto the bodies of those whose "place" it is to do that work.

I have argued that it is critical to understand this law of the household workplace if scholars, policy makers, and social movements are to be able not just to regulate domestic work but also to change the pluralist and deeply unequal norms. It is similarly critical to pay attention to the conclusion prevalent in several of the studies: "ambivalence characterizes the governance of private paid domestic work."[195] While domestic workers were acutely aware of the low status and stigma attached to their work, they also expressed the pride that they take in their own work and their ability to support their families, while acknowledging a degree of "self-distancing from their occupational status."[196] Rollins expresses the varying sense of "entrapment" that some (particularly older) domestic workers felt about their work.[197] And it is telling that Rollins underscores the fact that not a single one of the domestic workers she interviewed wanted her own daughter to become a domestic worker.[198]

Domestic workers' refusal to internalize their own servitude and their insistence upon the beauty and value of their own work are part of a resistance that frames their understanding of the injustice of their circumstances, their pride in their work and their ability to provide for their own families, and their defiant insistence in holding onto their dignity.

This discussion has three implications. First, theories of domestic workers' exceptionality may mislead us into thinking that domestic work offers no substantive challenge to mainstream labor regulation. The household workplace is presumed to be atypical in the contemporary economy. However, it is one of many sites of continuous availability to the needs of the employer, and of boundariless time and space. It is at our peril that we dichotomize it as the unfortunate relic of a time in which the "ritualized, social subordination" of the feudal household was organized through status.[199] What emerges through the ethnographies is that race, class, and gender are structuring factors that mark the bodies of Indigenous, postcolonial, and Black women as those who undertake domestic work. Domestic work makes it considerably harder to draw a neat line between subordination and servitude, and it places occupational status and associated social stigma uppermost in any credible account of labor law's evolution and future.

Second, those racialized and othered women who seem permanently stuck in domestic work challenge and shape the nature of the law of the household workplace. They have negotiated in the relative absence of state labor law and in its shadow. They force those concerned with equality to ask whether the line-drawing currently engaged in to identify the existence of subordination, rather than to emphasize its consequences, might be challenged. In other words, subordination has been accepted as labor law's defining feature in a social welfare regime that distributes entitlements but does so through inherently exclusionary uses of the male breadwinner model. Leading progressive labor law critiques have focused on the growth of atypical, precarious workers who increasingly fall outside of that classic model. Focusing on people who face intense subordination—so much so that the subordination reinforces their status—might lead us to reconsider the saliency of having that legal notion at the core of labor law.

Third, this chapter offers a reminder that merely including domestic workers in existing frameworks is not enough. The risk is that recurring hierarchies will continue to reassert themselves, inscribed on historically subordinated bodies or on newly emerging ones. Regulatory frameworks must look specifically at how to correct inequality. The process entails living with the uneasy coexistence of domestic work as both work like any other and work like no other. It entails rethinking specific regulation by the state and engaging with domestic workers' collective autonomy. The law of the household workplace was rendered more visible by the international standard setting process, led by a collective movement of domestic workers. They recognized that it is easier for workers to negotiate individually and collectively when there are additional—indeed, transnational—levers of support. Domestic workers improved their ability to negotiate, individually and collectively, with a new transformative, international labour law alongside emerging, reflexive state law then in the shadow of only a normalized, invisible but very present asymmetrical law of the household workplace.

Chapter 4

Searching for Law in Historical Cookbooks

> Legal voices are not necessarily the most important
> ones, and they may not express common under-
> standings and perceptions.
>
> —Carolyn Steedman, *Labours Lost*

Cookbooks—Really?

Often in labor law, we fail to imagine—much less recognize—the products of
the work that is care. Most successful care work disappears: food is consumed,
children are bathed and put to sleep, and a house is left clean and empty. Of
course, social reproduction and the continuation of humanity should speak
for itself, but the labor is largely rendered invisible. So the artifact that is the
written cookbook remains among the few enduring sources documenting the
care work that has in fact been done.[1] This is not without irony, for work that
leaves little time to write and that is performed by those who have largely been
denied a formal education. Yet both employers and domestic workers wrote
cookbooks. Those cookbooks have been preserved and can be read for distinct purposes. Consider that the cookbooks are sometimes accompanied by
sections on how to manage domestic labor in the household. This should
not be surprising, really. The household is where the people who actually
governed or later managed the domestic workplace were most likely to
turn to know what is expected of them. Moreover, as Steedman recounts in
her leading account of domestic workers as the working class, late eighteenth-
century English magistrates "administered" the law from within their
households: the "justicing room set aside in his own private house, *was* a court,

in the narrowest and most technical meaning of the word." Steedman adds
that the justicing room was not furnished with the usual "paraphernalia and
personnel" but was a meeting place for two or more magistrates to administer
the statute law.[2]

Throughout her work, Steedman pays particular attention to the kitchen.
She emphasizes the importance of the kitchen—like the courtroom—as a
space that "made and remade social relations on a daily basis" as well as "in
the moment, snatched by the servant, to say something about it at all, by means
of her pen." She goes so far as to frame it as a space that was "not the employer's premises, as a parlour," but also not the servant's. Although she quotes
the affirmation that the kitchen was actually nowhere, Steedman also points
to literary representations of the kitchen as a space where one might find
"another life enacted there," such as a networking meeting of London's Black
servants.[3]

For Steedman, the magistrates in those justicing rooms crafted the "law of
everyday life," and she discusses that law with nuance. But Steedman is interested in the broader employment relationship, and toward the end of her
pivotal work, she discusses a variety of forms of writing by domestic workers
and their employers, including poetry and satire. She also mentions "writing
cooks" and intimates that the cooks who wrote these works might not have
been well regarded. After all, they were concerned to treat their works as true
books, not only as manuals with clear instructions. They wrote "with their
own integrity as authors."[4] But questions remain. Is there everyday law in
those kitchens and in those cookbooks, too?[5] And can that everyday law be
transgressive?

Mrs. Beeton's 1861 book on *Household Management*, also published as
Beeton's Cookery Book, was on the shelves of most kitchens in Victorian, Ed-
wardian, and Georgian England. Colonial mistresses Flora Annie Webster Steel
and Grace Gardiner's classic work on Anglo-Indian housekeeping from 1890
compared the responsibilities of the colonial housekeeper to those of the
British colonial administrators; they were part of the same project of empire.
But how often is a cookbook, such as the one written by the free African
American woman and self-described "experienced cook" Malinda Russell,
considered a "culinary Emancipation Proclamation"?[6]

When I set out to write this book on the regulation of domestic work, I
knew I was looking for something other than Sir William Blackstone's 1765
categorization of the master-servant relationship in his *Commentaries on the
Laws of England* which included live-in (*intra maenia*) domestic workers.[7] Of
course, there are relevant and often interesting English cases and cases from

the colonies.[8] Consider an 1842 case from Canada-East, or modern-day Quebec: Mary Ann McDonough quit her job as a "wet nurse, and to do such work as would be required" for $6 per month when she was asked also to make the beds and sweep two rooms. This was not what she had been hired to do in her indenture. And these added tasks encroached on her own time: when refusing to make the beds, McDonough explained to her mistress that "she must go to church." McDonough was brought before a magistrate of the Court of Special Sessions "for refusing to obey the lawful commands as servant, in her duties to her master and mistress" and found to have deserted. She was also accused of taking into her possession and wearing cotton stockings that belonged to her mistress, although she insisted that they were presents from her employer. Although she was not imprisoned, which would have been customary at the time, she was fined.[9]

Lawyers and academics rightfully point to this kind of case for its insights on the law of master and servant. Cases can also give us a glimpse of the law of the household workplace, if we read the case diagonally, and at some level ethnographically. The *Lindsay v. McDonough* case certainly tells us something about McDonough's resistance in refusing to do work that did not fall within the usually delineated duties of a wet nurse. It also tells us of the severe consequence: losing or leaving her employment and being taken to court. We might even be able to intimate that it really was generally expected that domestic workers would take on all work required of them by their master, urgently or not, that flowed more generally from the "nature of domestic service."[10] A contemporary look at the facts of the case, with understandings gleaned from the ethnographies, might suggest another severe consequence: domestic workers who displease their employers by seeking to leave their service run the risk of being accused of petty theft.[11] And the question remains: how might we be able to find the "hidden transcript" of domestic workers, other than through the "distorting medium of their employers,"[12] who were invariably also magistrates deciding servants' cases?[13]

Douglas Hay and Paul Craven's monumental book on master and servant law has also unearthed the occasional court acknowledgement of informal, patriarchal, yet "virtually absolute control" over the plantation workforce, as well as court rationalizations—notably the purported acquiescence of the servants themselves—that allowed courts to tolerate "brutal private exploitation."[14] As their discussion of the plantation household reveals, domestic work is certainly not the only labor law sphere in which a master's extensive authority had been characterized as informal and tolerated or enabled by the state. Another historically relevant example was the captain of a ship at sea, including during the centuries-long transatlantic slave trade.[15]

Hay does point to English judicial and parliamentary reluctance, at least after 1797, to apply master-servant law to domestic workers.[16] The reluctance was not because the domestic work relationship lacked subordination: the household economy was regularized. The model of subordination was transferred outward from the household to the emerging labor market.[17] To apply state law to domestic work matters within the household was seen as "disruptive to household authority."[18] That is, legal pluralism is recognized, as is—implicitly—its asymmetry. There is a law of the household workplace, and the state will not unsettle it.

With the same brush, the legal pluralism can be ignored if the entire scholarly focus shifts immediately to patriarchal understandings of the family. It is usually recognized that the reference to household authority captures the position of the father as the head of the household and the family as a critical institution in maintaining social order. The household was also a sphere within which mistresses were entitled—indeed expected—to exercise control over their servants and maintain the social order that inscribed mistresses' own subordinated status. This has all been well established. What tends to be missed in the shift to the family and, by extension, to family law, is the extent to which the notion of household authority creates its own normative order within the domestic work relationship. That normative order—like others—operates in relation to and with the support of institutions of the state, notably the judiciary. As with master-servant law generally, whether or not it is applied by the state, the state tolerates it, rationalizes it, even depends on it. But what is it? How do we get to know the informal law that governs the household workplace?

In chapter 2, I argued that the informal is not necessarily the realm of disorder, but rather a realm embodying an interlegality that may well capture the ubiquitous and structural subaltern status of the informal. It is therefore not enough simply to change lenses and call the informal the norm. Rather, I have insisted on the need to focus on the historical and persisting invisibility of this particular master-servant relationship, an invisibility that is perpetuated through law despite domestic workers' everyday transgressions of it. I have wanted to know that law.

I was especially concerned about what some improbably optimistic readings of selected English cases were said to reveal about domestic workers' rights and general treatment in practice. Some of these optimistic accounts were mirrored in leading studies.[19] Hay and Craven, as well as Steedman, offer an important corrective by looking to the essentially penal enforcement of master-servant law, and beyond it.[20] Legal coercion is a "complex continuum of forms and practices."[21] As I discussed in chapter 3, I am particularly wary of drawing bright lines between free and unfree labor, and I welcome subtle accounts that refuse to dichotomize, allow for the high degree of differentiation across local work cultures, and are attentive to the role of state law in constructing and maintaining regimes for the supply and regulation of labor.[22] Even when penal master-servant law was on its way out in England, it thrived in the colonies. Historians have looked at records of desertion and advertisements for runaway servants or slaves. Hay and Craven look particularly at the penal enforcement of imprisonment for desertion, often with hard labor and that particular form of corporeal punishment that, in Hay's words, "branded the bodies of workers with a particularly emphatic mark of subordination."[23] They emphasize how class, age, race, and gender were "coded into the legislation and reified in differential rates of prosecution, conviction, and punishment."[24] Even when punishment rates were low, other forms of coercion—including what they call "private corporal punishment"—might be meted out by masters themselves.[25] In other words, we are back to the terms of the relationship in which domestic work and domestic workers remained largely invisible.

In surveying this history, I felt the need to get at something not altogether different but qualitatively distinct. I have sought to understand the domestic work relationship as an embodiment of the pluralist law of the household workplace. I have not yet been able to shake the feeling that we might overstate the role of formal, statutory, or judge-made law, and that there is more. Each and every time I look closely at the question of the reach of the state both historically and in the global South, I come up with a story of overreach. In other words, state law may not quite be as well known or as readily able to permeate social life as it might sometimes seem to be. Sometimes this conversation has to do with the limited ability to implement—that is, we look at law in terms of its effectiveness.[26]

However, my questions focus on the extent to which formal law may not necessarily be normatively controlling. This does not mean that its opposite is informality. Rather, it means that we need to look elsewhere, where pluralist law resides. Sometimes we can get a strong impression about the pluralist law that governs in a reported case—for example, why a servant took the weighty decision to desert a master's employ, refused to milk a cow, or protested the nonpayment of wages. As Steedman observes, "Local domestic servants were clear about what constitutes a reasonable workload and reasonable wages, and what work conditions ought to be like."[27] We learn what the state law is (requiring someone to be punished or not, or forced to return to the employer or not) and therefore what state actors think about the pluralist law of the household workplace, which of course may function within its shadows. We certainly learn that the penal master-servant law was anything but evenhanded and was deeply despised.

Court records can also provide important moments of significant visibility for domestic work, which are crucial starting points for a history of presence. Take, for example, the fact that a slave woman and domestic worker of African descent was tried, tortured, and hanged in Montreal in 1736 for setting fire to her master's home, and with it much of the city. That court record and the trial transcript that the historian Afua Cooper claims as a slave narrative became an incontrovertible record of a history of slavery in Canada, a country more accustomed to imagining itself as the promised land at the end of the historic Underground Railroad to freedom.[28] Similarly, the legal historian and labor lawyer Lea VanderVelde recalled that the infamous US Supreme Court decision in *Dred Scott* involved another litigant, Harriet Scott.[29] VanderVelde seeks to tell Harriet Scott's story, that of an African American domestic servant "who was Dred Scott's wife and nobody's slave."[30] By telling that story, she challenges the boundary and unearths the ways in which slaves sued for their own freedom—and, until the *Dred Scott* decision, usually won it.[31] In the process, VanderVelde relies on the dichotomy between enslaved servitude and free labor that permeates the literature on labor law on the periphery but that has largely been avoided in the field's broader discussions.

Both Cooper and VanderVelde struggle valiantly to allow enslaved domestic workers to speak in their own words, beyond the fragments that appear in court transcripts. The legal historian Lolita Buckner-Inniss poignantly captures both the challenge and significance of this historical work that at once acknowledges what it cannot know and resists invisibility: "If . . . history is twofold, consisting of either material objects or words, then I suppose that Harriet [Scott], if she is to be found at all, must be found in the speculative interstices of a recorded history that for the most part counts her as both insubstantial object and mute subject. However, if the choice is no historic Harriet at all and Harriet in the historic margins, then I'll take Harriet at the margins."[32]

In that tradition, I seek in this chapter to tell an alternative legal history of the domestic work relationship, recognizing that to do so we must be prepared to look at domestic work's margins. In other words, while I knew the historical laws and court records did not offer the full information about the law of the household workplace that I was seeking, I was not sure what I was looking for—that is, until I virtually stumbled across these cookbooks, as well as guides to the rights and duties of servants and books on household management.

In cookbooks, we have an archive that can explain what we do not usually learn: the law that governs the day-to-day relationship between domestic workers and their employers, and how the parties resisted and shaped that law. Desertion and suing for justice are certainly important forms of resistance, and the decision to use one or the other may well reflect the workers' gender and family status, as well as the physical surroundings in which the labor takes place.[33] However, I want to expose the everyday transgressions against the pluralist law of the household workplace that domestic workers themselves seek to act upon and change, with or without the state.

Through this study, I continue to affirm that there is law in the everyday domestic work relationship, though it may not be state law. I suggest that even when the master-servant relationship was generalized to extend beyond the household to cover all working people, including the formerly enslaved, the operation of the generalized law may ironically have come to exclude the paradigmatic domestic workers who constituted the working class.[34] In the domestic work relationship, it is more likely to be unwritten law (*ius non scriptum*) that governs, but the fact that it is unwritten does not mean that the parties do not know it. And even if it is unwritten or unspoken, it might still be enabled, or permitted, or tolerated by the state. State actors—including courts, magistrates, and colonial officers—perpetuate particular relationships of power and hierarchy upon which social order is maintained.[35]

I returned to my first intuition: to turn back to the abundant contemporary ethnographic sources that chronicle domestic workers' subordination, through the voices of both domestic workers and their employers. These sources offer an invaluable window into understandings of the law that surrounds the domestic work relationship. What was clear in these sources—despite some important regional variances—is that the domestic work relationship was remarkably similar across a range of locations and times.

Finding Legal Origin Stories in Cookbooks

I was a student of social history before I became a student of law. I knew from E. P. Thompson that one must look for the history of presence and pay close attention to where to find it. I have also followed Hay and Craven's reminder of the importance of moments of big transitions like the abolition of slavery, the emergence of the industrial revolution, and the advent of colonialism. It is around these moments of transition that a flurry of cookbooks and similar diaries and manuals appears, written by masters and mistresses and, remarkably, by domestic workers themselves. This chapter does not seek to offer a comprehensive survey but instead offers a close look at a selection of eight cookbooks, diaries, and manuals, spanning 1826–1902, four written by employers, and four written by workers.

My research has been greatly facilitated by a resurgence of interest in cookbooks by scholars in the field of food studies and, more specifically, culinary history. To them, "A cookbook . . . is rarely purely utilitarian" but rather a way to understand work, lives, and relationships in a given place and time.[36] In particular, there has been renewed attention to reclaiming women's history via the documentation that some have left. In the United States, scholars note the first appearance in 1796 of a cookbook using Indigenous, Native American ingredients like cornmeal and cranberries, and observe that in the 1840s a "cookbook industry" emerged, in an attempt to retrace the cultural patrimony of the antebellum South.[37] This has meant that poorly preserved cookbooks are increasingly being digitized and rendered accessible. This is the good fortune of this project, and I have taken seriously the invitation to read the whole cookbooks, not just searching for the law but really seeking to respect how the authors repeatedly made "something outta nuttin."[38]

Alternative Readings of Masters' and Mistresses' Cookbooks

Many of the cookbooks and related documents including rights and duties of servants were written by masters and mistresses. And a few contained no recipes at all—designed very much as doctrinal statements of the law. Consider barrister-at-law Henry Baylis's *The Rights, Duties and Relations of Domestic Servants and their Masters and Mistresses*, which appeared in its first edition in 1857 and was amplified and issued in six subsequent editions through 1906. Baylis cites Blackstone and a substantial list of cases on the domestic work relationship. He offers a detailed digest of that law. His work extends beyond the terms of hire for domestic servants, their termination of employment, masters' and mistresses' responsibility for accidents to the domestic worker, and their vicarious liability for their workers' actions to third parties. Baylis also offers guidance that seems more intent on shaping behavior than interpreting the cases. For example, he counsels prompt payment of wages, as it "sets a good example to servants" and can prevent dishonesty. He suggests that masters' or mistresses' motives and intentions in prosecuting a servant for suspected petty theft might be called into question, so they should not prosecute them without "reasonable grounds."[39] His work lies at the intersection of taking the available cases seriously while operating on the household relationship; it hints at the work that is resolutely unhinged from the court-rooms and located in the kitchens and appears to build from—or toward—the law actually found and applied there.

There are still other cookbooks and manuals in what emerged as the field of household management, or domestic economy. They tend to reinforce Victorian separations between domestic work and the sanctity of the family captured in the upstairs-downstairs divide, while offering glimpses of the limits in the face of societal change wrought by industrialization and the decreased economic sustainability of rural (or, in the US context, Southern planter) economies. Writing what she subtitles a "Downstairs History of Britain from the Nineteenth Century to Modern Times," Lucy Lethbridge notes: "Below the surface of the social changes of the twentieth century, this inequality, right at the heart of the family home, began to chafe. Yet servants also squeeze awkwardly into the big narrative of twentieth-century labour history. Despite the great numbers of working-class women employed as domestics, servants have been viewed as standing outside working-class political movements."[40]

This section foregrounds four of the books written from and for the kitchens.

Employment Relations Law for the Household

Mrs. Seely's Cook Book: A Manual of French and American Cookery: With Chapters on Domestic Servants, Their Rights and Duties, and Many Other Details of Household Management is a rather earnest book from the United States published in the early twentieth century and written by a woman who also ran a placement agency for domestic servants.[41] It is perhaps not surprising that the book reads a bit like a labor relations textbook—this was business, after all. The section on the rights and duties of servants opens with a pay table itemizing the lowest daily wage of $0.33 per day through to the highest monthly wage of $100.[42] Servants are immediately framed as legal subjects: "Before the law of this country servants of various kinds stand upon the same footing."[43] Servants are also represented in images, but this is the United States in the early twentieth century: it matters that in the book's photographs, the domestic workers tend to be white.[44]

There is no room for equivocation: the framework of this book is that of employment law and employment relations. The first chapter is titled "General Relations of Employers and Servants in the Home and before the Law." The starting point of this cookbook subsumes the domestic work relationship within an employment relationship, and Seely stresses the need for agreement between the employer and the employee about the terms of service. She considers a one-week trial period to be "usual," framing the arrangement as one that "is to go on by the month"—consistent with the pay tables that suggest a month is the typical pay period.[45] She also stresses the importance of having a "clear understanding between master and service at the time of engagement."[46] This is consistent with her affirmation that "in housekeeping order is a first law."[47] That is not to say that the parties are equal and each bargain for their terms, and Seely elaborates on the difference: "A servant has a right to ask questions about the place in a respectful manner. . . . Masters cannot expect efficient servants to be indifferent to the duties they are undertaking, and to their surroundings. . . . A servant should tell what he or she expects as a part of his place. . . . But a servant should not have a right to dictate what he or she will or will not do. The employer has the right of naming duties. Servants are at liberty to accept them or not, as they wish."[48]

Seely moves immediately from conditions of hire to counsel employers on the terms of discharge. It is particularly significant, given the development of at-will employment in US common law, that Seely's framework refers to "unjust" discharge and dismissal "without just cause" or for "sufficient cause." According to her, the servant must give notice (two or three days if appointed by the week, and one week if appointed by the month) and forfeits the wages of the term if he or she leaves without providing that notice.[49]

The question of references addressed by Seely offers an opportunity to think about the relationship. According to her, letters of reference were not a requirement of the employment relationship, so a master or mistress is not bound to give one. She does, however, advocate for careful wording should a master or mistress provide a letter of reference for someone who is not considered to be good. She insists that letters should be truthful and alludes to the penalty in state law for a person who forges a letter or impersonates a master or mistress to provide a reference, revealing the social contestation that surrounded this particular practice.

On the specific or "generally recognized duties" within the household context, Seely contemplates that the workplace is organized around a hierarchy of servants. The posts are highly gendered, and reporting to the mistress or to the master also seems to depend on gender. The "well-bred and well educated" housekeeper—who "is, under the mistress, head of the house" and responsible for hiring and discharging all servants—is to "have few rules, but those few rules must effectively be kept."[50] She is to be fully supported by the "heads of the house," who Seely refers to consistently in the plural to include the master and the mistress. The duties of the butler, while not immediately parallel to those of the housekeeper, are comparable, as he has charge of "the under menservants or footmen."[51] Status is closely policed—for example, through close attention to the demarcations of the uniforms each category of servant is expected to wear (the book is replete with images).

Another consistent pattern in Seely's account is the early time when work is to start. For example, the housekeeper is to be up early, ensuring that all those under her charge are at their work by 7:00 a.m. There are occasional references to when some servants may have an afternoon to "go out," although in some cases the expectation is that meals will be prepared by the cook and ready for another servant, likely the kitchen maid, to cook.[52] However, there is limited attention paid to when servants are to cease their work. Indeed, Seely admits that a lady's maid might need to sit up a "good deal" at night, so "she must strive to get what rest she can, and good-temperedly support any inevitable fatigue." The recompense is not time off or additional pay; instead, Seely notes that "a cheerful, kindly performance of her duties, and deference, obedience, industry, and strict honesty will be apt to secure for her a friend in her mistress and a happy home under all ordinary circumstances."[53] Living in is therefore a recurring theme, even for male servants such as coachmen and stablemen, and unabashedly explained as a way to "insure the convenience of the family, and to prevent the men's being away at meals, etc."[54]

Finally, there is a real effort to itemize and systematize the wide range of responsibilities assumed by individual categories of servants, but every now and then, as the responsibilities seem vast, the precision seems to be recognized as ultimately in vain. For example, discussing the duties of the lady's maid, Seely itemizes skills like "tolerably good dressmaker and a good hairdresser" and tries to build a chronology for the day, but ultimately she concedes that "very little instruction can be given" on what this servant is required to do when her mistress has not summoned her.[55] Seely states: "Different mistresses have different needs and make different demands upon maids."[56] The responsibilities of the lady's maid seem to be summed up as follows: she needs to "remain in attendance until she is dismissed" and she needs to to maintain a "respectful manner," for example, by standing when her mistress enters the room.[57]

Imposing Colonial Order in the Household

The Complete Indian Housekeeper and Cook was initially published in 1888, and due to its popularity, it went through ten editions. The 1890 edition has been preserved by Cambridge University Press as a book of enduring scholarly value. It was written by two longtime residents of India, Flora Annie Webster Steel and Grace Gardiner, characterized by the editors of the series in which their book appeared as well-traveled "witty" women of "lively intelligence" whose work provides valuable insight into life and attitudes in "British India."[58] The book is true to its title, *Giving the Duties of Mistress and Servants, the General Management of the House and Practical Recipes for Cooking in All Its Branches*.[59] Steel and Gardiner addressed their volume "to the English girls to whom fate may assign the task of being house-mothers in India's foreign strand." By this they meant not the domestic workers, of course, but the "young housekeepers in India"—that is, the "English ladies in this country" who come to India newly married, "to begin a new life, and take up new responsibilities under absolutely new conditions."[60] For the authors, the "art of making a home" was not to be undervalued; rather, it was a talent that even the most intelligent women knew to cultivate and value.[61] None other than Queen Victoria proclaimed in 1889 that "though the domestic question is treated entirely from an Indian point of view, few women could fail to find useful hints in this handy little volume; for the girl prepared to follow her newly-trothed lord to the distant East, it would be hard to fancy a more useful little parting gift."[62]

The authors decide to focus on the division of labor in Bengal and northern India, noting that the manner of life in Bombay and Madras is considerably different and requires a distinct classification.[63] However, they then do not hesitate to generalize, stating that despite classification differences, the outline will be useful throughout India, and they go so far as to offer a comparative table of wages for Bengal, Bombay, and Madras.

The book is an unvarnished how-to on governing the colonial household in India, outlining the duties and responsibilities of mistresses and servants alongside other such practical matters as keeping the storeroom free of black ants and other insects; preparing appropriate conserves; hosting dinners, luncheons, and tennis parties; and, of course, cooking, with recipes alongside. The duties of servants are followed by a chapter on cows and dairy, and "hints to missionaries and others living in camp and jungle" precede more hints on the "management of young children."[64]

On many levels, the detailed enumeration of duties of the overwhelmingly male colonial workforce is very much about chronicling the roles and responsibilities of each of the dozens of categories of servants attached to any given household.[65] Along with detailed descriptions of who should accomplish what specific tasks and how to avoid leather cracking and wash stains out of carpet are reminders of the trust required in certain servants, the hierarchy of servants, and the importance of paying certain workers slightly more than the going rate to secure a staff member who is "presentable, and who is both fit to, and capable of, receiving orders direct."[66] This hierarchy of servants is also inflected with racialized hierarchies, operating through the authors' framings of Islam and Hinduism.[67]

Is it plausible that the authors understood themselves to be setting down the "laws of the household"?[68] Local customs in households are mentioned by the authors with disdain and derision. This was empire: the colonial household was not to emulate local conditions but to impose a different order understood to be superior, at least in the households of the colonizers. There was no need to reason with local staff members about "delusions current in cook-houses in India, such as the belief that it is the yolk of the egg which clears soup."[69] Steel and Gardiner advise that "autocratic high-handedness is the only weapon of any avail."[70] The necessary laws were built expressly, avowedly, and with sarcastic humor on prevalent racialized stereotypes, couched in maternalism: "The secret lies in making rules, and keeping to them. The Indian servant is a child in everything save age, and should be treated as a child; that is to say, kindly, but with the greatest firmness. The laws of the household should be those of the Medes and Persians, and first faults should never go unpunished."[71]

Servants were understood by the authors to have "dirty" and "evil" habits.[72] Mistresses were therefore primarily responsible for the "decency and health" of their household. Servants were to be educated into duty, with physically induced ridicule as the go-to punishment for resistance.[73] Indeed, resistance was taken by the mistresses to be a further indication of Indian servants' supposed childlike nature: they were seen to gain "a certain satisfaction in the idea that at any rate they have been *troublesome*."[74] Mistresses needed to command respect, and no detail should be forgotten—even that the ayah or lady's maid should "never forget to *salaam* to her mistress, and ask if anything is wanted."[75] Servants were to live in in special quarters designated for them. However, they were not entitled to live with anyone other than their immediate families, and this was to be strictly policed by mistresses.[76] Living and cooking quarters were to be regularly inspected by the mistress.

The rules for servants were plentiful and precise, filled with governmental minutiae and reflections on time and duty management for each category of worker. Consider the following detailed description of part of the duties of every *khitmaghar* (table waiter):

> Everything required for each meal should be in the dining room before that meal is announced, and a running accompaniment of washing should be ruthlessly repressed. If milder measures fail, lock the pantry door before sitting down to meals for a few days, and fine one piece for every missing article . . . he should not lay the table for any meal more than one hour before that meal is to be served. He should not device ingenious patterns with the spare silver. He should not attempt to fold

up the cloth unaided. . . . He should not wash up glasses, china, plates and silver in one small degchi with a rag tied to a stick. He should not clean the table and lay it for the next meal whilst the family is at the table. He should not use the table napkins as kitchen cloths. He should not conceal, or attempt to conceal, a dirty duster about his person when waiting at table. He should not leave things to be washed up till they are wanted. Finally, he should not say the kettle is boiling when it is not. This is an inexcusable offence, but universal.[77]

The act of household governance in the colony was unabashedly for the English mistresses' comfort. The authors acknowledge the conundrum of needing to embody the tidiness and resourcefulness that they sought in servants, while acknowledging that to do everything themselves would not only constitute a failure but defeat the original intent: to secure "smooth working, quick ordering, and subsequent peace and leisure to the mistress."[78] Their advice: "Never do work which an ordinarily good servant ought to be able to do. If the one you have will not or cannot do it, get another who can."[79]

The authors pay close attention to time management, adding without a hint of irony that the time before washing up after breakfast and "laying" of lunch "is quite sufficient leisure for any but the idle."[80] Interestingly, most servants' time is not counted in hours and may be thought of as boundariless.[81] However, the duties of the *dirzie* (tailor) are characterized briefly, as "to give his mistress eight hours *at least* of steady sewing work." Sundays off are anticipated as "usual," but the mistress is then advised that this servant's daily hours should be longer than eight, presumably on the other days—he is expected to be in place by 8:00 a.m. and working until 5:00 p.m., with a one-hour break for food in the middle of the day.[82]

Like a colonial precursor to modern human resource management techniques, the authors mention a plethora of practices designed to allocate tasks and ensure the responsibility of the domestic staff. Consider this advice, which appears alongside the need to clean silver and empty water carafes on a nightly basis: "Silver should be counted over every night, and glass and china once a week. If a breakage is not reported, and the mistress discovers it, cut the *bak-shish* money remorselessly; not so if it is reported, since accidents will occur."[83]

The authors' classic work includes tips on how to reduce the number of servants. In their opinion, "nothing, in fact, upsets the smooth working of a household more than too much leisure, or a too minute division of responsibility."[84] Avoiding divided responsibility becomes an important theme: it is also how a mistress can hold a servant accountable, attribute fault, and even award praise. Praise, however rare, was how one pleased those servants upon whom

"the comfort of life depends," such as the servant who would through methodical work organization rise early enough to get to market ("the bazaar")
so as to have a well-cooked meal ready by breakfast time.[85] There is no question that the advice is self-serving managerialism, and demeaning remedies to
keep servants cooking over a hot fire in temperatures above 100 degrees Fahr-
enheit, for example, populate the text.[86] The authors add: "A good cook is not
made, he is born; so if you are lucky enough to find one, do anything to keep
him—short of letting him know that you are anxious to do so!"[87] The recognition that cooks have real significance is shown in chapter 16, in which the
authors write quite expressly about mistresses' need to persuade their cooks.
The chapter is presented as "advice to the cook." While still unshakeably con-
descending, the authors use a different tone, meant to persuade. The mistresses
start with a colonial acknowledgment: "Most likely you belong to a family of
khanasmahs, cooks, and khitmatghars."[88] Foodborne illness is the core of the
authors' concern; they estimate that it contributes to half of the illnesses in
the world. But comfort for the household takes precedence in their reasoning: "if the dinner is badly cooked, your mistress will be angry, the master will
have an indigestion, and be cross; everything will go wrong, and whose fault
will it be? *Yours*."[89]

Briefly, the authors are explicit about their objective of imposing the rules
of conduct of "a reasonable human being."[90] Moreover, mistresses' responsibilities are framed to parallel those of colonial administrators. The authors
leave no room for doubt: the Indian household was a site of colonial governance within the British Empire.[91]

Recording Colonial Household Ways In Diaries

Although similar in genre, a different tone emerges from *Hilda's Diary of a Cape
Housekeeper,* which moves in autobiographical diary form from January to
December 1902 in colonial South Africa.[92] Hildagonda Duckitt was a South
African–born woman with British and Dutch ancestors. Her grandfather was
sent to South Africa from Surrey in 1800 to form part of the colonial administration. Duckitt grew up on a Cape farm, and though her book does not
purport to set out the law of the household workplace, her work provides
insights into the organization of households and domestic responsibility
before the founding of the Republic of South Africa and the formal state
adoption of apartheid in 1910. She writes: "We had about fifty milch cows on
the farm, and the dairy work was more irksome than at the present time. . . .
The supervision of the dairy was left to one of the daughters of the house—
the churning and washing-up being done by a very capable coloured woman,

while we creamed or skimmed the pans of milk. . . . What lovely cream and butter it was! Every week the surplus was sent for sale to Cape Town."[93]

In her sometimes idyllic portrait of life in the wine country of "soft green vineyards and . . . wooded glens," where ostriches roamed about in small numbers amid bountiful harvests, servants emerge only sporadically.[94] We are told of the thirty servants who accompanied Duckitt's grandfather on his voyage from England to the Cape and the farm laborers whose food was rationed[95] and who were "allowed" to go home for a few weeks at the end of March, when "everything after a long South African summer has burnt-up."[96] Herdsmen lived with their wives in "comfortable cottages and gardens, near the kraals, which were bedded down with straw."[97] And "there were cellars running under the house. Some of the dark ones were used for storing choice bottled wines, potatoes, etc., and the front ones, which had nice windows, were used by the servants of the family—emancipated slaves and their descendants. One charming Malay woman had been the nurse, and was devoted to the family. The butler, 'Old Charles,' was a negro from the East Coast. How exquisitely he kept the silver and polished the cut-glass dishes and goblets on the sideboards, and all the small panes of glass in the large bright window."[98]

Through this diary, we observe that "laundry work at the Cape still continues to be largely done by Malay women in wash-houses put up by the Municipality in Cape Town."[99] Duckitt laments that "servants are not plentiful or good, and to any mistress who has tact and patience I would say, get a young white or coloured girl and train her."[100] Yet Duckitt affirms that her family always "trained young servants to help the elder ones," adding that sometimes an orphan was indentured to the family, and they would teach them all to read and write and work.[101]

Duckitt recalls that in the Cape Colony, unlike some other regions where "native 'boys' and coolies" are employed, "we have a mixed coloured population" that includes women who "as a rule, make very good cooks, but few stay with a mistress longer than twelve months."[102] Interwoven with pay scales, advice on training servants, and an expression of her preference for home-made bread (for which she has a recipe, and which we learn is baked on Tuesdays and Fridays by "our man cook Abraham"), Duckitt advises against using "native"—in this case meaning coloured women—servants to care for children, asserting that while they are faithful and attached, "they have not, as a rule, been trained in habits of obedience and truthfulness themselves, and consequently are not capable of training children."[103]

More recipes follow, and then Duckitt endorses a friend's plan to develop a circulating library of books on "domestic economy," exchanging books at fortnightly tea parties, to enable the "heads of households to get new ideas in this way and keep up with the times." We learn of Bengal chutney with sugar made into syrup, as well as sweet potatoes that are plentiful by April; Miss Breda's fish sambal and incubating chickens; vineyards filled with grapes that are successfully exported to England and the use of dates in Southern Arabia, which include an "exceedingly unpalatable dish out of green dates mixed with fish" by "the very poor" for "their own table."[104] Duckitt takes care to thank the mistresses whose recipes she quotes, seeking forgiveness for those who are omitted in a work designed to reach colonial homes "not only in South Africa but round the globe, and perhaps in old England itself."[105] Given the colonial logic with which this work is inscribed, it is not surprising that no domestic worker is thanked.

Everyday Laws

It is important to underscore the popularity of many of these books. *Miss Beecher's Domestic Receipt Book* was written by Catharine Esther Beecher—a pioneer of work on the domestic economy who was also the sister of Harriet Beecher Stowe, the author of *Uncle Tom's Cabin*—could be found across US households. The book was meant to shape everyday behavior and could even come across as moralizing. For example, Miss Beecher says, "A woman should be *ashamed* to have poor bread, far *more so*, than to speak bad grammar, or to have a dress out of the fashion."[106] However, a premium is placed on systematic planning of the household.

Several strategies to convince domestic workers to enter service are explicitly set out, which makes sense given that there were times when the popularity of domestic labor among rural and urban workers waned and its economic sustainability was called into question. Domestic workers are told that they "never can find a place in this world where everything will be just as you want it, and that it is a bad thing for you, as well as for your employers, to keep roving about from one place to another. Stay where you are and try to make those things that trouble you more tolerable, by enduring them with patience."[107]

Beecher acknowledges the frequent turnover of domestic workers and advises housekeepers not only to "keep stores under lock and key" but also to explain the need to do so to domestic workers (who might otherwise find it offensive) as a form of protection both for the household and for honest hired people (who would be protected against suspicion).[108] Beyond the usual detailed descriptions of job responsibilities for domestic servants, Beecher highlights the importance of the management of domestics. Her advice is to avoid extremes, either of severity or of becoming so fearful of displeasing a domestic that the worker is given authority and control: "A housekeeper thus described this change in one whom she hired: 'The first year, she was an excellent servant; the second year, she was a kind mistress; the third year, she was an intolerable tyrant!'"[109]

In very specific, studied ways, the manual trains housekeepers on how to ensure that a relationship of subordination is retained. For Beecher, this is facilitated by ensuring that domestic workers are hired "on trial, in order to ascertain whether they are willing and able to do the work of the family in the manner which the housekeeper wishes."[110] Maintaining the relationship also meant adaptations, and it is telling that Beecher counsels housekeepers to live in the size of house that suits the availability of good domestics, rather than attempting to live in a large house in a place where "good domestics" are scarce.[111]

Every Cook Can Govern: Reading Domestic Workers' Narratives through Cookbooks

Cookbooks and manuals on the rights and duties of servants were written not only by mistresses and housekeepers, but also by domestic workers. Recently, the award-winning food writer Toni Tipton-Martin spent over a decade amassing and analyzing the recipes in cookbooks by African Americans. She has been able to highlight the significant omission of the contributions of African Americans to the culinary history of the US south, while challenging the stereotypical mammy myth of the Aunt Jemima imagery.[112] Tipton-Martin uncovers culinary pasts through remembered traditions, embodied in the women who cooked according to the sometimes hidden knowledge passed down to them through and beyond plantation kitchens.[113]

Yet Tipton-Martin does more than challenge the Aunt Jemima stereotype—she challenges, or decodes, the Jemima code, which she quite deliberately understands in normative terms as an "arrangement of words and images" that reduced knowledge and skill to instinct and enacted the invisibility of African American chefs, cooks, and cookbook authors.[114] Tipton-Martin is careful to acknowledge that the authors whose books she foregrounds "did not intend for their work to symbolize the legions of African Americans who used food and commerce for independence."[115] She adds that those who wrote represent the myriad of unnamed people who challenged societal limits and imbued "other invisible cooks . . . with wisdom and knowledge."[116]

As a legal academic, I have looked at the cookbooks somewhat differently, recognizing that none appears to have been studied as a basis to gain insight into the law that was understood to govern the household as a workplace.

I acknowledge my own need to take care, in reading the cookbooks in ways that they might not have been intended, to understand the law of the household workplace. By reading each cookbook (including the recipes) and trying to read between the lines, I affirm that we learn a little more about how domestic workers navigated the domestic work relationship and, in some ways, transgressed it—even in the act of mastering and writing their métier's laws.

Robert Roberts's Directions to Servants and Masters

It is of undeniable historical significance that one of the first books of any kind written by an African American author to have been published by a major US publisher was Robert Roberts's 1827 major work on household management, *The House Servant's Directory*. Written when slavery was still legal throughout most of the Western world, the book by a free Black man was published in Boston and New York. Roberts was reportedly a butler in the household of Christopher Gore, who served as a senator and the governor of Massachusetts.[117] Roberts refers to his own experience among some of the first families in England, France, and the United States. Calling domestic service a "station in life," he addresses the book endorsed by his own former master to the younger generation of household servants, to explain both how to "give satisfaction to their employers, and gain a good reputation for themselves."[118] He focuses on cultivating and retaining good character.

The book is overwhelmingly a how-to. From the benefits of early rising to servants, correcting a bad taste or sourness in wine, going to market, and "a wash to give a brilliant lustre to plate," Roberts provides an important overview of the kind of responsibilities that await household servants.[119] Domestic work is understood to be an art and is presented as intimately linked to the masters' health, well-being, and fortune. The responsibilities resting on the various household workers is so significant, and the advice on dutiful service so complete (with an emphasis on "good management in every respect"), that a reader might be forgiven for asking when the servant is expected to sleep.[120]

The text reflects its times and has as its dominant theme submission to employers (as well as to visitors to their household).[121] The good servant is as attentive to the master's family as possible, and this advice permeates the various technical rules, like how to know whether a bed is damp or not when traveling.[122] Roberts counsels against servants' harboring a "revengeful spirit" or assaulting "the reputation of their benefactors."[123] The text moves, for example, from how to fix a roast that is a little underdone to getting credit for cooking meals to perfection, serving a master with integrity, and never undertaking "more work than you are quite certain you can do well," interspersed with an abundance of clichés.[124] However, the message remains clear: the servant should provide dutiful service and use self-control. The word "slave" does appear in the book, but it is used to urge servants not to let their anger get the better of them and "never to be a slave to passion."[125]

Roberts does not deny the existence of injustices, acknowledging that there may be more "difficulties, trials of temper" in domestic work than in any other station in which the employees might enter at a different stage in life.[126] Biblical references abound, and particularly telling is the reference to Jacob, who was treated unjustly in the house of Laban. Roberts encourages members of the younger generation to do their duty honestly and faithfully, reasoning that it is "much better to be the oppressed than to stand in the place of the oppressor."[127] Using the example of Jacob again, Roberts tells young people to bide their time, knowing that, in due course, their patience will be rewarded. He encourages servants to maintain a clean appearance, while urging his "young friends" to avoid the "pride and folly" that might lead them to run into debt on clothing, encouraging them instead to save.[128]

Most of Roberts's admonitions to the younger generation of servants is presented at the outset, in a detailed preface, but he also speaks to masters. Nestled between chapters containing instructions on how to choose fish and directions on how to make a fire of coal, Roberts addresses "a word to heads of families." He starts by asserting that "might is right" and affirming that a servant must adjust to the masters' will—"new masters, new laws."[129] Yet Roberts's plea—relying on a mixture of noblesse oblige and enlightened self-interest—is for masters to treat their servants amiably and liberally: "At least, show them that according to their pains, will be their gains."[130] Virtue in female servants is to be encouraged by paying them a liberal wage.[131] Roberts pointedly discourages employers from discharging a good servant for a slight offense and calls on masters not to impose any commands "but what are reasonable."[132]

Roberts characterizes the household workplace as one replete with health risks:

To say nothing of the deleterious vapours and pestilential exhalations of the charcoal, which soon undermine the health of the heartiest, the glare of a scorching fire, and the smoke so baneful to the eyes and the complexion, are continual and inevitable dangers: and a cook must live in the midst of them, as a soldier on the field of battle, surrounded by bullets, and bombs, and Congreve's rockets, with this only difference, that for the first, every day is a fighting day, that her warfare is almost always without glory, and most praiseworthy achievements pass not only

without reward, but frequently without even thanks; for the most con-
summate cook is, alas! Seldom noticed by the master, or heard of by the
guests.[133]

Again speaking to masters, Roberts advises that the "man of fashion" should
take the "greatest care" to ensure that his cook's health is "preserved."[134] He
provides health and safety advice about the design of the kitchen and makes
clear that a cook's role is so important that no other responsibilities should be
required of that worker.[135] The book ends with advice on using brick loaf or
biscuits to clean spots from wallpaper; the reader is advised to take care not
to damage "the fabric of the paper-hangings, or the figures on it."[136]

This book is a product of its time, and it reflects the importance of voice
but also its limits in the period before the Civil War, when even emancipated
African Americans had their place—even if that place might involve serving whites by professionally managing other servants. It is possible to salute
Roberts's professionalism, as does Tipton-Martin, who tours the grounds
from which he wrote the book that became so popular it was reprinted in
1828 and 1843, and a copy of it was found in President Andrew Jackson's library in the Hermitage, his Tennessee home.[137] However, Tipton-Martin also
recognizes the effect of the context on the voice and notes some everyday
transgressions in the attempt not only to tell, but also to shape, the law of the
household workplace via the persuasive pen.

Complete Servants?

Roberts's book somehow seems to avoid the predictability that may seem unavoidable in *The Complete Servant*, first published in 1825 by the former servants Samuel and Sarah Adams. Samuel was educated in a public (foundation)
school, and in 1770 he entered service as a footboy. He remained in service
for fifty years, becoming a groom, footman, valet, butler, and house steward.
His wife, Sarah, began as a maid of all work, and after twenty years became a
housekeeper in a large establishment. Both were able to call on the assistance
of members of their employer's family as they wrote the book, although the
introduction to the reproduction suggests that their sole memorial appears to
be the book. Their work is "respectfully addressed to the heads of families,"
imploring them to be "firm, without being severe, and kind, without being
familiar."[138] Yet even this book contains clear expectations. It starts with wages,
giving a detailed classification of what kind of domestic worker a household
can afford and how much the worker is to be paid. And it provides wages by
category throughout the book, stopping to note under "the man cook" that

the Duke of York pays Monsieur Ude, his French cook, 500 pounds per annum.[139] The Adamses also gently remind heads of household that they are not only employers but also patrons of the servants—expected, for example, when servants fall ill not only to "remit their labour, but render them all the assistance of proper medicine, food, and comfort, in their power."[140] This is, of course, unmistakably framed as an appeal to noblesse oblige on behalf of the "poor dependent creatures" who "may have nowhere to go to"—but the expectation is made clear.[141]

Beyond the first five pages, which are framed as a dedication, the book focuses on advice to servants in general. It is replete with clichés that confirm the message that domestic servants are to "devote themselves to the control of those whom they engage to serve."[142] A servant will "accept even their admonitions as pleasing proofs of their desire to make her useful to them, and to enhance her own confidence and consequence."[143] While acknowledging that the work of a servant of all work is "one continued round of activity," in the same sentence the authors comment that "industry becomes habitual, and she will reap the benefit of it throughout life. To be content is the main thing."[144] They provide the example of a well-trained hall porter, respected for his "close tongue," "inflexible countenance," and ability to see all but say nothing: "It is recorded of the porter of a minister of state, who died in the morning, that, on being asked in the afternoon if the fact were true, he replied that really he could not tell, but if the party would give him his card, he would make enquiry, and let him know."[145]

Early rising is "indispensably necessary," and punctuality and cleanliness are stressed throughout.[146] The Adamses use of the language of "leisure" is telling: "The Housekeeper will employ the little leisure time she may have before the servants' dinner hour, which in most families is generally early, in preparing the best pastry, or in doing any other things she can assist in, preparatory to the family dinner; at any rate, she will look around and see that the household business is, everywhere, going on regularly, and the culinary preparations getting forward."[147] "Leisure" comes again after dinner has been served, but the housekeeper is advised to use that time to begin to think about the next day.

The Adamses' book is also full of recipes, including guidance on how to choose meat, butter, and cheese; preserve milk or fruit; make British wines or vinegar (the housekeeper's task) or manage foreign wines (the butler's); distill water; and produce one-third more bread from a given quantity of grain. The authors inform us that the common strawberry is a natural dentifrice, and that a mixture of cloves, cedar, and rhubarb is excellent for perfuming clothes. They teach the reader how to extinguish a fire that may have burned the clothes and provide remedies for a bruised eye or a wasp's sting. The management of infant children is also addressed, including tips for "hardening children" to face every species of fatigue and hardship when they become adults—such as having a nurse keep the child "as little in her arms as possible"[148] Who were they seeking to persuade?

We learn that in addition to wages, the head nurse can expect perquisites at christenings. It is telling, moreover, that the Adamses include governesses, who are likely to be teachers in seminaries, as well as "the unsettled daughters of respectable families of moderate fortune, who have received a finished education."[149]

This book allows textured voices to come through. After setting out the cook's catechism—a one-page dictionary ranging from browning to stock—the Adamses acknowledge that the kitchen maid or undercook in many families has the hardest position in the house and admonish the cook to "avoid all cruelty, and no custom or usage should be an excuse for any practices, by which living and sensitive creatures are to be put to wanton and unnecessary torture."[150] The book also contains a number of etchings that satirize domestic service and give a glimpse at the power relations and sexual harassment or abuse. In one, a kitchen maid in uniform stands with hands on her hips, looking straight ahead. On the ground is a broken plate. Her expression is less dismay than defiance. The caption reads, "likely to answer."[151] In another, a female servant of all work is held by the hand by a man pointing to his lip, who says, "You've miss'd your tip." The servant's eyes register consternation, if not terror.[152]

The book ends with the servants' hall, and the Adamses explain the hierarchy at the table if all household workers are sitting together. It also contains an acknowledgment: "The servants' hall is a little world by itself."[153]

Tunis Campbell's Guidance

Tunis Gulic Campbell's *Hotel Keepers, Head Waiters and Housekeepers' Guide* was published in Boston in 1848. Campbell was a powerful actor in Reconstructionist politics in Georgia and is better known for that activity than for his cookbook and guide. In part because of his prominent role, we have a more complete biography for him than for some of the other authors discussed in this chapter. Born in New Jersey in 1812, he attended an Episcopal school in New York and was a trained missionary who expected to go to Liberia. However, he grew disenchanted with the planned removal of African Americans to Africa, "having long since determined to plant our trees on American soil."[154] Instead, he became a social worker, reformer, and abolitionist and participated in antislavery causes. For example, he toured with Frederick Douglass as an anticolonization and abolitionist lecturer; as a member of the Georgia State Senate, he urged ratification of the Fifteenth Amendment to the US Constitution to prevent people being barred from voting on the basis of race, color, or previous condition of servitude; and he testified against the Ku Klux Klan in a committee of the US Congress. In addition, he worked in a hotel in New York, first as a steward and then as a principal waiter. He subsequently worked at the Adams House, which is affiliated with Harvard University. It is there that he wrote his guide.

Campbell's book was intended both for hotels and private families, and it starts by affirming the centrality of order to the domestic sphere. Most of the book is about how to provide proper service at various moments in the day. It is detailed and systematic, giving more details about protocol than many of the other books I consulted. Campbell even calls for regular drills, understandably in the hotel context and not in private households. Nor does Campbell neglect the feature that makes these books valuable go-to references and that serves the function of establishing the author's credibility: he includes a number of recipes, for making corn bread and brown celery sauce; making mutton taste like venison; preparing lobster sauce or oyster soup; and roasting a cod's head or larks. At the end of the book Campbell includes certificates attesting to his character, intellect, and qualifications.

Campbell is clear about certain employer responsibilities. One is to avoid hiring "cheap help" and instead seeking out the best, while providing employees with reasonable compensation. His reason is utilitarian: the servants will then provide good and equal service, rather than "planning to defraud him [the employer] of an hour or two, that they may make a little extra to help out their wages."[155] He addresses employers' attitudes, affirming that "servants must be conciliated by kindness, as nothing can be gained by harsh treatment. Kindness secures their good will, while harshness makes them careless eye-servants." It is on this basis that he argues for rules and regulations to be established for all servants in a house and to be enforced "firmly but calmly."[156] Campbell goes so far as to advise hotel owners to make sure that not only travelers but also their servants are pleased by their stay at a hotel: "It should always be seen to by the proprietor himself, that his steward provides such things for the servants generally as will make them comfortable, both as to lodging and food; as such little attentions are more highly thought of by them than money in many instances by domestics."[157]

Campbell writes with the authority of one who is able to command respect for servants, because he is so clearly able to assert order: "Teach them never to run. . . . Permit no racing, as it is attended with great danger of slopping gravies and sauces upon guests."[158] Of all the cookbooks written by workers,

Campbell's conveys a sense of professionalism while deftly avoiding preaching subservience. But then, consider his station. Campbell's guide is "one of the earliest manuals written by any American on the supervision and management of first-class restaurants and hotel dining rooms."[159]

Born Free: Malinda Russell's Emancipation Proclamation

A different genre of cookbook appeared in the United States after the Civil War: compilations of recipes submitted by women and sold to raise funds for a range of causes, but initially for war widows and orphans.[160] The first cookbook published by an African American woman, Malinda Russell's *A Domestic Cook Book: Containing a Careful Selection of Useful Receipts for the Kitchen by Malinda Russell, an Experienced Cook*, belongs in this genre. First published in 1866, it is a beautiful book, with approximately 265 recipes for such dishes as cold water biscuits, sweet potato slice pie, rich black cake, and fricasseed catfish—as well as a ginger-pop beer that Tipton-Martin likens to West African recipes.[161] Russell also includes a number of medical cures and advice on making household preserves.

Most compelling, however, is that Russell writes her own "short history of the author" in her own voice.[162] She starts by telling the reader that she was born free. We learn that her grandmother, also named Malinda Russell, was a member of one of the first families set free by a Mr. Noddie of Virginia. The author's mother, Karen, was born after her mother's emancipation, so Karen's "children are by law free."[163] Born in eastern Tennessee, the author lost her mother when she was quite young, and she set out for Liberia when she was about nineteen. However, she was robbed by a member of the party with whom she was traveling, so she was forced to end her journey in Virginia. There, she began to cook and travel with ladies as a nurse. In her short history, Russell reproduces the entire contents of a certificate of good character that she was given when she set out for Liberia.

Although she married in Virginia, her husband, Anderson Vaughan, lived only four years after their wedding. She had one child who was disabled. She used her maiden name after her husband's passing. She appears to have had a succession of businesses: a laundry house in Virginia; a boarding house in Tennessee, where she moved after her husband's death; and then a successful pastry shop. However, her savings were taken from her by force in 1864 "by a guerrilla party" during the Civil War. In light of her "Union principles," she left the South and fled to Michigan "until peace is restored" in Tennessee—where she intended to try to recover at least part of her property.[164]

This, Russell explains, "is one reason why I publish my Cook Book, hoping to receive enough from the sale of it to enable me to return home." She made sure to credit Fanny Steward, "a colored cook of Virginia," with teaching her the trade. The experienced cook ends by affirming the following about the "valuable" recipes that she was advised to publish: "I know my book will sell well where I have cooked, and am sure those using my receipts will be well satisfied."[165] Russell's work represents a powerful challenge to invisibility and is rightly described by Tipton-Martin as embodying an emancipatory spirit.

That said, there is little in Russell's cookbook that seeks to set out the rights and duties of servants—and that is the point. Russell did not see herself as a servant. We learn that she was a woman who spent a lifetime seeking to establish professional autonomy instead of pursuing various forms of domestic work. She opened several related businesses before finally, late in life, seeking to sell her recipes, in a context in which options for African American women were exceedingly limited. Russell might also have engaged in precisely the kind of resistance that has been misused to fuel stereotypes about magical, innate, or haphazard approaches to cooking by African Americans that was part of the omnipresent Aunt Jemima stereotyping. Russell challenged a prevailing practice in which African American cooks' recipes were published by white cookbook authors, without any attribution beyond the cooks' first names. According to the historian Rebecca Sharpless, this practice served to "erase the women's identities and, in fact, conflate them with their work."[166]

By refusing to give fully exact proportions and detailed stepwise directions in many of her recipes, Russell may well have affirmed another art—improvising—as in jazz, a higher skill requiring a sophisticated knowledge of the entire composition. This helps prevent appropriation. Russell was born free, and her cookbook was for an audience of people who knew how to cook—and possibly like the women who taught her. The book suggests that its author was a woman who sought to carve out a life on the basis of her labor without legal subordination in any particular master's house.[167]

Tellingly, Russell's life decisions are not anomalous among those rare African American women who published cookbooks between 1800 and 1960: as Sharpless notes, none appears to have been written by a cook in a private home.[168] Indeed, W. E. B. Du Bois's 1899 *Philadelphia Negro* contained a special report on domestic service, noting that of the options available to ex-slaves, one was to enter commercial life and another was to "develop certain lines of home service into more independent and lucrative employment,"[169] notably as caterers. Sudie Holton's experience, in the form of a rare transcript preserved from 1939 by the Federal Writers' Project, is an illustration both of this quest for greater independence and of the code of invisibility that even more autonomous workers could rarely transgress. Her story is recounted by the writer and journalist James Larkin Pearson, who had hired Holton to cater a dinner in 1939 in Guilford, North Carolina. This story comes close to being in Mrs. Holton's own voice, but it is invariably mediated by Pearson's positionality. We learn right from the start that "Sudie" (not "Mrs. Holton") helps "the wife." But we also learn that Holton would "not take a regular job but was willing to work for a few hours or day at a time." Below is the story Pearson tells:

> Sudie Holton came over to the house last Sunday morning to help the wife with a company dinner. It was very special company and we were anxious to have everything just right. We didn't know anything about Sudie except that she was a very neat, light-skinned, colored woman about 45, who lived in the respectable part of the Negro settlement nearby. She had been recommended as being a really good cook who would not take a regular job but was willing to work for a few hours or day at a time. We were soon to learn that Sudie could swing a wicked skillet. Her biscuits were delectable morsels of feather-lightness and her fricasseed chicken and gravy beggared description.
>
> Sudie's clothes were very plain but as clean as a new pin and her quiet efficiency as she presided in kitchen and dining room inspired complete confidence that the occasion would be a notable success. Watching her, you could pretty well imagine what her home would be like, humble but shiningly clean, with books on a shelf or some kind of musical instrument, perhaps an old piano. As she went swiftly about her preparations in the kitchen we heard her singing in a really beautiful contralto voice.
>
> One of the dinner guests that day was a flashy young chap with an overgrown superiority complex and disagreeable habit of spouting foreign words at all times. He was not highly educated and was not exactly proficient in his own native tongue but he had memorized a few foreign phrases which he used to confound some less [?] enlightened listener. We considered it the worst possible taste but had found no way to break him of this unfortunate habit.
>
> True to form, the youngster began to show off to the other guests but they were not sufficiently impressed to please him. Then Sudie's neatly uniformed figure and quiet dignity seemed to challenge his attention. As she placed a plate before him our pseudo-linguist turned toward her and let loose one of his pet volleys of Spanish, then darted a sly wink at the rest of us. Without an instant's hesitation the colored

woman looked him in the eye and replied in Spanish. She not only replied to his memorized phrase but made some further remarks for which he had no answer. His mouth dropped open and he blushed a bright red. Sudie stood holding the plate of hot biscuits and waiting courteously for his reply. With a convulsive swallow and sheepish grin he handed her a line of school-boy French phrases. As casually as if it were all part of her day's work she fed him French until he choked. Even to our ignorant ears her tone and accent were far superior to his. Our smart guy had enough and just sat open-mouthed and goggle-eyed. The rest of us were tickled pink by the turn of events. "Sudie," I cried, "Where did you learn to speak such excellent French and Spanish?" "Oh, I studied modern languages several years at college," she answered composedly. "My German is not so good, but I have taught both French and Spanish."

"You've been to college?" I stammered. "You are a teacher?" "Of course. Why not?" "Go on," I urged, "Tell us all about it and what you are doing in our kitchen."

"I studied Spanish at Bennett College and took my last year of French at Columbia. I also studied music there. Is it so surprising that a Negro woman has happened to get some education? I wanted something better for myself than my poor mother had. She was just somebody's Negro cook and I lived in a shanty 'on the lot' with her. She was contented enough with her fate but my father had been white and I was always restless and dissatisfied. Mammy sent me to school whenever it was possible and I saved every penny I could and worked my way through college, cooking, dishwashing, sweeping, hairdressing, mending, anything I could get to do. I loved to study and lessons were easy." "And you taught?" "Yes, I taught French and Spanish in the colored high schools for three or four years, and I taught music for about the same length of time at a small Negro college in South Carolina. I was interested in Dramatics too and tried to develop some Negro folk-plays." "Why did you give up teaching for this . . . this cooking?"[170]

Yes, Pearson asked the same question, twice. And according to Pearson's account, Holton continued her story, prefaced by "Well, it's the old story": her husband (an educated man who was also a teacher) had a World War I injury that required her to abandon her own teaching and care for him; she could combine providing that care with the profession of caterer; and they hoped that their two daughters would "go on where their father and I left off." Then the narrative changed. Pearson recounts: "Here Sudie realized that she had been the center of attention for some time and she picked up the plate of cold biscuits. There was a wicked twinkle in her black eyes as she looked at the crest-fallen young would-be linguist and then dropped into a rich dialect. 'Bress yo' hearts, folkses, the biscuits am cold an' old Sudie done talked her fool head off. "Souse me, suh. 'Scuse me, Ma'am, an' I'll fotch some hot ones.'"[171]

Although we learn this story through Pearson's mediated narration that heaps condemnation on the rude guest, it seems clear that Holton's final address was to the entire room. She had exposed palpable contradictions in the order of the world that made the domestic work relationship so ubiquitous, easy, and natural. She had become too visible. She had exposed her own transgression of and through the mask.

The cookbooks written by domestic workers challenged their invisibility, without quite leaving them so fully exposed. The cookbooks are self-mediated archives: reminders of the workers' presence and their hard work and skill, robust challenges to stereotypes, examples of a multiple consciousness method used by the workers. I read them in particular as affirmations that domestic workers transgressed, and in the process attempted to shape the law of the household workplace.

Cookbooks: Interesting Digression, or Pivotal Basis for Reframing?

I have examined cookbooks, but of course most of the labor of domestic work—including the art of cooking—would have been passed down orally, through intergenerational, personal relations[172] in very specific spaces of exchange: kitchens that likely belonged to others but that could also be reframed as the space of "others"—that is, the domestic workers.[173] This is particularly the case for enslaved workers, who were legally and forcibly denied literacy. Instead, knowledge was transferred orally and physically, embodied in paid and unpaid work.

Permeating all of the texts, however, is the unavoidable question: who was expected to read them?[174] The texts written by masters or mistresses are explicitly designed for their (often younger) peers, although there are interesting changes in the subject—for example, when Steel and Gardiner address cooks. The vast majority of domestic workers could not read or write and were not well placed to challenge their exploitation using means familiar to other categories of labor such as the strike—although even the rumor of a strike could strike fear in the hearts of employers. Given the extent of the work chronicled in these cookbooks, surely there was an expectation that they could lead masters to sit up and pay attention. From presidential libraries to colonies abroad, the books circulated widely and were noticed.

There are few antebellum narratives from free or enslaved people of African descent, so Russell's cookbook is not only a surprise but a rare gem. The surprise may be particularly acute if one recognizes that although 100,000 recipe collections were printed in the course of two centuries in the United States, only approximately 200 were credited to African American cooks and writers.[175] Yet surprise at the rarity of a book like Russell's should not obscure the more general surprise of the legal scholar accustomed to looking for law elsewhere. This is a matter of perspective. The duties and rights of domestic workers and their employers are found where those most concerned—the parties to the relationship—are likely to look for them: in cookbooks likely found on their kitchen shelves.

It also makes sense, from the perspective of housekeepers and to some extent domestic workers, that duties and sometimes rights of servants, as well as general principles of household management, would be included in those books or produced separately and broadly distributed through the widely available print media of the industrial revolution in the expanding European colonies as well as the United States immediately before the Civil War and after emancipation. The household did not stand outside of the industrial revolution, nor did relationships of domestic servitude simply transform themselves after emancipation. Managing the colonial household was very much a part of the work of enacting empire.

It is also possible that I am making a bigger to-do about this than is necessary. Magistrates and justices did not hesitate to rely on a range of doctrinal sources, and they frequently relied on manuals prepared to help them render their decisions. The manuals on the rights and duties of servants—written, in Baylis's case, by a lawyer—would seem to serve a similar purpose, without recipes, even if they were addressed at least in part to mistresses (and, where literate, servants). How different, then, is it to turn to a cookbook that also sets out at least some of the rights and duties of servants and their masters or mistresses? The difference is not only in the ingredients but also in the space. That is, the source of law is the actors in the relationship themselves, in the household workplace—notably, the kitchen.

One must come to terms with how strange it must seem for those concerned with finding law and telling legal origin stories to recognize that the accompaniment of recipes with rules—recipes, too, are codes—has all but been forgotten, overlooked, or dismissed.[176] While my focus is different than Tipton-Martin's (she is concerned with rewriting culinary history), we have the same core concern: like Tipton-Martin, I challenge the invisibility of this labor, in my case to understand and decode the law of the household workplace by giving space to the everyday transgressions that for the subaltern included writing a book of one's own. And to quote Steedman, "[m]odern critics have scarce got the measure of the insubordination."[177]

Labor law sources are acknowledged to be heterogeneous, with the specificity of regulation emerging from the workplace—often taken to mean the industrial shop floor.[178] In other words, if labor law has managed to equalize the bargaining relationship, it centers the parties' collective autonomy. While the state has the duty to ensure the exercise of collective autonomy, the state and its law are neither the most important nor the most essential elements of the realization and exercise of that autonomy.[179]

The fact that the master-servant relationship was profoundly unequal does not mean that there was only state law or that there was an absence of resistance—everyday transgressions that might be individual or collective forms of resistance, beyond those traditionally seen as desertion, suing, or union organizing. The main question of this chapter has been how we can begin to see that other law, which might be the law by which the parties live and work, and how it has shaped the domestic work relationship. The courts may have helped to shape it, to give the law of the household workplace the force of law beyond it.

As this selective survey has shown, there are some features of the attempt to regulate the domestic work relationship that these cookbooks allow us to see quite clearly. For example, each cookbook attests to the significance of the search for order. Seely states that order is the first law, and the search for order permeates each framing of the rules by those who work in domestic settings. Yet we see the elusiveness of order in the magnitude of the responsibilities and the increasingly apparent limits in the ability to itemize and systematize them. The work seems boundariless when the expectations are so great. The masters or mistresses stress their ability to exert authority, or control as markers of full subordination. There is little wonder that each of the cookbooks or manuals written by workers stresses employers' responsibility to act amiably, liberally, and reasonably; to pay well; and to take care of a sick employee. However, it is perhaps in Webster Steel and Gardiner's colonial Indian cookbook that we witness the call for rules of conduct of a reasonable human being mapped against an expectation that the servant will devote virtually all of his or her time to the master's household's well-being.

If there is one overwhelming and interrelated constant, it is the extent of the master's or mistress's control over their domestic worker's time. It becomes unabashedly clear that the live-in relationship is to the employer's benefit. The boundarilessness of time is assumed; leisure might be mentioned but the details demonstrate that it is illusory for most domestic workers. Might it be a slight everyday transgression—written into the science of the book—for Adams and Adams to counsel holding the child as little as possible, for the child's good?

Of course, an exhaustive study would be more attentive to the contours of place and time. It might even tell a different kind of origin story, one that compared and contrasted the cookbook rules with those emerging from magistrates in the same place. But that is a project for another book. I am interested chiefly in being able to see more about the day-to-day regulation of the domestic work relationship within or beyond the shadow of state law. This chapter confirms my intuition that there was much to see and learn—as well as make and taste—in the shadow of state law. That is the law that the Domestic Workers Convention and the Domestic Workers Recommendation could hardly ignore but sought to influence. It is little wonder that some of the thorniest issues, including working time and wages, are part of the understandings that were such a big part of the law of the household workplace as seen in the cookbooks.

CHAPTER 5

Tough Spots at the International Labour Conference

> The task . . . is not to discard rights but to see through
> them or past them so that they reflect a larger
> definition of privacy . . . so that privacy is turned from
> exclusion based on self-regard into regard for another's
> fragile, mysterious autonomy.
>
> —Patricia J. Williams, *The Alchemy of Race and Rights*

This chapter focuses on the relationship between the law of the household workplace and the international standard-setting process. The International Labour Conference is a space for dialogue between social actors on questions of social importance, also known as social dialogue. The conference offered a space to challenge the process of rendering domestic workers invisible that is so central to the unequal law of the household workplace.

The previous two chapters offered opportunities to think more closely about the law of the household workplace that has prevailed historically and remains strong in many contemporary contexts around the world. Legal anthropologist Sally Falk Moore has affirmed that "a court or legislature can make custom law" while "a semi-autonomous social field can make law its custom."[1] In this book, I have reframed this widely accepted proposition. Without calling it custom, I have tried to understand the law of the household workplace from the inside and to pay attention to the places from which it has emerged and to which it has traveled. I have treated it as law that has been applied to the domestic work relationship, not necessarily via the courts, but via the kitchens. I have certainly not discounted how easy it might well have been for legislatures or courts in the past simply to draw on the unequal law of the household workplace and to make it the law of the land in decisions rendered. They might even have shaped its direction. Falk Moore

ASYMMETRICAL LAW OF THE HOUSEHOLD WORKPLACE
TO BE UNSETTLED

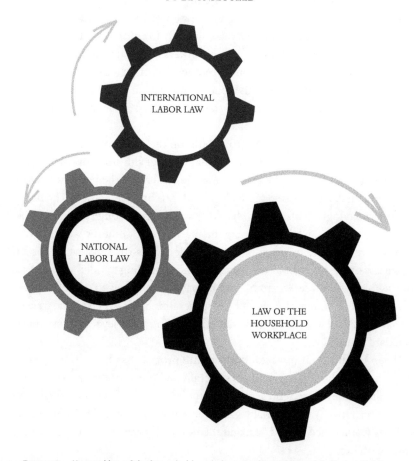

FIGURE 4.   Unequal law of the household workplace. Credit: Author and Emily Ann Painter.

speaks of the "processes of regularization" that constitute the active ways in which "conscious efforts are made to build and/or reproduce durable social and symbolic orders."[2]

The ILO *Law and Practice Report* surveyed the specific laws on the books in a range of countries that merely regularized or normalized the unequal law of the household workplace. Others had general laws that either excluded domestic workers or included them in such a broad manner that they were de facto excluded. In each of these cases, the law of the household workplace remained untouched and dominant, as figure 4 illustrates.

The transformation could therefore not simply be a matter of formalizing informality by normalizing the law that already prevailed, or even tempering it somewhat. As the *Law and Practice Report* emphasized, domestic workers do not lack structure and regulatory control: "On the contrary, their lives and work are regulated by strong non-state norms regarding work in the employer's household, which vary significantly from one cultural context to the next but which result in domestic workers being among the most marginalized workers—and for whom decent work is often a distant aspiration."[3] It seemed imperative to create the space to undertake a qualitatively different exercise by deliberately decentering state law to deepen the understanding of the law of the household workplace.

The international standard setting built on the different process that was set in motion: that of building a transnational legal framework sufficiently compelling that it would be able to unsettle the law of the household workplace and enable the transnational legal order to become settled. The deceptively simple logic explained in chapter 1 was to treat domestic workers like any other workers, while addressing the specificity of domestic work. It was a substantive equality framework, which undermines the reliance on the unequal law of the household workplace. Without needing to call that law of the household workplace "custom" and by paying attention to its defining features across a number of geographical spaces, this book has taken the transnational workplace as a site for governance, including at the level of international standard setting.

Even the international standard-setting process has had a transgressive impact. Even though the workers generally did not speak in the conference committee, they were represented, and their spatial silencing was challenged as an alternative transnational legal order was being built. The International Labour Conference helped "expand the political space available for transformative politics."[4]

With the new transnational legal order on decent work for domestic workers, the framework looks more like the diagram in figure 5, which seeks to capture the dynamic character of transnational normative change.

This multilevel governance framing of transnational legal ordering incorporates the insight of Harold Koh, an international lawyer and former dean of Yale Law School, that states themselves will "come into compliance with international norms if transnational legal processes are aggressively triggered by other transnational actors in a way that forces interaction in forums capable of generating norms, followed by norm-internalization."[5] Chapters 5 and 6 explore the shift and the enabling role of transnational actors like domestic workers' social movements. This chapter, therefore, returns to Geneva, to the International Labour Organization (ILO) and the International Labour Conference (ILC) committee meetings of June 2010 and June 2011.

TRANSNATIONAL LEGAL ORDER ON DECENT
WORK FOR DOMESTIC WORKERS TO BE SETTLED

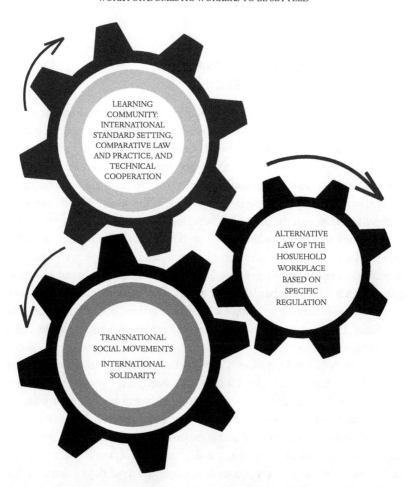

FIGURE 5. Alternative transnational legal order on decent work for domestic workers.
Credit: Author and Emily Ann Painter.

In those meetings, some of the most problematic assumptions about the law of the household workplace were laid bare, as one delegate or another tried to explain the supposedly commonsense understandings that had traditionally governed domestic work. In the same meetings, actors who had already understood and accepted the shift that was under way—formally, the workers' representative and a number of governmental representatives; and informally, a broad range of civil society actors—were able to explain the transition, negotiate and guide the actors on the committee to help the alternative legality take hold. The transition could be seen particularly clearly in the dialogue related to pivotal regulatory topics: working time and labor migration.

Workers on Labor Law's Margins Challenge Boundarilessness

The ILC committee had to tackle the boundarilessness of domestic workers' time, and everyone knew it. Working time took the ILC's secretariat back to reckoning with its first international labor standard, the Hours of Work (Industry) Convention, 1919 (No. 1).[6] Working time is also one of the thorniest issues for labor regulation generally. A report on the changing nature of work initiated by the European Commission, known as the Supiot Report, succinctly captures the work that the notion of "working time" performs in modern labor law: "The reference to 'working time,' on the one hand, limits the employer's hold on the worker's life and, on the other, allows the employer to evaluate his services. Time is simultaneously a limit to worker obligations and a standard against which to value what labour is worth. The legal limitation of working hours and the model for working life thus defined lead to 'working time' and 'free time' being regarded as contradictory terms and unpaid work being virtually ignored."[7]

The notion of working time is constructed around the standard employment relationship (SER), in which time is exchanged for wages in a full-time relational contract.[8] Under this model, providing overtime pay is the traditional way to adapt working time to employer needs, constructed as necessarily exceptional and thus both limited and compensated accordingly. Working time has become highly flexible in many industrialized market economies and is considered to be the primary source of the broader tendency to demand flexibility in employment.[9]

In their 1897 account of industrial democracy in the United Kingdom, Beatrice Webb and Sidney Webb charted the various ways in which a standard rate approach to the uniformization of time was carried out in industrializing sectors. They identified a range of trade unions that at the time insisted on pay by the piece instead of the hour, which was considered to have prevented sweated work or more work without more pay. The decision to favor a piece rate approach or a wage approach depended on the nature of the work carried out and the ability to use the standard rate to bargain collectively.[10] The self-regulating power of wage rates resurfaced as a reason why piecework based compensation might ultimately be insufficiently refined to avoid workers' economic exploitation.[11]

The Webbs added that the normalization of the working day through restrictions on hours of work was not common among "professional brain-workers" such as lawyers, doctors, and architects, although they did have minimum fee scales.[12] The Webbs dated the first calls to limit the length and regularity of the working day in the United Kingdom to the end of the eighteenth century. Their empirical analysis of the law of the shop captured the ways in which overtime pay—although cast as exceptional in legislation—tended to become a standard principle that resulted in downward pressure on the standard wage, while providing systematically longer hours for workers.[13] It also captured the extremely precarious nature of work for people for whom irregularity of work prevented the continuity of employment necessary to ensure their livelihood.[14] The ability of workers to undertake tasks in their own home rather than in a factory setting was also significant, and the Webbs noted that in the former context, "for good or for evil his [the worker's] working hours are determined by his own idiosyncracies."[15]

Yet for the Webbs, domestic workers were included not among the home workers, but rather among factory workers. They argued that "with regard to his domestic servants, the capitalist is free to determine the amount of toil solely with a view of keeping them in the highest possible efficiency."[16] This analysis is aligned with a regular feature of the law of the household workplace: "servants" would constantly be expected to be available to their "masters" to perform all required duties "within the reasonable limits of their physical strength and moral welfare."[17] But domestic workers have not fared like factory workers.

The international labor standard setting, in its focus on specific regulation as a strategy for equality and inclusion, challenged any assumption that the boundarilessness of domestic workers' time should simply be normalized. Acknowledging specificity, that assumption was problematized.

The problematization was accomplished by historicizing the assumption. For the feminist political economist Leah Vosko, the margins of the SER did not merely emerge. Rather, they were part and parcel of the original idea of an SER, which was part of the male breadwinner model that was dependent on a female caretaker's performing social reproduction within a nation-state structure that granted political citizenship to some, but not all, workers.[18] Vosko argues that a "gender contract" emerged and helped establish women's proper place in the family and workplace. Paid care workers and migrant women workers were also relegated to the margins.[19]

By leading the reader through a discussion of each of the standard pillars of the SER, including working time, Vosko shows how international labor standards of general applicability were actually geared to male citizens and helped "prepare the ground for ongoing exclusions on the basis of gender and citizenship status."[20] In other words, and as Falk Moore reminds us, "although universality of application is often used as one of the basic elements in any definition of law, universality is often a myth. Most rules of law, in fact, though theoretically universal in application, affect only a limited category of persons in a limited number of situations."[21] International labor conventions on hours of work in industry and employment helped standardize working time, while permitting exclusions that would affect working women.[22] Despite efforts to challenge exclusions—including the efforts by the ILO's Committee of Experts on the Application of Conventions and Recommendations to foster inclusion—it remains necessary to grapple with social reproduction.[23] Working time for domestic workers became a pivotal concern, at once a claim for inclusion within the SER and a call to build an "alternative imaginary" that starts with the workers who are most marginalized: domestic workers.[24]

With this analysis, it is hardly surprising that even when state labor law might prescribe limited working hours, and even when domestic workers were not expressly excluded by hours of work laws, domestic workers could rarely count on the state norms being applied to them. Sometimes courts have accepted the view that a different normative order was in play when the care of children or the elderly was at stake—at least in the household, and at least if the work was undertaken by servants.[25] The *Law and Practice Report* sought to cut through the trope that kept coming up: of course this is not about applying an industrial workplace model to domestic work. Nursing home workers, nurses, day care providers, and teachers might also recognize that their work has been historically undervalued, but few people would argue that working hour controls cannot or should not be applied to them. Something similar yet different was at play in discussions of servitude and needed to be challenged.

The ILO standard-setting process for decent work for domestic workers was designed as a high-priority matter to avoid the risk of reinforcing or reproducing inequality. On working time, it challenged the very margins and sources of exclusion that Vosko argues were part of the SER's development. This move challenged the international labor standards that were inclusive on their face but exclusionary in practice to live up to their promise of equality. Through the process, committee members were able to take the features that on their face defined modern labor and employment law and use them to distinguish decent work from servitude in the household context. Control over normal working time was a critical marker of that distinction. This is consistent with the fact that control over working time has been one of the deepest fault lines related to the regulation of work in many sectors of the economy, particularly the service industry. Working time is about boundaries that demarcate freedom: it may determine whether a worker will be considered to be full time or part time, entitled to certain employment benefits, or part of a bargaining unit of a union; and it may affect whether a worker has to work one job or several jobs to make ends meet. For those who are promised few hours, it has an impact on whether workers are perpetually expected to be available with no or few guarantees on how many hours they will work. For those expected to work many hours, it also affects whether they will have any time for themselves. In both cases, it affects work-life balance, not to mention the prospect of having clear moments for leisure and rest. How could it be that an historically marginalized category of workers could even hope to normalize their working hours in a way that would be consistent with international labor standards when some workers receive contracts with no hours or are otherwise perpetually on call?

Article 10 of the Domestic Workers Convention was crafted to ensure that domestic workers' working time would be in keeping with the principle of equal treatment for workers generally:

1. Each Member shall take measures towards ensuring equal treatment between domestic workers and workers generally in relation to normal hours of work, overtime compensation, periods of daily and weekly rest and paid annual leave in accordance with national laws, regulations or collective agreements, taking into account the special characteristics of domestic work.
2. Weekly rest shall be at least 24 consecutive hours.
3. Periods during which domestic workers are not free to dispose of their time as they please and remain at the disposal of the household in order to respond to possible calls shall be regarded as hours of work to the extent determined by national laws, regulations or collective agreements, or any other means consistent with national practice.

Critics were quick to recognize that while article 10(1) emphasizes a norm for working time, article 10(3) contains the particularly challenging acknowledgment of "on call" work and requires it to be remunerated.[26] The negotiated text that provided room for national laws, regulations, collective agreements, or other means consistent with national practice lessened the normative control of the ILO. This could be read as simply kicking the ball back to the national level.

The negotiation of this provision came at a central moment of regulatory and jurisprudential debate within the European Union on standby time and on-call duty.[27] Many people asked whether it went far enough in challenging that law of the household workplace and wondered how far the challenge could go. The provision raised concerns about retaining unitary notions of time in international standard setting for this particularly marginalized group of workers who would were ill placed to negotiate better terms than what the ILO standards could provide. In other words, breaking out of a unitary approach to time that is gendered male ran the risk of being particularly disadvantageous to those women who might need it the most.

These are the right questions to ask, and they underscore the indeterminacy inherent to all experimentalist engagements with law reform, even those that seek transformation.[28] In interviews, a French trade unionist who had negotiated the working time provision in the French national collective agreement that influenced the international standard-setting process explained the importance of arriving at an arrangement that addressed this feature of working time that is of particular importance to domestic workers.[29] Otherwise, the workers tended not to be remunerated at all, as the ethnographic studies discussed in chapter 3 also suggest. The more detailed and protective mechanism on standby time found in Article 14 of the South African Sectoral Determination No. 7 and related concerns were identified in the *Law and Practice Report*.[30]

It matters that the principle throughout the interpretation of the international standard setting, which is reinforced in article 10(1), is that the Domestic Workers Convention is an equal treatment standard. The regulation of domestic work is to be understood alongside—rather than as distinct from—the regulation of other categories of workers. It requires that domestic workers be treated no less favorably than other categories of workers who may find themselves not free to leave their workplace. This includes firefighters; police officers; and a variety of medical, health care, and nursing professionals. It includes day-care workers who watch over sleeping children. In any case, article 10(3) clearly accomplished two things. First, it acknowledged a prevalent practice: domestic workers tend to be required to stay in the house where they work. The provision helped make this practice visible. Second, it recognized that the time is time worked and must be paid. This already was a change from the asymmetrical law of the household workplace. I would argue that it must be interpreted through the lens of inclusivity and equality.

Other details on how to regulate working time were relegated to the nonbinding, supplementary Domestic Workers Recommendation. Paragraph 8 of the recommendation is perhaps the clearest indication that members acknowledge that more guidance is needed to be able to unsettle the law of the household workplace. That paragraph calls for members to "consider developing practical guidance" with organizations of representative domestic workers and employers of domestic workers on hours of work, overtime, and standby periods consistent with article 10(3). It also calls for records to be kept and remain freely available to domestic workers.

The working hours issue is of course intimately linked to wages, and article 11 of the Domestic Workers Convention requires domestic workers to be covered by minimum wage laws where they exist and their remuneration to be established "without discrimination based on sex."[31] Strategies that focused on creating solidarity among different categories of workers and that underscored the skill involved in performing domestic work helped clarify the importance of this provision.[32] However, other United Nations bodies raised the flag that flies throughout the *Law and Practice Report*, underscoring the fact that to redress wage discrimination against domestic workers, it will be important to add that there should be no discrimination on the basis of race or national origin.[33] I remain concerned about the persistent failure to problematize racialization, even when gender is addressed.

A particularly interesting provision on working time is paragraph 13 of the Domestic Workers Recommendation. It does a lot to expose the law of the household workplace by asking a simple question: Whose vacation is this anyway? It states in the most matter-of-fact way that "time spent by domestic workers accompanying the household members on holiday should not be counted as part of their paid annual leave." The wording of Paragraph 13 should be too obvious to need to be made explicit. However, it lays bare the way that many employers may have approached bringing a domestic worker along on their vacation—as if the domestic worker and her needs could be subordinated to those of the family through the convenient application of a logic that looks like a family logic—like one of the family. Domestic workers will tell you otherwise, as the ethnographies in chapter 3 showed. Paragraph 13, like many other provisions in the Domestic Workers Recommendation, acknowledges the profound inequality of bargaining power between domestic workers and their employers and makes the practice visible while regulating to change it.

More broadly, the approach of the Domestic Workers Convention and the Domestic Workers Recommendation to the regulation of time represents a marked departure from traditional arrangements, which have regularized or normalized inequality in the domestic work relationship. Rather than legitimizing lengthy working hours for domestic workers as a means of enabling employers to achieve what they perceive as a suitable work-life balance, article 25(1)(c) of the recommendation calls for "the concerns and rights of domestic workers [to be] taken into account in the context of more general efforts to reconcile work and family responsibilities."

Tackling Labor Migration in a Generalist Standard

The new convention and recommendation were not framed as international labor standards for migrant workers. Instead, they were framed as workers' rights instruments. The success of international treaties on migrant workers has not been phenomenal, and I did not want to let the convention get mired in those debates. No one doubted that migration was a significant contemporary feature in domestic work. As the sociologist Robyn Magalit Rodriguez argues, it is the defining feature, and it is characteristic of a neoliberal approach to development that turns the state into a form of labor broker, dependent on remittance-based strategies that wind up servicing debt rather than generating local opportunities.[34] As discussed in chapter 3, Rhacel Salazar Parreñas refers to these "care inequities" in the global economic landscape as a form of "care resource extraction," pointing to a "systematic withdrawal of care from poor nations to rich nations in the global economy."[35] Parreñas explains what it means, particularly for undocumented domestic workers, to live under the constant threat of deportation. Many of them had few options to choose from besides domestic work.[36]

I fully acknowledge the contradictions associated with standard setting on decent work for domestic workers in the context of neoliberal approaches to migration and development that have taken attention away from the continuity between histories of slavery and colonialism, shifts from permanent migration to temporary migration schemes and the imperative of broader structural change.[37] Focusing on transborder migration might paradoxically draw attention away from the broader conditions that affect the range of workers who undertake domestic work. It might similarly draw attention away from working conditions common to migrant and local domestic workers. Crucial in every case, the working conditions take on special significance when the worker is a migrant domestic worker. Throughout the standard-setting process, the fact that domestic workers have been marginalized and require state action, but should not be subjected to paternalistic state framing of their need for protection, had to be emphasized.[38] The framework fostering equality and inclusion applied across the board and sought to reinforce domestic workers' roles as labor actors. The Domestic Workers Convention and the Domestic Workers Recommendation innovate, therefore, because they apply to all domestic workers, at least as defined in article 1 of the convention. That definition includes migrant domestic workers because it does not exclude them. The point of the instruments—and, some would argue, their success— is that they regulate domestic workers, including migrant domestic workers, as workers.[39]

Article 9 recognizes how space in the household workplace frames domestic workers' exercise of autonomy. It is a basic but salient example of the effort to offer concrete standards that foster domestic workers' autonomy:

Each Member shall take measures to ensure that domestic workers:

(a) are free to reach agreement with their employer or potential employer on whether to reside in the household;

(b) who reside in the household are not obliged to remain in the household or with household members during periods of daily and weekly rest or annual leave; and

(c) are entitled to keep in their possession their travel and identity documents.

In particular, paragraph a makes the "normalization" of a live-in requirement—so prevalent in many migrant domestic worker programs—seem immediately problematic. The need to move away from this live-in requirement elicited considerable discussion in both years of the International Labour Conference committee. In 2010, Canada's representative sought to introduce an amendment that would add "unless residence in the home is a condition of employment."[40] The justification was that "residing in the household could be a condition of employment, for example in the case of taking care of children, persons with disabilities or elderly persons."[41] The proposal was immediately supported by Rahman, the vice-chairperson of the employers' group, who added further text. The amendments were equally swiftly opposed by Halimah Yacob, the vice-chair of the workers' group, on the principle that the freedom of the parties to negotiate was being taken away. A lengthy discussion ensued.

The unmistakable subtext, of course, was the plethora of migration programs, including Canada's, that were built around the requirement that domestic workers would live in. This requirement in a number of countries is intimately linked to the logic of sponsorship by an employer of a specific domestic worker (which in some regions is referred to as the *kafala* system), although the system does not require migrants to live in for all occupational categories subject to it—in some cases, even including judges. For domestic workers, the requirement to live in is often assumed to be naturally linked to the fee paid by the employer and the kind of work expected of the domestic worker. Generally state mandated, it has enabled untold abuse. While variations and modifications have been lobbied for in different jurisdictions, the fundamental precepts remain the same.[42] That's what the domestic workers were hired for, that's where the labor market shortage was, and that's how one would get the kind of live-in availability that citizens of countries in the global North were less and less likely to be willing to provide. As seen in the ethnographic studies discussed in chapter 3, whenever domestic workers have had the chance, they tend to live out. This was a consistent way in which domestic workers challenged the law of the household workplace, and here was the ILO proposing to delegates that international law should make domestic workers' challenge to the law of the household workplace the basis of a new transnational starting point.

The provision survived, but it came back up for discussion in 2011, when the new vice chair of the employers' group, Paul Mackay, introduced an amendment. Yacob objected forcefully: "The purpose of the Article was to give domestic workers—who were often very vulnerable, highly in debt and intimidated—a bargaining position that was more equal to that of other workers. Governments needed to ensure that domestic workers were free to decide for themselves whether or not they wanted to live in a household."[43]

The discussion in 2011 was lengthy, and delegates introduced a dizzying array of subamendments. No one quite said they did not want domestic workers to be able to be free to decide whether or not to live out. However, a range of concerns arose. They included whether negotiations about living in should happen before a domestic worker takes up employment and whether or not the freedom to bargain collectively would be respected if the language were modified (the vice chairperson of the employers' group even worried that the provision could lead to industrial action in the household). Again, there could be little doubt about delegates' concern over the future of migration programs, but this too remained unsaid. It was as if no one was prepared to vocalize that domestic workers should essentially remain unfree by having to live with their employer against their will. Delegates took the time to engage in informal consultations and came up with language that mirrored Yacob's statement—that domestic workers "are free to reach agreement with their employer or potential employer on whether to reside in the household."[44] The provision was adopted. It is considered a core victory for domestic workers.

The ILO and its delegates did run the risk that the language of the employment relationship as applied to the definition of a domestic worker could be interpreted to exclude migrant workers in certain jurisdictions—but this point was barely raised.[45] The International Labour Conference's committee members discussed the definitions of domestic workers at length before turning to the provisions that focused on labor migration. National jurisprudence varies on the effects that migrant status has on the employment relationship, and the new instruments address this matter only indirectly. I hoped that the ILO's Committee of Experts would adopt a more inclusive view, in keeping with the purpose of the new standards to include domestic workers within the corpus of international labor law.

Of course, many provisions dealing with general application take on a special hue if you are a migrant domestic worker. It hardly seems necessary to invoke the legion of reports on the abuse faced by migrant domestic workers when you read that article 5 of the Domestic Workers Convention requires domestic workers to have "effective protection against all forms of abuse, harassment or violence." ILO standard-setting on violence at work promises to deepen these protections. The particulars provided for in article 7 are relevant to any domestic worker. If a domestic worker enters into an agreement overseas, it becomes all the more important to have details about the employer ahead of time, and article 7(j) includes the terms of repatriation, if applicable—clearly confirming that the entire provision applies to migrant domestic workers.

However, there are also a number of provisions that specifically apply to migrant domestic workers. For example, article 8(1) requires a migrant domestic worker to receive a written job offer in the form of an enforceable contract, to be delivered before the domestic worker migrates. But even when it relates to one of the most vexing transnational dimensions—private employment agencies that deal almost exclusively with migrant domestic workers—the provision remains applicable to all domestic workers.

The UN committee on migrant workers also issued a general comment, which calls private employment agencies the locus of much documented abuse.[46] Some constituents seemed to resent the conclusion that agencies' conduct was often problematic. The Domestic Workers Convention might have been thought of as an opportunity to redeem the agencies or remove some tarnish from their reputations, though that did not happen during the two-year discussions of what has become article 15 of the convention.[47] That article lists an extensive set of requirements to protect domestic workers, including migrant workers, from abuses and fraudulent practices and to ensure that any such abuses or practices are properly investigated. The provision was hotly debated, and in the first year the vice-chair of the employers' group introduced a motion to delete it. Others sought to move it out of the ratifiable convention and into the nonbinding recommendation, even though it was drawn largely from the text of an existing Private Employment Agencies Convention, 1997 (No. 181).

Several amendments and subamendments later, Virgil Seafield, the delegate from the government of South Africa and spokesperson for the Africa group, introduced a hypothetical domestic worker named "Anna," who would make several appearances during the proceedings to explain the significance of particular points. In this case, Seafield reasoned as follows: "A domestic worker—hypothetical 'Anna'—was placed in a household by an employment agency. For some unknown reason, 'Anna' was dismissed by the household, and tried to claim her rights under national law, but since it was not clear who her employer was and who had legal liability, she was not able to secure redress. This demonstrated that, to ensure effective protection of the domestic workers, the household and the employment agency should be made jointly and severally liable towards the worker."[48]

Seafield then introduced an amendment to delete language that had been proposed about a triangular employment relationship and emphasized the act of placement by the employment agency. Storytelling was used in the process as a political strategy and an advocacy method—similar to what Premilla Nadasen does in her historical ethnography on African American household workers.[49] In the case of the ILO, the approach helped keep the focus on the workers to ensure that participants saw the standard-setting process and its implications through domestic workers' eyes.

At the 2011 sessions, the US governmental member argued that article 15 should be aligned to the Private Employment Agencies Convention "to establish practical guidelines in favour of domestic workers and reputable employment agencies, and to curtail exploitative operators."[50] The representative from Human Rights Watch also argued that "the provisions on employment agencies should be consistent with" the Private Employment Agencies Convention and its accompanying recommendation, "and should prohibit agencies from charging domestic workers for recruitment costs incurred by employers, because that could lead domestic workers into debt and forced labour."[51]

The Private Employment Agencies Convention has not been wildly popular: after twenty years, only thirty-three member states have ratified it.[52] In article 3, it did lift the ban on recourse by ILO members to private employment agencies. However, it is still not clear how much the convention has helped regulate transnational agencies, as they continue to proliferate and may seem increasingly footloose in their ability to elude regulation by home or host states. The Domestic Workers Convention and the Domestic Workers Recommendation do not define private employment agencies or employers, and they have broad application.[53] But how is it that "public" employment agencies are never mentioned? As discussed in chapter 6, some key countries, like the Philippines, regulate domestic workers through a public overseas employment agency. Since the convention and recommendation are both framed to place responsibility on state actors, they should be seen to apply to public institutions like the Philippines Overseas Employment Administration, which is linked to the Philippines Department of Labor and Employment and is responsible for licensing private employment agencies—including those acting on behalf of foreign principals.[54]

It is also hard to overstate the importance of article 15(e) of the Domestic Workers Convention in addressing recruitment fees. The article simply and firmly challenges the asymmetrical law of the household workplace by stipulating unequivocally that "fees charged by private employment agencies [should not be] deducted from the remuneration of domestic workers." The wording is somewhat different from that in the Private Employment Agencies Convention and might lead to some interpretive challenges.[55] It was already the source of some confusion in the standard-setting process. Mackay suggested that "his concern was to ensure that such fees were not charged prior to employment but rather that they be paid after domestic workers started receiving remuneration accruing from their employment."[56] Yet article 15(1)(e) of the Domestic Workers Convention captures the essence of article 7(1) of the Private Employment Agencies Convention, 1997 (No. 181)—"private employment agencies shall not charge directly or indirectly, in whole or in part, any fees or costs to workers"—and calls each ILO Member to be proactive by "tak[ing] measures to ensure that fees charged by private employment agencies are not deducted from the remuneration of domestic workers."

Three potentially relevant factors emerge from the drafting history of the Domestic Workers Convention: it was considered important to be consistent with the Private Employment Agencies Convention, ensure enough flexibility in the instrument to promote its ratification, and respect differing national conditions. A fourth factor, articulated by the governmental delegate from Australia, was to ensure that the Domestic Workers Convention would not become a mere "snapshot of what already existed in national laws. The Committee should not just strive to work towards offering protection, but commit to ensuring protection to domestic workers."[57] The workers' amendment to the chapeau of article 15—which begins "to effectively protect domestic workers, including migrant domestic workers" and was introduced in response to this exchange[58]—should weigh heavily in any observation on this provision that the ILO's Committee of Experts might be called upon to provide.[59]

If dealing with agencies was not thorny enough, paragraph 26(4) of the Domestic Workers Recommendation broaches an issue that is of particular relevance to international officials: preventing abuse and violations of domestic workers' rights in cases where employers claim diplomatic immunity. While the issue had been raised in the *Law and Practice Report*, the International Labour Office did not present draft text for a provision of the convention or recommendation.[60] The matter was ultimately raised by the representative of the government of Hungary, on behalf of the European Union member states. They introduced a new provision by amendment to cover this issue at the very end of the very last session of the committee in 2011. While a revised version submitted by the United States and seconded by Australia was ultimately adopted, it is telling that the vice chairs of both the employers' and the workers' groups welcomed the initiative, and only a limited number of the ILO members from the global North actually spoke about it. Only the delegate from the government of Bangladesh went on record to object to the addition of such an important point when there had "been no time to carry out appropriate consultations at national level" and when, in his opinion, the matter should be addressed only by the United Nations.[61] The amendment was adopted.[62]

It bears emphasizing that the approach to migration in the Domestic Workers Convention and the Domestic Workers Recommendation differs from that in the key UN conventions, and even some other ILO standards on migrant workers. The UN's 1990 International Convention on the Protection of the Rights of All Migrant Workers and Members of Their Families, the ILO's Migration for Employment Convention (Revised), 1949 (No. 97), and the Migrant Workers (Supplementary Provisions) Convention, 1975 (No. 143) all tend to establish and reinforce separate sets of rights that depend on individuals' migration status—including whether or not they are documented.[63] That traditional approach has been heavily criticized for underscoring how few rights some migrant workers really have.[64]

Thanks to the contextualized approach adopted in the Domestic Workers Convention and the Domestic Workers Recommendation, the new transnational legal order goes beyond challenging abuse to identify mechanisms that states acting individually and collaboratively can build to harmonize social security contributions for migrant domestic workers. Paragraph 20(2) of the Domestic Workers Recommendation encourages members to "consider concluding bilateral, regional or multilateral agreements to provide, for migrant domestic workers covered by such agreements, equality of treatment in respect of social security, as well as access to and preservation or portability of social security entitlements."

Of course this provision, like so many other features of the convention and recommendation, will require enhanced international cooperation. In turn, that international cooperation requires a degree of international solidarity. I think one of the most significant measures that the constituents accepted focuses on cooperation to ensure that the provisions of the convention as a whole are effectively applied to migrant domestic workers, according to article 8(3). The cooperation theme is expanded upon throughout paragraph 26, the recommendation's final paragraph. Paragraph 26 calls for "enhanced international cooperation or assistance," which I read as one of the clearest affirmations of the emerging focus on international solidarity that I have seen in an international labor instrument. The constituents were careful to specify that the cooperation would be multilateral and transnational and occur at bilateral, regional, and global levels. Through this instrument, the constituents affirmed the transnational future of this international labor standard setting.

At Long Last, Centering Domestic Work

Domestic work—a topic once turned over to an eager intern in the ILO's labor law reform unit—now has its own drop-down menu on the ILO's main web page.[65] The standard-setting initiatives and the social movement related to them have brought a sense of urgency and meaning to a new form of international labor law that seeks social justice on the verge of the ILO's next centenary. The initiatives have also enabled international labor law to address the relationship between paid and unpaid care work, as well as work, rest, leisure, and life.[66] To achieve decent work for all domestic workers, including migrant domestic workers, it is necessary to look beyond the worker and the migrant to consider the human being, who has care responsibilities of her own.[67] The Domestic Workers Convention and the Domestic Workers Recommendation constitute an important step toward seeing domestic work in a contextualized and principled way.

They also reaffirm and repurpose social dialogue. The new international standards broaden the scope of who matters in the ILO's traditionally tripartite process, expanding and deepening the relevant community of practice. That community was put to the test in this standard-setting process, but social dialogue enabled a consensus and a real momentum to emerge.

Something else happened around the standard setting on decent work for domestic workers that should not be overlooked. Members did not just adopt a convention and a recommendation. They also quickly but purposefully adopted a resolution to make decent work a reality for domestic workers worldwide. It is a short but important document that states:

> The General Conference of the International Labour Organization at its 100th Session,
> Having adopted the Domestic Workers Convention and Recommendation, 2011,
> Acknowledging the specific conditions under which domestic work is carried out,

> Recognizing the importance and urgency of ensuring decent work
> conditions for domestic workers worldwide,
> Invites the Governing Body of the International Labour Office to
> request the Director-General to consider, subject to the availability of
> resources, cost-effective measures to
> (a) Promote, through appropriate initiatives, the widespread ratification
>   of the Convention and the effective implementation of the Convention
>   and Recommendation;
> (b) Support governments and employers' and workers' organizations in
>   the sharing of knowledge, information and good practices on domestic
>   work;
> (c) Promote capacity building of governments and employers' and
>   workers' organizations to ensure decent working conditions for
>   domestic workers;
> (d) Encourage cooperation with regard to the promotion of decent work
>   for domestic workers between the International Labour Organization
>   and other relevant international organizations.[68]

This resolution has been at the core of the ILO secretariat's ongoing efforts to ensure decent work standards for domestic workers. The International Labour Conference has given the International Labour Office a framework it can use to support constituents' efforts to make decent work for domestic workers a reality. Constituents have been assured that the Office has the means to play a pivotal role in shaping this new transnational legal order of the rapidly approaching future.

The consensus on working time and living conditions forged when the Domestic Workers Convention and the Domestic Workers Recommendation were being negotiated led to a critical shift away from the unequal law of the household workplace and toward a "new legal common sense."[69] ILO constituents and the social movements for domestic workers' rights helped establish a transgressive transnational legal order through and alongside the adoption of the convention and recommendation. The provisions on working time are a crucial part of that work. They help to normalize domestic workers' working hours through specific and general working-time regulation. The negotiated, normative consensus on the meaning of decent work for domestic workers in the convention and recommendation is part of domestic workers' broader political mobilization for societal enfranchisement.

However, as I will discuss in the next chapter, there is little doubt that creative lawmakers can find ways to circumvent international standards and bring about unexpected consequences—even if they ratify the convention and profess to put it into their laws. Law is a limited tool for societal transformation, and international labor lawyers recognize the limits of standard setting on societal marginalization. The provisions on working time are sobering reminders that live-in domestic work may easily lead, in practice, to significant abuse— including the range of forced labor practices now included in the ILO's Forced Labour Convention, 1930 (No. 29) and its 2014 Protocol. It is no wonder that some states have periodically experimented with an abolitionist strategy— that is, banning migration in light of egregious violations of domestic workers' human rights.[70]

CHAPTER 6

Beyond Ratification

Diffusing Decent Work for Domestic Workers

> We have managed to bring domestic workers to the
> ILO, and I am sure you will feel the spirit and see the
> hope and expression on our faces. We wanted to show
> you the importance of domestic workers, who
> contribute to building the economies of the world by
> looking after your families and your homes. We are
> sure that, for the first time, the delegates at this
> Conference could feel, hear and experience the unity
> among the domestic workers, and maybe we will
> convince you that united, we can move mountains.
>
> —Myrtle Witbooi

As soon as the Domestic Workers Convention
and the Domestic Workers Recommendation were adopted by the International Labour Conference in 2011—on June 16, which quickly became International Domestic Workers' Day—domestic workers began a global campaign
to secure twelve ratifications by International Labour Organization (ILO)
members by 2012. Uruguay, a leader on law reform for this sector, stepped up
to the plate first and ratified the convention on June 14, 2012. The Philippines
followed on September 5. The convention came into force one year after that
second ratification, on September 5, 2013.

The international standard setting was quickly recognized around the world
as historic and a fairly unbridled success for the movement for domestic
workers' rights and recognition. It offered a huge boost for ILO standard
setting at a time when some people had lost faith in the process. Because of the
daunting challenge of making decent work for domestic workers a reality (of
course, a convention alone cannot do that), there was a call for international
solidarity to promote and deepen technical cooperation, centered at the ILO.
While the dream of twelve ratifications by 2012 was not realized, the Domestic
Workers Convention has been ratified faster than many international labor
standards: there were twelve ratifications by early 2014, twenty-five by early

2018, and momentum remains high.[1] Moreover, the ratifications defy any obvious pattern: migrant-sending states have predictably ratified the convention, but so have migrant-receiving states. Members from the global South have ratified it alongside members from the global North. Most regions and subregions have had at least one ratification. However, North American and Australasian members have yet to ratify, despite the prominent role played by the United States, Canada, Australia, and New Zealand in the ILO committee's deliberations.

While the pace of ratifications has been spectacular for the ILO, it is equally important to think about what is happening around and beyond ratification. To do so, we need to look at a broad range of changes to labor law. The diffusion of a transnational legal order on decent work for domestic workers extends well beyond the ratification of the international labor standard by individual ILO member states: it includes a range of actions by a range of actors at a range of governance levels—the local, national, regional, multilateral, and international. Indeed, it moves beyond states to embrace the global.

Around and beyond Ratification

Both leading up to and following the adoption of the Domestic Workers Convention and the Domestic Workers Recommendation, there has been an outpouring of reform of international, regional, and domestic laws related to decent work for domestic workers. The norms vary widely and have different legal authority. They seem to suggest that actors and institutions (including national courts) are taking the standards seriously. Consider that on November 13, 2014, the Colombian Constitutional Court referred to the convention, in its first post-ratification decision on domestic workers, as "a human rights treaty, and, more specifically, an equality treaty. Its aim, clearly defined in the preamble, is to strive for domestic work to take place under decent conditions. To achieve this, many of its articles constitute specific articulations of the principle of equality."[2]

The court relied on this equality-based approach to domestic workers' rights to reverse its previous decision upholding a legislative exclusion of domestic workers from workplace bonuses because they did not work in "enterprises."[3] The focus on equality led the court to stress the specificity of domestic work as a reason for including it.

Most importantly, as they did at the ILO, domestic workers have insisted on being visible in a range of processes since the convention was adopted, forcing other legal actors to pay attention to the conditions of domestic workers. For example, in 2015 a domestic worker brought a case before the Committee on Economic, Social and Cultural Rights of the United Nations (UN). Her claim was pretty straightforward: she sought her basic labor right to social security under the International Covenant on Economic and Social Rights (ICESR) of 1966. According to article 9, "The States Parties to the present Covenant recognize the right of everyone to social security, including social insurance." There has never been a noncontributory pension program for domestic workers. The woman's claim is still pending.

So why did Ecuadorian domestic workers bring forward a case to the Committee on Economic, Social and Cultural Rights seeking social security in 2015? While there might be many reasons, it hardly seems unrelated that in 2013, Ecuador ratified the Domestic Workers Convention, and its article 14 is much more specific than article 9 of the ICESR. Domestic workers are to "enjoy conditions that are not less favorable than those applicable to workers generally in respect of social security protection." That is, domestic workers are to be treated like other workers. Article 14 also takes "due regard for the special characteristics of domestic work." That is because to include domestic workers, it might well be necessary to ensure that they have access to something like a noncontributory pension program, because the conventional model applied on the basis of contributions by employers might not generate the kind of resources needed to support the program. The convention does not make that determination for individual states. Rather, it sets out a framework: take into account the specificity and make sure that the conditions are substantively equal. In other words, article 14 offers an inclusive equality frame: work like no other, work like any other.

As the patterns of ratification demonstrate, law reform does not have to follow a predictable North-South logic of legal transplantation. There is a tendency to think that good laws flow from democracies in Europe or other industrialized democracies, and are picked up and tried out in developing countries.[4] In the area of domestic work, however, many industrialized countries' laws are outdated and at times colonial. They tend to reflect rather than challenge the unjust law of the household workplace, keeping an old order of domestic work firmly in place.[5] While labor law in some industrialized countries such as France is among the most original in the world, in many places domestic workers simply were not thought of as members of the working class who should be protected, but rather marginal workers who were often migrants and who could be largely ignored until they moved out of this nonproductive part of the economy and into productive employment.

Some states were quick to recognize the inequality in their laws and decided to reform them in the wake of the adoption of the Domestic Workers Convention and the Domestic Workers Recommendation.[6] Many of these changes have been prompted by dynamic, inspired social movements like that led by the National Domestic Workers Alliance in the United States, which has worked state by state as well as federally to remove domestic workers' exclusion from labor standards legislation and build a framework to promote the dignity of care work.[7]

Regulating decent work for domestic workers teaches us something else: diffusion is not a unidirectional affair.[8] It is not simply that the convention and recommendation have radiated outward. Rather, the transnational legal order was constructed in large measure because it recognized the unequal law of the household workplace and tapped into the social movements and local initiatives, regulatory and beyond, that helped displace that law. As more initiatives are implemented, it may become less easy to align them. We can also see ambivalence and at times reluctance to accept proposed changes, if not outright backlash. The nature of the reforms varies, but the quest for decent work for domestic workers is a reminder that what we are really seeking is social justice.[9]

After writing the *Law and Practice Report*, I conducted a series of studies that assessed the impact of domestic law reform on the international standard setting and the impact of the new transnational legal order on decent work on domestic workers on ongoing regulatory changes in different ILO member states. The five examples that I studied are admittedly somewhat eclectic, but they cover countries with large numbers of domestic workers. Among the five there is also a good mix of labor migration and internal domestic work populations and regulation at a range of governance levels. Many of these countries' approaches have intrigued me for years because of the regulatory innovations in place. Some of the innovations involve law reform, and I featured these countries prominently in the *Law and Practice Report* as regulatory innovators wanted to take a closer look at their implementation. In other cases, I had learned informally of regulatory practices that meant that even though laws remained largely unchanged, a range of administrative and even judicial practices were helping them evolve.

This chapter surveys how international initiatives have been diffused and then draws upon the insights of the five studies. I looked at specific regulation and alternative dispute resolution of the domestic work relationship in South Africa,[10] how France addressed the employment relationship through a collective labor regulation program,[11] the juxtaposition of discourse on contemporary forms of slavery in Europe and the regulation of domestic work

via the generalist courts in Côte d'Ivoire,[12] the proliferation of legislative simplification programs in Switzerland,[13] and the challenge of bilateral agreements
to govern domestic worker migration in the Philippines.[14]

Each example provides an opportunity to consider the interactive dynamics between locally set norms, social movement actors, and international
standard setting: that is, the dynamics of multilevel governance. Diffusion is
not taken to mean causation, but rather that norms are set as communities
of learning emerge. Sometimes—as in the context of regulating migration
through bilateral agreements—we realize that the old frameworks may be part
of the problem. If the framework is maintaining and upholding the unequal
law of the household workplace rather than dislodging it, then it is preventing the transnational legal order from being settled. The development of a
transnational legal order on decent work for domestic workers is both an
unsettling and a dynamic process.

In the *Law and Practice Report*, I argued that the specific regulation of domestic work should be simple, supportive, and smart. Drawing on insights on
the regulation of labor market informality from researchers affiliated with the
Women in Informal Employment: Globalizing and Organizing network, I
found that it is important to choose the appropriate level at which domestic
work should be governed. The report documented the extent to which domestic work is both localized—isolated as it is in individual homes—and characterized by considerable labor migration across national borders. It made
the following case:

> Regulating domestic work must offer a mix of international, regional
> and bilateral governance initiatives (notably, fostering collective bargain-
> ing) which are as close as possible to the reality experienced by domes-
> tic workers.
>
> Model contracts are a good example of the kind of initiative that can
> effectively buttress existing legislation but they are of little help if the
> regulatory framework and minimum standards do not exist. The need
> for a regulatory framework to improve domestic workers' employment
> conditions is the main theme of this report.
>
> The introduction of laws and regulations should not only fine-tune em-
> ployment conditions but also address abusive practices. Any new legis-
> lation on the subject must therefore take into account the distinctive
> character of domestic work and address it meaningfully through regu-
> lation that promotes equality with other wage earners.
>
> Clarity and simplicity are of the essence. Regulation should not be
> overly complex or unnecessarily detailed. It should seek to build the

capability of domestic workers to understand and defend their own rights.[15]

Mostly, though, the impulse to move forward has come through transnational campaigns to develop and marshal international law to foster law reform in individual states.[16] As I suggested earlier and in different parts of this book, there is a tendency to think that good examples will come from the advanced democracies of the global North and be shared with the rest of the world. That has been the direction too often taken in labor law reform initiatives, and some international labor standard-setting initiatives at the ILO were developed from law and practice reports that surveyed mainly countries in the global North. In contrast, decent work for domestic workers was built in large measure on regulatory experimentation that was under way in countries in the global South. In a number of those countries, regulatory innovation on domestic work has been spurred by a combination of social necessity and strong social movements.[17] The shift is transgressive.

Influencing the Transnational Legal Order: Specific Regulation in South Africa

In 2010, Gay McDougall, a UN independent expert on minority issues, organized a United Nations Forum on Minorities and Effective Participation in Economic Life and made a point of inviting Myrtle Witbooi—the general secretary of the South African Domestic Service and Allied Workers Union, leader of the International Domestic Workers' Network, and a former domestic worker—to speak. Witbooi's comments were poignant, and as she said, they came straight "from the heart":

> Domestic work is rooted in the global history of slavery. Yet it is work like any other. . . . In South Africa, we have the best labor laws. We have over a million workers, yet we are still treated as minorities and face exploitation daily by employers. We have a democratic government, an open door for workers. But we must remember they are also employers, so we need to remind them at times who we are. [Domestic workers] are a vital and much needed workforce of many countries yet they are still treated as workers with no voice, and are often denied training and access to further schooling. We now need to change it and make minority rights a reality. . . . We want social security . . . we want training centres . . . we want a decent living wage. There is so much that we want. What do we want from the ILO? We want our pride, our dignity,

our respect back as workers, mainly women. We want to walk tall, be proud as workers. After all, we were and still are there for all of you. We need the support of government, NGOs, social groups, business, labor. Minorities—yes perhaps but workers that belong, migrants, urban, rural—we are here to stay.[18]

When Witbooi ended her talk, the governmental delegates, academics, and NGO participants in the room were still, taking in the power of her words. The chair of the forum, leading population and global health expert Gita Sen, thanked her by saying that sometimes speeches from the heart are the most moving of all. The independent expert's recommendations were issued in time to be part of the momentum that led to the adoption of the Domestic Workers Convention and the Domestic Workers Recommendation.[19]

As Witbooi emphasized, South African law has been at the vanguard of domestic workers' rights. In 1991, the government of South Africa—newly emerging from a system of legal apartheid—recognized that it needed to respond to a particularly potent symbol of apartheid: Black women relegated to care for whites in segregated, gated communities, while their own children floundered in townships. The government could not promise these workers that they would be able to leave domestic work overnight, but it knew it needed to address the employment relationship. South Africa agreed to an official visit of the ILO's Fact-Finding and Conciliation Commission on Freedom of Association (FFCC). The FFCC produced a report that called domestic workers' exclusion from labor law "one of the most serious problems affecting freedom of association."[20] The FFCC added that while nothing in South African law prevented domestic workers from exercising their rights, "there is, at the same time, nothing which protects" their freedom of association. The South African government sought the ILO's guidance, both on the applicability of international labor standards and on comparative law experience regulating domestic work.[21] The ILO provided technical cooperation in the form of backstopping to a major labor law reform initiative that was led by the late leading labor law scholar and anti-apartheid activist, Sir Bob Hepple; the initiative resulted in significant innovation on labor law reform and labor institutions.[22]

The reforms included specific regulation of domestic workers' conditions of employment through the Basic Conditions of Employment Act (BCEA), No. 75 of 1997, as amended. South Africa built a progressive, comprehensive set of labor relations and basic conditions of employment legislation for workers generally. It also adopted a detailed regulatory text, the Sectoral Determination No. 7, on domestic workers in 2002, which is regularly updated. It is meant to be quite comprehensive and includes domestic workers under contract, those employed by employment agencies, gardeners, and chauffeurs. Sectoral Determination No. 7 provided a way to regulate minimum wages, including how they were calculated. It also included regulations on key aspects of the employment relationship such as working time, leave provisions, prohibitions of forced and child labor, and termination of employment.

The courts also played an important role in unsettling the unjust law of the household workplace and fostering some societal transformation. The innovative South African constitution includes a broad and creative range of social and economic rights and has been a major part of this process of transformative constitutionalism.[23] South Africa has made access to justice regarding the termination of employment a reality—an issue of ongoing struggle in many jurisdictions, including some in the global North.[24] It introduced the Commission for Conciliation, Mediation and Arbitration (CCMA), which offers a wide range of low-wage categories of workers (including domestic workers) a legal mechanism to use in their quest for recognition of their labor rights.

During visits to South Africa in March 2014, I had the opportunity to observe a number of conciliation sessions on the termination of employment, where I watched domestic workers and their former employers face one another across a table. In some cases, it felt as if it might have been the first time they had ever done that. In one case, the domestic worker was a single mother who lived in precarious housing and had trouble getting to work on time. She seemed barely able to meet her male employer's eyes. She sat next to an interpreter appointed by the CCMA and was able to address her employer in her own language—she might have had to address the employer in English or Afrikaans in the household—and state her claim, in her own words, to the commissioner who was there to really listen to her too.[25] The domestic worker had a chance to require her employer to see and hear her, in a formal context characterized by respect.[26] Of course, it was not hard to tell that this case would be settled: this woman had no job and children to feed; representatives of domestic workers report that some are not even be able to afford the transportation to get to their sessions.[27] There is a risk that the justice can be meted out a little too quickly, easily, or inexpensively. Yet it is significant that the case had been heard within a few weeks, rather than a few months or years. And as interviewees from domestic workers' associations in South Africa reminded me, although imperfect, the mechanisms were important to diffusing and settling the potentially transformative principle at the heart of the international standard setting: domestic work is decent work.[28]

I also met with CCMA commissioners and representatives of the Ministry of Labor, who were able to demonstrate the subtle, slow shift in perception of the relationship between domestic worker and employer, from a relationship of servitude to a decent work relationship—a shift that was taking place in the minds of both workers and employers.[29] The CCMA is well known, in part because of publicity campaigns but also because of word of mouth and the speed with which it works through over 100,000 cases per year involving a range of workplaces and a large number of domestic workers. Maybe the CCMA is a victim of its own success. One commissioner told me that sometimes they have barely thirty minutes to assess whether a case is going to be settled or not.[30]

The commissioners also recognized the latitude they enjoyed, which helped them encourage settlements. They stressed the importance of understanding the nuances in the domestic work relationship and the multiple sites of relative power. One commissioner referred to a case in which a domestic worker quit her job and came to the CCMA alleging sexual harassment in the workplace at the hands of her male employer. The male employer came to the hearing with his wife, who was also cited as the employer. She initially supported her husband until she saw the domestic worker's detailed account of the incidents. That case was settled quickly because both employers wanted it to go away. However, the commissioner felt that it was her responsibility to explain separately to the domestic worker that she could bring a constructive dismissal claim, although she would have to wait several more weeks before the case could move forward with the new claim. The domestic worker decided to accept what was likely to be a smaller settlement, rather run the risk of having to wait over eighteen months for the matter to be resolved in court. Clearly there was a trade-off, one that is all too familiar to labor lawyers and mediators in many parts of the world.

Through the CCMA dispute resolution mechanism, a dispute can be resolved within an hour. Even the notion of progressive discipline in the domestic work context has been introduced, with workers reinstated in their jobs. The significance of reinstatement for domestic workers can hardly be overstated. Domestic workers who might well have breached an employment obligation and who previously would easily have been dismissed with no recourse can come to the CCMA and see a labor law principle applied so that they get another chance, like any other worker in the formal economy. Below is how one CCMA commissioner described an "aha" moment related to a husband and wife who were both domestic workers on a farm: "It was the weekend off, everyone had a bit too much to drink, there was a fight, and it spilled over into the employer's premises, and . . . some things were damaged. Anyway they were both eventually just dismissed for it, because it was quite serious. The police were involved. . . . The farmer was quite sick about it . . . yes, they do parties on the weekends, and it's their time, and they can do what they want to—but they still . . . live on the property."[31]

Everything is in this case: working time, living space, and what actually should constitute serious misconduct warranting dismissal in the live-in domestic work relationship. Some of these are matters of enforcement to be addressed by the labor administration. Those issues were not tackled, at least directly, in the mediation. The commissioner recognized just how much it meant for the employers to be summoned, by the employees whom they had dismissed, to appear before the CCMA. The commissioner had a strong grasp of the broader relationship, having seen many times before how maternalism or paternalism played out in this kind of relationship and structured it. What is distinct in this instance, however, is that the relationship was mediated. It is not just the employer and employees who determine the law of the household workplace. Rather, the dispute resolution mechanism is fast, close, and cultivates the sense that domestic workers belong there. Its very existence says that this is a recognized employment relationship, subject to the rule of law in the workplace.

In this case, the commissioner decided to let the parties keep talking to each other, left the room, and gave them a bit of time, returning "at the end of the ten minutes, after I had some tea. . . . You separate the parties, make sure that the employees understand that it's not about those hurt feelings and everything you've done before. That if we're going to be arbitrating . . . these are the tests we need to apply. Not because I don't like you and I prefer them, but because that's what the law says. . . . Then having a minute with the employer about the fact that whether they [the employees] brought you here or not, it's actually to assist both parties. So what's happened? . . . Can they come back to work . . . ?"[32]

The parties settled with a warning and a six-month probationary period for the employees. It really does matter that the commissioner thought they "would've taken a final warning valid [for] twenty-five years if they had to."[33] The statement speaks volumes about life options in a country with high unemployment and stark income inequality. There is a risk in that knowledge: although it is designed to challenge the status quo, with such a stark power imbalance, the CCMA's work can both transform aspects of the relationship and maintain the structure of inequality that goes beyond its ability to resolve.

One of the clearest contributions of the combination of Sectoral Determination No. 7 and the CCMA proceedings appears to have been to bring home the "aha" moment that domestic work really is an employment relationship. Participants in proceedings may start by reciting the reasons why the relationship was in fact something else: "I gave you a fridge, or children's clothing, or paid your daughter's school fees."[34] Yet the CCMA process, through a law that sees the relationship differently, helps convey the fact that the relationship is not exclusively the terrain of unbridled employer discretion, the gift, and noblesse oblige. This kind of process has become widely known in the South African context, as the CCMA is a popular institution.

It would be unfair to move too quickly past this innovation, without recalling the extent to which it has had a significant influence on international standard setting.[35] Examples from Sectoral Determination No. 7 were discussed at length in the *Law and Practice Report*, alongside statistical studies suggesting that regulation did not foster job loss so much as reduced working hours for the same pay. The fact that South Africa has been more proactive than many other states in this field made a difference in the shape of the instruments that the ILO member states adopted. South Africa was an early ratifier of the Domestic Workers Convention, on June 20, 2013, and South African law on the regulation of domestic work suggests that there has been a real diffusion in that country of the transnational legal order on decent work for domestic workers. South African law on domestic work was established in a context that explicitly sought to transform the law of the household workplace, and that transformative ethos infused the international standard-setting process. The experience suggests that diffusion is not necessarily a unidirectional process. The transnational process is at once multipolar and multidirectional. With the literature about it proliferating, it is likely to be ongoing.

Of course, the success raises a serious question: are the CCMA's resolutions themselves sufficiently dissuasive? I got answers with varying hues from commissioners, domestic workers' association representatives, ministry of labor officials, and academics. South African scholars, particularly those affiliated with the Social Law Project in Cape Town, have been clear that the current laws are insufficient and fall short of compliance with the Domestic Workers Convention and the Domestic Workers Recommendation. They also argue that domestic workers' historical exclusion from labor regulation is currently part of the neoliberal unraveling of the standard employment relationship.[36] The specificity of domestic work is therefore relative; the perceived mismatch between traditional labor regulatory frameworks and the domestic work relationship is part of a continuum on which increasingly typical contingent work is found. It is important to see domestic work in a broader context.

There is an "historically self-conscious" character to the regulation of domestic work in South Africa. Although employers may be of any racial category in South Africa, virtually all domestic workers remain Black, and the occupation is overwhelmingly filled with women. Domestic work in South Africa still is performed by not only the temporally oppressed worker (in boundariless time) but also the spatially dispossessed subaltern in post-apartheid society: domestic workers represent a staggering 8.7 percent of the population.[37] In addition, the South African Domestic and General Workers Union—in its unpublished historical account titled "Crawling through the History of Common Law and BCEA [Basic Conditions of Employment Act] of Vulnerable Workers in South Africa"—recognizes that migrant domestic work poses its own challenges in a context of prevalent unemployment, contractualization of work relationships, and migration to Southern Africa from neighboring countries like Zimbabwe.[38] Despite the legislative action and enforcement policies, therefore, domestic work is a reminder that apartheid in South Africa was not just a legal or political system, but an economic and social one, too. Labor law resides where the legal and political intersect with the economic and social. Moreover, the starkness of racial subordination in South Africa should not lead it to be treated as unique to South Africa.[39] Labor migration in domestic work is just one feature that keeps racialization at the forefront. A new transnational legal order on domestic work has to reckon with the knowledge that the social transformation it brings is part of a bigger challenge to the persisting character of settler colonial relationships.

In a generation of South Africans who did not live during the period of legal apartheid, the labor regulation is called to account when it does not seem to have redressed persisting structural inequality. Some people argue that too much of the legislative reform focuses on protection, instead of on measures to enhance domestic workers' agency.[40] This is where the new international labor standards continue to offer guidance, and this is where further cooperative learning from comparative experience—including that of France—becomes a particularly interesting aspect of how the new transnational legal order on decent work for domestic workers can be diffused.

Collective Autonomy and the Collective Decree System in France

In this book I have acknowledged and explained domestic workers' marginalization, but I have insisted on exploring the myriad ways in which they exercise their agency. The reason is simple but crucial: even in conditions of abject servitude, domestic workers hold on to their humanity through resistance. Sometimes the sources and nature of the resistance may be misunderstood, which can lead an observer to miss how the workers themselves work for their emancipation.[41]

The *Law and Practice Report* showcased examples of domestic workers worldwide acting collectively whenever possible to combat exploitative working conditions, despite significant organizing difficulties. To give just a few examples, the general secretary of the New Delhi–based All India Domestic Workers' Union held a twenty-six-day hunger strike in 1959 to seek legislative reform. The National Union of Domestic Employees in Trinidad and Tobago registered in 1974 as a section of the Shipbuilders and Ship Workers Union, circumventing legislative failure to recognize domestic workers as workers for the purposes of collective bargaining. The Latin American and Caribbean Confederation of Household Workers was founded in 1988 with member organizations from thirteen countries to promote cooperation with trade unions and address cross-border organizing issues. Italian workers' and employers' organizations engage in collective bargaining through a national collective agreement.

The international standard setting emphasized the role of the state to remedy historical forms of marginalization, largely through protective legislative reform. The risk was that domestic workers' self-organization might seem unrealistic, an aspiration to be nodded to but largely ignored. But could the ILO—an organization that has put the freedom of association front and center of its normative universe—see itself as just regulating for domestic workers, and not also with them?

France was one of the few countries that we could turn to in the standard-setting process, as it offered a concrete example of a full-fledged specific regulation program based on a model of collective bargaining. I had looked closely at the French regulation when researching my 1998 ILO working paper and was carrying out a research project on French regulation of decent work for domestic workers when the ILO contacted me for the standard-setting process. As seen throughout this book, French regulation became another influential source of guidance on decent work for domestic workers.

The French approach is unique, mixing collective bargaining by unions and employers' organizations on the content of the standards that would apply with governmental extension of those standards to all domestic workers in France. The country's National Collective Agreement (known by its French acronym, CCN, for Convention collective nationale), which was in force at the time of the standard setting, had been adopted in 1999.[42] Its details show that those who negotiated it really paid attention to the specificity of the domestic work relationship: its provisions tackle everything from living conditions to working hours, workplace harassment to sickness, and accident coverage to occupational training.

In a country where the numbers of paid domestic workers tripled between 1990 and 2006, many initiatives have been undertaken to foster the so-called tertiary economy, and the regulation of domestic work is the focus of significant regulatory concern.[43] In France, domestic workers are regulated by the CCN, a legislative extension of collective agreements across defined territory. The instruments are commonly used in French labor law as a way to foster broad coverage of collectively negotiated standards for all enterprises in a particular occupation. The CCN offers specific regulation in the absence of generalized coverage under the main labor code. It emerged through the National Federation of Household Employers or FEPEM (Fédération des particuliers employeurs de France), an organization of employers established in 1949 that, at the time, included mainly professional women striving to combine work life with family responsibilities. They did so by seeking both to regulate and professionalize the often young and invariably working-class women on whom they depended.[44] Collectively negotiated with four signatory unions, the CCN was joined in 2009 by an employer federation representing several of the multinational work agencies that are significant actors in the French and broader European domestic work market, the Union of Household Employers (known by the French Syndicat du particulier employeur, or SPE). Accompanying the CCN are a universal service check mechanism that simplifies the payment of social security contributions and accessible labor courts that enforce the CCN, called the Conseil des Prud'hommes.

It is intriguing that someone like Moroccan-born Fatima Elayoubi, who wrote so compellingly about her experience as an immigrant domestic worker in French households, never mentioned this framework. However, this did not surprise me for two reasons. The first reason is that migrant workers are in many ways excluded from the system designed to protect them. In December 2010, I met with the parties who had negotiated the creation of the CCN and a member of the Conseil des Prud'hommes, which hears a range of cases involving domestic workers and their employers. Everyone showed an intimate understanding of the problems faced by domestic workers and their individual employers and identified regulatory measures that turn the relationship away from one of constant availability and toward a regulated work model. The model worked to the extent that it could be understood, diffused broadly, and (relatively) easily followed by those covered under it. Yet representatives of the trade unions, which are all affiliated with the major union federations in France, reflected on the limited success they had in organizing the workers who are covered by the CCN. They lamented that they tended to meet the workers only when disputes arose; labor inspection to verify compliance seemed rare. There was little assurance that undocumented workers could gain access to the Conseil des Prud'hommes. Migrant workers were therefore at least de facto excluded and worked under dire conditions.[45]

The second reason might seem paradoxical: sometimes, regulatory mechanisms become a new social norm built on equality that is so seamless and so well accepted as part of a broader workplace governance norm that the past exclusion of domestic workers is what becomes unseen. Elayoubi had a nervous breakdown at work. Her employment as a contractual house cleaner working for several employers remained extremely onerous. She writes in her book, *Prière à la lune*, that she was able to obtain social protection because at least some of her employers who hired her to clean their houses formally declared her as a worker, for at least some of the hours, and paid the appropriate deductions. This is the point of the simplified contribution mechanism through service checks (rather than simply paying domestic workers in the informal cash economy) on which the CCN provisions are built. I believe it is crucial to pay attention to these mechanisms, however technical, because they are part of how you can change the unequal law of the household workplace and replace it with social norms that construct a transnational legal order that unsettles the unequal law of the household workplace and replaces it with transformative alternatives.

The French regulatory experiences held many potential lessons and helped make it possible that the Domestic Workers Convention and the Domestic Workers Recommendation would be constructed to offer concrete examples of collective autonomy. Given the centrality of the fundamental freedom of association and the effective exercise of collective bargaining in the ILO's mission, it was worth explaining how the fundamental freedom can be made real for domestic workers and exploring the challenges. While some people might understandably ask whether domestic workers should want collective autonomy in the manner in which it has been embraced in the past, I would suggest that domestic workers offer an opportunity to change our understanding of collective autonomy. This is part of their everyday transgression: domestic workers remind us that collective autonomy is fundamentally relational. They also remind us why it is absolutely necessary to think about who is included in collective relationships. Through a discussion of one of the few existing collective governance examples—the deeply imperfect but historically rooted French collective decrees model—the trade-off, even in a transnational context, should not be whether we choose protection or autonomy. Instead, we should be working to reconcile protection and autonomy for domestic workers. Worker agency is not optional.

The late labor law scholar Pierre Verge adopted a relational approach to labor law, one that focused less on private law notions of the contract and more on a concrete acknowledgment of the subordinated execution of work. His was a holistic, integrated vision of labor law, and the notion of collective autonomy was a critical part of it.[46] Collective autonomy is not provided by the state through law. Rather, it emerges—like freedom of association—from social reality, or as Max Weber understood it, as an "empirical legal order."[47] Collective autonomy also emerges in relation to a range of institutions and actors in labor relations that are necessary to support it.[48] The main point is that collective autonomy is a pluralist form of regulation, a "locus for the production of standards" in, by, and about the workplace.[49]

Domestic workers are socially marginalized, which contributes to making the inequality of bargaining power in their relationships with their employers obvious. Collective agreements emanate from the context where the asymmetrical law of the household workplace has applied, but they are meant to unsettle that law and contribute to equalizing the relationship. The French experience is a reminder of the kind of institutions and actors that can be necessary to build a framework to support domestic workers' exercise of collective autonomy. However, there is another paradox arising from the French example. Despite its active participation in the International Labour Conference and this regulatory innovation, France has not yet ratified the Domestic Workers Convention, while a number of other European states (including Belgium, Finland, Germany, Ireland, Italy, and, as discussed below, Switzerland) have. European countries have been encouraged to do so both by European human rights bodies and for its members, the European Union itself.

Right before the 2011 International Labour Conference, the forty-seven members of Europe's leading regional human rights organization, the Council of Europe, took action. The Parliamentary Assembly of the Council of Europe adopted Resolution 1811 and Recommendation 1970 on Protecting Migrant Women in the Labour Market.[50] The documents called for domestic work to be recognized as real work, which included eliminating discrimination and involving migrant women in the development of immigration and social policy. Recommendation 1970 even "encouraged the governments of member states to actively participate in the drafting of the ILO's future convention on domestic workers and to adhere to its provisions."[51] And they did!

After the Domestic Workers Convention and the Domestic Workers Recommendation were adopted, it was time for the twenty-eight members of the European Union to get involved. The European Economic and Social Committee recommended that member states ratify the convention. The committee also focused on an extremely important part of the standard-setting measures, designed to tackle the undeclared dimension of domestic work. It endorsed legalizing undeclared work through "fiscal aid measures and simple declaration schemes."[52] By 2016, the European Parliament had adopted the Resolution on Women Domestic Workers and Carers in the EU.[53]

The resolution lists two pages' worth of international and regional treaties (including the Vienna Convention on Diplomatic Relations) as well as resolutions; preparatory work (including the *Law and Practice Report*); and, of course, the Domestic Workers Convention and the Domestic Workers Recommendation. It provides quite a comprehensive list of the many aspects of the decent work deficit in domestic work, and pays attention to undocumented domestic workers.

It would appear that the message of the international standard setting has been effectively communicated. But there is another set of social factors that the European Parliament's resolution identified: the rights of the aging European population "to a range of in-home, residential and other community support services," the burden of household responsibilities that rest disproportionately on women, and the "reduced public investment in the care sector" since the financial and social crisis.[54] The resolution states that households need "affordable female domestic workers and carers." These are the bases of the arguments supporting recognition, and regulation, of the tertiary economy.

While some people celebrate the tertiary economy, others are quick to name it as consisting of a series of unrelated occupations reframed as personal care services. As François-Xavier Devetter, Thierry Ribault, and Florence Jany-Catrice have argued, what unites the people in these occupations is not so much their work as it is their shared history of marginalization. In France, for example, workers like Elayoubi are overwhelmingly racialized immigrant women doing backbreaking, spirit-murdering work.[55] Moreover, it is a source of concern that the French union representatives whom I met in 2010 had not been as successful at including domestic workers in their ranks as social movements that explicitly concerned themselves with the rights of undocumented migrants.[56] The labor market is racialized and segmented: too many workers—including undocumented migrant workers from the global South—have largely been left out. There has been a political decision to group this work together legislatively, based on a policy framework that promotes social cohesion. Yet there is concern that the occupations can be developed only on the basis of structural economic inequality that relies on and reinforces historical, social, and gender inequalities.[57] The tertiary economy might be both created and sustained on the basis of the consistent exclusion of these workers from standard forms of employment.[58]

The European Parliament's resolution is of course careful to balance the factors leading parliamentarians to want to expand personal care services with the recognition that "domestic workers and carers have the right to a decent life, which takes into account their need to have a good work, family and life balance, especially for live-in domestic workers, and must enjoy the same social and employment rights as other workers."[59] The resolution raises an important question about the Domestic Workers Convention and the Domestic Workers Recommendation: do these instruments strike a plausible balance, or might the European Parliament's resolution signal instead that the momentum for decent work for domestic workers is being instrumentalized, to make it easier to privatize care while allowing states to sidestep the responsibility to offer collectively provided care to those who need it?[60]

These issues are inseparable from paid domestic work, even if they go beyond the scope of the ILO instruments, and they raise serious questions about why the instruments may be receiving support in some quarters. Will social movements be able to keep their focus on how social services should be delivered by the state, rather than implicitly asking whether states should be providing these services at all? Internal to the way that domestic work in private households is currently structured, does the European Parliament's resolution address the fact that the new international labor standards go a considerable distance toward challenging the suggestion that live-in domestic work may well be compatible with this decent work framing? What measures would have to be taken to make sure that domestic workers can have work-life balance, particularly in circumstances where they are required or expected to migrate without their families? Will the measures leave enough space for domestic workers to exercise collective autonomy to set the standards that will frame how their work is regulated, establishing a locus for new standards that reflects the transgressive character of the new transnational legal order on decent work for domestic workers?

In the context of the Domestic Workers Convention and the Domestic Workers Recommendation, the European Parliament's resolution offers an opportunity to shift the focus. I have argued elsewhere that the equality lens in the new international labor standards is "substantive and inclusive rather than abstract and undifferentiated."[61] The convention and recommendation seek to move us away from standards that simply project the unjust law of the household workplace onto the transnational level. Individual states like France retain a lot of latitude to continue to innovate but may also be ambivalent about future directions. On the one hand, France is at the forefront of unsettling the unjust law of the household workplace, and does so through a vehicle that can foster collective autonomy. On the other hand, it is actively promoting its tertiary economy with well-organized interest groups, including those major transnational agencies that are significant members of the SPE. They may already find the existing CCN to be constraining. Ratification of the Decent Workers Convention could weigh in the balance. In its focus on substantive inclusion, it should redirect attention to the need to prevent the persisting exclusions of the most marginalized domestic workers who need the protections the most.

What About Slavery Discourse? Juxtaposing *Siliadin v. France* with Labor Law Enforcement on Domestic Work in Côte d'Ivoire

Noting that "states derived from former colonies and former colonial powers have roughly twice as many domestic workers per capita as states that were not part of the former imperial project," the historian Bernard Higman seeks to identify what structural features may characterize periods of slavery and freedom.[62] In other words, he looks for patterns of inequality and focuses on income inequality. Yet inequality is often gendered female and racialized Black.[63]

Siwa-Akofa Siliadin is one of those most marginalized domestic workers. She was brought to France from Togo in January 1994, when she was just fifteen years old, on a tourist visa. She was expected to work without pay to reimburse the cost of her airplane ticket. Her initial "employer" is referred to as a French national of Togolese origin. The employer promised to regularize her immigration status and send her to school, but instead her passport was confiscated, and she was soon loaned to another household, which decided to keep her. This is how the European Court of Human Rights (ECHR) described her life:

> She worked seven days a week, without a day off, and was occasionally and exceptionally authorised to go out on Sundays to attend mass. Her working day began at 7:30 a.m., when she had to get up and prepare breakfast, dress the children, take them to nursery school or their recreational activities, look after the baby, do the housework and wash and iron clothes. In the evening she prepared dinner, looked after the older children, did the washing up and went to bed at about 10.30 p.m. In addition, she had to clean a studio flat, in the same building, which Mr. B. had made into an office. The applicant slept on a mattress on the floor in the baby's room; she had to look after him if he woke up. She was

never paid, except by Mrs. B.'s mother, who gave her one or two 500 French franc (FRF) notes.[64]

Almost two years later, in December 2015, Siliadin managed to escape and was given shelter for five or six months by a Haitian national, according to ECHR reports. She continued to do domestic work but was given appropriate food and shelter and was paid a salary. Yet Siliadin decided to return to Mr. and Mrs. B.'s household, after some intervention from her extended family, on the promise that her immigration status would be regularized.

But her status was not regularized, and the exploitative conditions continued well into 1998, when Siliadin confided in a neighbor. The neighbor alerted the Committee against Modern Slavery, which filed a complaint with a prosecutor. The police searched Mr. and Mrs. B.'s house and laid two charges under the criminal code, which made it an offense "to obtain from an individual the performance of services without payment or in exchange for payment that is manifestly disproportionate to the amount of work carried out, by taking advantage of that person's vulnerability or state of dependence."[65] The criminal code also made it an offense punishable by imprisonment and a fine "to subject an individual to working or living conditions which are incompatible with human dignity by taking advantage of that individual's vulnerability or state of dependence."[66]

Siliadin v. France became the first case in which the ECHR found that a domestic worker had been subjected to conditions of forced and compulsory labor and held in servitude.[67] The court found that France had failed to provided Siliadin with the protections accorded by article 4 of the European Convention on Human Rights, as the criminal law did not afford her sufficient, effective protection.[68] The court did not find that she had been held in conditions of slavery.

Commentators have tended to focus on whether that last decision was right. Was she a slave? How has the discourse on slavery been used in the European human rights context? Siliadin's case had worked its way through the Paris Court of First Instance (Tribunal de Grande Instance), the Paris Court of Appeal, and the highest French court (the Court of Cassation, or Cour de Cassation), before it got to the ECHR. I am particularly concerned with the way that the different levels of courts characterized Siliadin's work and, through it, the domestic work relationship. As I discuss below, those characterizations tell us something about the qualitative differences between a framework that emphasizes slavery and servitude and one that emphasizes labor law.

While critical of Mr. and Mrs. B., the first two courts' framing seemed to normalize working time aspects of the law of the household workplace. Both of the decisions recognized that Siliadin was marginalized and dependent on her relationship with Mr. and Mrs. B. They acknowledged that her fear of arrest and deportation by French authorities was cultivated by Mr. and Mrs. B., who also gave her no resources. The Paris Court of First Instance recognized that she received no or very inadequate remuneration, so it was able to establish that the first offense had been committed. However, the court had a hard time establishing that her conditions were incompatible with human dignity, a necessary part of the second offense. Clearly, she worked long hours. She had very little free time. But "any person who remained at home with four children necessarily began her work early in the morning and finished late at night." She could go to mass, and she had "moments"—yes, "moments"—of respite during the day.[69] In the absence of insults or harassment, or having to work at a furious pace, the court found that this was not a violation of human dignity. As to accommodation, the court acknowledged that she did not have her own room or a space for her personal use. She slept with the children. This constituted a lack of consideration, but did it infringe on human dignity? The court reasoned that, given how many people in Paris did not have their own rooms, it would have to look to something else—such as unhealthy or dangerous conditions, or a lack of heating—to find an infringement of human dignity.

Mr. and Mrs. B. appealed. The Paris Court of Appeal investigated further and noted that Siliadin was an illegal immigrant in France and was not paid for her work. But it also noted that she was proficient in French, which she had learned in Togo, could find her way around Paris, and even had a "degree of independence" since she took "the children"—that is, Mr. and Mrs. B.'s children—to and from school and sports activities and could attend Mass, go shopping, and contact her uncle by telephone. She could come and go, without coercion, despite her young age. The court heard testimony from family members, who mentioned other aspects of the relationship that would sound familiar to many knowledgeable about the governance of the domestic work relationship in various parts of the world, including many former French colonies in West Africa. For example, Mrs. B.'s mother mentioned that she would give Siliadin small sums of money at family celebrations. Siliadin's uncle said that she was free to call him from a telephone booth, was in good health and adequately dressed, and always had some money. He said that Mrs. B. told him that she was setting aside a certain sum of money each month to build up a "nest egg" for "the girl" (meaning Siliadin), who was aware of the practice when she left. Surely, this was not slavery. Remarkably, the court acquitted Mr. and Mrs. B. of both charges.[70]

The focus of the inquiry turned to whether Siliadin had any freedom, and—deeply problematically—if she did, whether her relationship to Mr. and Mrs. B could be characterized by human dignity. Lost was the fact that she worked for almost fifteen hours a day, seven days a week. In other words, there was no reference to the normativity that labor law establishes. What would it mean to question the law of the household workplace—whose roots in slavery and colonialism are unmistakable—from a perspective that sees its incompatibility with labor law? What if, in other words, the focus had been on whether this constituted decent work?

Of course, Siliadin appealed, with the support of the Committee against Modern Slavery (CCEM). The CCEM had taken up cases of victims of domestic slavery from a range of francophone West African countries (Benin, Côte d'Ivoire, and Togo) as well as from India, Madagascar, Morocco, the Philippines. and Sri Lanka. The Court of Cassation recognized that the Paris Court of Appeal had paid too little attention to the victim's vulnerability and dependence. It found that both offenses had been committed and sent the case to the Versailles Court of Appeal, instructing it to entertain only requests for compensation, not imprisonment. It essentially accepted the decision of the Paris Court of First Instance and awarded damages both for repayment of wages and in recognition of the psychological trauma caused to Siliadin. Ultimately, it was through a labor case that a sum for arrears in salary and leave pay was awarded.

The matter did not end there. As explained above, a case was brought against France to the ECHR for failing to comply with its substantive obligations to protect Siliadin against slavery or servitude or forced or coerced labor under article 4 of the European Convention on Human Rights. Monetary compensation is insufficient when forced or coerced labor, slavery, or servitude are involved.

In addition to a broad swath of relevant international treaties, the ECHR cited a litany of reports and recommendations on domestic slavery in France and at the level of the Council of Europe that called attention to the seriousness of a problem that persisted despite the abolition of slavery in Europe over 150 years earlier. The court advocated "zero tolerance" for slavery in Europe, emphasizing the need to recognize domestic work as real work by requiring a legally enforceable contract, health insurance and leisure and personal time for domestic workers, and family life and social rights for the workers' children. The ECHR was clear: the obligation of the state under article 4 in this case required effective prosecution and the prospect of imprisonment. To assess whether Siliadin's condition fell under the scope of article 4, it looked to the definition of forced or compulsory labor in the ILO's Forced Labour

Convention, 1930 (No. 29) which require the work to have been "exacted . . . under the menace of penalty" and that Siliadin had "not offered . . . voluntarily" to do it. The EHCR had little difficulty finding that "an adolescent girl in a foreign land fearing arrest from the police" (since Mr. and Mrs. B. had failed to regularize her status) met both criteria for forced labor.[71] It also had little difficulty finding that servitude means an obligation to provide one's services, imposed through the use of coercion.[72] But French law was tightened in the process, and Siliadin's legal status in France was regularized. This happened before the ECHR rendered its decision.

The criminal charge of slavery or servitude is highly significant and offers a strong challenge to the kind of exploitative behavior to which Siliadin was subjected. Yet as with many approaches that privilege criminalization, the focus on contemporary slavery extends the arm of the punitive state without necessarily challenging the underlying structural conditions that make particular forms of work organization pervasive. The anxiety over contemporary slavery in Europe specifically, and the global North more generally, is inseparable from a globalization that fails to grapple with the freedom of movement and renders people illegal. The failure to call for permanent residency rights for migrants—including migrant domestic workers—is deeply, and broadly, implicated.[73] We may choose to condemn the "employers" who just happen to be of Togolese origin, and consequently who just happen to enable race at once to be highly symbolically visible and, in a twist of historical irony, ignored as former colonial and enslaving powers like France render justice through liberal democratic courts for a single, marginalized African worker.

We might be forgiven for losing sight of why someone like Siliadin and the millions of migrant domestic workers in precarious situations around the world are so easily subjected to this treatment and may even return to highly exploitative conditions: they have been rendered illegal under the law, and they are exploitable precisely because they are subject to deportation at any time. Their agency in leaving limited life options in the global South in search of better ones in the global North creates a constructed vulnerability. The fact that they must travel under precarious conditions simply is not the most crucial point.

Paradoxically, the contemporary focus on slavery as illegal may allow us to forget that the centuries-long transatlantic slave trade was a global and legal institution. By zeroing in on slavery and trafficking as crimes committed by individual actors, rather than turning attention to the deeply compromised governance of temporary migration, we do an injustice to the historical memory of slavery. It is not surprising that the focus on contemporary slavery seems to divert attention from historical practices of marginalization, despite the prevalence and significance of racial stratification in domestic work.[74] As Bridget Anderson astutely observes, modern slavery and trafficking discourse depoliticizes; that is, it focuses on the individualized victim, placing her beyond politics.[75] Globalization has re-racialized the world.[76] Yet the language of racialization seems to have disappeared from discussions of contemporary slavery.

Mr. and Mrs. B. were rightly condemned for practices that are unfortunately all too common in many regions in the world, including in Europe and in former French colonies in West Africa like Côte d'Ivoire. But while reports of forced labor conditions in child domestic work in Côte d'Ivoire have been widely circulated, research into attempts by local actors (including judges) to challenge abusive practices and regulate decent work for domestic workers is rare. It seemed imperative to take the time to look closely at those efforts. This study focuses in particular on the labor side of the governance equation in a place like Côte d'Ivoire, as a way to push back against the easy tropes of savior Europe in a sea of unregulated, racialized others. Once again, the insights from the study confirm the intuition that transnational learning on decent work for domestic workers should also come from places in the global South.

Côte d'Ivoire has no law specifically regulating domestic workers. It has a general labor code that is broadly applicable to workers—who are defined to include any physical person, whatever his or her sex, race, or nationality, who works for remuneration under the direction or "authority" of another physical or moral person, be they public or private, who is the employer.[77] Yet as discussed in chapter 2, it is not surprising that, as a former French colony, Côte d'Ivoire has applied its labor laws to those workers (typically male domestic workers) who were among the colonial migrant workers who became urbanized. Although the demographics of the situation have changed, and employers in urban settings are also from Côte d'Ivoire as well as other regions or countries (including diplomats), the typical domestic worker is still Ivoirian.

In research that I undertook with a team in Côte d'Ivoire in 2013, we unearthed records of fifty court cases involving domestic workers, some from first-level courts in several major urban centers, including Abidjan and Bouaké, and some from appellate-level courts.[78] The cases were decided before the Domestic Workers Convention and the Domestic Workers Recommendation were adopted by the ILO, and while Côte d'Ivoire faced one of its most destabilizing political crises, which lasted from 1999 to 2011. The cases are significant not only because of how many we found, but also because they so consistently supported domestic workers' rights. They were, of course, a drop in the proverbial bucket when compared with the ubiquity of the domestic work relationship, including child domestic work, in contemporary Côte d'Ivoire. They were also likely to reflect the cases of domestic workers who had the most favorable financial conditions and who stood to be able to collect monetary damages from their (often foreign) employers. Yet through the cases—which we supplemented with interviews of labor inspectors, judges, representatives of trade unions and employer organizations, and actors in the broader civil society—we could see that a real attempt had been made to apply labor law to the domestic work relationship. Most commonly, this was done by alleging that a worker's termination had taken place without a valid reason being given by the employer. In one case, the employer tried to convert a worker hired to guard the house into a laborer on the employer's plantation, without the worker's consent. Another employer accused a domestic worker of stealing without a shred of evidence. In both instances, the labor courts found the terminations to be abusive and awarded damages to the workers.

The courts have also repeatedly enforced minimum wage laws and tended to award significant monetary damages when they found that employers had failed to register domestic workers in the collective workplace accident and social security program (the Caisse Nationale de Prévoyance Sociale). For example, in a 2011 case, a domestic worker usually worked each day until 6:00 p.m. Then she would go to school, where she was pursuing a professional degree. Her employer had recently married and sought to have her stay later, until 7:00 p.m. She refused, and a labor court agreed with her that there was a significant modification to her terms of employment so that the dismissal that resulted was abusive. The decision was confirmed by the Abidjan Court of Appeal. The employer was forced to pay the worker damages, as well as the difference between the salary that she had been earning and the minimum wage.[79]

The labor courts have also paid attention to the context of the domestic work relationship. As is the case in South Africa, they do not require domestic workers to come with a written contract (in any event, written contracts are rare). They have tended to interpret oral contracts to favor the worker, treating them as employment contracts of indefinite duration. The courts have also resisted any probationary period that is not in writing: if the employer did not take the trouble to write it down so it was clear to both parties, then the court would not enforce it.

As one judge remarked during an interview, the employers tended to be surprised that they could even be brought before the labor court. After all, they had provided the domestic worker with a place to live and some level of comfort. They had done the domestic worker a favor. Surely this was not really an employment relationship?[80] In one case, the employer had no difficulty admitting that the domestic worker had actually worked for him as a house guardian, but he said that he considered the house guardian to be a member of the family, pointing to the fact that he had cared for the worker during an illness. So why was the case even before the labor court? The house guardian had been fired summarily when he refused to wash the employer's car while still on medically prescribed sick leave. The labor court therefore was not only in a position to recognize the termination, but it also clarified to the employer that this was an employment relationship that was covered by article 2 of the labor code.[81] Labor inspectors said similar things. Employers who found themselves at the negotiating table with a domestic worker who would not be expected to eat with them at their dinner table but who now expected to reach a mediated agreement with them often had an "aha" moment, resulting in a true paradigm shift.

It is worth stressing, however, that interviewees were usually quite sensitive to the broader economic context. Even those who welcomed the adoption of specific regulatory texts underscored the difficulty of regulating decent work conditions in a context in which precarious, contingent, and, in some cases, highly abusive working conditions reign, and in domestic work—where the employer's exposure to risk at work might not be considered, rightly or wrongly, significantly different from the employee's. Although they did not have quantitative data, labor inspectors pointed out that many if not most of the employers brought before them for informal reconciliations were foreign nationals or workers from international organizations. Those employers' capacity to pay would generally be significantly greater than that of the average Ivoirian national.[82]

Of course, the cases from Côte d'Ivoire were not always decided in domestic workers' favor or always in a manner consistent with the Domestic Workers Convention and the Domestic Workers Recommendation. In particular, the courts had a hard time with some complex scenarios. What should be done when domestic workers' own child care needs collided with the employers' family responsibilities? How does one even begin to calculate overtime pay? Labor inspectors and judges concurred that a specific regulatory law would be helpful, one that would reflect the Domestic Workers Convention—which Côte d'Ivoire has still not ratified—and the Domestic Workers Recommendation. Drafts of the proposed legislation available at the time were less progressive than international standards and even some of the labor court decisions; one draft required domestic workers' contracts to be in writing to be valid, which would have undermined the courts' tendency to interpret the absence of a written contract in the employers' favor. It remained important to be able to work through what it really means not simply to have specific regulations, but ones that challenge the asymmetrical law of the household workplace. The level of nuance developed by the specialist Ivoirian labor administration and judges needed to be more widely known, including by those well-meaning employers of domestic workers who sought to change the law legislatively, from the top down.

There was little doubt in my interviews in Côte d'Ivoire in late 2013, and after reading of the drafts of specific regulatory texts, that decent work for domestic workers was being widely diffused immediately after the adoption of the Domestic Workers Convention and the Domestic Workers Recommendation. The work of a range of actors in the labor administration and labor courts was increasingly being shared, considered, and discussed. Diffusion of a new transnational legal order on decent work for domestic workers might well have been fostering this growing legal consciousness, but people's ability to build on what was already being done would seem central to its ability to change the law of the household workplace and build one of several necessary, regulatory bases from which to keep challenging the most intransigent forms of abuse in the domestic work relationship. As discussed at the outset of this section, taking the various forms of inequality seriously is another.

Ratification as International Solidarity in a Context of Labor Migration: Incentives for Formalizing Domestic Work in Switzerland

Switzerland ratified the Domestic Workers Convention on November 12, 2014, and it entered into force in that country one year later. Switzerland called its ratification an act of international solidarity.[83] After all, the country had studied its laws and considered them to be generally in conformity with international law. If it was already in compliance, then ratification would mostly be to show solidarity with the international community on this pressing issue and to allow others to learn from the Swiss example.

In addition, Swiss regulatory initiatives had influenced the ILO's standard-setting process. In the *Law and Practice Report*, I had highlighted instances in which emerging Swiss initiatives could offer some guidance to the international community. For example, the *Law and Practice Report* discussed provisions in the Swiss standard employment contracts (SECs), notably the one from the Canton of Geneva.[84] The SECs largely reflected the basic civil law principles in the Swiss code of obligations but applied them specifically to the domestic economy. As Switzerland facilitated the free movement of people back and forth from the European Union, it became concerned that wages might be undercut through unfair competition from workers coming in particular from Eastern Europe.[85] It started to rely on the SECs to apply mandatory minimum wages in an attempt to prevent the feared race to the bottom on wages.

The Canton of Geneva's SEC basically deemed any person who undertakes household tasks of a familial or housekeeping nature, whether on a full-time or part-time basis, to be an employee within the scope of the regulation. The definition of domestic work in the Domestic Workers Convention remains broad, although the language of "employment relationship" was added to the definition.[86] This SEC, along with South Africa's Sectoral Determination No. 7, helped me justify proposing an inclusive definition of domestic work for the questionnaire.

The Canton of Geneva's SEC also seeks to cover migrant domestic workers, whether or not they are documented. It was accompanied by measures to simplify employers' registration of domestic workers, whether or not they are documented migrants. As in France, a service check model was adopted to facilitate the calculation and transfer of social security payments. Also as in France, the mechanism can be circumvented by declaring fewer hours than are actually worked.[87] Article 11 of the Canton of Geneva's SEC is careful to specify the conditions of any room and board furnished to domestic workers. It specifically mentions that domestic workers are entitled to a room with a door that has a lock, proper heating and sanitary facilities, and natural light. These conditions make sense for Switzerland, as they do for many other parts of the world. In an international instrument, it was important to respect North-South differences but not fall into the trap of accepting the disparity that tends to exist between the places where domestic workers are expected to live and sleep and the spaces occupied by their employers in the same household. ILO committee members ultimately agreed to the language in article 6 in the Domestic Workers Convention, which calls for "decent living conditions that respect their privacy," but included careful attention to what those decent living conditions mean in paragraph 17 of the nonbinding Domestic Workers Recommendation:

When provided, accommodation and food should include, taking into account national conditions, the following:
(a) a separate, private room that is suitably furnished, adequately ventilated and equipped with a lock, the key to which should be provided to the domestic worker;
(b) access to suitable sanitary facilities, shared or private;
(c) adequate lighting and, as appropriate, heating and air conditioning in keeping with prevailing conditions within the household; and

(d) meals of good quality and sufficient quantity, adapted to the
extent reasonable to the cultural and religious requirements,
if any, of the domestic worker concerned.

These contributions were important, but they in no way meant that Swiss
law fully complied with the convention and recommendation. It became necessary to acknowledge that Swiss labor law as it relates to domestic workers
also created exclusions. One was the exclusion of domestic workers from most
of the content of the Swiss code of obligations. This means that domestic
workers have different access to occupational safety and health and pregnancy
protections and have less advantageous maximum working hours.[88] Not only
is it incomplete, but the SEC mode of regulation can become confusing and
at times contradictory due to overlapping federal and cantonal jurisdiction.
Switzerland is a small country. It is entirely possible that a domestic worker
could be paid the minimum wage of the Canton of Jura by an employer who
is a banker in the morning and the minimum wage of the Canton of Geneva
by an employer who is a diplomat in the afternoon.

It was always understood that questions of this nature would have to be
resolved nationally, in keeping with a set of new international norms that help
make decent work for domestic workers a transnational reality. The Canton
of Geneva's SEC states, in relation to article 321 of the Swiss code of obligations, that the domestic worker must conform to the order of the household.
However, the fact that the household order must equitably take into account
the interests of each party suggests that something has happened here: the
normative order of the household is a pluralist one to which labor law applies.
Is the focus on the requirement of equity a nod to the need to remain consistent with decent work for domestic workers, as provided by the Domestic
Workers Convention and the Domestic Workers Recommendation?

The basic point is simple: Switzerland may have ratified the convention as
an act of solidarity, but its ratification provides an opportunity for learning
about the new transnational legal order on decent work for domestic workers. The Swiss regulatory model, in all its complexity, has informed both the
development of international standard setting and its ongoing diffusion.
However, this learning is not unidirectional. As Gabriela Medici argues,
Switzerland also stands to benefit from comparative learning and sharing of
information related to migration,[89] and it can learn from some of the international work on women migrant workers related to the convention.[90] For example, the UN Committee on the Elimination of Discrimination against
Women issued General Recommendation No. 26 on women migrant workers in late 2008, taking a human rights approach to migration and applying

the principles of gender equality to analyze the factors affecting women's migration.[91] In its recommendations, the committee itemized states' common responsibilities, as well as responsibilities of domestic workers' countries of origin, countries through which the workers passed, and their destination countries. Some recommendations were quite practical—for example, providing rights-based pre-departure training to women migrant workers. Some showed the extent of the problem, like the recommendations that temporary shelters should be made available for women migrant workers who wished to leave abusive employers and that strong legal measures should be implemented to ensure the workers' access to justice. Others seemed not to go quite far enough, requiring states to train their diplomatic and consular staff to ensure that they fulfill their responsibility to protect the rights of women migrant workers abroad. Nothing is said about potential abuse by those officials. Some recommendations seemed disconnected from the problem, calling for a list of "authentic, reliable recruitment agencies" to be provided and a uniform information system about available jobs abroad to be established.

The UN Committee on the Protection of the Rights of All Migrant Workers and Members of Their Families also got involved, issuing its first comment on the topic of migrant domestic workers in February 2011, in advance of the annual International Labour Conference.[92] The committee cited the *Law and Practice Report* and made the point that the proposed definition of domestic workers in what is currently article 1 of the Domestic Workers Convention included migrant domestic workers. It argued that "any distinction made to exclude migrant domestic workers from protection would constitute a prima facie violation of the Convention."[93] While it covered the classic migration dimensions of the challenge, it also provided the kind of detail on labor law that shows how much it was influenced by the ILO's process. The committee recommended that the rights of migrant domestic workers be dealt with within the larger framework of decent work for domestic workers.[94] In this regard, the committee considered that domestic work should be properly regulated by national legislation to ensure that domestic workers enjoy the same level of protection as other workers.[95]

Switzerland has a lot to offer if it implements these initiatives.[96] The ILO, headquartered in Geneva, has helped make progress by getting its own house in order: it established an internal code of conduct on how its own international officials—diplomats and others—should treat the domestic work relationship. Ultimately, then, the Swiss invocation of "international solidarity" came to mean something different: that the diffusion of regulatory innovation in the new transnational legal order on decent work for domestic workers is

ongoing and should be fostered in communities of learning that crisscross the
global North and the global South.

Do Bilateral Agreements Help Build or Challenge the New Transnational Legal Order? The Philippines in an Asymmetrical World of Domestic Worker Migration

The Philippines has been at the forefront of learning and innovating on labor
migration, if only because of the sheer number of people involved: 10,455,788
Filipinos were working and living overseas in 2011, according to the International Federation of Red Cross and Red Crescent Societies.[97] Thus, it is not
surprising that the Philippines played an active role in negotiations over the
Domestic Workers Convention and the Domestic Workers Recommendation.
A different representative of the country's government presided over the
International Labour Conference committee during 2010 and 2011, and that
government was the second ILO member to ratify the convention, on September 5, 2012.

Moreover, the Philippines has one of the most coordinated migration policies in the world, and workers from the Philippines occupy a distinct market
position relative to nationals of other countries. This is in large measure
because the government has negotiated some of the terms of their movement
through bilateral agreements. The Migrant Workers and Overseas Filipinos
Act encourages the Philippines Overseas Employment Administration (POEA)
to enter into bilateral agreements and requires that the receiving country
must have in place labor laws that protect the rights of migrant workers.[98]
They also must have ratified multilateral conventions on the protection
of migrant workers to receive such workers—including migrant domestic
workers—from the Philippines. Currently, the POEA has over twenty signed
agreements, but concerns about their ability to improve living and working
conditions abound.[99]

Some people have argued that the new international labor standards on decent work for domestic workers have given the Philippines the latitude to use
its bilateral agreements to ensure better protection for domestic workers'
rights, but the litany of newspaper reports on how Filipina migrant domestic
workers are treated in some of the countries with agreements in place leaves
room for a critical reassessment.[100] For example, Jakati Pawa, a forty-four-year-
old college graduate and mother of two, migrated to Kuwait in 2002 to work
as a domestic worker and was executed by the government of Kuwait in Jan-

uary 2017. Although she maintained her innocence to the end, she had been convicted of the killing of her employer's adult daughter in 2007, despite serious questions about whether the DNA used as evidence matched Pawa's. The Philippine labor secretary acknowledged, as several have before him, that while domestic workers "leave the country with the promise of a better life for their families, unfortunately they are confronted with their worst nightmare."[101] He raised the possibility of imposing a ban on Filipina domestic workers' migrating to Kuwait.

This would hardly be the first time that the Philippines had threatened or imposed a ban. The country has never been able to rely on bilateral agreements alone: it knows that their success is anything but ensured and that even threatening a ban can have consequences. Although the Philippines provides the single largest number of domestic workers to many countries worldwide as part of its remittance-based strategy, it is far from the only supplier in this market. Make no mistake about it: the supply of domestic workers is a labor market in the most economically calculated ways.

Less than a month after the Domestic Workers Convention was adopted, the Philippines launched a targeted effort to obtain a mandatory standard employment contract and a monthly minimum wage of US$400 with the Gulf Cooperation Council states (Bahrain, Kuwait, Oman, Qatar, Saudi Arabia, and the United Arab Emirates).[102] Indonesia had already put in place a moratorium on its domestic workers going to Saudi Arabia, and Saudi Arabia did not wait for the Philippines to act: it preemptively banned migrant domestic workers from both Indonesia and the Philippines, even though workers from the Philippines and Indonesia constituted the bulk of the domestic workers in Saudi Arabia at the time.[103] However, they could be replaced by workers from Ethiopia, who in turn could be replaced by workers from Kenya.

In December 2014, I interviewed representatives of international, governmental, human rights, and civil society organizations as well as of a trade union of domestic workers and a domestic worker agency in Nairobi, Kenya.[104] Respondents underscored the extent of the initiatives taken to curb and regulate emigration by Kenyan domestic workers into highly precarious work: there were attempted migration bans, initiatives to create a one-stop shop through which to channel labor migration, statements by leading human rights actors, sermons from pulpits, attempts to establish a code of conduct and coordinate the numerous agents who might be part of the chain of contractors involved in a domestic worker's recruitment, and a national task force to address the problem. The challenge of seeking to regulate decent work for domestic workers seemed insurmountable in the context of highly porous borders, with migrant domestic workers coming through Kenya from other countries in the region, bound for the Persian Gulf region and beyond. Actors sought comparative experience, and the Philippines was cited as a good example. But the question of how much could actually be resolved unilaterally persisted.

The interviewees knew that the choice of countries from which to obtain migrant workers was anything but random or abstract. Levels of economic development interacted with racial hierarchies and affected migrants' selection, conditions of work, and treatment. In particular, migrant workers from Kenya and some other sub-Saharan African countries are reported to be relegated to the most physically demanding, "dirty" forms of domestic work, and to work for the lowest pay.[105] Like the everyday law of the household workplace, there is nothing natural about this racialization. It perpetuates hierarchy and inequality and becomes invisible because it is seen as natural and goes largely unchallenged. The shift in governance level to the transnational just accentuates this inequality, reproducing it in households around the world. Domestic workers from the African continent were less expensive, the labor requirements for their recruitment were perceived to be more lax, and their governments' demands were not considered to be excessive.[106]

The Philippines cultivated, through its predeparture training, the perception that its citizens were the domestic workers of choice and thus able to command a higher salary than most others. Over time, it has also sought to direct its domestic workers toward destination countries that had gateways to permanent residency, like Canada.[107] But as Rhacel Salazar Parreñas in particular has documented, migrant domestic workers' experiences are anything but linear, and the geopolitical reasons surrounding migrants' decisions to move are complex and rarely limited to poverty.[108] Moreover, if a state declares a ban on immigration from another country, domestic workers from that country will not necessarily immediately leave; instead, they may well go underground. Even without a ban, there was real concern that domestic workers would simply be forced to substitute contracts that comply with the POEA's negotiated terms—especially the minimum monthly salary—for less favorable contracts when they arrive in their destination country.[109] Supply continues to exceed demand.

Meanwhile, the Saudi case evolved: Saudi Arabia agreed to some employment contract conditions and lifted its ban in October 2012. The Philippine government eventually approved the migration of some 2,000 domestic workers to Saudi Arabia when the countries entered into a bilateral agreement. That agreement, signed in 2013 for a five-year period, has received some international praise, and not only because it refers to the Domestic Workers Convention. It also requires a minimum of twenty-four consecutive hours for a weekly rest day, forbids the confiscating of migrants' passports, and provides for repatriation at no cost to domestic workers. One of the most important innovations is that it requires employers to deposit domestic workers' pay directly into their bank accounts.[110] But despite its detail, it does not live up to the standards in the convention, which to date has not been ratified by Saudi Arabia or any other Gulf Cooperation Council country. It falls particularly short on labor inspection and measures for implementation. Human rights organizations have lamented that little has changed on the ground for domestic workers since the agreement was adopted and suggest that with the oil crisis, the abuse has gotten worse.[111]

In the meantime, Sri Lanka imposed a ban on domestic workers' emigration to Saudi Arabia when the domestic worker Rizana Nafeek was executed. And while Saudi Arabia stepped up its recruitment of Ethiopian domestic workers, by October 2013 it was Ethiopia's turn to ban its domestic workers from traveling to Saudi Arabia due to allegations of widespread torture and sexual violence. Ethiopia has also insisted that Saudi Arabia sign a memorandum of agreement with it—something that Qatar, Kuwait, and Jordan were quicker to do.[112] By January 2016, Uganda had joined other countries, including Indonesia and Ethiopia, in banning the emigration of domestic workers to Saudi Arabia, citing widespread abuse.[113] In April 2017, the Philippines was considering renewing its ban on sending domestic workers to Saudi Arabia.

The limits of temporary migration strategies built around bilateral agreements are not only illustrated by the cycle of bans. However, those strategies underscore the collective action challenges associated with attempting to address decent work for domestic workers on a bilateral basis. The negotiation–labor ban cycle compels attention to some of the most egregious dimensions of the emphasis on temporary migration. But it deflects attention away from more structural questions linked to the model of development at the center of temporary migration to provide care.

This section has suggested that the alternative transnational legal order on decent work for domestic workers has started to unsettle some of the content of the bilateral agreements. Domestic workers' social movements continue to call for ratification as a way for countries like Kenya to seek international support to curtail abuse.[114] A more significant test will be their ability to provide meaningful alternatives to bilateral negotiations, punctuated by individual bans.

One alternative flowed through a courageous court action undertaken by domestic worker Evangeline Banao Vallejos, a native of the Philippines and married mother of five children.[115] Banao Vallejos worked overseas in Hong Kong as a domestic worker for twenty-two years. She respected the provisions of each of her temporary work visas, returning home when legally necessary to get another visa. Finally, on September 30, 2011, only months after the Domestic Workers Convention was adopted, she applied for the equivalent of permanent resident status through the courts along with another domestic worker, Daniel Domingo, as the law did not give her the right to permanent residency despite the length of her stay. In a hopeful moment for many people in similar shoes—government figures cited in the decision suggested that an estimated 117,000 domestic workers had been in Hong Kong for a similar period of time—the Hong Kong High Court granted her permanent residency status.

In its decision, the court took note of the fact that she had in fact "stayed and resided in her employers' respective residences" while caring for families in Hong Kong.[116] That decision relied on international law, citing the UN International Covenant on Civil and Political Rights.[117] It did not cite the Domestic Workers Convention, but of course that convention was not in force at that point, and China has not ratified it. However, the decision was reversed on appeal to the Court of Appeal of the High Court.[118] The landmark case was heard before the Hong Kong Court of Final Appeal in February 2013. In a decision that some commentators understood in its reasoning to have less to do with the domestic workers who appealed and more to do with the constitutional relationship between mainland China and Hong Kong under the Basic Law of the Hong Kong Special Administrative Region of the People's Republic of China, the appellate court's decision was maintained by the Court of Final Appeal in a unanimous ruling. The decision affirmed that the natural and ordinary meaning of the key term "ordinarily resident" in article 2(2)(2) of the Immigration Ordinance, Cap. 225, was not decisive in this case. Instead, the court applied a purposive and contextual analysis directly to the immigration scheme through which foreign domestic helpers entered Hong Kong. In somewhat circular reasoning, the court concluded that the immigration scheme was "qualitatively so far-removed from what would traditionally be recognized as 'ordinary residence' as to justify concluding that [foreign domestic helpers] do not, as a class, come within the meaning of 'ordinarily resident'" in the law.[119] Decent work for domestic workers was not part of the analysis. Or perhaps the unjust law of the household workplace in domestic work was so ubiquitous, and the logic remained so unchallenged, that the call for decent work for domestic workers that resided in the shadow of Banao's case could all too readily still be rendered invisible.

Focusing on the migration of domestic workers underscores both the role of state policies and the importance of looking at decent work for domestic workers transnationally, notably beyond the traditional framework of bilateral agreements. The Philippines' experience to date suggests that there are severe limits to efforts to address the decent work deficit in domestic work conclusively, alone, in a context where there are multiple countries of origin, plural migration corridors, and a significant range of intermediaries. Precarious conditions are multiplied, and regulatory and judicial options are narrow. While courts can play a pivotal role in unsettling the asymmetrical law of the household workplace by drawing on the alternative legal order, they can also perpetuate invisibility. It must be acknowledged that the structure of temporary labor migration is at once one of the most pressing concerns, yet one on which the new transnational legal order on decent work for domestic workers—despite the provisions discussed in chapter 5—offers the least guidance for change.

As I discuss in the conclusion, international solidarity is necessary to enable the alternative transnational legal order on decent work for domestic workers to begin the process of unsettling the asymmetry associated with current migration schemes.

A Tapestry of Diffusion

This chapter has offered a tapestry rather than a string of causality on the diffusion of norms on decent work for domestic workers. The norms do not radiate outward from the center that is the ILO or move from the global North to the global South in the manner often expected in the traditional transplantation literature. Rather, they have emerged from a range of sites of contestation, often through concerted social action. They have informed and been informed by domestic work activism across borders. They are, however, allowing the new transnational legal order on decent work for domestic workers to become recognized and understood as the appropriate regulatory framework to be applied in the household workplace.

In the years since the adoption of the Domestic Workers Convention and the Domestic Workers Recommendation, the global campaign for decent work for domestic workers has been a catalyst for ongoing learning. Regulatory reform has also been a reminder of both the indeterminacy and risk of regression in these reforms: in an era of neoliberal economic policies, standard employment is becoming less and less the norm and is being replaced by a growing range of precarious work. Domestic work continues to reside at the extreme of that range. Yet international standard setting on decent work for domestic workers, and the diffusion of related norms, may well be part of the process of building alternatives. In this regard, the diffusion may be less about domestic work specifically and more about building the future of transnational labor law in an era of ever more precarious work from the bottom up.

Conclusion

Thinking Transnationally

> Bhima doesn't hear them. She is taking her orders
> from a different authority now, following the fluttering
> sound in her ears, the sound of her flapping wings, the
> sound of learning how to fly. Freedom.
>
> —Thrity Umrigar, *The Space between Us*

This book has discussed the household as a site of labor law, a workplace for those who work not for love and historically for little money. I suggest that these features do not allow us to conclude that there is a sharp dichotomy between domestic work and most other forms of work covered by labor law. Rather, this book has shown that the values and assumptions inherent in the domestic work relationship should lead us to take the prospect of continuity between this historically laden work and contemporary understandings of precarious work in the new economy particularly seriously. The book started with a recognition that the work of social reproduction enables and sustains labor markets. It also sustains our humanity. Yet paid domestic workers are required to labor under conditions that reinforce and reproduce patterns of structural inequality, transnationally.

This book has focused on the labor law related to domestic work in the household. It has explained the law of the household workplace and examined aspects of that law closely, through ethnographic sources and historical cookbooks. It has refused stark dichotomizations between subordination and servitude to emphasize how both have become normalized over time to render domestic workers' needs invisible. It has, however, resisted drawing a direct line between the historical and ethnographic material and the contemporary context. Rather, it has canvassed an eclectic mix of sources to suggest that there is something about our ways of knowing that needs to be laid bare so that we can unsettle the unjust law of the household workplace and allow an alternative transnational legal order to emerge through responsive international labor standards, domestic workers' social movements, and a transformative standard-setting and norm diffusion process.

Mostly, this book has emphasized ongoing change. The formation and diffusion of an alternative transnational challenge is a continuing struggle of social practice.[1] This book has closely considered transnational social movement action by one of the most societally marginalized groups—domestic workers—to seek standard setting that could help transform the way the workplace is governed. The transformation has happened in one of the oldest (and some people might say most unlikely) international organizations: the International Labour Organization (ILO). This book has taken seriously the social justice claim that decent work applies to all, as the basis for a specific, equality-enhancing standard for domestic workers.

This book has focused on the ILO at the eve of its centenary. This international organization offers at once a traditional understanding of the role of states in international law, and—in its inclusion of employers and workers alongside governments—a unique vision of transnational participation. I have not focused on the ILO as the bearer of a traditional normative hierarchy that would trump all other law-making. In fact, although the state has remained very present throughout the study, I have worked hard to decenter it. This has not been terribly difficult to do once domestic workers themselves are centered. Even in the face of laws that claim universal application, states in many parts of the world have protested that domestic work simply cannot be governed by them. And domestic workers have not been represented.

I have both challenged that starting point and kept the focus on the actors—domestic workers and their supporters—who have operationalized the transnational to bring change. The ILO's tripartite structure builds in dialogue with social partners: workers and employers. I have considered domestic workers' marginalization from the vantage point of that unique international structure but focused on how domestic workers' social movements worked through and beyond the existing but restrictive model of ILO tripartism to create space for their own inclusion. This book has explained how a transnational legal order on decent work for domestic workers has been built, in a manner that addressed rather than sidestepped unequal power relations. The new transnational legal order was built to dislodge the asymmetry. It relied on multidirectional learning from ILO Members that had experimented significantly with regulating decent work for domestic workers. The standard-setting transgressed directional presumptions, to move in many cases from countries in the global South to those in the global North. The new transnational legal order unsettles the unequal law of the household workplace. It seeks to transform the domestic work relationship on an ongoing basis.

That said, this book has also been sanguine about limits. It is important to recall labor law scholar Lizzie Barmes's prescient observation that law may re-embed and extend the very forms of subordination it was designed to challenge.[2] It has been important to tell the backstory of how the Domestic Workers Convention and the Domestic Workers Recommendation were drafted to produce a norm that could at least start undoing some of the specific ways in which domestic work becomes a site of subordination. Domestic workers know that the direction of globalization, and consequently transnational governance, is indeterminate and contains multiple, deeply imperfect spaces for counterhegemonic contestation. They used one—the ILO—and their accomplishments have been remarkably significant. Domestic workers' social movements have shown through the ILO standard-setting process that to look at the transnational as a site of pluralism is to look for the spaces that may well be pried open to imagine another world.

Neither are domestic workers and the advocates who work with them naïve about a neoliberal governance moment that so intimately affects the way many travel halfway around the world, only to wind up in private households that are ostensibly beyond the reach of any state. They know that they navigate across borders under some of the most precarious conditions, while goods and capital have robust international protection. Labor and migration are both treated as domestic concerns or private matters. To a limited extent, the Domestic Workers Convention and the Domestic Workers Recommendation refocus attention on states' responsibility to act in relation to the range of actors, including employment agencies, that profit from these precarious conditions that are anything but natural—rather, they are politically constructed to shift risk to the most marginalized.

Regulating decent work for domestic workers was part of holding open limited spaces for transnational governance. The standard setting crossed borders and governance levels, once again showing that not only the construction of the new transnational legal order, but also its diffusion, is multidirectional. This book has canvassed some of the examples of ILO Members that are able to continue to learn from the process of diffusion. The international standard setting in this sense became the basis for a broad community of learning, calling upon an approach that can be characterized as international solidarity.

I think it is meaningful that paragraph 26 of the Domestic Workers Recommendation encourages member states to "take appropriate steps to assist one another in giving effect to the provisions of the Convention through enhanced international cooperation or assistance or both, including support for social and economic development, poverty eradication programmes and universal education." This is a direct call for international solidarity. International solidarity is at the heart of a broad understanding of what development can mean. According to this vision of international solidarity, labor law is development.[3] The broad vision of development is one of the ways in which decent work for domestic workers has offered a transnational challenge to labor law.

The new convention and recommendation do not call into question the reliance on temporary migration programs as states' current preferred policy approach. We have seen how states facilitate the neoliberal governance of societally marginalized women in policies that seek to grow the tertiary economy. The new standards do not address the structural reasons that lead historically marginalized groups to predominate in domestic work—indeed, to be objectified as embodying domestic work. It is often thought that domestic work is a relic, left over from an earlier time. We are in a moment not only of paid domestic work's prevalence in the global South, but also of a resurgence of paid domestic work in industrialized market economies. Labor migration to perform domestic work has increased significantly to become a policy response to workers, including women workers expected to be perennially available on the formal market. Care, rather than being reincorporated in the framing of what we all do as humans, is externalized. Of course, the patterns of who does the work remain historically laden; they produce or reproduce racialized patterns of relationship between particular places in the global South and hegemonic states there or in the global North. Those patterns, far from humanizing the relationships of work, normalize patterns of inequality.

Is it too much to imagine that the beleaguered, occasionally sidelined, and inherently reconciliatory ILO could play a more overt role in challenging these structural patterns? Perhaps these issues speak to limits inherent to the tripartite, dialogue-based structure of the ILO. They might equally have been failures of courage in a moment when the international organization feared sustained institutional challenge or renewed marginalization by the member states it needs to take it through its next century. But the ILO's 1919 Constitution and the annexed 1944 Declaration of Philadelphia are bold social justice texts that reaffirm that labor is not a commodity and hold the ILO responsible for examining and considering all international economic and financial policies in light of its fundamental objective to secure peace on the basis of social justice. Article II of the Declaration of Philadelphia affirms that "all human beings, irrespective of race, creed or sex, have the right to pursue both their material well-being and their spiritual development in conditions of freedom and dignity, of economic security and equal opportunity." Maybe there is a different lesson from the standard setting on decent work for domestic workers that turned out to be more robust than many people had expected. In this moment of deep discontent about the direction of neoliberal globalization, it is time for the ILO to act with the courage of its constitutional convictions.

Throughout the book, I have kept attention on the unmitigated success: the standard-setting process and the standards themselves have galvanized a transnational movement of domestic workers. Neither the process nor the result defines that social movement, and I would argue that the social movement should not necessarily confine its objectives to what is contained within the Domestic Workers Convention and the Domestic Workers Recommendation. This has several implications.

The first is that while standard setting was framed to emphasize the human rights case for equality-based inclusion in labor law, domestic workers need not apologize for or limit themselves to making their claims through a framework that has not only advantages but clear limits. Domestic workers' activism embodies rights in struggle.[4] Part of what domestic workers have done by claiming inclusion is to transgress a framework that did not prioritize their concerns. By claiming that they both do work like any other and work like no other, they hold the standards to achieving substantive equality. In fact, some members of the labor community reacted with astonishment to the idea that domestic workers could achieve a strong international labor convention and recommendation, when some of the mainstream workers—those in auto manufacturing and a wide range of precarious work—see themselves as struggling. Could it be that domestic workers who are at once paradigmatic employees and the embodiment of exclusion made the claim for a decent minimum wage seem obvious and made it possible to see why settling a new norm of working time in domestic work that is largely consistent with historical international standards was a basic marker of freedom?

The second implication may resemble a moment faced by the US civil rights movement when it became important to move beyond the most blatant political inclusion claims and address broader structural dimensions of social justice.[5] Needless to state, there was significant and persistent resistance to that move. The parallel is not perfect, to the extent that decent work for domestic workers embraces the full range of components that are included in the corpus of international labor law. Those components include social protection—the battlefront on which many of the current cases are moving forward, as seen in chapter 6. The Domestic Workers Convention and the Domestic Workers Recommendation are surprisingly substantive instruments, which member states need to work with closely to foster respect for their terms. Where the parallel works is in the call for structural change. If domestic work is decent work, it should not remain racialized as other. This recalls the dual meaning of subordination that has been used throughout this book. In other words, decent work for domestic work must challenge the racialized segmentation of the work. This includes taking seriously the concerns of domestic workers who called within the standard-setting process for access to a broad range of life options and who rarely aspire to have their daughters perform the same work. Ai-jen Poo of the National Domestic Workers Alliance insists on the humanity of care. She is on to something that we can ill afford to lose sight of.[6]

The third implication takes us full circle. It is about taking the transnational so seriously that we rethink what governance level is appropriate for matters deemed to be domestic. This includes labor itself and certainly affects labor migration. Nancy Fraser has theorized the importance of addressing representation, including political representation. She cautions against using an inappropriate level to raise justice concerns. She also emphasizes that the question of the frame is a political choice.[7] In this moment of deep societal discontent over the direction of globalization and its many exclusions, Fraser underscores the importance of emancipatory social movements in struggles over who should bear globalization's risks.[8] Standard setting on decent work for domestic workers focused on many governance levels, but the prevailing assumption in most international labor standard setting is that states bear primary responsibility, in consultation with labor and employers who form part of the national whole for the purposes of international labor regulation.

Before the standard setting for decent work for domestic workers, it might have seemed improbable that domestic workers would be the ones to direct us to a place where the need to rethink the transnational would seem so obvious. But we have seen that domestic workers do a lot of border crossing: between production and reproduction, histories of subordination and servitude and their contemporary legacies, the national and the transnational, and state law and the law of the household workplace. Domestic workers embody the transnational that they have helped to build. They are also well placed to call for a transnational labor law that rethinks how people move and under what conditions. The limits of bilateral agreements coupled with a proliferation of international and regional texts affirming domestic workers' rights might signal that this is the time to make a different kind of case. The energy alone needed to identify and punish the proliferation of rogue recruitment agencies should reorient policy from the individualized solutions to the structural. I acknowledge that liberalizing migration within a framework of reasonable labor market access for the movement of people, with a premium on rights of permanent migration, may seem a particularly unlikely direction in the current moment of significant backlash against current migration flows.[9]

It is worth taking the time, before concluding, to consider the barebones sketch of how the decent work framework in the Domestic Workers Convention and the Domestic Workers Recommendation could be understood on the basis of three insights. First, it would have to be built on an acknowledgment of the structural inequality of global migration and seek to pay attention to ensure a level of burden sharing through international solidarity among states.[10] Second, it would build on article 16 of the convention, which requires that "each Member shall take measures to ensure, in accordance with national laws, regulations and practice, that all domestic workers, either by themselves or through a representative, have effective access to courts, tribunals or other dispute resolution mechanisms under conditions that are not less favourable than those available to workers generally." It would incorporate the commitment to cooperate at regional and global levels found in paragraph 26 of the recommendation, referenced above, which recommends forms of international solidarity. And third, it would spotlight a particular gender and trade concern by acknowledging that most social reproduction is undertaken by women, and that a majority of migrant women workers cross borders to provide care, as a crucial element of inclusive trade policies.[11]

A decent work complement to reasonable labor market access would seek to operationalize at a multilateral or regional level matters that were ill-suited to bilateral resolution.[12] This might be one of domestic workers' next frontiers. The goals would be to foster complementarity and hold open alternative spaces to seek an equitable mediation of social policy in economic policy.[13] All of these reflections embrace border crossing. They all entail thinking transnationally,[14] about the spaces that can be held—or pried—open. None is romantic. As law remains central to globalization, thinking about transnational labor law should avoid overstating the disruptive power of plural sources of law.[15] Decent work for domestic workers will simply not happen unless the transnational solidarity that brought the issue to the ILO's standard-setting table is sustained, and unless domestic workers themselves remain front and center.

POSTFACE

My mother, Muriel Blackett, was a formidable cook. But in her ninetieth year, she is happy not to have to cook anymore. My grandmother, Daisy Stoute, was a domestic worker in Barbados prior to its independence. She worked long hours cooking for others. She could not have raised her children without the help of her firstborn daughter, my mother—who from the age of six cooked the meals and washed the clothes of her younger brothers. Although she excelled at primary school, my mother was not able to take up a scholarship to attend high school and instead stayed home to care for her youngest, sickly brother. In adolescence, she was taken in by a relative, ostensibly to keep her out of harm's way, but she wound up working harder than ever. She clung to her church community and became a seamstress. When the opportunity presented itself for her to go to Canada under the country's first modern immigration program to admit racialized permanent residents from the global South—the Foreign Domestic Worker Movement program—she took it.[1]

Entry to Canada was offered on the basis of the stereotype written into the text of the 1955 *Memorandum of Understanding*. The logic was clear: what else would Black "girls" want to do with their lives other than work as maids in white households?

I remember thumbing through my mother's training manual on how to be a good maid under the program. Her little blue notebook was meticulously handwritten during the night courses that were offered in preparation for coming to Canada:

Week 1, Monday 8.5.61, menu, tea bread and butter, followed with good habits of working in the kitchen on Thursday 11th May—1. Wash your hands, 2. Put on an apron and cap, . . . 8. Use separate spoons for stirring and tasting, 9. Keep a bucket or garbage can for scraps; don't throw scraps out of the window, . . . 16. Clean up your work space when you are finished.

Week 2, Tuesday 16.5.61, Dusting, 2. Dust high places first and work methodically round the room. . . . Walls. Sweep walls with a cob-web broom. . . . Sweep with long even strokes from top downwards, first removing all pictures etc. . . .

Week 3, Tuesday 23.5.61, Silver, Wash with warm, soapy water, dry well, Clean with ammonia. . . . Wednesday May 24th 1961, To Iron a Pillow Case (1) Stretch into Shape. . . .

Week 4, How to cook a complete meat course in a presto, 2 lbs beef, 25–30 minutes, potatoes (cut in quarters), 5 minutes, carrots (cut in quarters), 5 minutes. . . .

Week 5, Friday 8.6.61, Daily cleaning of the Bedroom, 1. Strip the bed, arch the mattress, and leave the room to air . . . , Weekly, . . . 7. Take down curtains, pin up long curtains. . . .

Week 6, Tuesday 13.6.61, Bathrooms, 2. Clean bath, basin and lavatory according to kind. . . . 4. Scrub floor and rubber mats, 5. Polish floor, clean window, replace mats. . . .

Week 7, Wednesday 21.6.61, Laundry. Washing and finishing a variety of children's wear. . . . Stains removal. . . .

Week 8, Monday 26.6.61, Pinwheel Sandwiches. . . .

Week 9, Friday 7.7.61, Fine Material, Laundering of Silk Articles. . . . They should be washed by the method of kneading and squeezing. . . .

Week 10, Shepherd's Pie. . . .

Week 11, Wednesday 19.7.61, Darning a Hole, the darning in the other direction must be close enough so that the hole when filled will be similar to the web of the thread in the garment.

Within weeks of completing the exam for the course, Mom had landed in Canada.

I forgot about that book, and for years focused instead on the activism and the theoretical work on the regulation of domestic work. It is my daughter—who decided to interview her Granny on her experience as an immigrant to Canada—who literally brought the book home for me as a gift from my mom. Reviewing it, I recalled with a mixture of horror and amusement that as a child, I had taken the liberty of adding some of my own recipes to my mom's, using my best cursive writing to live up to her high standards. I also found a five-cent ticket from the Barbados transport board that Mom must have used to attend the night courses after her daily work as a seamstress was done. When I asked her about the notebook and training, Mom quipped that the trainers acted as if she and the other women didn't know how to do anything.

My mother traveled, as did the norms about the household workplace and domestic workers' proper place. Indeed, Mom's training for domestic work in Canada sounded a lot like the instructions in the cookbooks that I reviewed to write this book. In particular, stereotypes about domestic workers' invisibility were pervasive. Ironically, stereotypes were part of the reason Canada offered the workers permanent residency in the first place—what else would these Black women from the Caribbean do with their lives except serve others, the Cabinet Document on the admission of domestics from the British West Indies inferred.[2]

I knew from listening to my mother and other women from the Caribbean that these women had other ideas. Like many women from the English-speaking Black community in Montreal in which I grew up, my mother spent her two years in service—a requirement of the immigration scheme—and then immediately moved on. One Black community member recounted at a Montreal-based fiftieth anniversary commemoration of the program that she had "sailed the seas" before settling down and starting a family. Before the program became progressively more restrictive, other women—like the Honourable Jean Augustine, the first African Canadian woman to be elected to the Canadian House of Commons and the first to serve in the federal cabinet—continued their formal education and rose to great heights in society. Still others, like the group known as the Jamaican mothers, challenged the stereotypes written into the law, which deemed them to be single and childless, and sought to expel them from Canada when they showed they had lives of their own.[3]

Like many of the Black women of Caribbean heritage who came to Canada through the program, my mother married my father, John Richard Blackett, an ordained minister whom she got engaged to marry before leaving Barbados. She quickly found a job as a seamstress in Montreal's then-thriving clothing industry. As was common at that time, she was fired when she became pregnant with me. After I was born, she moved to a unionized job in a public hospital. She was a phenomenal mother to my sister and me and taught our equally formidable father to cook more than a few basic essentials. However, though she has allowed my daughter and son to come to "Granny's cooking school" during school breaks, she only taught her own daughters to cook once we had finished our formal education, established ourselves professionally, and started our own families. Both my parents were adamant that their daughters would have the kind of opportunities in life that they had been denied. And let's face it: my mother took great pride in being the excellent cook in the family.

My parents and many other women and men in our community had hard lives, but they were far from the passive victims in books like Kathryn Stockett's The Help. The Help is written through a white employer's eyes, and it stereotypes African American domestic workers in many ways—including by resurrecting the mammy myth discussed in chapter 4.[4] In The Help, agency lies in the hands of enlightened whites. The women who were domestic workers that I have known in my family, community, and activism, transgressed the everyday, commonsense law of the household workplace.

This book has been about that transgressing, through which domestic workers have fundamentally challenged transnational labor law to become something bigger, more deeply rooted, and more demanding than the field of labor law might ever have imagined. While at some level this book is not quite my mother's story, it could not have been written without her.

First, Mom believed in me enough when I was a law student and domestic worker activist to help me when my own savings in Canadian dollars plummeted relative to then-strong European currencies. She gave me the money that she had been saving with a trusted group of West Indian women in the hospital where she worked so that I could take up an initially unpaid internship at the International Labour Organization (ILO). The outstanding members of the team where I had the good fortune to land in 1993—particularly my supervisor, Anne Trebilcock, and my internship coordinator, Shauna Olney—took my work with the Montreal Household Workers' Association seriously and asked me to research the regulation of domestic work at the request of the government of South Africa. South Africa was just emerging from apartheid, and the government realized that domestic workers would not simply be able to leave their jobs overnight. South Africans also recognized that the relationship between domestic workers and their employers had come to epitomize apartheid's explicit social stratification. The research I did became the ILO's first contemporary study of the regulation of domestic work, and in it I argued for specific regulation. My report was ultimately revised and published in 1998. It was on the basis of that publication that, ten years later, I was asked by the ILO to become its chief expert on setting standards for the working conditions of domestic workers.

Second, I could not have done the work that I did without the intimate knowledge of domestic work that I gained from Mom and our community. That knowledge has shaped the way I have come to see this world, relate to other workers' life aspirations and resistances, and understand what decent work looks and feels like. It has also meant that as I have traveled—as I have done often—I have repeatedly sought to sense and learn from and about the domestic work relationships, sometimes as an observer or a temporary member of a household workplace, and sometimes as an employer. I have wanted to understand them as a pluralist intent on shedding a Western colonial gaze—to learn about employers' views, while paying close attention to domestic workers' social expectations and navigations in their context, whether that be Switzerland, Côte d'Ivoire, Colombia, Tunisia, the United States, or Canada. I formulated many of the intuitions in this book during my travels, including that the asymmetry of the law of the household workplace is strikingly similar across contexts and has to be unsettled to be transformed.

My mother's experience meant that I was always aware of the fact that everyone has power and that power is unevenly distributed. I am also struck by how many people—academics, international officials, and friends—have at some point (and I can tell when the conversation will turn to this) wanted to share their personal experience of having hired a domestic worker or been raised by a domestic worker. Most of them seem to want me to validate their view that close attention must be paid to this employment relationship lest it turn into social subordination. I remember one conversation with a colleague who is dear to me. He spoke of "all the tiny violations of labor law" that characterized what he thought was a respectful relationship. The implications of calling domestic work an employment relationship were becoming clear. These experiences have influenced how I understand the domestic work relationship, and over time and after countless experiences and exchanges, my belief that it is necessary to understand the law of the household workplace before one can hope to change it.

As I raised my own children while holding a full-time academic position, I was grateful to be able to rely on the excellent public early childhood care system in Quebec. My spouse mostly lived overseas, and my good fortune was to be able to count on Lucien Smith, a recently retired Montrealer of Barbadian heritage who had come to Canada as a domestic worker and then worked in a unionized hospital job, bought her own home and raised her own family, to work with me to take care of my family on weekday afternoons and evenings. My mother's experience alongside my activism helped me to be scrupulous about ensuring equitable working conditions, avoiding easy tropes of the "like one of the family" variety, and working to build a relationship of respect. But I would have failed miserably had I tried to disabuse my young children of their conclusion that "Auntie Lucien" (the traditional form of address that children of Caribbean heritage use toward adults in the community as a sign of respect, whether or not they are related to them) was one of their grandmothers.

Third, Mom's experience strengthened my resolve to resist invisibility in the process of setting international standards. I got involved in that process because it has been one of my lifelong goals to shift the regulatory narrative to challenge domestic workers' invisibility. It has been an honor to have played a role in setting international labor standards for decent work for domestic workers. I would not have been able to do it the same way without Mom, a shared history of community and struggle, and my own life experiences. The process necessarily involved a team of people within and beyond the ILO, and it is important that its success came through the combined efforts of many. But throughout the work, out of respect for my mother and aunties and community, it has become important to me to resist attempts to make my own labor invisible, resist intellectual dispossession and recolonization, and resist becoming "the help." Sisters and brothers, I know you hear me. 'Nuf said.

APPENDIX 1

A Note on Terminology

The use of the terms "domestic work" and "domestic workers" should be explained, as the language surrounding this occupation has varied greatly over time and according to geographical and cultural context. Their meaning can therefore vary from one country to another.

The language used in this report has the virtue of updating the archaic terms of "maid" and "servant" that clearly implied direct subservience. The shift to "worker" is particularly significant for the ILO, which is responsible for improving the conditions of all workers.

Some parts of the world have already moved away from the language of "domesticity," because of its pejorative connotations and the tendency to undervalue care work. Others, on the other hand, have opted to retain the concept of "domestic" work and note that the word has its place in the language of international relations, side by side with that of the individual state. Others again prefer to speak of "private household," but this risks institutionalizing a distinction between public and private regulation that has already been superseded by the ILO's Home Work Convention, 1996 (No. 177).

The decision of some countries to espouse the concept of "home care" has some real advantages, but it also comes with problems. Although theoretically the language is gender neutral, perhaps for that very reason it does not readily conjure up the image of a gardener or chauffeur. It may be something of a euphemism, too, masking the broad range of menial household duties that

domestic workers are called upon to undertake, while tasks of a more uplift-
ing nature are reserved for members of the family, generally the mother. However, the real virtue of this language is the inherent principle that caring is a
form of work. Indeed, some academics speak of "caretaking" rather than caregiving," to emphasize the skills associated with care work and the importance of their remuneration.

In other countries again, the terms used are "household helper" or "household aide," a formulation that unfortunately takes the emphasis away from
the notion of "worker" and runs the risk of "de-skilling" the occupation. A
number of civil associations have therefore preferred "household work" as a
linguistic solution. But here there is a real danger of confusion with the term
"home work" employed in past standard-setting exercises—a confusion that
is aggravated by the problem of translation into other languages.

Be that as it may, the language chosen for the future instrument must reflect the wide range of responsibilities and skills required in domestic work.

This report by the Office abides by the Governing Body's decision to refer
to decent work for "domestic workers," in keeping with the usage of the ILO's
supervisory bodies and other ILO reports. As far as possible, the report has
also updated references in past ILO documents to "servants" and "maids."

That said, it must be made clear that the International Labour Conference
is at liberty to adopt a Convention with a different title and that ILO Members, in consultation with their representative employers' and workers' organizations, might retain the authority to use the terminology most suited to
their local context. Self-definition, particularly by those doing the work, is crucial. The important thing is that the workers who come within the scope of
the proposed international instrument should benefit effectively from the protection it affords.[1]

Text of the Domestic Workers Convention and Domestic Workers Recommendation

C189—Domestic Workers Convention, 2011 (No. 189)
Convention concerning decent work for domestic workers
Entry into force: 05 Sep 2013
Adoption: Geneva, 100th ILC session (16 Jun 2011)
Status: Up-to-date instrument (Technical Convention)
Convention may be denounced: 05 Sep 2023–05 Sep 2024

Preamble

The General Conference of the International Labour Organization, Having been convened at Geneva by the Governing Body of the International Labour Office, and having met in its 100th Session on 1 June 2011, and

Mindful of the commitment of the International Labour Organization to promote decent work for all through the achievement of the goals of the ILO Declaration on Fundamental Principles and Rights at Work and the ILO Declaration on Social Justice for a Fair Globalization, and

Recognizing the significant contribution of domestic workers to the global economy, which includes increasing paid job opportunities for women and men workers with family responsibilities, greater scope for caring for ageing populations, children and persons with a disability, and substantial income transfers within and between countries, and

Considering that domestic work continues to be undervalued and invisible and is mainly carried out by women and girls, many of whom are migrants or members of disadvantaged communities and who are particularly vulnerable to discrimination in respect of conditions of employment and of work, and to other abuses of human rights, and

Considering also that in developing countries with historically scarce opportunities for formal employment, domestic workers constitute a significant proportion of the national workforce and remain among the most marginalized, and

Recalling that international labour Conventions and Recommendations apply to all workers, including domestic workers, unless otherwise provided, and

Noting the particular relevance for domestic workers of the Migration for Employment Convention (Revised), 1949 (No. 97), the Migrant Workers (Supplementary Provisions) Convention, 1975 (No. 143), the Workers with Family Responsibilities Convention, 1981 (No. 156), the Private Employment Agencies Convention, 1997 (No. 181), and the Employment Relationship Recommendation, 2006 (No. 198), as well as of the ILO Multilateral Framework on Labour Migration: Non-binding principles and guidelines for a rights-based approach to labour migration (2006), and

Recognizing the special conditions under which domestic work is carried out that make it desirable to supplement the general standards with standards specific to domestic workers so as to enable them to enjoy their rights fully, and

Recalling other relevant international instruments such as the Universal Declaration of Human Rights, the International Covenant on Civil and Political Rights, the International Covenant on Economic, Social and Cultural Rights, the International Convention on the Elimination of All Forms of Racial Discrimination, the Convention on the Elimination of All Forms of Discrimination against Women, the United Nations Convention against Transnational Organized Crime, and in particular its Protocol to Prevent, Suppress and Punish Trafficking in Persons, Especially Women and Children and its Protocol against the Smuggling of Migrants by Land, Sea and Air, the Convention on

the Rights of the Child and the International Convention on the Protection
of the Rights of All Migrant Workers and Members of Their Families, and

Having decided upon the adoption of certain proposals concerning decent
work for domestic workers, which is the fourth item on the agenda of the session, and

Having determined that these proposals shall take the form of an international
Convention; adopts this sixteenth day of June of the year two thousand and
eleven the following Convention, which may be cited as the Domestic Workers Convention, 2011.

Article 1

For the purpose of this Convention:

   (a) the term *domestic work* means work performed in or for a household
       or households;
   (b) the term *domestic worker* means any person engaged in domestic work
       within an employment relationship;
   (c) a person who performs domestic work only occasionally or sporadically
       and not on an occupational basis is not a domestic worker.

Article 2

   1. The Convention applies to all domestic workers.
   2. A Member which ratifies this Convention may, after consulting with
      the most representative organizations of employers and workers and,
      where they exist, with organizations representative of domestic
      workers and those representative of employers of domestic workers,
      exclude wholly or partly from its scope:
      (a) categories of workers who are otherwise provided with at least
          equivalent protection;
      (b) limited categories of workers in respect of which special problems
          of a substantial nature arise.
   3. Each Member which avails itself of the possibility afforded in the
      prece ding paragraph shall, in its first report on the application of the
      Convention under article 22 of the Constitution of the International

Labour Organisation, indicate any particular category of workers thus excluded and the reasons for such exclusion and, in subsequent reports, specify any measures that may have been taken with a view to extending the application of the Convention to the workers concerned.

Article 3

1. Each Member shall take measures to ensure the effective promotion and protection of the human rights of all domestic workers, as set out in this Convention.
2. Each Member shall, in relation to domestic workers, take the measures set out in this Convention to respect, promote and realize the fundamental principles and rights at work, namely:
   (a) freedom of association and the effective recognition of the right to collective bargaining;
   (b) the elimination of all forms of forced or compulsory labour;
   (c) the effective abolition of child labour; and
   (d) the elimination of discrimination in respect of employment and occupation.
3. In taking measures to ensure that domestic workers and employers of domestic workers enjoy freedom of association and the effective recognition of the right to collective bargaining, Members shall protect the right of domestic workers and employers of domestic workers to establish and, subject to the rules of the organization concerned, to join organizations, federations and confederations of their own choosing.

Article 4

1. Each Member shall set a minimum age for domestic workers consistent with the provisions of the Minimum Age Convention, 1973 (No. 138), and the Worst Forms of Child Labour Convention, 1999 (No. 182), and not lower than that established by national laws and regulations for workers generally.
2. Each Member shall take measures to ensure that work performed by domestic workers who are under the age of 18 and above the minimum age of employment does not deprive them of compulsory

education, or interfere with opportunities to participate in further education or vocational training.

Article 5

Each Member shall take measures to ensure that domestic workers enjoy effective protection against all forms of abuse, harassment and violence.

Article 6

Each Member shall take measures to ensure that domestic workers, like workers generally, enjoy fair terms of employment as well as decent working conditions and, if they reside in the household, decent living conditions that respect their privacy.

Article 7

Each Member shall take measures to ensure that domestic workers are informed of their terms and conditions of employment in an appropriate, verifiable and easily understandable manner and preferably, where possible, through written contracts in accordance with national laws, regulations or collective agreements, in particular:

(a) the name and address of the employer and of the worker;
(b) the address of the usual workplace or workplaces;
(c) the starting date and, where the contract is for a specified period of time, its duration;
(d) the type of work to be performed;
(e) the remuneration, method of calculation and periodicity of payments;
(f) the normal hours of work;
(g) paid annual leave, and daily and weekly rest periods;
(h) the provision of food and accommodation, if applicable;
(i) the period of probation or trial period, if applicable;
(j) the terms of repatriation, if applicable; and
(k) terms and conditions relating to the termination of employment, including any period of notice by either the domestic worker or the employer.

Article 8

1. National laws and regulations shall require that migrant domestic workers who are recruited in one country for domestic work in another receive a written job offer, or contract of employment that is enforceable in the country in which the work is to be performed, addressing the terms and conditions of employment referred to in Article 7, prior to crossing national borders for the purpose of taking up the domestic work to which the offer or contract applies.
2. The preceding paragraph shall not apply to workers who enjoy freedom of movement for the purpose of employment under bilateral, regional or multilateral agreements, or within the framework of regional economic integration areas.
3. Members shall take measures to cooperate with each other to ensure the effective application of the provisions of this Convention to migrant domestic workers.
4. Each Member shall specify, by means of laws, regulations or other measures, the conditions under which migrant domestic workers are entitled to repatriation on the expiry or termination of the employment contract for which they were recruited.

Article 9

Each Member shall take measures to ensure that domestic workers:

(a) are free to reach agreement with their employer or potential employer on whether to reside in the household;
(b) who reside in the household are not obliged to remain in the household or with household members during periods of daily and weekly rest or annual leave; and
(c) are entitled to keep in their possession their travel and identity documents.

Article 10

1. Each Member shall take measures towards ensuring equal treatment between domestic workers and workers generally in relation to normal hours of work, overtime compensation, periods of daily and

weekly rest and paid annual leave in accordance with national laws, regulations or collective agreements, taking into account the special characteristics of domestic work.

2. Weekly rest shall be at least 24 consecutive hours.
3. Periods during which domestic workers are not free to dispose of their time as they please and remain at the disposal of the household in order to respond to possible calls shall be regarded as hours of work to the extent determined by national laws, regulations or collective agreements, or any other means consistent with national practice.

Article 11

Each Member shall take measures to ensure that domestic workers enjoy minimum wage coverage, where such coverage exists, and that remuneration is established without discrimination based on sex.

Article 12

1. Domestic workers shall be paid directly in cash at regular intervals at least once a month. Unless provided for by national laws, regulations or collective agreements, payment may be made by bank transfer, bank cheque, postal cheque, money order or other lawful means of monetary payment, with the consent of the worker concerned.
2. National laws, regulations, collective agreements or arbitration awards may provide for the payment of a limited proportion of the remuneration of domestic workers in the form of payments in kind that are not less favourable than those generally applicable to other categories of workers, provided that measures are taken to ensure that such payments in kind are agreed to by the worker, are for the personal use and benefit of the worker, and that the monetary value attributed to them is fair and reasonable.

Article 13

1. Every domestic worker has the right to a safe and healthy working environment. Each Member shall take, in accordance with national laws, regulations and practice, effective measures, with due regard for

the specific characteristics of domestic work, to ensure the occupational safety and health of domestic workers.

2. The measures referred to in the preceding paragraph may be applied progressively, in consultation with the most representative organizations of employers and workers and, where they exist, with organizations representative of domestic workers and those representative of employers of domestic workers.

Article 14

1. Each Member shall take appropriate measures, in accordance with national laws and regulations and with due regard for the specific characteristics of domestic work, to ensure that domestic workers enjoy conditions that are not less favourable than those applicable to workers generally in respect of social security protection, including with respect to maternity.

2. The measures referred to in the preceding paragraph may be applied progressively, in consultation with the most representative organizations of employers and workers and, where they exist, with organizations representative of domestic workers and those representative of employers of domestic workers.

Article 15

1. To effectively protect domestic workers, including migrant domestic workers, recruited or placed by private employment agencies, against abusive practices, each Member shall:

   (a) determine the conditions governing the operation of private employment agencies recruiting or placing domestic workers, in accordance with national laws, regulations and practice;

   (b) ensure that adequate machinery and procedures exist for the investigation of complaints, alleged abuses and fraudulent practices concerning the activities of private employment agencies in relation to domestic workers;

   (c) adopt all necessary and appropriate measures, within its jurisdiction and, where appropriate, in collaboration with other Members, to provide adequate protection for and prevent abuses of domestic workers recruited or placed in its territory by private employment agencies. These shall include laws or regulations that specify the respective obligations of the private employment agency and the household towards the domestic worker and provide for penalties, including prohibition of those private employment agencies that engage in fraudulent practices and abuses;

(d) consider, where domestic workers are recruited in one country for work in another, concluding bilateral, regional or multilateral agreements to prevent abuses and fraudulent practices in recruitment, placement and employment; and

(e) take measures to ensure that fees charged by private employment agencies are not deducted from the remuneration of domestic workers.

2. In giving effect to each of the provisions of this Article, each Member shall consult with the most representative organizations of employers and workers and, where they exist, with organizations representative of domestic workers and those representative of employers of domestic workers.

Article 16

Each Member shall take measures to ensure, in accordance with national laws, regulations and practice, that all domestic workers, either by themselves or through a representative, have effective access to courts, tribunals or other dispute resolution mechanisms under conditions that are not less favourable than those available to workers generally.

Article 17

1. Each Member shall establish effective and accessible complaint mechanisms and means of ensuring compliance with national laws and regulations for the protection of domestic workers.

2. Each Member shall develop and implement measures for labour inspection, enforcement and penalties with due regard for the special characteristics of domestic work, in accordance with national laws and regulations.

3. In so far as compatible with national laws and regulations, such measures shall specify the conditions under which access to household premises may be granted, having due respect for privacy.

Article 18

Each Member shall implement the provisions of this Convention, in consultation with the most representative employers and workers organizations, through laws and regulations, as well as through collective agreements or additional measures consistent with national practice, by extending or adapting existing measures to cover domestic workers or by developing specific measures for them, as appropriate.

Article 19

This Convention does not affect more favourable provisions applicable to domestic workers under other international labour Conventions.

Article 20

The formal ratifications of this Convention shall be communicated to the Director-General of the International Labour Office for registration.

Article 21

1. This Convention shall be binding only upon those Members of the International Labour Organization whose ratifications have been registered with the Director-General of the International Labour Office.
2. It shall come into force twelve months after the date on which the ratifications of two Members have been registered with the Director-General.
3. Thereafter, this Convention shall come into force for any Member twelve months after the date on which its ratification is registered.

Article 22

1. A Member which has ratified this Convention may denounce it after the expiration of ten years from the date on which the Convention first comes into force, by an act communicated to the Director-General

of the International Labour Office for registration. Such denunciation shall not take effect until one year after the date on which it is registered.

2. Each Member which has ratified this Convention and which does not, within the year following the expiration of the period of ten years mentioned in the preceding paragraph, exercise the right of denunciation provided for in this Article, will be bound for another period of ten years and, thereafter, may denounce this Convention within the first year of each new period of ten years under the terms provided for in this Article.

Article 23

1. The Director-General of the International Labour Office shall notify all Members of the International Labour Organization of the registration of all ratifications and denunciations that have been communicated by the Members of the Organization.

2. When notifying the Members of the Organization of the registration of the second ratification that has been communicated, the Director-General shall draw the attention of the Members of the Organization to the date upon which the Convention will come into force.

Article 24

The Director-General of the International Labour Office shall communicate to the Secretary-General of the United Nations for registration in accordance with Article 102 of the Charter of the United Nations full particulars of all ratifications and denunciations that have been registered.

Article 25

At such times as it may consider necessary, the Governing Body of the International Labour Office shall present to the General Conference a report on the working of this Convention and shall examine the desirability of placing on the agenda of the Conference the question of its revision in whole or in part.

Article 26

   1. Should the Conference adopt a new Convention revising this Convention, then, unless the new Convention otherwise provides:

      (a) the ratification by a Member of the new revising Convention shall ipso jure involve the immediate denunciation of this Convention, notwithstanding the provisions of Article 22, if and when the new revising Convention shall have come into force;

      (b) as from the date when the new revising Convention comes into force, this Convention shall cease to be open to ratification by the Members.

   2. This Convention shall in any case remain in force in its actual form and content for those Members which have ratified it but have not ratified the revising Convention.

Article 27

The English and French versions of the text of this Convention are equally authoritative.

    R201—Domestic Workers Recommendation, 2011 (No. 201)
    Recommendation concerning Decent Work for Domestic Workers
    Adoption: Geneva, 100th ILC session (16 Jun 2011)
    Status: Up-to-date instrument

Preamble

The General Conference of the International Labour Organization,
Having been convened at Geneva by the Governing Body of the International Labour Office, and having met in its 100th Session on 1 June 2011, and
Having adopted the Domestic Workers Convention, 2011, and
Having decided upon the adoption of certain proposals with regard to decent work for domestic workers, which is the fourth item on the agenda of the session, and
Having determined that these proposals shall take the form of a Recommendation supplementing the Domestic Workers Convention, 2011;

adopts this sixteenth day of June of the year two thousand and eleven the following Recommendation, which may be cited as the Domestic Workers Recommendation, 2011.

1. The provisions of this Recommendation supplement those of the Domestic Workers Convention, 2011 ("the Convention"), and should be considered in conjunction with them.

2. In taking measures to ensure that domestic workers enjoy freedom of association and the effective recognition of the right to collective bargaining, Members should:

   (a) identify and eliminate any legislative or administrative restrictions or other obstacles to the right of domestic workers to establish their own organizations or to join the workers' organizations of their own choosing and to the right of organizations of domestic workers to join workers' organizations, federations and confederations;

   (b) give consideration to taking or supporting measures to strengthen the capacity of workers' and employers' organizations, organizations representing domestic workers and those of employers of domestic workers, to promote effectively the interests of their members, provided that at all times the independence and autonomy, within the law, of such organizations are protected.

3. In taking measures for the elimination of discrimination in respect of employment and occupation, Members should, consistent with international labour standards, among other things:

   (a) make sure that arrangements for work-related medical testing respect the principle of the confidentiality of personal data and the privacy of domestic workers, and are consistent with the ILO code of practice "Protection of workers' personal data" (1997), and other relevant international data protection standards;

   (b) prevent any discrimination related to such testing; and

   (c) ensure that no domestic worker is required to undertake HIV or pregnancy testing, or to disclose HIV or pregnancy status.

4. Members giving consideration to medical testing for domestic workers should consider:

   (a) making public health information available to members of the households and domestic workers on the primary health and disease concerns that give rise to any needs for medical testing in each national context;

    (b) making information available to members of the households and domestic workers on voluntary medical testing, medical treatment, and good health and hygiene practices, consistent with public health initiatives for the community generally; and

    (c) distributing information on best practices for work-related medical testing, appropriately adapted to reflect the special nature of domestic work.

5. (1) Taking into account the provisions of the Worst Forms of Child Labour Convention, 1999 (No. 182), and Recommendation (No. 190), Members should identify types of domestic work that, by their nature or the circumstances in which they are carried out, are likely to harm the health, safety or morals of children, and should also prohibit and eliminate such child labour.

(2) When regulating the working and living conditions of domestic workers, Members should give special attention to the needs of domestic workers who are under the age of 18 and above the minimum age of employment as defined by national laws and regulations, and take measures to protect them, including by:

    (a) strictly limiting their hours of work to ensure adequate time for rest, education and training, leisure activities and family contacts;

    (b) prohibiting night work;

    (c) placing restrictions on work that is excessively demanding, whether physically or psychologically; and

    (d) establishing or strengthening mechanisms to monitor their working and living conditions.

6. (1) Members should provide appropriate assistance, when necessary, to ensure that domestic workers understand their terms and conditions of employment.

(2) Further to the particulars listed in Article 7 of the Convention, the terms and conditions of employment should also include:

    (a) a job description;

    (b) sick leave and, if applicable, any other personal leave;

    (c) the rate of pay or compensation for overtime and standby consistent with Article 10(3) of the Convention;

    (d) any other payments to which the domestic worker is entitled;

    (e) any payments in kind and their monetary value;

    (f) details of any accommodation provided; and

    (g) any authorized deductions from the worker's remuneration.

(3) Members should consider establishing a model contract of employment for domestic work, in consultation with the most representative

organizations of employers and workers and, where they exist, with organizations representative of domestic workers and those representative of employers of domestic workers.

(4) The model contract should at all times be made available free of charge to domestic workers, employers, representative organizations and the general public.

7. Members should consider establishing mechanisms to protect domestic workers from abuse, harassment and violence, such as:

   (a) establishing accessible complaint mechanisms for domestic workers to report cases of abuse, harassment and violence;

   (b) ensuring that all complaints of abuse, harassment and violence are investigated, and prosecuted, as appropriate; and

   (c) establishing programmes for the relocation from the household and rehabilitation of domestic workers subjected to abuse, harassment and violence, including the provision of temporary accommodation and health care.

8. (1) Hours of work, including overtime and periods of standby consistent with Article 10(3) of the Convention, should be accurately recorded, and this information should be freely accessible to the domestic worker.

   (2) Members should consider developing practical guidance in this respect, in consultation with the most representative organizations of employers and workers and, where they exist, with organizations representative of domestic workers and those representative of employers of domestic workers.

9. (1) With respect to periods during which domestic workers are not free to dispose of their time as they please and remain at the disposal of the household in order to respond to possible calls (standby or on-call periods), Members, to the extent determined by national laws, regulations or collective agreements, should regulate:

   (a) the maximum number of hours per week, month or year that a domestic worker may be required to be on standby, and the ways they might be measured;

   (b) the compensatory rest period to which a domestic worker is entitled if the normal period of rest is interrupted by standby; and

   (c) the rate at which standby hours should be remunerated.

   (2) With regard to domestic workers whose normal duties are performed at night, and taking into account the constraints of night work, Members should consider measures comparable to those specified in subparagraph 9(1).

10. Members should take measures to ensure that domestic workers are entitled to suitable periods of rest during the working day, which allow for meals and breaks to be taken.

11. (1) Weekly rest should be at least 24 consecutive hours.

(2) The fixed day of weekly rest should be determined by agreement of the parties, in accordance with national laws, regulations or collective agreements, taking into account work exigencies and the cultural, religious and social requirements of the domestic worker.

(3) Where national laws, regulations or collective agreements provide for weekly rest to be accumulated over a period longer than seven days for workers generally, such a period should not exceed 14 days for domestic workers.

12. National laws, regulations or collective agreements should define the grounds on which domestic workers may be required to work during the period of daily or weekly rest and provide for adequate compensatory rest, irrespective of any financial compensation.

13. Time spent by domestic workers accompanying the household members on holiday should not be counted as part of their paid annual leave.

14. When provision is made for the payment in kind of a limited proportion of remuneration, Members should consider:

(a) establishing an overall limit on the proportion of the remuneration that may be paid in kind so as not to diminish unduly the remuneration necessary for the maintenance of domestic workers and their families;

(b) calculating the monetary value of payments in kind by reference to objective criteria such as market value, cost price or prices fixed by public authorities, as appropriate;

(c) limiting payments in kind to those clearly appropriate for the personal use and benefit of the domestic worker, such as food and accommodation;

(d) ensuring that, when a domestic worker is required to live in accommodation provided by the household, no deduction may be made from the remuneration with respect to that accommodation, unless otherwise agreed to by the worker; and

(e) ensuring that items directly related to the performance of domestic work, such as uniforms, tools or protective equipment, and their cleaning and maintenance, are not considered as payment in kind and their cost is not deducted from the remuneration of the domestic worker.

15. (1) Domestic workers should be given at the time of each payment an easily understandable written account of the total remuneration due to them and the specific amount and purpose of any deductions which may have been made.

    (2) Upon termination of employment, any outstanding payments should be made promptly.

16. Members should take measures to ensure that domestic workers enjoy conditions not less favourable than those of workers generally in respect of the protection of workers' claims in the event of the employer's insolvency or death.

17. When provided, accommodation and food should include, taking into account national conditions, the following:

    (a) a separate, private room that is suitably furnished, adequately ventilated and equipped with a lock, the key to which should be provided to the domestic worker;

    (b) access to suitable sanitary facilities, shared or private;

    (c) adequate lighting and, as appropriate, heating and air conditioning in keeping with prevailing conditions within the household; and

    (d) meals of good quality and sufficient quantity, adapted to the extent reasonable to the cultural and religious requirements, if any, of the domestic worker concerned.

18. In the event of termination of employment at the initiative of the employer, for reasons other than serious misconduct, live-in domestic workers should be given a reasonable period of notice and time off during that period to enable them to seek new employment and accommodation.

19. Members, in consultation with the most representative organizations of employers and workers and, where they exist, with organizations representative of domestic workers and those representative of employers of domestic workers, should take measures, such as to:

    (a) protect domestic workers by eliminating or minimizing, so far as is reasonably practicable, work-related hazards and risks, in order to prevent injuries, diseases and deaths and promote occupational safety and health in the household workplace;

    (b) provide an adequate and appropriate system of inspection, consistent with Article 17 of the Convention, and adequate penalties for violation of occupational safety and health laws and regulations;

    (c) establish procedures for collecting and publishing statistics on accidents and diseases related to domestic work, and other statistics considered to contribute to the prevention of occupational safety and health related risks and injuries;

    (d) advise on occupational safety and health, including on ergonomic aspects and protective equipment; and

    (e) develop training programmes and disseminate guidelines on occupational safety and health requirements specific to domestic work.

20. (1) Members should consider, in accordance with national laws and regulations, means to facilitate the payment of social security contributions, including in respect of domestic workers working for multiple employers, for instance through a system of simplified payment.

(2) Members should consider concluding bilateral, regional or multilateral agreements to provide, for migrant domestic workers covered by such agreements, equality of treatment in respect of social security, as well as access to and preservation or portability of social security entitlements.

(3) The monetary value of payments in kind should be duly considered for social security purposes, including in respect of the contribution by the employers and the entitlements of the domestic workers.

21. (1) Members should consider additional measures to ensure the effective protection of domestic workers and, in particular, migrant domestic workers, such as:

    (a) establishing a national hotline with interpretation services for domestic workers who need assistance;

    (b) consistent with Article 17 of the Convention, providing for a system of pre-placement visits to households in which migrant domestic workers are to be employed;

    (c) developing a network of emergency housing;

    (d) raising employers' awareness of their obligations by providing information on good practices in the employment of domestic workers, employment and immigration law obligations regarding migrant domestic workers, enforcement arrangements and sanctions in cases of violation, and assistance services available to domestic workers and their employers;

    (e) securing access of domestic workers to complaint mechanisms and their ability to pursue legal civil and criminal remedies, both

during and after employment, irrespective of departure from the
country concerned; and

(f) providing for a public outreach service to inform domestic
workers, in languages understood by them, of their rights,
relevant laws and regulations, available complaint mechanisms
and legal remedies, concerning both employment and immigration law, and legal protection against crimes such as violence,
trafficking in persons and deprivation of liberty, and to provide
any other pertinent information they may require.

(2) Members that are countries of origin of migrant domestic
workers should assist in the effective protection of the rights of these
workers, by informing them of their rights before departure, establishing legal assistance funds, social services and specialized consular
services and through any other appropriate measures.

22. Members should, after consulting with the most representative
organizations of employers and workers and, where they exist, with
organizations representative of domestic workers and those representative of employers of domestic workers, consider specifying by
means of laws, regulations or other measures, the conditions under
which migrant domestic workers are entitled to repatriation at no
cost to themselves on the expiry or termination of the employment
contract for which they were recruited.

23. Members should promote good practices by private employment
agencies in relation to domestic workers, including migrant domestic
workers, taking into account the principles and approaches in the
Private Employment Agencies Convention, 1997 (No. 181), and
the Private Employment Agencies Recommendation, 1997 (No. 188).

24. In so far as compatible with national law and practice concerning
respect for privacy, Members may consider conditions under which
labour inspectors or other officials entrusted with enforcing provisions applicable to domestic work should be allowed to enter the
premises in which the work is carried out.

25. (1) Members should, in consultation with the most representative
organizations of employers and workers and, where they exist, with
organizations representative of domestic workers and those representative of employers of domestic workers, establish policies and
programmes, so as to:

(a) encourage the continuing development of the competencies and
qualifications of domestic workers, including literacy training as

appropriate, in order to enhance their professional development and employment opportunities;

(b) address the work-life balance needs of domestic workers; and

(c) ensure that the concerns and rights of domestic workers are taken into account in the context of more general efforts to reconcile work and family responsibilities.

(2) Members should, after consulting with the most representative organizations of employers and workers and, where they exist, with organizations representative of domestic workers and those representative of employers of domestic workers, develop appropriate indicators and measurement systems in order to strengthen the capacity of national statistical offices to effectively collect data necessary to support effective policymaking regarding domestic work.

26. (1) Members should consider cooperating with each other to ensure the effective application of the Domestic Workers Convention, 2011, and this Recommendation, to migrant domestic workers.

(2) Members should cooperate at bilateral, regional and global levels for the purpose of enhancing the protection of domestic workers, especially in matters concerning the prevention of forced labour and trafficking in persons, the access to social security, the monitoring of the activities of private employment agencies recruiting persons to work as domestic workers in another country, the dissemination of good practices and the collection of statistics on domestic work.

(3) Members should take appropriate steps to assist one another in giving effect to the provisions of the Convention through enhanced international cooperation or assistance, or both, including support for social and economic development, poverty eradication programmes and universal education.

(4) In the context of diplomatic immunity, Members should consider:

(a) adopting policies and codes of conduct for diplomatic personnel aimed at preventing violations of domestic workers' rights; and

(b) cooperating with each other at bilateral, regional and multilateral levels to address and prevent abusive practices towards domestic workers.

APPENDIX 3

International Standard-Setting Timeline

DATE	STAGE	ACTION
March 2008	301st session of the ILO Governing Body	Put standard setting on decent work for domestic workers on the ILO's conference agenda
March 2008– April 2009	*Law and Practice Report* including questionnaire *(Report IV(1)* or White Report)	Established the case for standard setting and proposed the first draft—in the form of questions to the ILO's member states—of the core elements that would be used in the Decent Work Convention and the Decent Work Recommendation
June 2009– March 2010	Report IV(2) or Yellow Report;	Recorded ILO member states' responses to the questionnaire, which became the basis of the first discussions at the 99th Session of the International Labour Conference
June 2010	99th Session of the International Labour Conference (ILC)	First round of committee discussions on decent work for domestic workers. The discussions are recorded in ILC, Provisional Record 12.
August 2010	Conclusions—Report IV(1) or Brown Report	On the basis of the conclusions of the 99th Session of the ILC, the draft text of the Convention and Recommendation were prepared for discussion at the 100th Session
June 2011	100th Session of the International Labour Conference, Report of the Conference Committee	Second round of committee discussions on decent work for domestic workers. The discussions are recorded in International Labour Conference, Provisional Record 15.
June 16, 2011	Domestic Work Convention "C189" and Domestic Work Recommendation "R201"	100th General Session of the International Labour Conference formally adopted the new Convention and Recommendation. June 16th has become International Domestic Workers' Day.
September 5, 2013	Domestic Work Convention enters into force	Two ratifications were required for the Domestic Workers Convention to enter into force one year after. They were received from Uruguay (June 14, 2012) and the Philippines (September 5, 2012).
January 31, 2018	25th ratification of Convention No. 189, by Brazil	Convention No. 189 enters into force in Brazil on January 31, 2019

Note: This timeline condenses and presents some of the constitutionally mandated steps to focus on key moments in and beyond the process of creating International Labour Organization (ILO), "C189" and "R201." The *Law and Practice Report* is International Labour Conference, "Report IV(1)."

APPENDIX 4

The Foregrounded Ethnographies

To contextualize the household workplace, I rely on a selection of seven of the leading, contemporary ethnographies. While many excellent ethnographies have emerged since the International Labour Organization completed its standard setting, I focus below on a selection of those that I relied upon before the adoption of the Domestic Workers Convention and the Domestic Workers Recommendation in 2011. I also vary the regional focus. In particular, although a great deal of excellent work has been done on domestic workers in the United States, I wanted to show the global nature of the regulatory phenomena and to focus on domestic workers from a range of regions worldwide. While studies of domestic worker migration abound, I emphasize a selection of those studies that offer special insight into the employment relationship. Some of the authors of the foregrounded ethnographies follow in the tradition of earlier leading works that have propelled generations of analysis of domestic work.[1] Many of these influential early ethnographic studies similarly informed my international work, so it should not be surprising that references to them appear throughout this book.[2]

1. Judith Rollins, *Between Women: Domestics and Their Employers*, 1985

The earliest of the foregrounded studies, and among the most cited works on the contemporary domestic work relationship, Rollins's ethnography is set in the Boston, Massachusetts, area (including suburbs) in the early 1980s and is based on in-depth interviews with twenty employers and twenty domestic workers.[3] Uniquely, it is also based on Rollins's own experience. She placed advertisements in newspapers and performed domestic work for ten employers—who varied by location, ethnicity, and income level—in September 1981 and from early November to mid-May 1982. She did not disclose that she was a researcher but led her employers to believe that she was a full-time domestic worker. Rollins explains her decision "to submerge myself in the situation before even designing the research in order to sensitize myself to the experience of domestic work and of relating to a female employer . . . especially [to increase] my appreciation for the variety of types of relationships created by different personalities and the hints of salient issues of the interpersonal dynamics between mistresses and employees."[4]

2. Mary Romero, *Maid in the U.S.A.*, 1992

Romero's first chapter discusses the "intersection of biography and history" and includes a forthright discussion of the author's intellectual journey as someone who grew up knowing many women who cleaned other people's houses.[5] Romero interviewed twenty-five live-out Chicana household workers employed mainly in cleaning services in the greater Denver, Colorado, area. She situates the structure of domestic work within an analysis of capitalism. She captures relational dynamics and in particular considers that the "struggle over the work process is aimed at developing new interactions with employers that eliminate aspects of hierarchy along the lines of gender, race, and class."[6]

3. Christine Chin, *In Service and Servitude: Foreign Female Domestic Workers and the Malaysian Modernity Project*, 1998

In her critical interdisciplinary approach to domestic work as part of Malaysia's development strategy, Chin devotes a chapter of her book to the "infrapolitics" of domestic service.[7] Chin conducted fieldwork in 1994 in both rural and urban settings and conversed with domestic workers at a number of locations in Kuala Lumpur. She interviewed Filipina and Indonesian domestic workers and observed some middle-class Malaysian employers. She also interviewed Malaysians (notably of Chinese descent) who had either worked as domestics or hired them. Chin also interacted with employment agencies, apparently posing as a potential domestic employer to obtain information.

4. Jacqueline Andall, *Gender, Migration and Domestic Servitude: The Politics of Black Women in Italy*, 2000

In 1992 and 1993, Andall interviewed twenty-nine migrant domestic workers living in Rome and hailing from Cape Verde, Ethiopia, Eritrea, or Somalia.[8] Ten additional interviews were undertaken of Cape Verdean women in Rotterdam, the Netherlands, in 1996. Those women had all migrated to Italy in the period between 1969 and 1979 and had subsequently left Italy. Andall also interviewed a broad range of key informants, including members of a national organization for domestic workers that has been active throughout the period since World War II and that has negotiated a collective agreement for domestic workers.

5. Pierette Hondagneu-Sotelo, *Doméstica: Immigrant Workers Cleaning and Caring in the Shadows of Affluence*, 2000

Hondagneu-Sotelo conducted a study of Latina immigrant domestic workers and their employers, examining her subjects' lives in Los Angeles and its suburbs in the mid- to late 1990s.[9] Specifically, she interviewed thirty-seven employers and twenty-three employees, along with three specialized legal attorneys and five domestic employment agency employees. The study is complemented by nonrandom survey data of 153 domestic workers who responded to a questionnaire administered in public places. The questionnaire covered basic demographic information (country of origin, years in the United States, marital status, and number of children and where they reside), previous work experiences, and information on wages and hours. She also drew on the available census data.

6. Daiva K. Stasiulis and Abigail B. Bakan, *Negotiating Citizenship: Migrant Women in Canada and the Global System*, 2005

The role of a major postindustrial state in labor migration is at the center of Stasiulis and Bakan's analysis.[10] The authors offer a small-scale study of both West Indian and Filipina domestic workers in Toronto, with a complementary study of immigrant nurses in Toronto from the same regions and countries, in the mid-1990s. While their analytical focus on two occupational sites for care is the negotiation of citizenship, notably rights, they interrogate the "transnational character of migrants' lives—their labor strategies, family-households, political practices, sense of community and diasporic consciousness" in Canada.[11] Much of the discussion of the negotiated citizenship occurs in the context of the pursuit of rights in courts.

7. Shireen Ally, *From Servants to Workers: South African Domestic Workers and the Democratic State*, 2009

Ally conducted her study in Johannesburg from February 2004 to August 2005.[12] She collected the life histories of approximately sixty domestic workers whom she interviewed and followed for over a year. Ally sought to attain an adequate sampling of African and Coloured women who worked in private households, excluding the mainly male gardeners and chauffeurs. Although her focus on workers and the state meant that she did not include employers as part of the research design, she did take care to include workers whose employers reflected contemporary South Africa—they were African, Coloured, Indian, and white and from the working, middle, and upper classes. The workers in her study had live-in and live-out arrangements and performed full- and part-time work.

General Reflections

I wish to emphasize that none of these scholars ignores her own identity. Each is critically self-conscious about her social location, which is an integral part of her ethnographic analysis. My engagement with their work is part of the tradition of embodied knowledge. I engage with and in some cases argue against the "narratives of analysis" of the relationship between the law of the household workplace, collective action, and state-based law proffered by the scholars who carried out the ethnographies.[13] Through this process, I study the domestic work relationship to understand its law.

Scholarship on the regulation of domestic work is proliferating. We are fortunate in this field to have a solid body of ethnographic work that has already been undertaken. The focus on ethnographies reflects my hope to encourage legal scholarship on the domestic work relationship to take the painstakingly constructed body of qualitative empirical analysis not as background, or worse, as irrelevant or anecdotal, but rather as vital to understanding the governance of the relationships as work, and to begin to sense the law that applies to the relationships. It is at least complementary to the single court decision analyzed at great length for its legal principle or to extensive exegesis of a statute, and it allows us to understand what resides at least in the shadow of state law, if not beyond it.

Focusing on the ethnographies may make it more difficult, too, to sidestep their careful attention to intersecting identities by conveniently reframing domestic work to focus on gender alone. Each of the ethnographic studies discussed above engages with racialization and migration as it intersects with gender and class. Each does so in a way that implicates state law and policies that frame domestic workers' working lives and their exercises of citizenship.

Finally, it should be underscored that the authors of the ethnographies quite systematically engage with each other's work, across country, region, and time—drawing parallels or underscoring particularities and distinctions. Their careful work has consolidated our knowledge of the domestic work relationship. The scholarship exemplifies a perspective articulated by Evelyn Nakano Glenn in her study of three generations of Japanese American women in domestic service: that the similarities in the structure of the domestic work relationship is of overriding importance in any assessment of labor systems in liberal market economies.[14] Sociohistorical variables across space, time, and circumstance become naturalized—fixed, unmovable, and transhistorical.[15] Glenn refers to the structural features that, alongside the ideologically enforced binary of the private home and the public workplace, result in the burden of care being differentially distributed along identity lines. I would argue that the identity-based features intersect with a critical structuring feature identified by Glenn, the history of unfreedom that surrounds paid care in the household by others. Indeed, all of the authors of the ethnographies discussed here point to the extent to this unfreedom: the association of care work with slavery and confinement in the United States, apartheid in South Africa, indentured and other forms of forced labor in former colonies, and disadvantaged castes and other forms of exclusion in different societies at different times—all become part of the unseen but prevalent pattern. The critical point is that the pattern of othered women taking care of wealthier households is so prevalent in domestic work that these features become expected and commonplace, and the work is viewed as these women's natural place. In the process, it renders domestic workers invisible.

Glossary of Terms

B

Blackstone's *Commentaries on the Laws of England*

Influential work on the development of English law, drafted by Sir William Blackstone in the eighteenth century. It was the first methodical treatise on the common law.

Bretton Woods Institutions

The International Bank for Reconstruction and Development (World Bank) and the International Monetary Fund, which were formed as a result of the Bretton Woods Conference of 1944—a meeting of the Allied nations after World War II to decide on postwar financial regulations.

C

Caisse Nationale de Prévoyance Sociale (CNPS)

Translated into English as the National Social Security Fund, this organization manages Côte D'Ivoire's social security program, which includes the provision of retirement pensions and maternity protection to private-sector employees.

Collective autonomy

The process involved when workers' and employers' organizations regulate their own interactions, most commonly expressed through the freedom of association and the right to bargain collectively.

Commission for Conciliation, Mediation and Arbitration

A South African dispute resolution body established under the Labour Relations Act of 1995, which mediates and arbitrates labor disputes.

Conseil des Prud'hommes

France's first-level labor court, which hears disputes related to the execution or dissolution of private work contracts between employees and employers.

Convention

A legally binding international treaty adopted by an international organization that may be ratified by Members. See also *recommendation*.

Council of Europe

A regional human rights organization founded in 1949, comprising forty-seven European member states, twenty-eight of whom are currently members of the separate and distinct political and economic European Union. The European Court of Human Rights is part of the Council of Europe and rules on individual or state allegations of violations of the civil and political rights set out in the European Convention on Human Rights.

F

Fact-Finding and Conciliation Commission on Freedom of Association

The International Labour Organization's (ILO's) Fact-Finding and Conciliation Commission on Freedom of Association was established in 1950 and consists of independent experts. Its mandate is to examine any allegation of infringements of trade union rights referred to it by the Governing Body of the ILO.

G

Global Labour Institute

A network of trade unions and other civil society organizations based in Geneva.

Gulf Cooperation Council (GCC)

The Gulf Cooperation Council (GCC) is a political and economic alliance between Bahrain, Kuwait, Oman, Saudi Arabia, the United Arab Emirates, and Qatar.

I

International Domestic Workers' Federation (IDWF)

Initially the International Domestic Workers' Network (IDWN) was established in 2006 to push for standard setting on decent work for domestic workers. In 2013 in Montevideo the Federation was formed. As of April 2018, the IDWF had 67 affiliates from 54 countries, representing 600,000 domestic workers organized in trade unions, other associations and networks, and cooperatives.

International Labour Organization (ILO)

Established in 1919, the International Labour Organization is the only United Nations agency to bring together representatives of governments, employers, and workers from 187 member states to set labor standards, develop policies, and devise programs promoting decent work. Its permanent secretariat is called the International Labour Office. It has a governing body and holds an annual International Labour Conference.

International Union of Food, Agricultural, Hotel, Restaurant, Catering, Tobacco and Allied Workers' Association (IUF)

The International Union of Food, Agricultural, Hotel, Restaurant, Catering, Tobacco and Allied Workers' Association is an international federation of trade unions representing workers employed in agriculture and plantations; the preparation and manufacture of food and beverages; hotels, restaurants, and catering services; and all stages of tobacco processing.

L

Latin American and Caribbean Confederation of Household Workers (CONLACTRAHO)

A confederation of twenty-three Latin American and Caribbean domestic workers' unions and associates founded in 1988.

League of Nations

An intergovernmental organization founded in 1919 with the goal of maintaining world peace through collective security, disarmament, negotiation, and arbitration. It was replaced by the United Nations.

N

National Domestic Workers Alliance

A US-based organization made up of over sixty affiliates, which mobilizes, defends, and promotes the rights of domestic workers.

P

Philippines Overseas Employment Administration (POEA)

The government body that oversees and regulates the emigration of foreign domestic workers from the Philippines.

R

Recommendation

A nonbinding guideline issued by an international body. See also *convention*.

S

Sectoral Determination

The regulation that governs the setting of minimum wages, conditions of employment, and other labor issues in South Africa.

Social Dialogue

The process through which trade unions and employer organizations interact and negotiate, often in collaboration with governments, to influence work-related issues, labor market policies, social protection, and a range of economic and fiscal policies. The practices are institutionalized at the ILO and have been widespread in some European countries. The ILO has fostered social dialogue in various regions of the world.

Standard Employment Contracts (SEC)

In Switzerland, acts passed by the Federal Council or State (cantonal) Council, which regulate the conditions of employment in a given occupation.

Standard Employment Relationship (SER)

A relationship between employee and employer that includes full-time, long-term employment in a physical location.

Statute of Artificers

An act passed in the United Kingdom in 1563 that regulated workers through the imposition of maximum wages, restrictions on workers' freedom of movement, and other measures.

Swiss Code of Obligations

The portion of the Swiss civil code that regulates contract law and corporations.

T

Tripartite

Shared by or involving three parties. The International Labour Organization is organized on a tripartite basis, including representatives of governments, employers, and workers in its constitutional and organizational structure.

V

Vienna Convention on Diplomatic Relations

An international treaty passed in 1961 that created a framework for diplomatic relations between independent states.

W

Westphalian sovereignty

Also referred to as state sovereignty, the principle that each nation-state has sovereignty over its territory and domestic affairs, to the exclusion of all external powers. Westphalian sovereignty also posits that each state (no matter how large or small) is equal in international law. The term originated in the series of treaties known collectively as the Peace of Westphalia, which ended Europe's Thirty Years' War in 1648.

WIEGO

The Women in Informal Employment: Globalizing and Organizing network, established in 1997, is a collective of membership-based organizations (such as trade unions, cooperatives, and workers' associations) that represent informal workers; researchers and statisticians who carry out research, data collection, or data analysis on the informal economy; and practitioners from development agencies who provide services to or shape policies toward the informal workforce.

Notes

Introduction

1. The ILO's Governing Body has fifty-six titular members (twenty-eight representing governments, fourteen representing employers, and fourteen representing workers) and sixty-six deputy members (twenty-eight representing governments, nineteen representing employers, and nineteen representing workers). Ten of the titular government seats are held permanently by representatives of states of "chief industrial importance" (Brazil, China, France, Germany, India, Italy, Japan, the Russian Federation, the United Kingdom, and the United States). Constitution of the International Labour Organization, 15 U.N.T.S. 35, 1919, Article 7; International Labour Organization, *Composition of the Governing Body of the International Labour Office* (as elected on June 12, 2017), accessed September 5, 2017, https://www.ilo.org/wcmsp5/groups/public/@ed_norm/@relconf/@reloff/documents/meetingdocument/wcms_083528.pdf. Representatives to fill the other eighteen seats are elected every three years by the International Labour Conference, most recently in June 2017. Employer and worker members are elected in their individual capacities. The Governing Body meets three times per year, in March, June, and November. It decides ILO policy, sets the agenda for the International Labour Conference, drafts the Programme and Budget of the Organization to be submitted at the conference, and elects the Director-General. See, generally, International Labour Organization, *Composition of the Governing Body*, GB.05 (2017–2020) Rev.5.

2. See, for example, Silvera, *Silenced*; Romero, *Maid in the U.S.A*; Thornton Dill, *Across the Boundaries of Race and Class*; Hondagneu-Sotelo, *Doméstica*.

3. See, for example, Cock, *Maids and Madams*; Chaney and Castro, *Muchachas No More*.

4. See, for example, Enloe, *Bananas, Beaches and Bases*; Anderson, *Britain's Secret Slaves*; Giles and Arat-Koç, *Maid in the Market*; Bakan and Stasiulis, *Not One of the Family*; Chang, *Disposable Domestics*.

5. Elayoubi, *Prière à la Lune*.

6. Elayoubi, 67, 83 (quote translated by the author).

7. International Labour Office, *Report IV(1): Decent Work for Domestic Workers* (hereafter referred to as *Law and Practice Report*).

8. International Labour Office, "Who Are Domestic Workers?," accessed August 15, 2018, https://www.ilo.org/global/topics/domestic-workers/WCMS_209773/lang—en/index.htm. In International Labour Office, *Domestic Workers across the World*, the estimate was "at least 52.6 million men and women across the world in 2010" (19). The ILO has had to work through disagreements about how domestic work is counted. See, for example, Schwenken and Heimeshoff, *Domestic Workers Count*.

9. See, e.g., Magnus, "The Social, Economic, and Legal Conditions of Domestic Servants: I." Magnus discusses early immigration schemes in Europe.

10. International Labour Office, "Who Are Domestic Workers?"; United Nations Development Programme, *Human Development Report 2009*; United Nations Department of Economic and Social Affairs, "International Migrants by Age." So far, the ILO has offered the following caveat: "Due to data limitations, it is not possible to give a reliable estimate of the share of migrants among domestic workers, but as the examples cited in this chapter show, it can be substantial." International Labour Office, *Domestic Workers across the World*, 24.

11. International Labour Office, *Law and Practice Report*. It is crucial to note that some domestic workers are men (often from racial or ethnic minority groups). See, for example, McGregor, "'Joining the BBC.'"

12. Parreñas, *Children of Global Migration*, 13–14.

13. Rodriguez, *Migrants for Export*, xvii.

14. World Bank, *Migration and Remittances*, 1–2, 18.

15. Pete Pattisson, "Beirut Death of Nepalese Migrant Worker Lila," *Guardian*, January 30, 2012, https://www.theguardian.com/news/video/2012/jan/30/beirut-death-nepalese-migrant-video.

16. An early example is Enloe, *Bananas, Beaches and Bases*. Various accounts are discussed in detail in chapter 3.

17. Poo, *Age of Dignity*, 84.

18. See Demaret, "Decent Work for Domestic Workers." See also Trebilcock, "Using Development Approaches to Address the Challenge of the Informal Economy for Labour Law."

19. Constitution of the International Labour Organization, 15 U.N.T.S. 35, 1919. Annex: Declaration concerning the aims and purposes of the International Labour Organization (Declaration of Philadelphia).

20. There are 189 numbered conventions. The Maritime Labour Convention, adopted in 2006, is not numbered. The ILO has also adopted a number of protocols. See Maupain, *The Future of the International Labour Organization in the Global Economy*.

21. Rodríguez-Piñero, *Indigenous Peoples, Postcolonialism, and International Law*. See also W. Simpson, "Standard-Setting and Supervision."

22. See Gallin, "The ILO Home Work Convention." As of September 5, 2018, the Home Work Convention had been ratified by only ten ILO members, despite strong governmental support for its adoption.

23. Doumbia-Henry, "The Consolidated Maritime Labour Convention." The ILO estimates the number of seafarers worldwide at 1.2 million ("Milestone Ratifications of Seafarers' Labour Rights Charter"). According to the International Maritime Organization, "the worldwide supply of seafarers in 2010 was estimated to be 624,000 officers and 747,000 ratings" ("'Go to Sea!'"). The International Transport Workers Federation estimates that only 2 percent of seafarers are women ("Women Seafarers").

24. See Doumbia-Henry, "The Consolidated Maritime Labour Convention."

25. International Labour Office, *Decent Work*.

26. While some of these views could be mirrored in opening statements of the ILO's Committee on Domestic Workers in 2010, it was remarkable to see the extent to which positions shifted over the two-year discussions. See chapters 1 and 5.

27. Nadasen, *Household Workers Unite*, 56. Nadasen's account serves as an important corrective to the paradoxical reference to domestic workers in Ralph Ellison's classic pre–civil rights era novel, *Invisible Man*, as little more than the bearers of trivial gossip about their employers.

28. For example, Alana Erickson Coble wrote: ("No matter how desperate, domestics continued to reject live-in work. Independence was more important to them" (*Cleaning Up*, 56). And Shireen Ally noted that the shift to live-out work constituted a way to claim "incredibly important autonomy from employers and the capacity to maintain an independent familial life" (*From Servants to Workers*, 52).

29. See International Labour Office, *Law and Practice Report*, para. 265.

30. B. Webb and S. Webb, *Industrial Democracy*, 676.

31. Nadasen, *Household Workers United*, 108.

32. See, for example, the discussion of Ally's work in chapter 3.

33. Nadasen, *Household Workers United*, 108–9.

34. Nadasen, 108 and 118–19. The domestic worker organizers subsequently changed the name of their organization to the National Domestic Workers of America, dropping the word "union." Eileen Boris and Jennifer Klein analyze the parallel and overlapping discussion of home care worker organizing (*Caring for America*, 124).

35. See Nadasen, *Household Workers United*. See also Briones, *Empowering Migrant Women*.

36. See, for example, the close analysis of the scheme in place in Belgium by Defourny and colleagues ("Does the Mission of Providers Matter on a Quasi-Market?" and "Les titres-services").

37. The specific example is discussed in Van Walsum, "Regulating Migrant Domestic Work in the Netherlands." See also Stasiulis and Bakan, *Negotiating Citizenship*, 75. The persisting racialized hierarchy is discussed in chapters 3 and 6.

38. Pape, "ILO Convention C189," 194.

39. ILC, 20th Sess., Record of Proceedings. A list of "Resolutions adopted at the International Labour Conference (1919–2015)" is available at https://www.ilo.org/global/about-the-ilo/how-the-ilo-works/departments-and-offices/jur/legal-instruments/WCMS_428590/lang—en/index.htm (accessed 30 Sept. 2018). For a discussion of ILO's attempts over time to regulate domestic work, see A. D'Souza, "Moving towards Decent Work for Domestic Workers," 42.

40. In its first report on the application of the convention, Belgium declared that it had excluded domestic workers. See International Labour Office, *Law and Practice Report*, 22, table II.2.

41. ILC, 27th Sess., *Record of Proceedings*.

42. ILO, *Resolution Concerning the Conditions of Employment of Domestic Workers*, June 30, 1948, ILC, 31st Sess., *Record of Proceedings*, p. 464 and Appendix VII and XVI.

43. ILC, *Resolution Concerning the Conditions of Employment of Domestic Workers*, 49th Sess., 23 July 1965, Official Bulletin (Geneva), Vol. XLVIII, No. 3, July 1965, Supplement 1, 20–21..

44. International Labour Office, "The Employment and Conditions of Domestic Workers in Private Households." In addition, Erna Magnus analyzed results from surveys in Great Britain, Germany, Switzerland, the United States, and Sweden ("The Social, Economic, and Legal Conditions of Domestic Servants: I" and "The Social,

Economic, and Legal Conditions of Domestic Servants: II"). See also Elliott, "The Status of Domestic Work in the United Kingdom"; Miller, "Household Employment in the United States."

45. See Human Rights Watch, "I Won't Be a Doctor,'" "'It's a Men's Club,'" "'We Can't Refuse to Pick Cotton,'" and "'Working Like a Robot.'"

46. Blackett, "Making Domestic Work Visible," 29. See also A. D'Souza, "Moving towards Decent Work for Domestic Workers," 58.

47. International Labour Office, *Decent Work*.

48. Pape, "ILO Convention C189," 194.

49. Governing Body of the ILO, "Decisions of the 301st Session," item 2.

50. Blackett, "Introductory Note," 250.

51. Darian-Smith, *Laws and Societies in Global Contexts*, 317.

52. D. Roberts, *Killing the Black Body*. Arlie Hochschild did not initially include domestic work in her pathbreaking study of emotional labor, *The Managed Heart*.

53. Shaffer and Halliday, *Transnational Legal Orders*, 11.

54. Of course, this is the same tradition that that the Rev. Dr. Martin Luther King Jr. embodied in the civil rights movement and the poor people's campaign, and that is at the heart of the Black radical tradition. See King, *Where Do We Go from Here?*; Harding, *There Is a River*; Lawrence, "The Word and the River."

55. Crenshaw, "Demarginalizing the Intersection of Race and Sex" and "Mapping the Margins."

56. Ehrlich, *Fundamental Principles of the Sociology of Law*, 498.

57. Matsuda, *When the First Quail Calls*, 7; de Sousa Santos, *Toward a New Legal Common Sense*, 417–38.

58. Shaffer and Halliday, *Transnational Legal Orders*, 11.

59. Guha-Khasnobis, Kanbur, and Ostrom, "Beyond Formality and Informality," 13.

60. S. Hall, *The Fateful Triangle*, 33.

61. Blackett, "Introduction."

62. There are parallel inspirations in framings of Indigenous sovereignty. See L. Simpson, *Dancing on Our Turtle's Back*, 40.

63. C. L. R. James, *Every Cook Can Govern*, in *A New Notion*. It is worth acknowledging, however, that in his discussion of ancient Greek democracy and equality James seems to minimize the democratic challenge of the initial small number of household slaves, focusing only somewhat more on the later challenge of freeing labor of the growth of slavery in commerce and industry, which he still considered to be quite limited (141).

64. Barmes, *Bullying and Behavioural Conflict*, 266.

65. International Labour Office, *Law and Practice Report*, para. 25.

66. For example, Darcy du Toit argues that "all workers may need an alternative model of regulation" ("Constructing an Integrated Model," 350).

67. See Blackett, "Review of *Exploited, Undervalued—and Essential*," 803.

1. Establishing a Transgressive Transnational Legal Order

Epigraph: Vanessa Williams, "'Unbought and Unbossed': Shirley Chisholm's Feminist Mantra Is Still Relevant 50 Years Later," *Washington Post*, January 26, 2018.

1. I discuss this role elsewhere (Blackett, "Introduction," note 32):

> A number of McGill students and recent graduates supported me as research assistants for the ILO's Decent Work for Domestic Workers. I take this opportunity to acknowledge in particular Tatiana Gomez, LL.B. and B.C.L., 2008, who provided research assistance throughout the short, intense drafting period from summer to fall 2008. I also thank Maude Choko, currently a D.C.L. candidate at McGill, and undergraduate law students Alika Hendricks, LL.B. and B.C.L., 2009, and Mae Nam, current LL.B. and B.C.L. candidate, for targeted research assistance. Colleagues at the ILO provided crucial back-stopping support, notably by identifying some of the legislative sources and statistical data, obtaining memoranda of understanding, and information on the use by member states of flexibility clauses, compiling most of the charts and tables, and writing the chapter on "the ILO and other international initiatives" (chapter IX). One ILO official subsequently published his survey of memoranda of understanding. See Naj Ghosheh, "Protecting the Housekeeper: Legal Agreements Applicable to International Migrant Domestic Workers" (2009) 25 *International Journal of Comparative Labour Law and Industrial Relations* 301.

2. International Labour Office, *Report IV(1): Decent Work for Domestic Workers* (hereafter referred to as *Law and Practice Report*), para. 56, citing an opinion from the Office of the Legal Adviser dated July 29, 2002. The basic idea was that the ILO, which has adopted hundreds of international labor standards since 1919, did not exclude categories of workers from the scope of its standards unless it specifically said that it did. When I looked at the actual exclusions reported to the ILO, I realized they were not as significant or widespread as some people had thought. At least in theory, domestic workers were considered to be workers like any other in terms of most international labor standards. And in ILO practice, the supervisory bodies had repeatedly interpreted international labor standards to include domestic workers.

3. Freedom of Association and Protection of the Right to Organise Convention, 1948 (No. 87); Right to Organise and Collective Bargaining Convention, 1949 (No. 98); Equal Remuneration Convention, 1951 (No. 100); Discrimination (Employment and Occupation) Convention, 1958 (No. 111); Forced Labour Convention, 1930 (No. 29); Abolition of Forced Labour Convention, 1957 (No. 105); Minimum Age Convention, 1973 (No. 138); Worst Forms of Child Labour Convention, 1999 (No. 182).

4. International Labour Office, *Law and Practice Report*, chapter 2.

5. International Labour Office, *Law and Practice Report*, paras. 55–81.

6. International Labour Office, *Law and Practice Report*, para. 82.

7. International Labour Office, *Law and Practice Report*, paras. 45–47. See also Blackett, "Promoting Domestic Workers' Human Dignity," 247.

8. P. Smith, "Work Like Any Other"; Mundlak and Shamir, "Bringing Together or Drifting Apart?"; Einat Albin, "From 'Domestic Servant' to 'Domestic Worker.'"

9. International Labour Office, *Law and Practice Report*, para. 337.

10. See Tuck and Yang, "Decolonization Is Not a Metaphor," 6.

11. The historical approach is familiar to activists and advocates who have fought for comparable worth, or equal pay for work of equal value.

12. International Labour Office, *Law and Practice Report*, para. 40.

13. International Labour Office, *Law and Practice Report*, para. 325. I also proposed that a convention be modeled after the Maritime Labour Convention, 2006 (International Labour Organization, "Maritime Labour Convention"). The new convention would be ratifiable like other conventions, but ILO member states would be bound in the traditional international law sense only to parts of it, while other parts would provide recommendations or guidance. The proposal was offered to enable the ILO to retain an ongoing role in tackling the law of the household workplace with established targets and close guidance flowing through implementation of the proposed convention. I hoped it would enable the ILO to guide innovation across governance levels—locally, nationally, bilaterally, and regionally. However, the questionnaire was ultimately drafted as two separate instruments, which set the wheels in motion for a more conventional pair of instruments. There was little room for discussion during the conference committees of the prospect of rebuilding a combined instrument, once the responses to the questionnaire came in and the draft conclusions were prepared.

14. Fish, *Domestic Workers of the World Unite!*, 93. Unfortunately, Fish's attribution of the writing of the *Law and Practice Report* inaccurately attributes the writing to ILO director Manuela Tomei, whose background is in sociology and languages, and suggests that the ILO legal official Martin Oelz (who was not even hired into the relevant unit when I was writing the report) contributed to its writing.

15. Some might call the ILO corporatist, because it reflects an older vision of the relationship that business and labor should play in setting government policy.

16. See Murray, *Transnational Labour Regulation*.

17. The organization and its executive director, Ai-jen Poo, have come to represent a vision of care work imbued with a deep humanity. The slogan "lead with love" affirms the dignity of domestic workers in their work that is essential to us all. See Blackett, "Introduction."

18. International Labour Office, *Law and Practice Report*, paras. 48–52. The report provided a detailed comparative analysis of the laws of seventy-two ILO member states, whose inhabitants made up 80 percent of the world's population. It offered a theoretical framework for understanding how domestic work can be regulated and made a case to the ILO's constituency—its tripartite deliberative community of governments, workers' representatives, and employers' representatives—in favor of moving forward on standard setting through a binding convention, supplemented by a nonbinding recommendation. The constituency responded to a detailed questionnaire in the report, on the basis of which the new international labor standards were negotiated.

19. International Labour Office, *Law and Practice Report*, 34 (Box III.2). See also Chuang, "The U.S. Au Pair Program."

20. ILC, 99th Sess., *Provisional Record 12*, para. 135.

21. ILC, 99th Sess., *Provisional Record 12*, para. 142.

22. International Labour Office, *Law and Practice Report*, para. 38.

23. Quoted in Nadasen, *Household Workers Unite*, 114.

24. See International Labour Office, *Law and Practice Report*, para. 245. See also Maria Luz Vega Ruiz, "L'administration et l'inspection du travail." The *Labour Inspection (Agriculture) Convention*, 1969 (ILO No. 129) specifically provides that when the worker's

and employer's home is also the workplace, it may be liable to inspection. The only qualification is consent of the operator of the undertaking or a special authorization issued by the competent authority.

25. International Labour Office, *Law and Practice Report*, para. 250.

26. *Ley Sobre Normas Para la Regulación del Trabajo Doméstico*, Act No. 18.065 (2006); *Law and Practice Report*, 74, Box VII.1.

27. ILC, 100th Sess., *Provisional Record 15*, para. 713.

28. ILC, 100th Sess., *Provisional Record 15*, paras. 716–17. Article 12 of the *Universal Declaration of Human Rights* states: "No one shall be subjected to arbitrary interference with his privacy, family, home or correspondence, nor to attacks upon his honour and reputation. Everyone has the right to the protection of the law against such interference or attacks."

29. Leary, "The Paradox of Workers' Rights," 26–27.

30. See, for example, Kolben, "Labor Rights as Human Rights?" See also Radha D'Souza, who argues from a Marxist tradition in *What's Wrong with Rights* that to inherit a rights-based system does not mean social movements must claim rights, rather than the real thing: social justice.

31. ILC, 100th Sess., *Provisional Record 15*, paras. 561–562.

32. International Labour Organization, "C189."

33. ILC, 99th Sess., *Provisional Record 12*, para. 553.

34. ILC, 99th Sess., *Provisional Record 12*, paras. 553–601, especially 583 and 587.

35. For an important early discussion of tripartism, tripartism plus, and social dialogue, see Trebilcock, *Towards Social Dialogue*. See also Fashoyin, "Tripartite Cooperation, Social Dialogue and National Development."

36. Pape, "ILO Convention C189."

37. Faina Milman Sivan discusses the selection process for representative organizations of workers and employers at the ILC ("Freedom of Association in Deliberative Spaces").

38. International Domestic Workers Federation, "Ratify C189." See also Bonner, "Domestic Workers around the World."

39. See, for example, Chaney and Castro, *Muchachas No More*.

40. Pape, "ILO Convention C189," 195.

41. International Labour Conference, "Standing Orders of the International Labour Conference," article 56, para. 9.

42. See paragraph 25.1 of the Domestic Workers Recommendation.

43. Quoted in ILC, 99th Sess., *Provisional Record 12*, para. 60.

44. ILC, 99th Session, *Provisional Record 19*, 39.

45. "Ne m'appelez pas: boy!," *Le Temps*, Geneva, June 11, 2011, https://www.letemps .ch/monde/ne-mappelez-boy.

46. ILC, 99th Sess., *Provisional Record 12*, paras. 12–14.

47. ILC, 99th Sess., *Provisional Record 12*, para. 15.

48. ILC, 99th Sess., *Provisional Record 12*, paras. 66, 89, 107. Several government representatives voted with the employers' group, including representatives of a number of Gulf States, India, Indonesia, Malaysia, New Zealand, and Panama. In the following session, the government representative of New Zealand apparently felt the need to take the floor to explain why that country's government supported the amendment

and pledged to work constructively toward a convention (see ILC, 99th Sess., *Provisional Record 12*, para. 110).

49. ILC, 99th Sess., *Provisional Record 12*, para. 875. The representative of the government of Namibia hoped "that one social partner did not have the desire to prevent the Committee from concluding its discussion of the proposed Recommendation." ILC, 99th Sess., *Provisional Record 12*, para. 882.

50. Quoted in ILC, 99th Sess., *Provisional Record 12*, para. 891. See also paras. 869–892.

51. ILC, 99th Session, *Provisional Record 19*, 41. See also pp. 35, 40–41.

52. Quoted in ILC, 100th Sess., *Provisional Record 15*, para. 1278.

53. The employers' group would also have amended the provisions allowing an ILO Member to denounce its ratification of the convention; see articles 22–24 of the Domestic Workers Convention. ILC, 100th Sess., *Provisional Record 15*, para. 767). According to article VIII of the Maritime Labour Convention: "This Convention shall come into force 12 months after the date on which there have been registered ratifications by at least 30 members with a total share in the world gross tonnage of ships of at least 33 per cent" (International Labour Organization, "Maritime Labour Convention"). And according to article IX, denunciation could take place after ten years (ILC, 100th Sess., *Provisional Record 15*, para. 767).

54. ILC, 100th Sess., *Provisional Record 15*, paras. 767–86.

2. What's Informality Got to Do with It?

1. *Standard Bank of SA Ltd. v. Caster Transport CC and Others* (2014), paras. 3–6. Further challenging the view that this decision was somehow pedantic or a matter of form rather than substance, (at para 7) the judge ordered that a written apology be made to each defendant as part of the remedy (ibid., para. 7).

2. Martin Chanock criticizes the tendency to see the system of apartheid in South Africa as exceptional (*The Making of South African Legal Culture 1902–1936*, 361).

3. On the universal basic income, see, e.g., Standing, *Basic Income*; Davala et al., *Basic Income*.

4. See Vosko, *Managing the Margins*. See also the discussion of working time in chapter 5.

5. Domestic workers typically earn around 40 percent of average wages in a given country, although the level relative to average wages varies between 63.8 percent in Honduras in 2006 and only 14.0 percent in Botswana in 2005–06 (International Labour Office, *Domestic Workers across the World*, 67).

6. Jean Comaroff and John Comaroff, *Theory from the South*, 3.

7. Comaroff and Comaroff, 1; R. D'Souza, "The 'Third World,'" 503. I have suggested elsewhere that "[t]o neglect regulatory 'reform' in Africa and the African diaspora might be to the broader peril of the discipline [of labor law]." Blackett, "Introduction: Labor Law and Development," 308.

8. International Labour Office, *Dilemma of the Informal Sector*, 3.

9. Trebilcock, "Using Development Approaches to Address the Challenge of the Informal Economy for Labour Law," 65.

10. F. Cooper, *Decolonization and African Society*, 2.

11. Cooper, 277 and 467.

12. Cooper, 290.

13. Mbembe, *On the Postcolony*, 25.

14. See, notably, Prebisch, "The Economic Development of Latin America and Its Principal Problems." See also Frank, *Capitalism and Underdevelopment in Latin America*.

15. See Chua, "The Privatization-Nationalization Cycle."

16. Abi-Saab, "The Newly Independent States and the Scope of Domestic Jurisdiction," 90.

17. Fakhri, *Sugar and the Making of International Trade Law*, 148.

18. Ruggie, "Taking Embedded Liberalism Global." More recent scholarship in the global North stresses that there is no uniform approach, but rather a variety of forms of capitalist development. See P. Hall and Soskice, *Varieties of Capitalism*. See also Fraser, "A Triple Movement?" Moreover, Fakhri insists that the embedded liberalism compromise emerged not only through the "negotiation of interests within the global North, but also by tensions between the North and South; also, it had more room for development concerns than originally described" (147).

19. Pahuja, *Decolonising International Law*, 81. This important work traces the transition in approaches to development through international law, focusing on the UN and Bretton Woods Bodies. My work on decolonizing labor law traces this transition through the work of the ILO.

20. However, Arthur Lewis took pains to characterize the subsistence economy and theorize its relationship to distribution, accumulation, and growth in both closed and open economies. In particular, Lewis recognized the transnational dimensions of his findings in the open economy, which included the immigration of unskilled workers:

> In the classical world all countries have surplus labour. In the neo-classical world labour is scarce in all countries. In the real world, however, countries which achieve labour scarcity continue to be surrounded by others which have abundant labour. Instead of concentrating on one country, and examining the expansion of its capitalist sector, we now have to see this country as part of the expanding capitalist sector of the world economy as a whole, and to enquire how the distribution of income inside the country and its rate of capital accumulation, are affected by the fact that there is abundant labour available elsewhere at a subsistence wage. ("Economic Development with Unlimited Supplies of Labour," 176)

21. Hart, "Informal Income Opportunities and Urban Employment in Ghana"; International Labour Office, *Employment, Incomes and Equality*, 5.

22. ILO, *Employment, Incomes and Equality*, 6.

23. ILO, 6.

24. Bangasser, "The ILO and the Informal Sector," 28.

25. Boris, *Home to Work*.

26. Kouadio, "Stratégies résidentielles d'une catégorie de citadins du bas de l'échelle de qualification."

27. See, for example, Calleman, "Domestic Service in a 'Land of Equality.'"

28. Indeed, a dominant figure in many francophone West African states affected by structural adjustment and a brutal overnight 50 percent currency devaluation was

the civil servant in the very formal economy who had not received a salary in months but continued to report for work in the morning, only to sell produce or engage in similar activities in the informal economy after the workday. The employee, in other words, is also an informal economy worker. This worker's salary and social supports followed not a Western paradigm of supporting only a nuclear family but played a much broader role that adjustment measures failed to anticipate. See Blackett, "Beyond Standard Setting," 464.

29. Chen, Vanek, and Carr, *Mainstreaming Informal Employment and Gender in Poverty Reduction*, 19.

30. See Chen, Vanek, and Carr. One important example of this work is the construction of global value chains—for example, in the production, transformation, and marketing of products based on shea butter from West Africa.

31. See LaHovary, "The Informal Economy and the ILO."

32. This includes paying attention to the Hernando de Soto–inspired extension of property rights to informal title and the fact that the structural, transnational dimensions of informality is left out. See de Soto, *The Mystery of Capital*. See also K. Meagher, "Cannibalizing the Informal Economy."

33. Trebilcock, "International Labour Standards and the Informal Economy," 590.

34. See Melissaris, "The More the Merrier?"

35. Radha D'Souza problematizes a pluralism that resembles the violence of the colonial enterprise of codifying customary law and its contemporary comparison in the relationship between the coexistence of suprastate economic constitutionalism and a persisting pluralism for others ("The 'Third World' and Socio-Legal Studies," 503).

36. Chanock, *The Making of South African Legal Culture 1902–1936*, 249–50; see also 271.

37. H. P. Glenn, "A Transnational Concept of Law," 840. Sally Falk Moore recognizes the "weight put on the association of law with the historical development of the state" and "the attribution of custom and customary law both to early European peoples and to colonial subjects" (*Law as Process*, 15). However much I am inclined to agree with her on giving terminological weight to the state, I find it is impossible to overlook the fact that she considers "complex societies" separately (which may also have displaced attention from the more capacious notion of social spheres), as a way to reflect conventional usage and the construction of the category (law) as "a category of our own culture" (*Law as Process*, 17). What the critical legal pluralist school represented by the work of Roderick Macdonald accomplishes, by dislodging the easy starting assumption about prior authority, is to question such divisions of humanity. See Kleinhans and Macdonald, "What Is a *Critical* Legal Pluralism?," 25.

38. Darian-Smith, *Laws and Societies in Global Contexts*, 12.

39. Pierre Verge and Guylaine Vallée, *Un droit du travail?*, 101. In its most expansive version, the law of the shop is understood through the notion of collective autonomy. Although the state has a duty to ensure the exercise of collective autonomy, that is neither the most important nor the single essential element of its realization and exercise. See Arthurs, "Labour Law without the State?"

40. Belley, "Georges Gurvitch."

41. James Atleson situates the power to manage as beyond contracts and rooted in older notions of property as giving status (*Values and Assumptions in American Labor Law*).

42. Ehrlich, *Fundamental Principles of the Sociology of Law*.

43. Interview with two domestic workers in Abidjan, Côte d'Ivoire, December 20, 2013. In accordance with university ethics requirements, the interviews with domestic workers were conducted in confidence, and the names of the workers are withheld accordingly.

44. Belley, "L'avenir du droit et des juristes," 520.

45. Zumbansen, "Transnational Legal Pluralism," 149. See also Rittich, "Formality and Informality in the Law of Work," 114.

46. De Sousa Santos, *Toward a New Legal Common Sense*.

47. Stuart Hall discusses discourse as an "overall view of human conduct as always meaningful" (*Fateful Triangle*, 31), and the meanings "organize and are inscribed within the practices and operations of relations of power between groups" (*Fateful Triangle*, 47).

48. Falk Moore defines semiautonomy as the ability to "generate rules and customs and symbols internally, but . . . it is also vulnerable to rules and decisions and other forces emanating from the larger world by which it is surrounded. The semi-autonomous social field has rule-making capacities, and the means to induce or coerce compliance; but it is simultaneously set in a larger social matrix which can, and does, affect and invade it, sometimes at the invitation of persons inside it, sometimes at its own instance" (*Law as Process*, 54–55).

49. Falk Moore, *Law as Process*, 6.

50. Falk Moore, 48.

51. Shireen Ally refers to this as a form of legislative statecraft (*From Servants to Workers*). *Everyday Transgressions* supports the implicit challenge to deferential characterizations of law in a particular context that leave out the deliberate dimensions of law making. See Webber, "Legal Pluralism and Human Agency."

52. Davies and Freedland, *Labour Legislation and Public Policy*, 664.

53. Rajagopal, *International Law from Below*, 258. Of course, de Sousa Santos remains deeply skeptical about what the modern state can retain, but he also builds a "sociology of emergence" that moves beyond critical discrediting to reconstructive possibilities (*Epistemologies of the South*, 164).

54. Belley, "L'avenir du droit et des juristes," 501.

55. Gunther Teubner's sophisticated theorization of pluralist transnational legal systems centers on the underevaluated character of the collision of regimes of norms, but it conceptualizes the fields as autonomous rather than semiautonomous. Teubner's notion of law as an autopoietic system anticipated the move beyond conflicts of state law in the classic sense of private international law to a different global collision between social sectors. In his analysis of the fragmentation of global law, Teubner does not turn to a replication of private international law methods or to a reductionist approach to political pluralism. Combining a reflexive method, in which processes of "norming" are applied to the norms themselves while eschewing aspirations of reaching a metalevel at which problems may be solved, his pluralist description of law is built instead on a framework that emphasizes simple normative compatibility rather than hierarchical unity of law, attention to legal irritants in law making, and a decentralized approach to the conflicts of laws. See Teubner, *Autopoietic Law*.

3. Subordination or Servitude in the Law of the Household Workplace

1. Fanon, *Black Skin, White Masks*, 111–12. See also Bhabha, "Remembering Fanon," S. Hall, *Fateful Triangle*, 80; Coulthard, *Red Skin, White Masks*; Butler, "Endangered/Endangering."

2. Elayoubi, *Prière à la Lune*, 73.

3. Elayoubi, 72–74.

4. Hooks, "Eating the other"; Razack, *Looking White People in the Eye*. Razack's focus is educational settings.

5. Hooks, "Eating the other," 28.

6. Bhabha adds that identification itself "is a place of splitting" through which Fanon captures the ambivalence associated with responding to the colonizer's call to identify as different, as one of us—a doctor, a teacher, a lawyer? In other words, *Black Skin, White Masks* is "not the Colonialist Self or the Colonized Other, but the disturbing distance in-between that constitutes the figure of colonial otherness—the White man's artifice inscribed on the black man's body." Bhabha, "Remembering Fanon," xxviii.

7. Hooks, 37.

8. Ally, *From Servants to Workers*, 1 and 2. Eve the maid is a character in the popular satirical South African comic strip *Madam and Eve*, created by Stephen Francis and Rico Schacherl. See G. Smith, "*Madam and Eve*." See also Blackett and Galani Tiemeni, "Regulatory Innovation," 204.

9. Quoted in Ally, *From Servants to Workers*, 4.

10. Piketty, *Capital in the Twenty-First Century*.

11. Elsewhere I discuss the housing challenge and its impact on hearings before the Commission for Conciliation, Mediation and Arbitration (Blackett, "Decolonizing Labour Law," 90).

12. Quoted in Ally, *From Servants to Workers*, 1.

13. S. Hall, *The Fateful Triangle*, 81.

14. The foregrounded ethnographies are from 1985–2009. They are discussed in Appendix 4.

15. I hasten to add that similar moves have been made in legal scholarship. Stewart Macaulay's ethnographic analysis of business contracts has been a widely cited example. His account is based on interviews with sixty-eight entrepreneurs and lawyers representing forty-three companies and six law firms, most in Wisconsin. He reminded legal academe that in the quintessential arena of contracting parties with relatively equal bargaining power, entrepreneurs conduct their affairs through informal negotiations, without much if any reference to contracts, the law, or the background legal rules and sanctions that might prevail. That does not mean that state law, usually in the form of private law norms, ceases to be a force. It is omnipresent, but in the shadows. Other widely accepted norms seemed to be in play, and it is noteworthy to contemplate in the contemporary context the role apparently played by trust. See Macaulay, "Non-Contractual Relations in Business," 62–63.

16. This is a point that I develop in the context of an attempt to unify labor law regionally in West and Central Africa. See Blackett, "The Paradox of OHADA's Transnational, Hard Law, Labour Harmonization Initiative," 243.

17. See Rockman, *Scraping By*. Joanne Pope Melish presents a continuum rather than a dichotomization of slavery and freedom (*Disowning Slavery*. Christopher Tomlins em-

phasizes, even as he underscores the legal distinctiveness of chattel slavery, the fact that "the variegated legal culture of work and labor that empirical research exposes does not correspond to consistent conceptual polarities of free and unfree" (*Freedom Bound*, 9).

18. I discuss this further in Blackett, "Emancipation in the Idea of Labour Law."

19. Atleson, *Values and Assumptions in American Labor Law*. See also Simon F. Deakin and Frank Wilkinson, *The Law of the Labour Market*.

20. Deakin and Wilkinson, *The Law of the Labour Market*, 74. See also Fudge and Tucker, *Labour before the Law*.

21. Deakin and Wilkinson, *The Law of the Labour Market*, 78–79.

22. See VanderVelde, "Labor Vision of the Thirteenth Amendment." For Bruno Veneziani, commenting on domestic workers as "pre-industrial remnants" in the evolution of the contract of employment, "the truth is that the attention of legislators was concentrated on the factory system, which had generated a new social stratification among workers. In the domestic sphere in the civil law countries the old location conduction had to be applied, although it was meaningful only in the case of higher servants who, linked by a tie of subordination, could 'render services to the person employing them, but were not at their service.' In Britain the judges were reluctant, even under the guise of contract, to interfere with the patriarchal authority of the master within his own household" (Veneziani, "The Evolution of the Contract of Employment," 47). While "location" prevented the creation of a relationship in perpetuity, it did entail lengthy leasing of personal service. Moreover, while location was considered to reflect "equality between commodity and price," the notion of subordination itself was "a characteristic only of the relationship of domestic servants to their masters" (Veneziani, 63). It was understood both by the eighteenth-century French jurist Robert-Joseph Pothier and by Sir William Blackstone to comprise an obligation by domestic or menial servants to serve at any time and to be continuously available.

23. Blackstone, *Commentaries*.

24. Blackstone, 453.

25. Blackstone, 357. See also Baylis, *The Rights, Duties and Relations of Domestic Servants*, 1.

26. Blackstone, *Commentaries*, 358.

27. Blackstone, 358, citing Todd v. Kerrick, 8 Exch. 151.

28. Blackstone, 363–64.

29. *Commentaries*, 423. Blackstone's affirmation that "a slave, the instant he lands in England, becomes a free man: that is the law will protect him in the enjoyment of his person and his property" (424) was influential in *Somerset v. Stewart* (1772) 98 ER 499.

30. See, for example, Cairns, "Blackstone in the Bayous."

31. See Patterson, *Slavery and Social Death*, 24–25.

32. VanderVelde, "The Labor Vision of the Thirteenth Amendment."

33. See Cairns, "Blackstone, an English Institutist," 318.

34. For a critique of the failure to allow for a demarcation between forced labor and slavery, see Patterson, "Trafficking, Gender and Slavery."

35. Steedman, *Master and Servant*, 147–148. For Steedman, the earlier family rhetoric was in decline in the late eighteenth century as the language of contract prevailed. Even the language of servitude was subsumed into contractual logic. Steedman, 148.

36. Steedman, *Labours Lost*, 21.

37. Steedman, 21.

38. Steedman, 21–22.

39. Thompson, *The Making of the English Working Class*.

40. Thompson, 27.

41. Steedman, *Labours Lost*, 105–28, and *Master and Servant*, 13. It is of some interest that Blackstone, in his commentaries, cites the case of "a free woman of colour," the Mark Clark case from Indiana, in which the Indiana Supreme Court ruled that although the woman was purchased for indenture for twenty years, she petitioned that she was held illegally as a slave and was able to establish that her servitude was involuntary and in violation of Indiana's 1816 Constitution so was discharged of it. 1 Blackf. 122 (Indiana) 1821; Blackstone, *Commentaries*, Vol. 1, 426.

42. Steedman, *Labours Lost*, 22.

43. Steedman, 59–61.

44. Pope Melish, *Disowning Slavery*, 238. See also Hay and Craven, Introduction, 23 ("Ultimately the racial distinction in slavery dissolved the divide between free and indentured white laborers: whites were free, blacks were slaves, and indentured laborers disappeared from America.")

45. Cedric Robinson offers a pivotal rethinking of how this starting point is framed (*Black Marxism*). Elsewhere, I expand upon this critique as it applies to labor law (Blackett, "Emancipation in the Idea of Labour Law").

46. Macaulay, "Non-Contractual Relations in Business."

47. Stasiulis and Bakan, *Negotiating Citizenship*. 29.

48. Chin, *In Service and Servitude*, 142.

49. Some came from as far as Madagascar, and "even Asians" were enslaved as domestic workers during that time period (Ally, *From Servants to Workers*, 24). See also Cock, *Maids and Madams*; Gaitskel, et al., "Class, Race and Gender."

50. Quoted in Ally, *From Servants to Workers*, 23. Ally notes the interaction between migrant patterns (notably, the movement of English settlers to South Africa in 1820) and the abolition of slavery. But most white immigrant women swiftly married and moved out of domestic work. Ally also notes the impact of sensationalized "white peril" scares alleging sexual assault of white mistresses by African "houseboys" (*From Servants to Workers* 32–33).

51. Despite their deliberate omission from the past provisions in the Natives (Urban Areas) Act of 1923, special amendments were subsequently adopted in 1930 and 1937 to extend those controls to the women. See Ally, *From Servants to Workers*, 34.

52. Ally, 31 and 34–35. Intermediaries like church-run hostels were encouraged in the South African Native Affairs Commission Report to serve as state conduits that led African women into domestic work.

53. Ally, 38.

54. Ally, 3.

55. Chin, *In Service and Servitude*, 84.

56. Chin, 89.

57. Andall, *Gender, Migration and Domestic Service*. See also Veneziani, "The Evolution of the Contract of Employment," 46 (noting that the Italian Civil Code of 1865 "was criticized because the [domestic work] relationship appeared to be left to local customs and the conscience of the head of the household.")

58. Andall, *Gender, Migration and Domestic Service*.

59. Rollins, *Between Women*, 108.

60. Rollins, 7.

61. Hondagneu-Sotelo, *Doméstica*, 26. She is careful to add that the specific location is important to her analysis, given the varying intensity of income distribution in some cities.

62. Hondagneu-Sotelo, 6. She adds, however, that the demand for domestic workers comes from a broad swath of locations and social classes (8–9). See also Saskia Sassen, *The Global City*, 244.

63. Hondagneu-Sotelo, *Doméstica*, 7.

64. Hondagneu-Sotelo, 8.

65. Hondagneu-Sotelo, 14.

66. Romero, *Maid in the U.S.A.*, 7–10.

67. Romero, 93.

68. Romero, 93 and 122.

69. Stasiulis and Bakan, *Negotiating Citizenship*, 76.

70. Stasiulis and Bakan, 76–77.

71. Stasiulis and Bakan, 41.

72. Parreñas, *Servants of Globalization*, 30.

73. Parreñas, *Children of Global Migration*, 20 and 14.

74. Stasiulis and Bakan, *Negotiating Citizenship*, 48–51 and 63.

75. Stasiulis and Bakan, 162.

76. Rollins, *Between Women*, 92–93.

77. Hondagneu-Sotelo, *Doméstica*, 9.

78. Hondagneu-Sotelo, 63.

79. Hondagneu-Sotelo, 76–113.

80. See, for example, Tsikata, "Employment Agencies and the Regulation of Domestic Workers in Ghana."

81. Unavoidably, attention has turned to the forced labor dimensions in the recruitment process, in part based on trust-based referrals across national borders. The regulation of cross-border migration and agencies to redress forced labor is discussed in further detail in chapter 5.

82. Stasiulis and Bakan, *Negotiating Citizenship*, 75.

83. Hondagneu-Sotelo, *Doméstica*, 82.

84. Hochschild, *The Managed Heart*.

85. Hondagneu-Sotelo, *Doméstica*, 12.

86. For a historical account of employers in nineteenth-century US labor markets pitting different racialized groups of domestic workers against each other, see Urban, *Brokering Servitude*.

87. Colen and Sanjek, "At Work in Homes I: Orientations," 6.

88. Du Bois, *The Philadelphia Negro*, 93.

89. Rollins, *Between Women*. Of the women who were not from the South, one was from the West Indies, one was from Cape Cod (born in Cape Verde), and one was from Boston.

90. Parreñas, *Servants of Globalization*, 137.

91. E. Glenn, *Forced to Care*, 184.

92. Andall, *Gender, Migration and Domestic Service*, 237–38. This led to calls for a time of union solidarity with migrant women workers. However, Andall also notes the

flawed turn in the analysis offered by ACLI-COLF, when it assumed that there would be a "war amongst the poorest," as Italian women turned back to domestic work in the context of the economic crisis of the 1970s (*Gender, Migration and Domestic Service*, 238). For Andall, this showed a lack of appreciation of the nature of structural racial segregation. She critiques the union's inability to appreciate the nature of structural racial segregation and its ultimate decision to foreground gender. Andall demonstrates the problematic assumptions about gender solidarity between domestic workers and their employers that ensued and discusses the failure to appreciate how the presence of racialized men in work gendered as female did not suggest a more equitable distribution of care.

93. It is worth remembering that the international campaign to control working hours was framed in terms of eight hours of work, eight of leisure (understood as time for education and civic engagement, as well as family life), and eight of rest per day. See A. Thomas, *International Social Policy*, 54 and 63–65. The ILO convention focused on the hours of work in industry in terms of that framing.

94. See Vosko, *Managing the Margins*. See also Standing, *Beyond the New Paternalism*.

95. Romero, *Maid in the U.S.A.*, 127.

96. Chin, *In Service and Servitude*, 148.

97. Quoted in Andall, *Gender, Migration and Domestic Service*, 154–55.

98. Andall, 163.

99. Ministro el Lavoro e delle Politiche Sociali, "Contratto collectivo nazionale di lavoro sulla disciplina de rapport di lavoro domestic," 2013, http://www.colfebadan tionline.it/images/ccnllavorodomestico2013-2016.pdf. article 15.

100. Deakin and Wilkinson, *The Law of the Labour Market*, 74.

101. Rockman, *Scraping By*, 424.

102. Hondagneu-Sotelo, *Doméstica*, 83.

103. Some scholars reported that wages were more likely to be above the legal minimum for live-out workers than for live-in workers. See, for example, Hondagneu-Sotelo, 38.

104. Boris, *Home to Work*, 49.

105. Hondagneu-Sotelo, *Doméstica*, 35–36.

106. Rollins, *Between Women*.

107. Hondagneu-Sotelo, 82.

108. Romero, *Maid in the U.S.A.*, 129–30.

109. Rollins, *Between Women*, 67.

110. Rollins, 65.

111. Rollins, 72 and 75–76. Rollins asks whether the issue is linked to the availability of a large labor pool of black women, or whether the pay differential is deliberate.

112. Hondagneu-Sotelo, *Doméstica*, 55–57.

113. Van Walsum, "Regulating Migrant Domestic Work in the Netherlands."

114. Chin, *In Service and Servitude*, 88. Chin refers to this as a form of state "subsidy" (89).

115. Chin, 69–89.

116. Andall, *Gender, Migration and Domestic Service*, 131.

117. Hondagneu-Sotelo, *Doméstica*, 36. She adds that most of the women who take the live-in jobs are recent immigrants.

118. Hondagneu-Sotelo, 32.

119. Hondagneu-Sotelo, 33–35.

120. Hondagneu-Sotelo, 34.

121. Hondagneu-Sotelo, 34.

122. Andall, *Gender, Migration and Domestic Service*, 292–93.

123. Quoted in Andall, 159.

124. Andall, 155.

125. Andall, 130; see also 159. This included being woken up early in the morning to make a hot beverage for guests of the employer.

126. Andall, 151; see also 269.

127. Andall, 153. See also Calavita, *Immigrants at the Margins*.

128. Andall, *Gender, Migration and Domestic Service*, 201.

129. Andall, 203–14.

130. Chin, *In Service and Servitude*, 132–42.

131. Stasiulis and Bakan, *Negotiating Citizenship*, 94.

132. Romero, *Maid in the U.S.A.*

133. Magnus, "The Social, Economic, and Legal Conditions of Domestic Servants: I," 205, and "The Social, Economic, and Legal Conditions of Domestic Servants: II," 342.

134. Magnus, "The Social, Economic, and Legal Conditions of Domestic Servants: II," 342.

135. Deakin and Wilkinson, *The Law of the Labour Market*, 87.

136. Ministro el Lavoro e delle Politiche Sociali, "Contratto collectivo nazionale di lavoro," article 15, and Ministro el Lavoro e delle Politiche Sociali, "Lavora domestico: CCNL, 31 maggio 2017," http://olympus.uniurb.it/index.php?option=com_content&view=article&id=17315:17lavdomesaarco&catid=227&Itemid=139.

137. Andall, *Gender, Migration and Domestic Service*, 161.

138. Andall.

139. Andall.

140. Andall.

141. Hondagneu-Sotelo, *Doméstica*.

142. Although Arlie Russell Hothschild did not initially include domestic work in her path-breaking study of emotional labor, *The Managed Heart*, her subsequent study with Barbara Ehrenreich, *Global Woman*, focused on the domestic work relationship.

143. I use Martha Fineman's focus on "care taking" rather than "care giving" (*The Neutered Mother*).

144. Romero, *Maid in the U.S.A.*, 99.

145. Romero, 88.

146. Romero, 88 and 90.

147. Romero, 113.

148. Romero, 3–4.

149. Romero, 93.

150. Romero, 12.

151. Romero, 4.

152. See, for example, Rollins, *Between Women*; Andall, *Gender, Migration and Domestic Service*, 115.

153. Romero, *Maid in the U.S.A.*; Hondagneu-Sotelo, *Doméstica*, 10. See also Rollins, *Between Women*; Andall, *Gender, Migration and Domestic Service*, 105.

154. Romero, *Maid in the U.S.A.*, 110.

155. Romero, 4.

156. Ally, *From Servants to Workers*, 1.

157. Chin, *In Service and Servitude*, 135.

158. Romero, *Maid in the U.S.A.*, 151.

159. Romero, 125.

160. Romero, 117.

161. Chin, *In Service and Servitude*, 131.

162. Stasiulis and Bakan, *Negotiating Citizenship*, 98.

163. Romero, *Maid in the U.S.A.*, 124–25. Dumont-Robillard, *Accès à la justice pour les travailleuses domestiques migrantes?*

164. Quoted in Romero, 100.

165. Cedric Robinson notes that "the racial mythology that accompanied capitalist industrial formation and provided its social structures engendered no truly profound alternatives" (*Black Marxism*, 316).

166. Quoted in Romero, *Maid in the U.S.A.*, 124–25.

167. Rollins, "And the Last Shall Be First."

168. Parreñas, *Children of Global Migration*, 194.

169. International Labour Office, *Report IV(1): Decent Work for Domestic Workers (Law and Practice Report)*, para. 265.

170. Ally, *From Servants to Workers*, 162

171. Stasiulis and Bakan, *Negotiating Citizenship*, 6. The authors add that Filipina live-in domestic workers were similarly organizing against their oppressive labor market conditions.

172. Stasiulis and Bakan, 84–85.

173. Stasiulis and Bakan, 141.

174. Rollins, "And the Last Shall Be First."

175. Rollins, *Between Women*, 227.

176. Rollins, 231.

177. Thornton Dill, *Across the Boundaries of Race and Class*, 33.

178. Ally, *From Servants to Workers*, 111.

179. Ally, 54–55.

180. Parreñas, *Children of Global Migration*, 194.

181. Andall, *Gender, Migration and Domestic Service*.

182. Quoted in Andall, 158.

183. Chin, *In Service and Servitude*, 149.

184. Chin, 151–58.

185. Parreñas, *Servants of Globalization*, 150.

186. Parreñas, 151.

187. Parreñas, 152.

188. Parreñas, 153–55.

189. In the US context, Rollins mostly reveals stories of relationships that were "neither problematic nor extraordinarily positive" (*Between Women*, 126). However, she also presents some remarkable stories that give a sense of the employer's absolute power to terminate the employment relationship. For example, she tells the

story of one domestic worker who got drunk on the job and was literally taken out of the house and, because the employer did not know where she lived (how's that for labor market informality?), dropped off at the police station. The story continues only because later in life the employer became an alcoholic herself. She told Rollins, "I keep thinking of that poor woman and what's become of her" (quoted in *Between Women*, 123). When another employer noticed that small amounts of money—coins—regularly went missing from her pocketbook, she said, "I just fired her [the domestic worker]. It just made me very nervous" (quoted in *Between Women*, 125).

190. Andall, *Gender, Migration and Domestic Service*.

191. Quoted in Rollins, *Between Women*, 125.

192. Chapter 6 shows some of the changes that have helped reframe the domestic work relationship.

193. *Re Peterboro Lock Manufacturing*, 1953, 1501 (Bora Laskin J., as he then was).

194. Calavita, *Immigrants at the Margins*, 74.

195. Hondagneu-Sotelo, *Doméstica*, xi. Thornton Dill writes: "Contrary to popular imagery, the overriding attitude expressed toward the occupation was not disdain or loathing, but ambivalence" (*Across the Boundaries of Race and Class*, 83).

196. Hondagneu-Sotelo, *Doméstica*, 12.

197. Rollins poignantly describes one younger domestic worker, Ms. Owens, who referred to the beauty she saw in the work that her mother did as a domestic worker (*Between Women*, 112).

198. Rollins, *Between Women*, 107–14. See also Hondagneu-Sotelo, *Doméstica*, 12. Some of the ethnographies nonetheless documented patterns of mothers—even those who had migrated across globe—reluctantly having to train their own daughters to perform domestic work. See Andall, *Gender, Migration and Domestic Service*.

199. McKeon, *The Secret History of Domesticity*, 212.

4. Searching for Law in Historical Cookbooks

1. Rebecca Sharpless notes that it is not entirely surprising that documentation about the conditions of domestic work would come via cookbooks: cooking produces a product, however ephemeral. Its components can be identified, quantified, represented, and thus remembered (*Cooking in Other Women's Kitchens*).

2. Steedman, *Labours Lost*, 173. Steedman frames her concern as "the regulation of, and intervention, in employment relationships outside of the confines of the statutes as well as within them," including a particular set of adjudications of disputes concerning domestic servants by magistrate Sir Gervase Clifton. Steedman, *Labours Lost*, 183.

3. Steedman, *Labours Lost*, 355, 301, 302. In reference to the "networking" meeting, Steedman cites Aleyn Lyell, *Johnsonian Gleanings, Part II*.

4. Steedman, *Labours Lost*, 287. Interestingly, a figure reproduced by Steedman shows three maidservants processing food in a kitchen, with one of them apparently using an "instruction manual" (274).

5. For Rod Macdonald, "Relationships are the bedrock of law." Macdonald, *Lessons of Everyday Law*, 3. For Macdonald, everyday law can be found in any number of ordinary encounters. Everyday law's richness and subtlety, its implicit and explicit character,

and its capacity for injustice, need to be addressed in discussions of legal normativity. Macdonald, *Lessons of Everyday Law*, 6.

6. Russell, *A Domestic Cook Book*; Tipton-Martin, "Breaking the Jemima Code," 120.

7. Blackstone, *Commentaries on the Laws of England*, Vol. 1, 357. Carolyn Steedman insists that Blackstone contrasts the life of domestics, characterized as "menial servants," not with that of charwomen or other domestic workers who lived out, but rather with workers undertaking nondomestic service "under contract . . . and who were subject, like menials, to the substantial and extensive law of service" (*Master and Servant*, 178).

8. A famous decision by Lord Mansfield—*R. v. Brampton (Inhabitants)* (1777) 23 Digest 77, 536 (1777) Cald Mag Cas. 11 (K.B)—found that a master could act on his own authority to dismiss his unwed, pregnant domestic servant, rather than seek prior approval of a magistrate. The decision expressly turned on public morals and disregarded the general custom that prior authorization from a magistrate was required. It also raised jurisdictional concerns if domestic servants (or servants other than those in what was then called husbandry) were not in fact covered under the Statute of Artificers. See Hay, "England 1562–1875," 110–11. Steedman suggests that most other eighteenth-century magistrates considered that it did apply. See Steedman, *Labours Lost*, 178.

9. *Charles Lindsay v. Mary Ann McDonough* (May 27, 1842), A.N.Q.M., W.S.S.(R.) Nos. 464 and 465. The summons dated May 23, 1842, indicates that McDonough was charged both with having "refused and neglected to perform your full duties and to obey the lawful commands" of Lindsay and his wife, and with "divers faults and misdemeanors . . . by illegally taking in your possession and wearing divers articles of wearing apparel belonging to your said Mistress." The fine appears to be a percentage of the cost of the suit. See also Craven, "Canada, 1670–1935," 191; Pilarczyk, "The Law of Servants," 816; Pilarczyk, "Too Well Used," 517.

10. Magnus, "The Social, Economic, and Legal Conditions of Domestic Servants: I," 190. Baylis suggests in England that "whether the employer or servant be bound to provide washing, and in what way, will probably depend on the particular circumstances of the case; but in order to prevent future dispute, there should be at the time of hiring a distinct understanding on this, as well as other similar points." Baylis, *The Rights, Duties and Relations of Domestic Servants*, 3.

11. In *Lindsay v. McDonough*, witness testimony was taken. However, it is worth noting that even well after this case was decided, when the Civil Code of Lower Canada was adopted in 1866, a master's oath as to the conditions of engagement and the fact of payment of wages, along with his detailed statement, would suffice in the absence of written proof; the matter might even be deferred to the master in the absence of an oath. Civil Code of Lower Canada, article 1669; amended in 1878 and finally in 1889 when a master's oath could be refuted "in the same manner as any other testimony." *Code civil—Civil Code, 1866–1980, An Historical and Critical Edition*. Montreal: McGill University, 1981.

12. Munn, "Hong Kong, 1841–1870," 367.

13. Pilarczyk, "Too Well Used;" Pilarczyk, "The Law of Servants."

14. Hay and Craven, "Introduction," 48, 49. See also Fick, *The Making of Haiti*.

15. See, for example, Rediker, *Between the Devil and the Deep Blue Sea*; Grandin, *Empire of Necessity*.

16. Hay, "England," 89. This applied to domestic servants and any other occupations not specifically listed in the Statute of Artificers.

17. McKeon, *The Secret History of Domesticity*, 219–22. McKeon maps the ritualized social subordination of the servant by the master that took place in seventeenth-century England, to challenge any stable notion of a public-private divide, however real and locally useful.

18. Hay, "England," 67.

19. In particular, Beatrice Webb and Sidney Webb's classic 1897 work, *Industrial Democracy*, adopts a theoretical framework that is built on a methodological rootedness in the world as it is observed. This allowed them to see, for example, that "notwithstanding the constant demand for servants in private households, the women who cook, scrub, clean, or wait in the common run of hotels, boarding-houses, lodgings, coffee-shops, or restaurants, are as ill-paid, as ill-treated, and as overworked as their sisters in other unorganised occupations" (*Industrial Democracy*, 676). Their approach also enabled them to offer a prescient critique of the doctrine of supply and demand insofar as domestic work was concerned: "A doctrine which results in the community getting only thirty-seven hours' work a week out of the well-nourished Northumberland coal-hewer, and only thirty-three hours a week out of the highly-paid flint glass maker, whilst forcing the laundry-women to toil for seventy hours, and the chronically underfed chain and nail operatives for eighty hours, stands self-condemned" (583). The authors "pause . . . for a moment, in our analysis of the industrial machine, to examine the case of the domestic servant" (674). But their look beyond women in industry is all too brief and reflects the scholarly paradox of the time: domestic work by women in upper- and middle-class households was perceived to be well paid and to be performed in good working conditions. The Webbs turned to the dominant scholarly interpretation of industry, which challenged workers' need for trade unions. The Webbs challenged that argument and in the process chastized mainstream scholars:

> It is, we think, somewhat discreditable to English economists that they should have gone on copying and recopying from each other's lectures and textbooks the idea that this rise in wages among the domestic servants of the well-to-do classes constitutes any argument against the validity of the case for Trade Unionism in the world of competitive industry. We can only attribute it to the fact that male economic lecturers and text-book writers have seldom themselves experienced the troubles of housekeeping, either on a large or a small scale, whilst the few women economists have hitherto suffered from a lack of personal knowledge of the actual relations between capitalists and workman in the profit-making world. (676, n.1)

Their critique did not, however, lead them to challenge the starting assumption about wages and working conditions in domestic service. Without conducting the same kind of study that characterizes much of their work, the Webbs argued that there was "no analogy between the engagement of domestic servants to minister to the personal comfort of the relatively rich, and the wage-contract of the operative employed by the profit-maker" (674). The most important consideration, they argued, was the absence of price pressure within the household context—domestic service is for the use of the household and is not for sale, they reasoned. The link between reproductive work and the ability to produce in the labor market might well have been obscured in the transition from rural domestic opulence and very large household establishments that employed many domestic workers in a household economy, and the role of domestic work in freeing up industrialists to participate fully in market activities beyond the household. Wages paid to excellent, trustworthy servants were described as virtually spontaneously being raised (676).

Continuing to use this logic, the Webbs argued that domestic employees (unlike industrial wage laborers) had bargaining power that was relatively equal to that of their employers. The authors presumed that the employer was the mistress of the house, and that she was less than knowledgeable and rather more preoccupied with other affairs. This left mistresses at the mercy of their domestic employees, considered to be better placed to undertake the bargain. The Webbs go so far as to refer to the employers as "helpless": "the alternative to the well-to-do woman of doing without a servant for a single day is perhaps as disagreeable to her as the alternative to the servant of being out of place and the worry and inconvenience to the mistress of finding another servant is at least as great as the discomfort to the servant of getting another situation" (Webb and Webb, *Industrial Democracy*, 676, 675).

In short, the Webbs considered that domestic workers' "personal comfort . . . in a typical middle-class household depends mainly on themselves; that of the mistress and her family depends to an enormous extent on the goodwill of her servants" (*Industrial Democracy*, 675).

20. Hay and Craven, Introduction. Steedman discusses the policing of society through the regulation of domestic work—that is, the "internal good ordering and management of society." *Labours Lost*, 199.

21. Hay and Craven, Introduction, 27. See also Pope, "Contract, Race and Freedom"; VanderVelde, *Redemption Songs*; Kotiswaran, "From Sex Panic to Extreme Exploitation"; Blackett, "Emancipation in the Idea of Labour Law."

22. See also Tomlins, *Freedom Bound*.

23. Hay, "England, 1562–1875," 97. See also Hay and Craven, Introduction.

24. Hay and Craven, Introduction, 36.

25. Hay and Craven, 47.

26. Turner, *The British Caribbean*, 307.

27. Steedman, *Labours Lost*, 195.

28. A. Cooper, *The Hanging of Angélique*.

29. *Dred Scott v. Sandford*, 60 U.S. (19 How.) 393 (1857).

30. VanderVelde, *Mrs. Dred Scott*, 9.

31. In *Redemption Songs*, VanderVelde chronicles the freedom suits that preceded the US Supreme Court decision.

32. Buckner-Inniss et al., review of *Mrs. Dred Scott*, 462.

33. VanderVelde, *Redemption Songs*; Grandin, *Empire of Necessity*.

34. Carolyn Steedman suggests further that "we would have had a very different history of this time and place if Adam Smith had not said that the servant's work was not work and if Karl Marx had not followed him, and said that we could discount service labour in our accounts of capitalist modernity" (*Labours Lost*, 355–56).

35. See Hernández, *Racial Subordination in Latin America*, 12–13. Hernandez deftly employs a "customary law" approach, in contradistinction to a more anthropological

"traditional law" framework that emphasizes parallel approaches. I explain below why I prefer a resolutely legal pluralist analysis rooted in counterhegemonic accounts of law and legal change.

36. Tipton-Martin, *The Jemima Code*, 4.

37. Fisher, *What Mrs. Fisher Knows about Southern Cooking*, 82.

38. Tipton-Martin, *The Jemima Code*, 7. I acknowledge VanderVelde's encouragement to me to do the same.

39. Baylis, *The Rights, Duties and Relations of Domestic Servants*, 35. He even discusses and lists training schools for domestic workers.

40. Lethbridge, *Servants*, xii; Steedman, *Labours Lost*.

41. Seely, *Mrs. Seely's Cook Book*.

42. Seely, 1–2.

43. Seely, 3.

44. My assertion about the representations of racial identity remains tentative, in part because the scanned reproduction of the original book leaves the images less than clear, but mostly because representations of identity are necessarily fluid when dealing with a concept that is constituted socially. For an important historical account, see Gross, *What Blood Won't Tell*. For a leading contemporary account, see Obasogie, *Blinded by Sight*.

45. Seely, *Mrs. Seely's Cook Book*, 2. Seely adds that a term longer than a year would need to be put in writing or be considered invalid, consistent with the treatment of indentures in other jurisdictions. See also Pilarczyk, "The Law of Servants and the Servants of Law."

46. Seely, *Mrs. Seely's Cookbook*, 3.

47. Seely, 6.

48. Seely, 4.

49. Seely, 4–5.

50. Seely, 8.

51. Seely, 13.

52. Seely, 23.

53. Seely, 13.

54. Seely, 27.

55. Seely, 11.

56. Seely, 12.

57. Seely, 12.

58. Steel and Gardiner, *The Complete Indian Housekeeper*, preface by Cambridge University Press.

59. Steel and Gardiner, *The Complete Indian Housekeeper*.

60. Steel and Gardiner, ix.

61. Steel and Gardiner, 8. The authors actually refer affirmingly to George Eliot in making this claim.

62. Quoted in Steel and Gardiner, 320. The *Lahore Civil and Military Gazette* commended the book as a valuable manual that is "extremely amusing and true to life" on Indian household management (quoted in Steel and Gardiner, 320).

63. Steel and Gardiner, *The Complete Indian Housekeeper*, 30.

64. Steel and Gardiner, 154, 160.

65. The authors note that the ayah is likely to be the only female servant in the household and insist that she should be treated as the equal "of any other servant in the house" (Steel and Gardiner, 66). They then explain why English nurses are typically brought in to educate children, and they express dismay at the thought of using Indian servants to raise children. They state that to maintain "cleanliness, decency and order . . . as in an Indian pantry or cookroom," the "whole secret lies in refusing to listen to the word *dastur,* or custom" (Steel and Gardiner, 67). See also Stoler, *Carnal Knowledge and Imperial Power.*

66. Steel and Gardiner, *The Complete Indian Housekeeper,* 72. The authors characterize the *malachi* (scullion) and the sweeper as "the only two servants who ever condescend to clean anything. Curiously enough in these cases, they acquire a strange similarity in dress and demeanour; possibly because, being everybody's slave, they lose all spirit and self-respect. Both slink from sight, and become furtive even in *their* methods of work, and both contrive to assimilate an incredible amount of pure griminess around their own persons" (Steel and Gardiner, 80). They advise against keeping this category of servant subservient to other servants, but if that must be done, they advise at different points in the book that this relationship should be turned into that of a "responsible servant on good wages," able to step in to cook "at the most critical moment" (60 and 61).

67. Webster Steel and Gardiner express strong views on prevalent perceptions of the two religions and characterize the functions of the ayah of the "sweeper caste" in relation to "Mohammedan" women (Steel and Gardiner, 64).

68. Steel and Gardiner, *The Complete Indian Housekeeper,* 3.

69. Steel and Gardiner, 3

70. Steel and Gardiner, 49.

71. Steel and Gardiner, 3.

72. Steel and Gardiner, 48.

73. Steel and Gardiner, 4. As if to illustrate their racialized paternalism, the authors recommend "castor oil" as "an ultimatum in all obstinate cases, on the ground that there must be some physical cause for inability to learn or to remember" (3, 4). Even an acknowledged "acute sense of justice" on the part of Indian servants was seen as illustrating their childlike character.

74. Steel and Gardiner, 10. Emphasis in the original.

75. Steel and Gardiner, 64.

76. The authors note: "This, on the other hand, is no reason why they should turn your domain into a caravanserai for their relations to the third and fourth generation. As a rule, it is well to draw a very sharp line in this respect" (Steel and Gardiner, 4).

77. Steel and Gardiner, 53–54.

78. Steel and Gardiner, 10.

79. Steel and Gardiner, 6. Moreover, the authors recommend hiring servants young and promoting them over time, but not keeping them too long to avoid the corruption that they stereotypically suggest is connected in the "Oriental mind" when a servant is taken into confidence.

80. Steel and Gardiner, 85.

81. Steel and Gardiner, 190. Consider the expectation that after a dinner party, at midnight or 1:00 a.m., a commendable cook would "appear in clean clothing and ask if all had gone well," and basically already know and take responsibility for the response (Steel and Gardiner, 231).

82. Steel and Gardiner, 79. The authors add that in the hot weather, working from 7:00 to 11:00 a.m. and 3:00 to 7:00 p.m. might be preferred (Steel and Gardiner, 96).

83. Steel and Gardiner, 57.

84. Steel and Gardner, 33–34. The authors pay attention even to how to train servants to take over certain responsibilities in the event that maladies, like malaria (ague) take over the kitchen, to ensure that service continues" (61).

85. Steel and Gardiner, 49. The authors observe: "For one mistress who makes a point of commending a well-cooked dish, how many are there who never dream of praise? And whose only criticism is unmeasured and often unreasonable blame?" (Steel and Gardiner, 70).

86. Steel and Gardiner, 51.

87. Steel and Gardiner, 51.

88. Steel and Gardiner, 185.

89. Steel and Gardiner, 185.

90. Steel and Gardiner, 54.

91. Steel and Gardiner, 11. Stoler, *Carnal Knowledge.*

92. Duckitt, *Hilda's Diary of a Cape Housekeeper.*

93. Duckitt, 9.

94. Duckitt, 18.

95. Duckitt, 9.

96. Duckitt, 7.

97. Duckitt, 9.

98. Duckitt, 19

99. Duckitt, 30.

100. Duckitt, 32.

101. Duckitt, 24. It is not apparent from the sentence structure whether Duckitt means that only the indentured servants were taught to read and write, as well as work, or if the young servants were taught as well.

102. Duckitt, 32.

103. Duckitt, 33.

104. Duckitt, 155.

105. Duckitt, 255.

106. Beecher, *Miss Beecher's Domestic Receipt Book,* 230.

107. Beecher, 231.

108. Beecher, 272. Beecher also draws attention to the "peculiar trials and peculiar duties" of American housekeepers faced with a "great influx of foreigners of another language and another faith"—but in the language of the day, she argues against trying to convince "an ignorant and feeble mind to do what it believes to be wrong," as that would be an obstacle to faithful service (Beecher, 290, 290 and 272).

109. Beecher, 270.

110. Beecher, 270.

111. Beecher, 274.

112. John Egerton explains the 1880s emergence of Aunt Jemima out of advertising inspired by blackface performance:

> As black women grew more self-assured and instrumental in the culinary
> arts of the post-bellum South, their white mistresses and masters had to find

an explanation for this anomaly; in a culture that considered all blacks to be inferior, there was no room for exceptional intelligence and skill. They needed a female counterpart to the loyal and compliant Uncle Tom—a mythic persona, a caricature for all seasons. She had to be humerous, stout, lighthearted, illiterately magical—stern enough to control the children without threatening them, dependable and loyal enough to assure mothers that the kitchen was in good hands, asexual enough to foreclose any wayward thoughts among the men of the house. . . . She was the dominant white majority's response to the prospect of black parity, or even superiority, in the kitchen. The image, the name, the code said it all: it had to be this way, or no way. ("Foreword," xi).

113. Tipton-Martin, *The Jemima Code*, 5. Tipton-Martin draws upon an emerging scholarship on African American women, their cuisine, and their community identity. See, for example, Witt, *Black Hunger*; Mendes, *The African Heritage Cookbook*.

114. Tipton-Martin, *The Jemima Code*, 2.

115. Tipton-Martin, 13.

116. Tipton-Martin, 13.

117. Russell, *A Domestic Cook Book*, xi.

118. R. Roberts, *The House Servant's Directory*, x.

119. Roberts, viii.

120. Roberts, 152.

121. Roberts, 69. Roberts also advises servants to be good to each other, calling it their "greatest comfort" (71).

122. Roberts, 110–12.

123. Roberts, 72, 141.

124. Roberts, 145–49. The tone in these pages is somewhat different, and Roberts's note that the remarks are extracted from an 1822 cookbook by William Kitchiner, *The Cook's Oracle*, helps explain the different writing style.

125. Roberts, xiii.

126. Roberts, x.

127. Roberts, xi.

128. Roberts, 78.

129. Roberts, 154.

130. Roberts, 156. However, Roberts warns masters not to trust servants with "the secret of their own strength" and to avoid familiarity, which according "to a proverb is accompanied by contempt."

131. Roberts, 157.

132. Roberts, 157.

133. Roberts, 158.

134. Roberts, 158.

135. Roberts, 158.

136. Roberts, 180.

137. Russell, *A Domestic Cook Book*, xi.

138. Samuel Adams and Sarah Adams, *The Complete Servant*, 10.

139. Adams and Adams, 141.

140. Adams and Adams, 18.

141. Adams and Adams, 12.

142. Adams and Adams, 20.

143. Adams and Adams, 65.

144. Adams and Adams, 105.

145. Adams and Adams, 150.

146. Adams and Adams, 102. Lucy Lethbridge adds that early rising fell disproportionately on female servants, an observation that is mirrored in the gendered description of job responsibilities (*Servants*, 47–49).

147. Adams and Adams, *The Complete Servant*, 29.

148. Adams and Adams, 88.

149. Adams and Adams, 92.

150. Adams and Adams, 78–79.

151. Adams and Adams, 79.

152. Adams and Adams, 104.

153. Adams and Adams, 174.

154. Duncan, *Freedom's Shore*, 15.

155. Campbell, *Hotel Keepers, Head Waiters, and Housekeepers' Guide*, 92.

156. Campbell, 93.

157. Campbell, 61.

158. Campbell, 66.

159. Quoted in Kat Eschner, "These Were the First Cookbooks Published by Black People in America" *Smithsonian Magazine*, October 11, 2017, https://www.smithsonianmag.com/smart-news/these-were-first-cookbooks-published-black-people-america-180965175/. See also Tipton-Martin, *The Jemima Code*, 12.

160. Haber, "Foreword," xiv.

161. Tipton-Martin affirms that Russell's book allows "black cooks to finally pull up a seat at the long table of Southern history—to share equally in the creation of its beloved cuisine" (Tipton-Martin, "Breaking the Jemima Code," 120).

162. Russell, *A Domestic Cook Book*, 3.

163. Russell, 3.

164. Russell, 4.

165. Russell, 4.

166. Sharpless, *Cooking in Other Women's Kitchens*, xxiv–xxv.

167. This insight mirrors Mary Romero's findings in *Maid in the U.S.A.*, discussed in chapter 3.

168. Sharpless, *Cooking in Other Women's Kitchens*, xix.

169. Du Bois, *The Philadelphia Negro*, 33. Du Bois's classic also includes a *Special Report on Negro Domestic Service in the Seventh Ward, Philadelphia*, written by Isabel Eaton.

170. Pinnix, Jones, and Pearson, *Sudie Holton*.

171. Pinnix, Jones, and Pearson.

172. Several important oral history accounts capture the skill and respect for the work that is part of the culinary legacy. Tipton-Martin singles out the Southern Foodways Alliance's oral history project (*The Jemima Code*, 3). She also argues that "to judge the black cook by a lack of schooling rather than as a miracle of memory and oral transmission is to miss what was truly accomplished: excellence across a range of skills, independence, and social mobility—not to mention the creation of really delicious food" (23).

173. Steedman, *Labours Lost*, 301, 351–54.

174. On late eighteenth-century England, for example, Steedman notes that "lady and gentlemen pamphleteers and cookery book writers" addressed domestic servants directly in kitchens, but they "were not disordered in their mind. Cottagers and household servants may have been the addressees of their texts, but few can have thought that the poor would read them." *Labours Lost*, 273, 275. Steedman adds that literate cooks were particularly useful, including in modest households. *Labours Lost*, 285.

175. Egerton, "Foreword," ix.

176. Tipton-Martin, *The Jemima Code*, 2.

177. Steedman, *Labours Lost*, 289. Steedman's reference is specifically to a late eighteenth-century domestic worker's book of poetry, Elizabeth Hands, *The Death of Amnon*. By looking to domestic workers' poetry, Steedman is able to unearth the social prejudice and social resentment voiced by domestic workers as well as employers. Steedman, *Labours Lost*, 301.

178. Verge and Vallée, *Un droit du travail?*

179. Arthurs, "Labour Law without the State?"

5. Tough Spots at the International Labour Conference

1. Falk Moore, *Law as Process*, 79.

2. Falk Moore, *Law as Process*, 40–41. Kate Meagher offers a critique of processes of normalization of the informal without actually improving the conditions of the workers. See Meagher, "Cannibalizing," 23.

3. International Labour Office, *Report IV(1): Decent Work for Domestic Workers* (hereafter referred to as *Law and Practice Report*), para. 39. See also Guha-Khasnobis, Kanbur, and Ostrom, "Beyond Formality and Informality," 4.

4. Rajagopal, *International Law From Below*, 23.

5. Koh, "Transnational Legal Process." Koh argues that a range of actors, including lawyers, have a responsibility to influence the direction of transnational law.

6. Although emblematic and the basis of much of the structure of labor codes around the world, the convention has beens ratified by fifty-two states, or little more than a quarter of the ILO's member states.

7. Supiot, *Beyond Employment*, 60.

8. There is a large body of literature on the SER. One of the earliest contributors to it is Ulrich Mückenberger ("Non-Standard Forms of Employment in the Federal Republic of Germany"). See also Bosch, "Working Time and the Standard Employment Relationship." For an account by a leading feminist political economist, see Vosko, *Managing the Margins*.

9. Alain Supiot issues an important caution about invoking the language of flexibility in regulatory debates:

> Management has readily understood this new pressing need for mobility and has therefore demanded "flexibility" in the employer-employee relationship. From a legal point of view, this whole idea of flexibility—a management term—does not have much meaning. It really only makes sense when referring to the principle of professional freedom as understood from its two sides: the freedom to set up a business and the freedom to work. The claim for flexi-

bility can then be understood in law as a demand for professional freedom to be enhanced within work organization. Labour law should take this demand into account and not stand in the way of the evolution of work organization methods. However, the fundamental question to be resolved today is not about increased flexibility (something that has already widely been taken up in legislation in a number of European countries) but about bringing the new imperatives of greater work freedom into line with the equally pressing need of every worker to enjoy a long-lasting real membership of the labour force which actually enables him to exercise individual initiative. (*Beyond Employment*, 26)

10. Webb and Webb, *Industrial Democracy*, 291.

11. Webb and Webb.

12. Webb and Webb, 324.

13. Webb and Webb, 349. The Webbs focused on women who were required to work nights.

14. Webb and Webb, 430.

15. Webb and Webb, 326. In this sense, the manual home worker was considered to be in a similar position to the professional (325).

16. Webb and Webb, 327.

17. Magnus, "The Social, Economic, and Legal Conditions of Domestic Servants: I," 206.

18. Parreñas notes that the partial citizenship of temporary migrant workers sets a "tone of exclusion from the host society" (*Servants of Globalization*, 21).

19. Vosko's account would have been strengthened had it relied more closely on work dealing with racialization, like the ethnographies I discussed in chapter 3.

20. Vosko, *Managing the Margins*, 48.

21. Falk Moore, *Law as Process*, 69.

22. However, Deirdre McCann and Jill Murray contend that the exclusions are not absolute, states can exclude categories of workers only after consulting with organizations of the employers and workers concerned, and the workers retain particular protections—and consequently, even though the archetype was the male breadwinner, the Hours of Work (Industry) Convention remains an important benchmark and identifies arrangements that would be considered nonstandard even by contemporary standards ("The Legal Regulation of Working Time in Domestic Work"). See also Murray, *Transnational Labour Regulation*.

23. See Blackett, review of *Managing the Margins*, 458.

24. Vosko, *Managing the Margins*, 224.

25. See Mundlak and Shamir, "Bringing Together or Drifting Apart?"

26. The most sustained critique comes from McCann, a leading specialist on working time who was on the staff of the unit responsible for the standard setting. She was involved in the preparatory work for the *Law and Practice Report*. In particular, she coordinated the team of short-term researchers based at the ILO and prepared a draft of sections of the chapter of the report that surveyed working time. Yet remarkably, her cogent analysis was not shared with me during the drafting of the report or the questionnaire that would be the basis of the proposed convention and recommendation. The working paper was co-authored with Professor Jill Murray and published after the *Law and Practice Report*'s finalization, and subsequent to the first discussion in June 2010. I

learned of it during a research visit to Melbourne, Australia, where I participated in a panel with Murray, who presented the insights. See McCann and Murray, "The Legal Regulation of Working Time in Domestic Work." See also McCann, "New Frontiers of Regulation."

27. See European Foundation for the Improvement of Living and Working Conditions, "Revisions to the European Working Time Directive"; Ales, Deinert, and Kenner, *Core and Contingent Workers in the European Union*.

28. David Kennedy assesses international legal experts' actions and responsibility, including in the face of law's potential dark side (*A World of Struggle*).

29. Blackett, "Transnational Labour Law and Collective Autonomy," 241; French National Collective Agreement, article 3. See also the discussion in chapter 6.

30. South African Sectoral Determination No. 7, section 14. See the discussion in chapter 6 and International Labour Office, *Law and Practice Report*, paras. 167–73.

31. See also United Nations, "Convention on the Elimination of All Forms of Discrimination against Women," article 11, para. 1(d).

32. Charlotte Yates addresses the particular challenge associated with organizing child-care workers—particularly in-home child-care providers—in her discussion of an organizing strategy of the British Columbia Government and Services Employees Union. She stresses that the union made the case for pay equity by stressing the professional aspects and professional development and skill required for child-care work ("Organizing Women in the Spaces between Home, Work and Community").

33. See International Labour Office, *Report IV(2)*. In her work on workplace integration, Cynthia Estlund has emphasized one aspect of why it is necessary to move beyond seeing gender and race as parallel claims. She notes that "gender . . . is a basis for stereotyping, discrimination, and social conflict, but not usually of spatial separation outside the workplace" (*Working Together*, 12).

34. See Robyn Magalit Rodriguez, *Migrants for Export*, xvii. Rodriguez also emphasizes the disciplining through nationalistic discourse that makes dutiful work overseas part of good Filipino citizenship (90).

35. Parreñas, *Children of Global Migration*, 13–14.

36. Parreñas, *Servants of Global Migration*, 23.

37. Domestic workers were of course colonial migrants, dispossessed and urbanized within their own lands. See Mamdani, *Citizen and Subject*, 218. See also Achiume, "Reimagining International Law."

38. Rodriguez, *Migrants for Export*, 102; Ally, *From Servants to Workers*, 88.

39. International Labour Organization, "ILO Multilateral Framework on Labour Migration," principles 8 and 9.

40. International Labour Conference, 99th Sess., Provisional Record 12, para. 462.

41. International Labour Conference, 99th Sess., Provisional Record 12, para. 462.

42. See Faraday, *Profiting from the Precarious*; Jureidini, *Domestic Workers in the Middle East*; Hastie, "The Inequality of Low-Wage Migrant Labour"; Parreñas, *Servants of Globalization*, 17.

43. ILC, 100th Sess., *Provisional Record 15*, para. 470.

44. ILC, 100th Sess., *Provisional Record 15*, paras. 471–94.

45. Practice varies widely. Compare the US case of *Hoffman Plastic Compounds, Inc. v. National Labor Relations Board* (2002) 535 U.S. 137 with the South African case of *Discovery Health Ltd. v. Commission for Conciliation, Mediation & Arbitration and Others* (2008) 29 ILJ 1480.

46. United Nations Committee on the Protection of the Rights of All Migrant Workers and their Families, General Comment No. 1 on Migrant Domestic Workers, CMW/C/GC/1 (23 Feb. 2011) para. 9. It is worth noting that the Council of Europe has called for member states to establish international cooperation among labor inspectors, police, and border guards. See Parliamentary Assembly of the Council of Europe, "Resolution 1534 (2007)."

47. The order of articles and paragraphs was revisited toward the end of the standard-setting process to ensure a logical progression of subjects.

48. ILC, 99th Sess., *Provisional Record 12*, para. 819.

49. Nadasen, *Household Workers Unite*.

50. ILC 100th Sess., *Provisional Record 15*, para. 24.

51. ILC, 100th Sess., *Provisional Record 15*, para. 49.

52. This is as of September 6, 2018. See International Labour Organization, "Table of Ratifications," https://www.ilo.org/dyn/normlex/en/f?p=1000:11300:0::NO :11300:P11300_INSTRUMENT_ID:312326. The convention has been subject to important critique. See, for example, Benjamin, "Beyond the Boundaries."

53. See the discussion in ILC, 100th Sess., *Provisional Record 15*, paras. 112–17.

54. See *Migrant Workers and Overseas Filipinos Act* of 1995, Rep. Act No. 9422 (2007), as amended. Not only does the act regulate "private sector participation in the recruitment and overseas placement of workers by setting up a licensing and registration system," but it also provides preemployment services and establishes a "system for promoting and monitoring the overseas employment of Filipino workers taking into consideration their welfare and the domestic manpower requirements" (section 23[b][1]).

55. See ILC, 100th Sess., *Provisional Record 15*, para. 745. While the vice-chair of the employers' group asserted that "there was no prohibition in Convention No. 181 against charging agency fees," article 7(2) permits exceptions only "in the interest of the workers concerned" and following consultations. I explore this point in more detail elsewhere. See Blackett, "The Decent Work for Domestic Workers Convention and Recommendation, 2011."

56. ILC, 100th Sess., *Provisional Record 15*, para. 745.

57. ILC, 100th Sess., *Provisional Record 15*, para. 729.

58. ILC, 100th Sess., *Provisional Record 15*, para. 746.

59. Article 37(1) of the ILO Constitution gives the International Court of Justice the authority to issue interpretations of the Constitution and ILO conventions (International Labour Organization, "ILO Constitution"). In its various activities, the Committee of Experts issues formal observations and responds to direct requests for advice. Given that the Committee of Experts was established in 1926 and has been issuing annual reports since 1932, the resulting body of guidance is formidable.

60. The *Law and Practice Report* noted that "although domestic workers are especially vulnerable, traveling as part of a diplomatic entourage does not protect them from arbitrary treatment and abuse" (para. 240) and referred to article 8 of the Council of Europe's recommendation on domestic slavery (Parliamentary Assembly of the Council of Europe, "Recommendation 1523"), which recommended amending the Vienna Convention to waive diplomatic immunity for all offenses committed in private life (International Labour Office, *Law and Practice Report*, para. 241).

61. ILC, 100th Sess., *Provisional Record 15*, para. 1244.

62. ILC, 100th Sess., *Provisional Record 15*, paras. 1237–44.

63. The United Nations General Assembly articulated an equality of treatment standard between "immigrants lawfully in its [a nation's] territory" and national workers, at least for a defined set of conditions of employment ("A/RES/45/158," article 6), and addressed equal treatment (ibid., article 10). Leah Vosko discusses three phases in international labor regulation on migrant workers and the current problems of exclusion ("Out of the Shadows?").

64. Dauvergne, *Making People Illegal.*

65. Blackett, "Making Domestic Work Visible." I discuss the origins of this working paper in the postface.

66. See Standing, *Global Labour Flexibility;* Nedelsky, *Law's Relations.*

67. Blackett, "Domestic Workers at the Interface of Migration and Development"

68. International Labour Conference, "Resolution Concerning Efforts to Make Decent Work a Reality for Domestic Workers Worldwide," 2011, ILC, 100th Sess., *Provisional Record 15,* para. 138, adopted on June 15, 2011, https://www.ilo.org/wcmsp5 /groups/public/—ed_norm/—relconf/documents/meetingdocument/wcms _162049.pdf.

69. De Sousa Santos, *Toward a New Legal Common Sense.*

70. See Blackett, "'The Space between Us,'" and the discussion in chapter 6.

6. Beyond Ratification

Epigraph: ILC, 99th Sess., *Provisional Record 19, 39.*

1. The list of ratifications is available at https://www.ilo.org/dyn/normlex/en/f?p =1000:11300:0::NO:11300:P11300_INSTRUMENT_ID:2551460 (accessed October 5, 2018). The following countries have ratified: Argentina, Belgium, Bolivia, Brazil, Chile, Colombia, Costa Rica, Dominican Republic, Ecuador, Finland, Germany, Guinea, Guyana, Ireland, Italy, Jamaica, Mauritius, Nicaragua, Panama, Paraguay, Philippines, Portugal, South Africa, Switzerland, and Uruguay. Adoption of the Decent Work Convention was been followed by ongoing transnational campaigns, including to seek fifteen ratifications by 2015 and then to maintain pressure on individual ILO member states to take decisive action. See Mather, "'Yes, We Did It!'"; Karin Pape, "ILO Convention C189," 200.

2. Sentencias C-871 (2014) (Colombian Constitutional Court), http://www .corteconstitucional.gov.co/relatoria/2014/C-871-14.htm. Colombia ratified the Domestic Workers Convention on May 9, 2014. The Colombian Constitutional Court specifically mentioned articles 3, 6, 10, 11, and 14 of the convention as reflecting the principle of equality.

3. Sentencia C-051 (1995) (Colombian Constitutional Court), http://www .corteconstitucional.gov.co/relatoria/1995/C-051-95.htm; and Sentencia C-100 (2005) (Colombian Constitutional Court), http://www.corteconstitucional.gov.co/relatoria /2005/C-100-05.htm. For an important discussion of the Decent Work Convention in Colombia and Spain, see Alvarado Bedoya, "El trabajo doméstico y del cuidado," 180–81.

4. I discuss assumptions about legal transplantation in chapter 2. See also Blackett, "Emancipation in the Idea of Labour Law."

5. See Macdonald and Kong, "Patchwork Law Reform."

6. Consider law reform in Colombia: Decreto No. 2346/1969 de 25 septiembre, por el que se regula el Régimen Especial de la Seguridad Social para los Empleados de Hogar (May 11, 2011). See Alvarado Bedoya, "El trabajo doméstico y del cuidado."

7. See Poo, *The Age of Dignity.*

8. See Teubner, "Legal Irritants."

9. Blackett, "'A New Thing,'" 289; Poblete, "The Influence of the ILO Domestic Workers Convention," 200–201. Consider also that the extension of the rights to domestic workers is cited as one of the reasons for President Jair Bolsonaro's popularity. Renaud Lambert, "Le Brésil estail fasciste?," *Le monde diplomatique*, November 2018, https//www.monde-diplomatique.fr/2018/11/LAMBERT/59236.

10. Blackett and Tiemeni, "Regulatory Innovation in the Governance of Decent Work for Domestic Workers in South Africa"; Blackett, "Decolonizing Labour Law."

11. Blackett, "Transnational Labour Law and Collective Autonomy for Marginalized Workers."

12. Blackett and Koné Silué, "Regulatory Innovation on Decent Work for Domestic Workers in Côte d'Ivoire"

13. Medici and Blackett, "Ratification as International Solidarity".

14. Blackett, "'The Space between Us.'"

15. International Labour Office, *Report IV(1): Decent Work for Domestic Workers* (hereafter referred to as *Law and Practice Report*), para. 338.

16. United Nations Committee on the Protection of the Rights of all Migrant Workers and Members of Their Families, "General Comment No. 1 on Migrant Domestic Workers Workers."

17. Rhacel Parreñas calls for more studies of domestic work outside of the global North (*Servants of Globalization*, 209).

18. United Nations Human Rights Council, "Forum on Minority Issues."

19. United Nations Human Rights Council, "Forum on Minority Issues."

20. ILO, Official Bulletin, Special Supplement, Vol. LXXV, 1992, Series B, 8 at para. 723.

21. In fact, as discussed in the postface, it was in response to a request for technical assistance that I was asked by the ILO in 1993 to prepare a study of ILO standards and comparative law examples on regulating domestic work. That study was subsequently revised, updated, and published (Blackett, "Making Domestic Work Visible"). That working paper focused primarily on regulatory innovation in France, Spain, and Zimbabwe.

22. See Hepple, *Labour Laws and Global Trade.*

23. Du Toit, *Exploited, Undervalued—and Essential.*

24. See Benjamin, "Beyond the Boundaries," 13, table 1. After analyzing data for 2002–12 from the Commission for Conciliation, Mediation and Arbitration, Benjamin found that roughly 80 percent of referrals to the commission each year were dismissal cases. Darcy du Toit reports that 89 percent of referrals were for unfair dismissal, with the remainder relating to discrimination, unilateral changes to the terms and conditions of employment, and unfair labor practices as defined by the South African Labour Relations Act. Du Toit, "Situating Domestic Work," 15.

25. The CCMA commissioners are reasonably representative of South Africa's racial diversity. While racial inclusion is a dimension of access to justice, one informant mentioned that some commissioners faced racism and general disrespect. Interview with CCMA commissioner 7D, March 2014.

26. This case is discussed in further detail in Blackett, "Decolonizing Labour Law," 92–93.

27. Interview with CCMA commissioner, March 2014.

28. Interview with domestic workers' representative, March 2014.

29. These interviews are discussed at length in Blackett and Tiemeni, "Regulatory Innovation in the Governance of Decent Work for Domestic Workers in South Africa."

30. Interview with CCMA commissioner, March 2014.

31. Interview with CCMA commissioner, March 2014. Domestic workers employed in the agricultural sector are excluded in Sectoral Determination No. 7 but are covered by Sectoral Determination No. 13: Farm Worker Sector (Section 1[3(a)] includes all workers on a farm, including domestic workers employed in a home on a farm).

32. Interview with CCMA commissioner, March 2014.

33. Interview with CCMA commissioner

34. Interview with CCMA commissioner.

35. The CCMA has been much studied, and its limits with respect to regional migrant domestic workers and collective representation are the subject of ongoing reflection. See Ally, *From Servants to Workers*; Laura Griffin, "Borderwork."

36. Bamu, "Nurturing a Culture of Compliance," 189.

37. Du Toit, "Situating Domestic Work," 1.

38. The unpublished booklet was provided to me during my interviews in March 2014. The precise quote is: "More educated youth are entering the domestic sector due to unemployment we also had competitions with our brothers from Zimbabwe that will work for less than what the wage act says, employers employ man because they can drive work in side and do gardening for woman that a very bitter struggle, Domestic workers prefer char or daily employment working for 10 employers per week. This increases the unemployment in this sector, because they work 2–4 hour per house no respect for the labor laws because there is no deduction" (n.p.).

39. On the importance of not exceptionalizing the South African experience, see Chanock, *The Making of South African Legal Culture 1902–1936*, 361.

40. See Ally, *From Servants to Workers*, 60–64.

41. See Fick, *The Making of Haiti*; Kelley, *Hammer and Hoe*.

42. Extended by Ministerial Order on March 2, 2000 (25th ed., IDCC, 2111) J.O. September 2010.

43. Devetter, Ribault, and Jany-Catrice, *Les services à la personne*, 18–19.

44. See Jacqueline Martin-Huan, *La longue marche des domestiques en France du XIXe siècle à nos jours*.

45. Dalmasso, "Le cadre juridique de l'activité de service à la personne."

46. Vallée, "La contribution scientifique de Pierre Verge à l'affirmation et à la recomposition du droit and travail," 21.

47. Weber, *Economy and Society*, 68.

48. This includes recognition by generalist courts, through constitutional protection. Some institutions (like labor relations boards or other specialized labor adjudicators) are products of the state, and others (like grievance arbitrators) are maintained by it. See Vallée, "La contribution scientifique de Pierre Verge à l'affirmation et à la recomposition du droit and travail," 26.

49. Verge, "Vers une graduelle 'continentalisation' du droit du travail?," 290–93.

50. Parliamentary Assembly of the Council of Europe, Protecting Migrant Women in the Labour Market, "Resolution 1811 (2011)" and "Recommendation 1970 (2011)."

51. Parliamentary Assembly of the Council of Europe, "Recommendation 1970 (2011)." See also the ILO Minimum Wage Fixing Recommendation, 1970 (No. 135), para. 3.3.

52. European Economic and Social Committee, Opinion, SOC/508-EESC-2014-1456.

53. European Parliament, T8-0203 /2016, 28 April 2016.

54. European Parliament, Resolution on Women Domestic Workers and Carers in the EU, 2015/2094(INI)

55. Devetter, Ribault, and Jany-Catrice, *Les services à la personne*, 18–19.

56. Blackett, "Transnational Labour Law and Collective Autonomy," 242.

57. Devetter, Ribault, and Jany-Catrice, 23.

58. Blackett, "'A New Thing,'" 289.

59. European Parliament, "European Parliament Resolution of 28 April 2016 on Women Domestic Workers and Carers in the EU."

60. See Hayes, *Stories of Care*; Louise Boivin, "Chèque service, normes du travail et liberté d'association" and "'Just in Time' Labour"; Glenn, *Forced to Care*; Trebilcock, "Challenges in Germany's Implementation." See also the response of the European Commission to the resolution, SP(2016)485, September 22, 2016.

61. Blackett, "'The Space between Us,'" 262.

62. Higman, "An Historical Perspective," 30.

63. In her critique of the literature on liberation from racial, gender-based. or other forms of inequality, Judith Rollins challenges the predominant focus on economic change. While "economic rearrangements" are important, a broader critique that insists on challenging structural inequality is essential to prevent old hierarchies from simply reemerging (*Between Women*, 6).

64. *Siliadin v. France* (2005) no. 73316/01 IHRL 2866, ECHR (France), at 3.

65. Article 225-13. The provision was amended on March 18, 2003, after a French National Assembly taskforce on the various forms of modern slavery reported on the ambiguity of the provisions, to read: "It shall be an offence punishable by five years' imprisonment and a fine of 150,000 euros to obtain from an individual whose vulnerability or state of dependence is apparent or of which the offender is aware, the performance of services without payment or in exchange for payment which is manifestly disproportionate to the amount of work carried out."

66. Article 225-14. The provision was also amended on March 18, 2003, to read: "It shall be an offence punishable by five years' imprisonment and a fine of 150,000 euros to subject an individual whose vulnerability or state of dependence is apparent or of which the offender is aware to working or living conditions which are incompatible with human dignity." And article 225-15 was added: "The offences set out in Articles 225-13 and 225-14 shall be punishable by seven years' imprisonment and a fine of 200,000 euros if they are committed against more than one person. If they are committed against a minor, they shall be punishable by seven years' imprisonment and a fine of 200,000 euros. If they are committed against more than one person, including one or more minors, they shall be punishable by ten years' imprisonment and a fine of 300,000 euros."

67. *Siliadin v. France* (2005) no. 73316/01 IHRL 2866, ECHR (France). The ECHR did not find that the case amounted to slavery in the traditional sense of the concept. The court was at pains to mention what should be an extraneous fact: that the employer, although a French national, was "of Togolese origin." The relationship of former imperial powers to the construction of race through the legacy of slavery and colonial dispossession is hinted at in phrases such as "contemporary forms of slavery" that are recast as the realm of racialized, "uncivilized" others.

68. The relevant sections of article 4 state that

1. No one shall be held in slavery or servitude.

2. No one shall be required to perform forced or compulsory labour. (European Court of Human Rights and Council of Europe. "European Convention on Human Rights")

69. *Siliadin v. France*, 4.

70. *Siliadin v. France*, 5–6.

71. *Siliadin v. France*, 32.

72. The ECHR has evolved in its case law since that point. See, for example, *C.N. and V. v. France* (2012) no. 67724/09, ECHR (France); *C.N. v. the United Kingdom* (2012) no. 4239/08, ECHR (France).

73. See Kotiswaran, "From Sex Panic to Extreme Exploitation."

74. Blackett, "Slavery is not a Metaphor."

75. Anderson, *Us and Them? The Dangerous Politics of Immigration Control*, 11, 138.

76. Darian-Smith, *Laws and Societies in Global Contexts*, 314.

77. During the time of my study, Loi no 95-15 du 12 janvier 1995 portant Code du travail (CIV), JORCI 23 February 1998, was in force. On July 20, 2015, Loi no 2015-532 du 20 juillet 2015 portant Code du travail (CIV), came into force.

78. The team included Assata Koné, a lecturer in the Faculty of Law, Université Houphouët Boigny, Abidjan; and Yéfoungnigui Silue, then studying for a master's degree at the Université Alassane Ouatarra de Bouaké.

79. Decision no. 68 (2011) Juris Social April 2012 (Abidjan, Côte d'Ivoire, C.A.).

80. Interviews with labor court judges, December 2013.

81. See Decision no. 109 (2000) Juris Social September 2002 (Bouake, Côte d'Ivoire, Labour C.).

82. Interview with labor inspectors, December 2013.

83. See Medici and Blackett, "Ratification as International Solidarity."

84. Canton of Geneva, "Contrat-type de travail avec salaires minimaux impératifs de l'économie domestique," December 13, 2011, https://www.ge.ch/legislation/rsg /f/s/rsg_j1_50p03.html. The standard employment contracts (SECs) are not model contracts but forms of state regulation. SECs were initially subsidiary regulatory texts, designed to deal with matters like the formation and nature of employment relationships. The consolidated version went into force January 1, 2012, and was still in force as of January 1, 2018 (Republic and Canton of Geneva).

85. See Medici and Blackett, "Ratification as International Solidarity," 200.

86. The Domestic Workers Convention ultimately included a definitional reference to the "employment relationship," which has been read by many to limit the scope beyond that contemplated in the Canton of Geneva's SEC.

87. Louise Boivin discusses similar circumvention practices in the use of model contracts in Quebec ("Réorganisation des services d'aide à domicile au Québec et droits syndicaux").

88. See Medici and Blackett, "Ratification as International Solidarity," 204–5.

89. Medici, *Migrantinnen als Pflegehilfen in Schweizer Privataushalten*.

90. Gabriela Naemi Medici offers a comprehensive analysis of labor migration in Switzerland (*Migrantinnen als Pflegehilfen in Schweizer Privataushalten*).

91. United Nations Committee on the Elimination of Discrimination against Women, "General Recommendation No. 26 on Women Migrant Workers." UN Doc. CEDAW/C/2009/WP.1/R, c.

92. United Nations Committee on the Protection of the Rights of all Migrant Workers and Members of Their Families, "General Comment No. 1 on Migrant Domestic Workers Workers." UN Doc. CMW/C/GC/1.

93. UN Committee on Migrant Workers, General Comment No. 1, para. 6.

94. UN Committee on Migrant Workers, General Comment No. 1, para. 6.

95. UN Committee on Migrant Workers, General Comment No. 1, para 13. The committee added that its recommendation was in line with the position of the UN Committee on Economic, Social and Cultural Rights, "The Right to Work," General Comment No. 18, para. 10.

96. Switzerland has played a leadership role in the Global Forum on Migration and Development and addressed migrant domestic work.

97. Leclerc, "Statistics on Labor Migration within the Asia-Pacific Region."

98. Migrant Workers and Overseas Filipinos Act of 1995, Rep. Act No. 10022 (2009), as amended, article 4.

99. Some bilateral agreements are land- and some are sea-based. See Philippine Overseas Employment Administration, "Bilateral Labor Agreements (Landbased)." Nicola Yeates has identified bilateral agreements that apply to other categories of migrants and include arrangements for compensation and even forms of social financing between sending and receiving countries. For example, the Philippines and Qatar entered into an agreement that regulates not only migration but also the employment contract. The agreement makes clear to employers that they cannot introduce changes into the contract that they agreed to with the domestic worker unless those changes improve the worker's condition. See, e.g., Yeates, "The Globalization of Nurse Migration."

100. See Chavez and Piper, "The Reluctant Leader."

101. Quoted in Julie M. Aurelio, "Ban on Sending Filipino Domestic Helpers to Kuwait Eyed," *Inquirer*, January 28, 2017, http://globalnation.inquirer.net/152154/ban-sending-filipino-domestic-helpers-kuwait-eyed#ixzz4vtS850Uu.

102. See Migrant-Rights.org, "Avoiding Reform, GCC States Seek Alternative Sources of Labor"; Philippines Overseas Employment Administration, "Governing Board Resolution No. 7" and "Governing Board Resolution No. 1."

103. Tigno, "At the Mercy of the Market?," 23.

104. I conducted the on-site research with Dzodzi Tsikata, a professor at the at the Institute of Statistical Social and Economic Research of the University of Ghana and president of Council for the Development of Social Science Research in Africa; and Lyn Ossome, a senior research fellow at the Makerere Institute of Social Research, under a grant from the International Development Research Centre to the Labour Law and Development Research Laboratory (Grant No. 106616-00020603-020).

105. See, for example, de Regt, "Employing Migrant Domestic Workers in Urban Yemen"; McGregor, "'Joining the BBC (British Bottom Cleaners)'"; Lund, "Hierarchies of Care Work in South Africa"; van Walsum, "Regulating Migrant Domestic Work in the Netherlands.

106. Migrant-Rights.org, "Avoiding Reform, GCC States Seek Alternative Sources of Labor," February 11, 2013, http://www.migrant-rights.org/2013/02/11/avoiding-reform-gcc-states-seek-alternative-sources-of-labor/.

Reports indicate that 3,000 or so Kenyan migrant workers were registered with the Kenyan Embassy in Riyadh, but the actual numbers are likely considerably higher. See Joyce J. Wangui, "Pursuit of Greener Pastures in Saudi Arabia Spells Doom for

Kenyan Immigrants," December 20, 2011, https://diasporamessenger.com/2011/12 /pursuit-of-greener-pastures-in-saudi-arabia-spells-doom-for-kenyan-immigrants.

107. Those pathways have become "narrower and more precarious." See Faraday, *Canada's Choice*, 34; Gallerand and Gallié, "Travail non libre"; Hastie, "The Inequality of Low-Wage Migrant Labour"; Fudge, "Global Care Chains."

108. Parreñas, *Servants of Globalization* and *Children of Global Migration*. See also C. Thomas, "Migrant Domestic Workers in Egypt."

109. Graziano Battistella and Maruja Asis describe various ways in which bans can be circumvented ("Stemming Irregular Migration at the Source," 325).

110. Philippine Overseas Employment Administration, "Standard Employment Contract for Filipino Household Service Workers (HSWs) Bound for the Kingdom of Saudi Arabia," article 4. See also Encinas-Franco, "Filipino Women Migrant Workers and Overseas Employment Policy."

111. Center for Migrant Advocacy—Philippines, "Replies to LOI for the Philippines with a Focus on Women Migrant Workers," accessed August 4, 2018, http://tbinternet .ohchr.org/Treaties/CEDAW/Shared%20Documents/PHL/INT_CEDAW_NGO _PHL_24247_E.pdf., 8.

112. See Tesfaye Getnet, "Saudi Arabia's MoU Signature Necessary to Lift Travel Ban," *Capital* Ethiopia, September 5, 2016, http://capitalethiopia.com/2016/09/05 /saudi-arabias-mou-signature-necessary-lift-travel-ban/?pr=68257&lang=en.

113. "Ugandan Women Flown Home from Saudi Arabia amid Maid Ban," BBC News, January 26, 2016, https://www.bbc.com/news/world-africa-35409201.

114. See "Kenya Marks International Domestic Workers Day amid Rising Cases of Abuse," Africa News, June 17, 2018, http://www.xinhuanet.com/english/2018-06/17 /c_137259217.htm. Vicky Kanyoka, the Africa Regional Coordinator for the IDWF, explains the importance for Kenya of ratification of the Decent Workers Convention.

115. See Sally Hayden, "Inside the Underground Efforts to Liberate Saudi Arabia's Domestic Workers," *Vice News*, March 9, 2016, https://news.vice.com/article/inside -the-underground-efforts-to-liberate-saudi-arabias-domestic-workers.

116. *Vallejos Evangeline Banao and Commissioner of Registration* (2011) HCAL 124/2010 (Hong Kong, H.C.).

117. See Kevin Drew, "Court Rules on Side of Maids' Right to Residency," *New York Times*, September 30, 2011, http://www.nytimes.com/2011/10/01/world/asia/court -rules-on-side-of-maids-rights-to-residency.html.

118. *Vallejos Evangeline Banao v. and Commissioner of Registration* (2012) CACV 204/2011 (Hong Kong, C.A.). See "Hong Kong Government Wins Appeal in Maid Registry Case," BBC News, March 28, 2012, https://www.bbc.com/news/business -17532723; "Filipino Maid Takes Fight for Permanent Residency to Hong Kong's Top Court," *Guardian*, June 22, 2012, https://www.theguardian.com/world/2012/jun/22 /filipino-maid-hong-kong-court.

119. *Vallejos Evangeline Banao and Commissioner of Registration* (2013) CFA, FACV Nos. 19 & 20 of 2012, 25 March 2013, para. 89; "Hong Kong Maids Lose Residency Case," *Guardian*, March 25, 2013, https://www.theguardian.com/world/2013/mar/25/hong -kong-maids-residency-case. See also Davidov, *A Purposive Approach to Labour Law*, and the critical engagement in Harry Arthurs, et al., *Book Symposium*.

Conclusion

1. Brunnée and Toope, *Legitimacy and Legality in International Law*, 22.

2. Barmes, *Bullying and Behavioural Conflict at Work*, 266.

3. Blackett, "Emancipation in the Idea of Labour Law," 434.

4. Baxi, *Human Rights in a Posthuman World*, 29.

5. King Jr., *Where Do We Go from Here*.

6. Poo, *The Age of Dignity*. Jennifer Nedelsky radically rethinks the relationship between work and care so that care is the responsibility of everyone (*(Part)-Time for All*).

7. Fraser, *Scales of Justice*, 40; Achiume, "Reimagining International Law for Global Migration," 142; Mégret, "Transnational Mobility," 13.

8. Fraser, "A Triple Movement?," 131.

9. Blackett, "Development, the Movement of Persons, and Labour Law." Yong-Shik Lee refers to reasonable labor market access, but his focus is temporary migration programs, and it should be emphasized that he does not advocate including labor standards in the World Trade Organization (*Reclaiming Development*, 171–72).

10. United Nations Human Rights Council, *Resolution on Human Rights and International Solidarity*, A/HRC/RES/23/12, June 24, 2013. The vote was largely polarized between member states in the global South and those the global North. A discussion of the direction of the United Nations' mandate on international solidarity is beyond the scope of this book.

11. World Trade Organization. "Joint Declaration on Trade and Women's Economic Empowerment on the Occasion of the WTO Ministerial Conference in Buenos Aires in December 2017," https://www.wto.org/english/thewto_e/minist_e/mc11_e/genderdeclarationmc11_e.pdf.

12. Of course, identifying the optimal institutional home(s) for a transnational response would be particularly difficult. The problems of institutional fit that Bob Hepple identified at the WTO on the adjudication of labor rights would apply also to labor migration. Hepple, *Labour Laws and Global Trade*. Greater attention has been turned, recently, to the possibilities offered at the regional level. See, e.g., Deacon et al, eds., *World Regional Social Policy and Global Governance*; Blackett and Lévesque, *Social Regionalism in the Global Economy*. The *Global Compact for Safe, Orderly and Regular Migration* specifically references the Domestic Workers Convention, acknowledges the importance of a multilevel and, in particular, regional approach (adding that no state can address migration alone), and underscores the importance of international cooperation and solidarity. Its focus is on redressing "irregular" migration by promoting "regular" migration, including through a human rights approach. There is little room for interrogation of the fine line between regular but temporary migration schemes and persisting precarity. United Nations General Assembly, *Global Compact for Safe, Orderly and Regular Migration*.

13. Blackett, "'The Space between Us,'" 268–73, and "Development, the Movement of Persons, and Labour Law," 158–65.

14. Peer Zumbansen theorizes transnational law not as a field but as a methodology for keeping space open ("Transnational Legal Pluralism," 153).

15. David W. Kennedy, "The Mystery of Global Governance," 848.

Postface

1. The late, internationally celebrated sociologist Agnes Calliste notes that approximately a hundred women from Guadeloupe were brought to Quebec in the short period 1910–11 to serve as domestic workers, but the program was discontinued when rumors circulated that some of the women were single mothers ("Canadian Immigration Policy and Domestics from the Caribbean").

2. Canada Department of Foreign and International Trade, Admission of Domestics from the B.W.I. Memorandum from Minister of Citizenship and Immigration and Minister of Labour to Cabinet, Ottawa, June 7, 1955, Cabinet Doc. No. 131-55. Documents on Canadian External Relations.

3. *Elizabeth Lodge, Carmen Hyde, Eliza Cox, Elaine Peart, Rubena Whyte, Gloria Lawrence, and Lola Anderson v. Minister of Employment and Immigration*, [1979] 1 F.C. 775; 94 DLR (3d) 326.

4. See Association of Black Women Historians, "An Open Statement to the Fans of *The Help*," August 12, 2011, http://truth.abwh.org/2011/08/12/an-open-statement-to -the-fans-of-the-help/.

Appendix 1

1. Source: International Labour Office, *Report IV(1): Decent Work for Domestic Workers* (2010),15.

Appendix 4

1. See Thornton Dill, *Across the Boundaries of Race and Class* (a study of African American women who worked as domestic servants while Jim Crow conditions still prevailed in the United States); Cock, *Maids and Madams* (a study of South African domestic workers under apartheid).

2. The list of publications that have influenced my writing of the *Law and Practice Report* for the better is long—other important contemporary ethnographies that I reference in this book and other writing include Parreñas, *Servants of Globalization* and *Children of Global Migration*; Silvera, *Silenced*; Anderson, *Britain's Secret Slaves*; Chang, *Disposable Domestics*; Glenn, *Issei, Nisei, War Bride*.

3. Rollins, *Between Women*.

4. Rollins, 11–17.

5. Romero, *Maid in the U.S.A.*

6. Romero, *Maid in the U.S.A.*, 45.

7. Chin, *In Service and Servitude*, 125.

8. Andall, *Gender, Migration and Domestic Servitude*.

9. Hondagneu-Sotelo, *Doméstica*.

10. Stasiulis and Bakan, *Negotiating Citizenship*.

11. Stasiulis and Bakan, 2.

12. Ally, *From Servants to Workers*.

13. Stasiulis and Bakan, *Negotiating Citizenship*, 4.

14. E. Glenn, *Issei, Nisei, War Bride*, 95.

15. S. Hall, *The Fateful Triangle*, 58. Hall draws on Marx and Engels, *The German Ideology*.

SELECTED BIBLIOGRAPHY

Abi-Saab, Georges. "The Newly Independent States and the Scope of Domestic Jurisdiction." *Proceedings of the American Society of International Law at Its Annual Meeting* 84, no. 3 (1960): 84–90.

Achiume, Tendayi E. "Reimagining International Law for Global Migration: Migration as Decolonization?" *American Society of International Law Unbound* 111 (2017): 142–46.

Adams, Samuel, and Sarah Adams. *The Complete Servant: Being a Practical Guide to the Peculiar Duties and Business of All Descriptions of Servants, from the Housekeeper to the Servant of All-Work, and from the Land Steward to the Foot-Boy. With Useful Receipts and Tables.* London: Knight and Lacey, 1825.

Albin, Einat. "From 'Domestic Servant' to 'Domestic Worker.'" In *Challenging the Legal Boundaries of Work Regulation*, edited by Judy Fudge, Shae McChrystal, and Kamala Sankaran, 231–50. Oxford: Hart Publishing, 2012.

Ales, Edoardo, Olaf Deinert, and Jeff Kenner, eds. *Core and Contingent Workers in the European Union: A Comparative Analysis.* Oxford: Hart Publishing, 2017.

Aleyn Lyell, Reade. *Johnsonian Gleanings, Part II: Francis Barber, the Doctor's Negro Servant.* San Bernadino, CA: Ulan Press, 2011.

Ally, Shireen. *From Servants to Workers: South African Domestic Workers and the Democratic State.* Ithaca, NY: Cornell University Press, 2009.

Alvarado Bedoya, Claudia Patricia. "El trabajo doméstico y del cuidado: Informalidad y fronteras de laboralidad." PhD diss., Pompeu Fabra University, 2017.

Andall, Jacqueline. *Gender, Migration and Domestic Servitude: The Politics of Black Women in Italy.* Farnham, UK: Ashgate Publishing, 2000.

Anderson, Bridget. *Britain's Secret Slaves: The Plight of Overseas Domestic Workers in the United Kingdom.* London: Anti-Slavery International, 1993.

———. *Us and Them: The Dangerous Politics of Immigration Control.* Oxford: Oxford University Press, 2013.

Arthurs, Harry W. "The Hollowing out of Corporate Canada: Implications for Transnational Labor Law, Policy and Practice." *Buffalo Law Review* 57, no. 3 (2008): 781–802.

———. "Labour Law without the State?" *University of Toronto Law Journal* 45, no. 1 (1996): 1–45.

Arthurs, Harry W., Einat Albin, Simon Deakin, Guy Mundlak, Ruth Dukes, and Guy Davidov. "Book Symposium on Guy Davidov's A Purposive Approach to Labour Law," *Jerusalem Review of Legal Studies* 15, no. 1 (2017): 1–82.

Atleson, James B. *Values and Assumptions in American Labor Law*. Amherst, MA: University of Massachusetts Press, 1983.

Bakan, Abigail B., and Daiva Stasiulis, eds. *Not One of the Family: Foreign Domestic Workers in Canada*. Toronto: University of Toronto Press, 1997.

Bangasser, Paul E. "The ILO and the Informal Sector: An Institutional History." Geneva: International Labour Office, 2000. http://www.ilo.int/wcmsp5/groups/public/@ed_emp/documents/publication/wcms_142295.pdf.

Barmes, Lizzie. *Bullying and Behavioural Conflict at Work: The Duality of Individual Rights*. Oxford: Oxford University Press, 2016.

Battistella, Graziano, and Maruja M. B. Asis. "Stemming Irregular Migration at the Source: The Philippine Experience." In *Skillful Survivals: Irregular Migration to the Gulf*, edited by Philippe Fargues and Nasra M. Shah, 315–35. Cambridge: Gulf Research Center and European University Institute, 2017.

Baxi, Upendra. *Human Rights in a Posthuman World: Critical Essays*. Oxford: Oxford University Press, 2007.

Baylis, T. Henry, *The Rights, Duties and Relations of Domestic Servants and their Masters and Mistresses. With a Short Account of Servants' Institutions, &c. and their Advantages*. 4th Ed., with considerable additions by Edward P. Monckton. London: Butterworths, 1873.

Beecher, Catharine Esther. *Miss Beecher's Domestic Receipt Book*. New York: Harper and Brothers, 1846.

Belley, Jean-Guy. "Georges Gurvitch et les professionnels de la pensée juridique." *Droit et société* 4, no. 1 (1986): 353–71.

——. "L'avenir du droit et des juristes: Trois scénarios." *Revue générale de droit* 30, no. 3 (1999–2000): 501–21.

Benjamin, Paul. "Beyond the Boundaries: Prospects for Expanding Labour Market Regulation in South Africa." In *Boundaries and Frontiers of Labour Law: Goals and Means in the Regulation of Work*, edited by Guy Davidov and Brian Langille, 181–204. Oxford: Hart Publishing, 2006.

Bhabha, Homi K. "Remembering Fanon: Self, Psyche, and the Colonial Condition." Foreword to the 1986 edition. In Franz Fanon, *Black Skin, White Mask*. Translated by Richard Philcox. New York: Grove Press, 2008.

Blackett, Adelle. "Beyond Standard Setting: A Study of ILO Technical Cooperation on Regional Labor Law Reform in West and Central Africa." *Comparative Labor Law and Policy Journal* 32, no. 2 (2011): 443–92.

——. "The Decent Work for Domestic Workers Convention and Recommendation, 2011." *American Journal of International Law* 106, no. 4 (2012): 778–94.

——. "Decolonizing Labour Law: A Few Comments." In *Labour Law and Social Progress: Holding the Line or Shifting the Boundaries?*, edited by Roger Blanpain, Frank Hendrickx, and Darcy du Toit, 89–100. Alphen aan den Rijn, The Netherlands: Wolters Kluwer, 2016.

——. "Development, the Movement of Persons, and Labour Law: Reasonable Labour Market Access and Its Decent Work Complement." In *The Role of Labour Standards in Development: From Theory to Sustainable Practice?*, ed. Tonia Novitz and David Mangan, 143–65. Oxford: Oxford University Press, 2010.

——. "Domestic Workers at the Interface of Migration and Development: Action to Expand Good Practice." Paper presented at the Global Forum on Migrant and Development, Accra, Ghana, September 21–22, 2011.

——. "Emancipation in the Idea of Labour Law: Commoditization, Resistance and Distributive Justice beyond Borders." In *The Idea of Labour Law*, edited by Guy Davidov and Brian Langille, 420–36. Oxford: Oxford University Press, 2011.

——. "Introduction: Labor Law and Development; Perspectives on Labor Regulation in Africa and the African Diaspora." *Comparative Labor Law and Policy Journal* 32, no. 2 (2011): 303–10.

——. "Introduction: Regulating Decent Work for Domestic Workers." *Canadian Journal of Women and the Law* 23, no. 1 (2011): 1–45.

——. "Introductory Note to the Decent Work for Domestic Workers Convention, 2011 (no. 189) and Recommendation (no. 201)" (June 16, 2011). *International Legal Materials* 53, no. 1 (2014): 250–253. http://doi.org/10.5305/intelegamate .53.1.0250.

——. "Making Domestic Work Visible: The Case for Specific Regulation." Labour Law and Labour Relations Programme Working Paper No. 2. Geneva: International Labour Office, 1998. https://www.mcgill.ca/law/files/law /adelle_blackett_specific_regulation_98b09_500_engl.pdf.

——. "'A New Thing: Shall Ye Not Know It?': On Living Metaphors in Transnational Labour Law." In *The Daunting Enterprise of the Law: Essays in Honour of Harry Arthurs*, edited by Simon Archer, Daniel Drache, and Peer Zumbansen, 286–97. Montreal: McGill-Queen's University Press, 2017.

——. "The Paradox of OHADA's Transnational, Hard Law, Labour Harmonization Initiative." In *Social Regionalism in the Global Economy*, edited by Adelle Blackett and Christian Lévesque, 243–72. New York: Routledge, 2011.

——. "Promoting Domestic Workers' Human Dignity through Specific Regulation." In *Domestic Service and the Formation of European Identity: Understanding the Globalization of Domestic Work, 16th–21st Centuries*, edited by Antoinette Fauve-Chamoux, 247–73. Bern, Switzerland: Peter Lang Publishing, 2005.

——. "Regulatory Innovation on Decent Work for Domestic Workers in the Light of International Labour Organization Convention No. 189." *International Journal of Comparative Labour Law and Industrial Relations* 34, no. 2 (2018): 141–48.

——. Review of *Exploited, Undervalued—and Essential: Domestic Workers and the Realisation of Their Rights*, edited by Darcy du Toit. *Law and Society Review* 49, no. 3 (2015): 801–4.

——. Review of *Managing the Margins: Gender, Citizenship, and the International Regulation of Precarious Employment*, by Leah F. Vosko. *International Labour Review* 150, nos. 3–4 (2011): 457–61.

——. "Situated Reflections on International Labour Law, Capabilities, and Decent Work: The Case of Centre Maraîcher Eugène Guinois." *Revue québécoise de droit international (Hors série)* (2007): 223–44.

——. "Slavery Is Not a Metaphor." Review of *Contemporary Slavery: Popular Rhetoric and Political Practice*, edited by Annie Bunting and Joel Quirk. *American Journal of Comparative Law*, 66, no. 4 (2018, forthcoming).

——. "'The Space between Us': Migrant Domestic Work as a Nexus between International Labor Standards and Trade Policy." In *Linking Global Trade and Human Rights*, edited by Daniel Drache and Lesley A. Jacobs, 259–73. Cambridge: Cambridge University Press, 2014.

——. "Transnational Labour Law and Collective Autonomy for Marginalized Workers: Reflections on Decent Work for Domestic Workers." In *Research Handbook on Transnational Labour Law*, edited by Adelle Blackett and Anne Trebilcock, 230–44. Cheltenham, UK: Elgar Publishing, 2015.

Blackett, Adelle, and Thierry Galani Tiemeni. "Regulatory Innovation in the Governance of Decent Work for Domestic Workers in South Africa: Access to Justice and the Commission on Conciliation, Mediation and Arbitration." *International Journal of Comparative Labour Law and Industrial Relations* 34, no. 2 (2018): 203–30.

Blackett, Adelle, and Assata Koné-Silué. "Regulatory Innovation in the Governance of Decent Work for Domestic Workers in Côte d'Ivoire: Labour Administration and the Judiciary in a Generalist Code." *International Labour Review* 158, no. 1 (forthcoming, 2019).

Blackett, Adelle, and Christian Lévesque, eds. *Social Regionalism in the Global Economy*. New York: Routledge, 2011.

Blackstone, William. *Commentaries on the Laws of England*. Vol. 1. Oxford: Clarendon Press, 1765–69.

Boivin, Louise. "Chèque service, normes du travail et liberté d'association: Le cas du Québec." Montreal: Labour Law and Development Research Laboratory, 2017. https://www.mcgill.ca/lldrl/files/lldrl/boivin_cheque_service _working_paper24-08-17.pdf.

——. "'Just in Time' Labour: The Case of Networks Providing Home Assistance Service in Quebec." *International Journal of Comparative Labour Law and Industrial Relations* 32, no. 3 (2016): 301–21.

——. "Réorganisation des services d'aide à domicile au Québec et droits syndicaux: De la qualification à la disponibilité permanente juste-à-temps." *Revue internationale francophone: Nouvelles questions féministes* 32, no. 2 (2013): 44–56.

Bonner, Christine. "Domestic Workers around the World: Organising for Empowerment." Paper presented at the Social Law Project Conference, Cape Town, South Africa, May 7–8, 2010. http://wiego.org/publications/domestic -workers-around-world-organising-empowerment.

Boris, Eileen. *Home to Work: Motherhood and the Politics of Industrial Homework in the United States*. Cambridge: Cambridge University Press, 1994.

Boris, Eileen, and Jennifer Klein. *Caring for America: Home Health Workers in the Shadow of the Welfare State*. Oxford: Oxford University Press, 2012.

Bosch, Gerhard. "Working Time and the Standard Employment Relationship." In *Decent Working Time: New Trends, New Issues*, edited by Jean-Yves Boulin, Michel Lallement, Jon C. Messenger, and François Michon, 41–64. Geneva: International Labour Office, 2006.

Briones, Leah. *Empowering Migrant Women: Why Agency and Rights Are Not Enough*. Burlington, VT: Ashgate Publishing Company, 2013.

Brunnée, Jutta, and Stephen J. Toope. *Legitimacy and Legality in International Law.* Cambridge: Cambridge University Press, 2010.

Buckner-Inniss, Lolita, Sonia Lawrence, Emily Graham, Maneesha Dekha, and Kim Brooks. Review of *Mrs. Dred Scott: A Life on Slavery's Frontier,* by Lea VanderVelde. *Canadian Journal of Women and the Law* 24, no. 2 (2012): 458–75.

Butler, Judith. "Endangered/Endangering: Schematic Racism and White Paranoia." In *Reading Rodney King: Reading Urban Uprising,* edited by Robert Gooding-Williams, 15–22. London: Routledge, 1993.

Cairns, John W. "Blackstone, an English Institutist: Legal Literature and the Rise of the Nation State." *Oxford Journal of Legal Studies* 4, no. 3 (1984): 318–60.

——. "Blackstone in the Bayous: Inscribing Slavery in the Louisiana Digest of 1808." In *Re-Interpreting Blackstone's Commentaries: A Seminal Text in National and International Contexts,* edited by Wilfrid Prest, 599–622. Oxford: Hart Publishing, 2014.

Calavita, Kitty. *Immigrants at the Margins: Law, Race, and Exclusion in Southern Europe.* Cambridge: Cambridge University Press, 2005.

Calleman, Catherina. "Domestic Services in a 'Land of Equality': The Case of Sweden." *Canadian Journal of Women and the Law* 23, no. 1 (2011): 121–39.

Calliste, Agnes. "Canadian Immigration Policy and Domestics from the Caribbean: The Second Domestic Scheme." In *Race, Class, Gender: Bonds and Barriers,* edited by Jesse Vorst, 133–65. Toronto: Garamond Press; 1991.

Campbell, Tunis Gulic. *Hotel Keepers, Head Waiters, and Housekeepers' Guide.* Boston: Coolidge and Wiley, 1848.

Chaney, Elsa M., and Mary Garcia Castro, eds. *Muchachas No More: Household Workers in Latin America and the Caribbean.* Philadelphia: Temple University Press, 1989.

Chang, Grace. *Disposable Domestics: Immigrant Women Workers in the Global Economy.* Cambridge, MA: South End Press, 2000.

Chanock, Martin. *The Making of South African Legal Culture 1902–1936: Fear, Favour, and Prejudice.* Cambridge: Cambridge University Press, 2001.

Charlesworth, Hilary, and David Kennedy. "Afterword: And Forward—There Remains So Much We Do Not Know." In *International Law and Its Others,* edited by Anne Orford, 401–7. New York: Cambridge University Press, 2006.

Chavez, Jenina Joy, and Nicola Piper. "The Reluctant Leader: The Philippine Journey from Labor Export to Championing a Rights-Based Approach to Overseas Employment." In *Asian Leadership in Policy and Governance,* edited by Evan Berman and M. Shamsul Haque, 305–44. Bingley, UK: Emerald Group Publishing, 2015.

Chen, Martha Alter. "Recognizing Domestic Workers, Regulating Domestic Work: Conceptual Measurement, and Regulatory Challenges." *Canadian Journal of Women and the Law* 23, no. 1 (2011): 167–84.

Chen, Martha Alter, Joann Vanek, and Marilyn Carr. *Mainstreaming Informal Employment and Gender in Poverty Reduction: A Handbook for Policy Makers and Other Stakeholders.* London: Commonwealth Secretariat and International Development Research Centre, 2004.

Chin, Christine B. N. *In Service and Servitude: Foreign Female Domestic Workers and the Malaysian Modernity Project.* New York: Columbia University Press, 1998.

Chua, Amy. "The Privatization-Nationalization Cycle: The Link between Markets and Ethnicity in Developing Countries." *Columbia Law Review* 95, no. 2 (1995): 223–303.

Chuang, Janie A. "The U.S. Au Pair Program: Labor Exploitation and the Myth of Cultural Exchange." *Harvard Journal of Law and Gender* 36, no. 2 (2013): 269–343.

Cock, Jacklyn. *Maids and Madams: Domestic Workers under Apartheid*. London: Women's Press, 1989.

Colen, Shellee, and Roger Sanjek. "At Work in Homes I: Orientations." In *At Work in Homes: Household Workers in World Perspective*, edited by Roger Sanjek and Shellee Colen, 1–11. Washington, DC: American Anthropological Association, 1990.

Comaroff, Jean, and John L. Comaroff. *Theory from the South: Or, How Euro-America Is Evolving toward Africa*. Abingdon: Routledge, 2012.

Cooper, Afua. *The Hanging of Angélique: The Untold Story of Canadian Slavery and the Burning of Old Montréal*. Athens: University of Georgia Press, 2006.

Cooper, Esther Victoria. "The Negro Woman Domestic Worker in Relation to Trade Unionism." MArts thesis, Fisk University, 1940.

Cooper, Frederick. *Decolonization and African Society: The Labor Question in French and British Africa*. Cambridge: Cambridge University Press, 1996.

Coulthard, Glen Sean. *Red Skin, White Masks: Rejecting the Colonial Politics of Recognition*. Minneapolis: University of Minnesota Press, 2014.

Coutu, Michel. "La naissance du contrat de travail comme concept juridique: Max Weber et Hugo Sinzheimer, critiques de Philipp Lotmar." *Canadian Journal of Law and Society* 24, no. 2 (2009): 159–79.

——. "Max Weber on the Labour Contract: Between Realism and Formal Legal Thought." *Journal of Law and Society* 36, no. 4 (2009): 558–67.

Craven, Paul, "Canada, 1670–1935: Symbolic and Instrumental Enforcement in Loyalist North America." In *Masters, Servants, and Magistrates in Britain and the Empire, 1562–1955*, edited by Douglas Hay and Paul Craven, 175–218. Chapel Hill: University of North Carolina Press, 2004.

Crenshaw, Kimberlé, "Demarginalizing the Intersection of Race and Sex: A Black Feminist Critique of Antidiscrimination Doctrine, Feminist Theory and Antiracist Politics." *University of Chicago Legal Forum* 140, no. 1 (1989): 139.

——. "Mapping the Margins: Intersectionality, Identity Politics, and Violence against Women of Color." *Stanford Law Review* 43, no. 6 (1991): 1241–99.

Dalmasso, Raphaël. "Le cadre juridique de l'activité de service à la personne." In *Les services à la personne*, edited by Barnard Balzani, 27–39. Paris: Les études de la documentation française, 2010.

Darian-Smith, Eve. *Laws and Societies in Global Contexts: Contemporary Approaches*. New York: Cambridge University Press, 2013.

Dauvergne, Catherine. *Making People Illegal: What Globalization Means for Migration and Law*. Cambridge: Cambridge University Press, 2009.

Davala, Sarath, Renana Jhabvala, Soumya Kapoor Mehta, and Guy Standing. *Basic Income: A Transformative Policy for India*. London: Bloomsbury, 2015.

Davidov, Guy. *A Purposive Approach to Labour Law*. Oxford: Oxford University Press, 2016.

Davies, Paul, and Mark Freedland, *Labour Legislation and Public Policy*. Oxford: Oxford University Press, 1993.

Deacon, Bob, Maria Cristina Macovei, Luk Van Langenhove, and Nicola Yeates, eds. *World-Regional Social Policy and Global Governance*. New York: Routledge, 2010.

Deakin, Simon F. Review of *Values and Assumptions in American Labor Law*, by James B. Atleson. *Cambridge Law Journal* 44, no. 2 (1985): 321–22.

——. "What Exactly is Happening to the Contract of Employment?" Reflections on *The Legal Construction of Personal Work Relations*, by Mark Freedland and Nicola Kountouris. *Jerusalem Review of Legal Studies* 7, no. 1 (2015): 135–44.

Deakin, Simon F., and Frank Wilkinson. *The Law of the Labour Market: Industrialization, Employment, and Legal Evolution*. Oxford: Oxford University Press, 2005.

Defourny, Jacques, Arnaud Henry, Stéphane Nassaut, and Marthe Nyssens. "Does the Mission of Providers Matter on a Quasi-Market? The Case of the Belgian 'Service Voucher' Scheme." *Annals of Public and Cooperative Economics* 81, no. 4 (2010): 583–610.

——. "Les titres-services: Quelle qualité d'emploi et d'organisation du service?" *Regards économiques* 69 (2009): 1–16.

Demaret, Luc. "Decent Work for Domestic Workers—International Convention on the Way." *Labour Education* 3–4, nos. 148–49 (2007): 1–7. https://www.ilo.org/wcmsp5/groups/public/—ed_dialogue/—actrav/documents/publication/wcms_392019.pdf.

De Regt, Marina. "Employing Migrant Domestic Workers in Urban Yemen: A New Form of Social Distinction." *Hawwa* 6, no. 2 (2008): 154–75.

De Soto, Hernando. *The Mystery of Capital: Why Capitalism Triumphs in the West and Fails Everywhere Else*. New York: Basic Books, 2000.

De Sousa Santos, Boaventura. *Epistemologies of the South: Justice against Epistemicide*. Abingdon, UK: Routledge, 2016.

——. *Toward a New Legal Common Sense: Law, Globalization, and Emancipation*. Cambridge: Cambridge University Press, 2002.

De Sousa Santos, Boaventura, and César A. Rodriguez-Garavito. "Law, Politics, and the Subaltern in Counter-Hegemonic Globalization." In *Law and Globalization from Below: Towards a Cosmopolitan Legality*, edited by Boaventura de Sousa Santos and César A. Rodriguez-Garavito, 1–26. Cambridge: Cambridge University Press, 2005.

Devetter, François-Xavier, Thierry Ribault, and Florence Jany-Catrice. *Les services à la personne*. Paris: Éditions La Découverte, 2009.

Doumbia-Henry, Cleopatra. "The Consolidated Maritime Labour Convention: A Marriage of the Traditional and the New." In *Les normes internationales du travail: Un patrimonie pour l'avenir: Mélanges en l'honneur de Nicola Valticos*, edited by Jean-Claude Javillier and Bernard Gernigon, 319–34. Geneva: International Labour Office, 2004. http://www.ilo.org/wcmsp5/groups/public/—ed_norm/—normes/documents/publication/wcms_087423.pdf.

D'Souza, Asha. "Moving towards Decent Work for Domestic Workers: An Overview of the ILO's Work." ILO Bureau for Gender Equality Working Paper No. 2. 2010. https://www.ilo.org/wcmsp5/groups/public/@dgreports/@gender/documents/publication/wcms_142905.pdf.

D'Souza, Radha. "The 'Third World' and Socio-Legal Studies': Neo-Liberalism and Lessons from India's Legal Innovations." *Socil & Legal Studies* 14, no. 4 (2005): 487.

———. *What's Wrong with Rights: Social Movements, Law and Liberal Imaginations.* London: Pluto Press, 2018.

Du Bois, W. E. B. *The Philadelphia Negro: A Social Study.* Philadelphia: University of Pennsylvania Press, 1899.

Duckitt, Hildagonda J. *Hilda's Diary of a Cape Housekeeper: Being a Chronicle of Daily Events and Monthly Work in a Cape Household, with Numerous Cooking Recipes, and Notes on Gardening, Poultry Keeping, Etc.* London: Chapman and Hall, 1902.

Dumont-Robillard, Myriam. *Accès à la justice pour les travailleuses domestiques migrantes: Une illusion?* Montréal: Thémis, 2015.

Duncan, Russell. *Freedom's Shore: Tunis Campbell and the Georgia Freedmen.* Athens: University of Georgia Press, 1986.

Duplessis, Isabelle. "La mollesse et le droit international du travail: Mode de regulation privilégié pour société décentralisée." In *Governance, International Law and Corporate Social Responsibility*, edited by Jean-Claude Javillier, 1–23. Geneva: International Labour Office, 2007.

Du Toit, Darcy. "Constructing an Integrated Model for the Regulation and Enforcement of Domestic Workers' Rights." In Du Toit, *Exploited, Undervalued—and Essential*, 321–50.

———, ed. *Exploited, Undervalued—and Essential: Domestic Workers and the Realisation of Their Rights.* Pretoria, South Africa: Pretoria University Law Press, 2013.

———. "Situating Domestic Work in a Changing Global Labour Market." In Du Toit, *Exploited, Undervalued—and Essential*, 1–30.

Eaton, Isabel A. M. "Special Report on Negro Domestic Service in the Seventh Ward." In *The Philadelphia Negro: A Social Study*, by W. E. B. Du Bois, 425–509. Philadelphia: University of Pennsylvania Press, 1899.

Egerton, John. "Foreword: A Gallery of Great Cooks." In *The Jemima Code: Two Centuries of African American Cookbooks*, by Toni Tipton-Martin, ix–xii. Austin: University of Texas Press, 2015.

Ehrenreich, Barbara, and Arlie Russell Hochschild, eds. *Global Woman: Nannies, Maids, and Sex Workers in the New Economy.* New York: Henry Holt and Company, 2002.

Ehrlich, Eugen. *Fundamental Principles of the Sociology of Law.* New York: Arno Press, 1975.

Elayoubi, Fatima. *Prière à la Lune.* Paris: Bachari, 2006.

Elliott, Dorothy M. "The Status of Domestic Work in the United Kingdom: With Special Reference to the National Institute of Houseworkers." *International Labour Review* 63, no. 2 (1951): 125–48.

Ellison, Ralph. *Invisible Man.* New York, Random House, 1952.

Encinas-Franco, Jean. "Filipino Women Migrant Workers and Overseas Employment Policy: An Analysis From Women's Rights Perspective." *Asian Politics and Policy* 8, no. 3 (2016): 494–501.

Engle Merry, Sally. *Human Rights and Gender Violence: Translating International Law into Local Justice.* Chicago: University of Chicago Press, 2006.

Enloe, Cynthia. *Bananas, Beaches and Bases: Making Feminist Sense of International Politics*. 2nd ed. Berkeley: University of California Press, 2014.

Erickson Coble, Alana. *Cleaning Up: The Transformation of Domestic Service in Twentieth Century New York*. Abingdon, UK: Routledge, 2006.

Estlund, Cynthia. *Working Together: How Workplace Bonds Strengthen a Diverse Democracy*. Oxford: Oxford University Press, 2003.

European Foundation for the Improvement of Living and Working Conditions. "Revisions to the European Working Time Directive: Recent Eurofound Research." Dublin: European Foundation for the Improvement of Living and Working Conditions, 2008. https://www.eurofound.europa.eu/sites/default/files/ef_publication/field_ef_document/ef08101en.pdf.

Fakhri, Michael. *Sugar and the Making of International Trade Law*. Cambridge: Cambridge University Press, 2014.

Falk Moore, Sally. *Law as Process: An Anthropological Approach*. Boston: Routledge, 1978.

Fanon, Frantz. *Black Skin, White Masks*. Translated by Richard Philcox. New York: Grove Press, 2008.

Faraday, Fay. *Canada's Choice: Decent Work or Entrenched Exploitation for Canada's Migrant Workers?* Toronto: Metcalf Foundation, 2016.

——. *Profiting from the Precarious: How Recruitment Practices Exploit Migrant Workers*. Toronto: Metcalf Foundation, 2014.

Fashoyin, Tayo. "Tripartite Cooperation, Social Dialogue and National Development." *International Labour Review* 143, no. 4 (2004): 341–372.

Fick, Carolyn E. *The Making of Haiti: The Saint-Domingue Revolution from Below*. Knoxville: University of Tennessee Press, 1991.

Fineman, Martha Albertson. *The Neutered Mother, the Sexual Family and Other Twentieth Century Tragedies*. New York: Routledge, 1995.

Fischer-Lescano, Andreas, and Gunther Teubner. "Regime-Collisions: The Vain Search for Legal Unity in the Fragmentation of Global Law." *Michigan Journal of International Law* 25, no. 4 (2004): 999–1046.

Fish, Jennifer Natalie. *Domestic Democracy: At Home in South Africa*. New York: Routledge, 2006.

——. *Domestic Workers of the World Unite! A Global Movement for Dignity and Human Rights*. New York: New York University Press, 2017.

Fisher, Abby. *What Mrs. Fisher Knows about Southern Cooking: Soups, Pickles, Preserves, Etc.* With historical notes by Karen Hess. Bedford, MA: Applewood Books, 1995.

Frank, Andre Gunder. *Capitalism and Underdevelopment in Latin America: Historical Studies of Chile and Brazil*. New York: Monthly Review Press, 1967.

Fraser, Nancy. "From Exploitation to Expropriation: Historic Geographies of Racialized Capitalism." *Economic Geography* 94, no. 1 (2017): 1–17.

——. *Scales of Justice: Reimagining Political Space in a Globalizing World*. New York: Columbia University Press, 2009.

——. "A Triple Movement? Parsing the Politics of Crisis after Polanyi." *New Left Review* 81 (2013): 119–32.

Fudge, Judy. "Blurring Legal Boundaries: Regulating for Decent Work." In *Challenging the Legal Boundaries of Work Regulation*, edited by Judy Fudge, Shae McChrystal, and Kamala Sankaran. Oxford: Hart Publishing, 2012.

———. "Global Care Chains, Employment Agencies, and the Conundrum of Jurisdiction: Decent Work for Domestic Workers in Canada." *Canadian Journal of Women and the Law* 23, no. 1 (2011): 235–64.

Fudge, Judy, and Eric Tucker. *Labour before the Law*. Oxford: Oxford University Press, 2001.

Gaitskell, Deborah, Jody Kimble, Moira Maconachie, and Elaine Unterhalter. "Class, Race and Gender: Domestic Workers in South Africa." *Review of African Political Economy* 10, nos. 27–28 (1983): 86–108.

Gallerand, Elsa, and Martin Gallié. "Travail non libre et rapports sociaux de sexe—À propos des programmes canadiens d'immigration temporaire." *Canadian Journal of Law and Society* 33, no. 2 (2018): 223–41.

Gallin, Dan. "The ILO Home Work Convention—Ten Years Later." Paper presented at the Women, Work and Poverty: SEWA/UNIFEM Policy Conference on Home Based Workers of South Asia, New Delhi, January 18–20, 2007. http://www.wiego.org/sites/default/files/resources/files/Gallin-Homework-Convention-10Years-Later-speech-January2007.pdf.

Garcia, Ruben J. *Marginal Workers: How Legal Fault Lines Divide Workers and Leave Them without Protection*. New York: New York University Press, 2012.

Ghosheh, Naj. "Protecting the Housekeeper: Legal Agreements Applicable to International Migrant Domestic Workers." *International Journal of Comparative Labour Law and Industrial Relations* 25, no. 3 (2009): 301–25.

Giles, Wenona, and Sedef Arat-Koç, eds. *Maid in the Market: Women's Paid Domestic Labour*. Halifax, NS: Fernwood, 1994.

Glenn, Evelyn Nakano. *Forced to Care: Coercion and Caregiving in America*. Cambridge, MA: Harvard University Press, 2012.

———. *Issei, Nisei, War Bride: Three Generations of Japanese American Women in Domestic Service*. Philadelphia: Temple University Press, 1986.

Glenn, H. Patrick. "A Transnational Concept of Law." In *The Oxford Handbook of Legal Studies*, edited by Mark Tushnet and Peter Cane, 839–60. Oxford: Oxford University Press, 2005.

Grandin, Greg. *The Empire of Necessity: Slavery, Freedom and Deception in the New World*. New York: Henry Holt, 2014.

Griffin, Laura. "Borderwork: 'Illegality,' Un-bounded Labour and the Lives of Basotho Migrant Domestic Workers." PhD diss., University of Melbourne, 2010.

Gross, Ariela. *What Blood Won't Tell: A History of Race on Trial in America*. Cambridge, MA: Harvard University Press, 2009.

Guha-Khasnobis, Basudeb, Ravi Kanbur, and Elinor Ostrom. "Beyond Formality and Informality." In *Linking the Formal and Informal Economy: Concepts and Policies*, edited by Basudeb Guha-Khasnobis, Ravi Kanbur, and Elinor Ostrom, 1–20. Oxford: Oxford University Press, 2006.

———, eds. *Linking the Formal and Informal Economy: Concepts and Policies*. Oxford: Oxford University Press, 2006.

Haber, Barbara. "Foreword: Why Cookbooks Matter." In *The Jemima Code: Two Centuries of African American Cookbooks*, by Toni Tipton-Martin, xiii–xvii. Austin: University of Texas Press, 2015.

Hall, Peter A., and David Soskice, eds. *Varieties of Capitalism: The Institutional Foundations of Comparative Advantage.* Oxford: Oxford University Press, 2001.

Hall, Stuart. *The Fateful Triangle: Race, Ethnicity, Nation.* Cambridge, MA: Harvard University Press, 2017.

Halliday, Terence C., and Gregory Shaffer, eds. *Transnational Legal Orders.* Cambridge: Cambridge University Press, 2015.

Hands, Elizabeth. *The Death of Amnon. A Poem with an Appendix: Containing Pastoral and Other Poetical Pieces.* Coventry, UK: N. Rollason, 1789.

Harding, Vincent. *There Is a River: The Black Struggle for Freedom in America.* New York: Harcourt Brace Jovanovich, 1981.

Hart, Keith. "Informal Income Opportunities and Urban Employment in Ghana." *Journal of Modern African Studies* 11, no.1 (1973): 61–89.

Hastie, Bethany. "The Inequality of Low-Wage Migrant Labour: Reflections on *PN v FR* and *OPT v Presteve Foods.*" Special issue, *Canadian Journal of Law and Society / Revue Canadienne Droit et Société* 33, no. 2 (forthcoming): 243–59.

Hay, Douglas. "England, 1562–1875: The Law and Its Uses." In *Masters, Servants, and Magistrates in Britain and the Empire, 1562–1955,* edited by Douglas Hay and Paul Craven, 59–116. Chapel Hill: University of North Carolina Press, 2004.

Hay, Douglas, and Paul Craven. Introduction to *Masters, Servants, and Magistrates in Britain and the Empire, 1562–1955,* edited by Douglas Hay and Paul Craven, 1–58. Chapel Hill: University of North Carolina Press, 2004.

Hayes, L. J. B. *Stories of Care: A Labour of Law—Gender and Class at Work.* London: Palgrave, 2017.

Hepple, Bob. *Labour Laws and Global Trade.* Oxford: Hart Publishing, 2005.

Hernández, Tanya Kateri. *Racial Subordination in Latin America: The Role of the State, Customary Law, and the New Civil Rights Response.* Cambridge: Cambridge University Press, 2013.

Higman, Bernard W. "An Historical Perspective: Colonial Continuities in the Global Geography of Domestic Service." In *Colonization and Domestic Service: Historical and Contemporary Perspectives,* edited by Victoria K. Haskins and Claire Lowrie, 19–40. New York: Routledge, 2015.

Hochschild, Arlie Russell. *The Managed Heart: Commercialization of Human Feeling.* Berkeley: University of California Press, 1979.

Hondagneu-Sotelo, Pierrette. *Doméstica: Immigrant Workers Cleaning and Caring in the Shadows of Affluence.* Berkeley: University of California Press, 2001.

hooks, bell. "Eating the other: Desire and Resistance." In *Black Looks: Race and Representation,* 21–39. Boston: South End Press, 1992.

Human Rights Watch. "'I Won't Be a Doctor, and One Day You'll Be Sick': Girls' Access to Education in Afghanistan." October 17, 2017. https://www.hrw.org/report/2017/10/17/i-wont-be-doctor-and-one-day-youll-be-sick/girls-access-education-afghanistan.

——. "'It's a Men's Club': Discrimination against Women in Iran's Job Market." May 25, 2017. https://www.hrw.org/report/2017/05/25/its-mens-club/discrimination-against-women-irans-job-market.

——. "'We Can't Refuse to Pick Cotton': Forced and Child Labor Linked to World Bank Group Investments in Uzbekistan." June 27, 2017. https://www.hrw.org

/report/2017/06/27/we-cant-refuse-pick-cotton/forced-and-child-labor-linked-world-bank-group.

——. "'Working Like a Robot': Abuse of Tanzanian Domestic Workers in Oman and the United Arab Emirates." November 14, 2017. https://www.hrw.org/report/2017/11/14/working-robot/abuse-tanzanian-domestic-workers-oman-and-united-arab-emirates.

International Domestic Workers Federation. "Ratify C189." June 16, 2011. http://www.idwfed.org/en/campaigns/ratify-c189.

International Labour Conference. 20th Sess., *Record of Proceedings* (1936).

——. 27th Sess., *Record of Proceedings* (1945).

——. 31st Sess., *Record of Proceedings* (1948).

——. 99th Sess., *Provisional Record 12* (2010). https://www.ilo.org/wcmsp5/groups/public/—ed_norm/—relconf/documents/meetingdocument/wcms_141770.pdf.

——. 99th Sess., *Provisional Record 19* (2010). https://www.ilo.org/ilc/ILCSessions/99thSession/pr/WCMS_141972/lang—en/index.htm

——. 100th Sess., *Provisional Record 15* (2011). https://www.ilo.org/wcmsp5/groups/public/—ed_norm/—relconf/documents/meetingdocument/wcms_157696.pdf.

——. 100th Sess., *Provisional Record 30* (2011). https://www.ilo.org/ilc/ILCSessions/100thSession/reports/provisional-records/WCMS_158275/lang—en/index.htm.

——. 101st Sess., *Provisional Record 19*, revised (2012) (part 1). https://www.ilo.org/wcmsp5/groups/public/—ed_norm/—relconf/documents/meetingdocument/wcms_183031.pdf.

——. "Standing Orders of the International Labour Conference." November 7, 2006. http://www.ilo.org/public/english/standards/relm/ilc/ilc-so.htm.

International Labour Office. *Decent Work: Report of the Director General*. Geneva: International Labour Conference, 87th Session, 1999.

——. *The Dilemma of the Informal Sector: Report of the Director General*. Geneva: International Labour Conference, 78th Session, 1991.

——. *Domestic Workers across the World: Global and Regional Statistics and the Extent of Legal Protection*. Geneva: ILO, 2013. http://www.ilo.org/wcmsp5/groups/public/—dgreports/—dcomm/—publ/documents/publication/wcms_173363.pdf.

——. *Effective Protection of Domestic Workers: A Guide to Designing Labour Laws*. Geneva: ILO, 2012. https://www.ilo.org/travail/areasofwork/domestic-workers/WCMS_173365/lang—en/index.htm.

——. "The Employment and Conditions of Domestic Workers in Private Households: An ILO Survey." *International Labour Review* 102, no. 4 (1970): 391–401.

——. *Employment, Incomes and Equality: A Strategy for Increasing Productive Employment in Kenya*. Geneva: ILO, 1972.

——. *Report IV(1): Decent Work for Domestic Workers*. Geneva: International Labour Conference, 99th Session, 2010. http://www.ilo.org/wcmsp5/groups/public/—ed_norm/—relconf/documents/meetingdocument/wcms_104700.pdf.

———. *Report IV(2): Decent Work for Domestic Workers.* Geneva: International Labour Conference, 2010. http://www.ilo.org/wcmsp5/groups/public/—ed_norm /—relconf/documents/meetingdocument/wcms_104700.pdf.

———. *Report VI: Decent Work and the Informal Economy.* Geneva: International Labour Conference, 2002. http://www.ilo.org/public/english/standards/relm/ilc /ilc90/pdf/rep-vi.pdf.

International Labour Organization Governing Body. "300th Session: Report of the Director-General." November 2007. http://www.ilo.org/wcmsp5/groups /public/—ed_norm/—relconf/documents/meetingdocument/wcms _085051.pdf.

———. "Decision on the Second Item on the Agenda: Date, Place and Agenda of the 99th Session (2010) of the International Labour Conference." Record of Decisions of the 301st Session from March 2008, to May 16, 2008. http:// www.ilo.org/gb/decisions/GB301-decision/WCMS_093430/lang—en/index .htm.

———. *ILO Multilateral Framework on Labour Migration: Non-binding Principles and Guidelines for a Rights-Based Approach to Labour Migration.* Geneva: ILO, 2006. http://www.ilo.org/wcmsp5/groups/public/—asia/—ro-bangkok /documents/publication/wcms_146243.pdf.

James, C. L. R. *A New Notion: Two Works by C. L. R. James: Every Cook Can Govern; The Invading Socialist Society.* Edited by Noel Ignatiev. Oakland, CA: P. M. Press, 2010.

Jessup, Philip C. *Transnational Law.* New Haven, CT: Yale University Press, 1956.

Kelley, Robin D. *Hammer and Hoe: Alabama Communists during the Great Depression.* Chapel Hill: University of North Carolina Press, 1990.

Kennedy, David. *A World of Struggle: How Power, Law, and Expertise Shape Global Political Economy.* Princeton, NJ: Princeton University Press, 2016.

Kennedy, David W. "The Mystery of Global Governance." *Ohio Northern University Law Review* 34 (2008): 827–60.

King, Martin Luther, Jr. *All Labor Has Dignity.* Boston: Beacon Press, 2012.

———. *Where Do We Go from Here? Community or Chaos.* Boston: Beacon Press, 1967.

Kitchiner, William. *The Cook's Oracle; Containing Receipts for Plain Cookery.* London: Hurst, Robinson, and Co., 1822.

Kleinhans, Marthe-Marie, and Roderick A. Macdonald, "What Is a *Critical Legal Pluralism?" Canadian Journal of Law & Society* 12, no. 25 (1997): 25–46.

Koh, Harold. "Transnational Legal Process." *Nebraska Law Review* 75 (1996): 181–207.

Kolben, Kevin. "Labor Rights as Human Rights?" *Virginia Journal of International Law* 50, no. 2 (2010): 449–84.

Kotiswaran, Prabha. "From Sex Panic to Extreme Exploitation: Revisiting the Law and Governance of Human Trafficking." In *Revisiting the Law and Governance of Trafficking, Forced Labor and Modern Slavery,* edited by Prabha Kotiswaran, 1–56. New York: Cambridge University Press, 2017.

Kouadio, Anne-Marie. "Stratégies résidentielles d'une catégorie de citadins du bas de l'échelle de qualification: Les personnels domestiques féminins de la ville d'Abidjan." Council for the Development of Social Science Research in Africa, 2008.

LaHovary, Claire. "The Informal Economy and the ILO: A Legal Perspective." *International Journal of Comparative Labour Law and Industrial Relations* 30, no. 4 (2014): 391–411.

Lawrence, Charles, III. "The Word and the River: Pedagogy as Scholarship as Struggle." *Southern California Law Review* 65, no. 5 (1992): 2231–79.

Leary, Virginia A. "The Paradox of Workers' Rights as Human Rights." In *Human Rights, Labor Rights, and International Trade,* edited by Lance A. Compa and Stephen F. Diamond, 22–47. Philadelphia: University of Pennsylvania Press, 2003.

Leclerc, Anne E. "Statistics on Labor Migration within the Asia-Pacific Region." Presentation at the Red Cross Red Crescent Manila Conference on Labor Migration, Manila, the Philippines, May 12–13, 2015. http://www.ifrc.org /Global/Documents/Asia-pacific/201505/Map_Infographic.pdf.

Lee, Yong-Shik. *Reclaiming Development in the World Trading System.* 2nd ed. Cambridge: Cambridge University Press, 2016.

Lethbridge, Lucy. *Servants: A Downstairs View of Twentieth-Century Britain.* New York: Bloomsbury, 2013.

Lewis, Arthur. "Economic Development with Unlimited Supplies of Labour." *Manchester School* 22, no. 2 (1954): 139–91.

Lotmar, Philipp. *Der Arbeitsvertrag nach dem Privatrecht des Deutschen Reiches.* Leipzig: Duncker and Humblot, 1902–8.

Lund, Francie. "Hierarchies of Care Work in South Africa: Nurses, Social Workers and Home-Based Care Workers." *International Labour Review* 149, no. 4 (2010): 495–509.

Luz Vega Ruiz, Maria. "L'administration et l'inspection du travail dans le domaine du travail domestique: Les expériences de l'Amérique latine." *Canadian Journal of Women and the Law* 23, no. 1 (2011): 341–58.

Macaulay, Stewart. "Non-Contractual Relations in Business: A Preliminary Study." *American Sociological Review* 28, no. 1 (1963): 55–67.

MacDonald, Roderick A., and Hoi L. Kong. "Patchwork Law Reform: Your Idea Is Good in Practice, but It Won't Work in Theory." *Osgoode Hall Law Journal* 44, no. 1 (2006): 11–52.

Magnus, Erna. "The Social, Economic, and Legal Conditions of Domestic Servants: I." *International Labour Review* 30, no. 2 (1934): 190–207.

——. "The Social, Economic, and Legal Conditions of Domestic Servants: II." *International Labour Review* 30, no. 3 (1934): 336–64.

Mamdani, Mahmood. *Citizen and Subject: Contemporary Africa and the Legacy of Late Colonialism.* Princeton, NJ: Princeton University Press, 1996.

Martin-Huan, Jacqueline. *La longue marche des domestiques en France du XIXe siècle à nos jours.* Haute-Goulaine, France: Opéra Editions, 1997.

Marx, Karl, and Friedrich Engels. *The German Ideology.* Translated by C. J. Arthur. London: Lawrence and Wishart, 1970.

Mather, Celia. "'Yes, We Did It!' How the World's Domestic Workers Won Their International Rights and Recognition." Cambridge, MA: Women in Informal

Employment: Globalizing and Organizing, 2013. http://global-labour.net /documents/Mather_Yes%20we%20did%20it!_2013.pdf.

Matsuda, Mari. "When the First Quail Calls: Multiple Consciousness as Jurisprudential Method." *Women's Rights Law Reporter* 11, no. 1 (1989): 7–9.

Maupain, Francis. *The Future of the International Labour Organization in the Global Economy*. Oxford: Hart Publishing, 2013.

Mbembe, Achille. *On the Postcolony*. Berkeley: University of California Press, 2001.

McCann, Deirdre. "New Frontiers of Regulation: Domestic Work, Working Conditions, and the Holistic Assessment of Nonstandard Work Norms." *Comparative Labor Law and Policy Journal* 34, no. 1 (2012): 167–92.

McCann, Deirdre, and Jill Murray. "The Legal Regulation of Working Time in Domestic Work." Geneva: International Labour Office, 2010. https://www .ilo.org/wcmsp5/groups/public/—ed_protect/—protrav/—travail /documents/publication/wcms_150650.pdf.

McConnell, Moira L., Dominick Devlin, and Cleopatra Doumbia-Henry. *The Maritime Labour Convention, 2006: A Legal Primer to an Emerging International Regime*. Leiden, The Netherlands: Brill, 2011.

McGregor, Joann. "'Joining the BBC (British Bottom Cleaners)': Zimbabwean Migrants and the UK Care Industry." *Journal of Ethnic and Migration Studies* 33, no. 5 (2007): 801–24.

McKeon, Michael. *The Secret History of Domesticity: Public, Private, and the Division of Knowledge*. Baltimore, MD: Johns Hopkins University Press, 2005.

Meagher, Gabrielle. "A Struggle for Recognition: Work Life Reform in the Domestic Services Industry." *Economic and Industrial Democracy* 21, no.1 (2000): 9–37.

Meagher, Kate. "Cannibalizing the Informal Economy: Frugal Innovation and Economic Inclusion in Africa." *European Journal of Development Research* 30, no. 1 (2018): 17–33.

Medici, Gabriela Naemi. *Migrantinnen als Pflegehilfen in Schweizer Privataushalten: Menschenrechtliche Vorgaben und staatliche Handlungspflichten*. Zurich: Schulthess, 2015.

Medici, Gabriela Naemi, and Adelle Blackett. "Ratification as International Solidarity: Reflections on Switzerland and Decent Work for Domestic Workers." *Connecticut Journal of International Law* 31, no. 2 (2016): 187–215.

Mégret, Frédéric. "Transnational Mobility, the International Law of Aliens, and the Origins of Global Migration Law." *American Society of International Law Unbound* 111 (2017): 13–17.

Melissaris, Emmanuel. "The More the Merrier? A New Take on Legal Pluralism." *Social & Legal Studies* 13, no. 1 (2004): 57–79.

Mendes, Helen. *The African Heritage Cookbook*. London: MacMillan, 1971.

Miller, Frieda S. "Household Employment in the United States." *International Labour Review* 66, no. 4 (1952): 318–37.

Moore Coley, Soraya. "And Still I Rise: An Exploratory Study of Contemporary Black Private Household Workers." PhD diss., Bryn Mawr College, 1981.

Mückenberger, Ulrich. "Non-Standard Forms of Employment in the Federal Republic of Germany: The Role and Effectiveness of the State." In *Precarious Jobs in Labour Market Regulation: The Growth of Atypical Employment in Western*

Europe, edited by Gerry Rodgers and Janine Rodgers, 167–86. Geneva: International Institute for Labour Studies, 1989.

Mundlak, Guy, and Hila Shamir. "Bringing Together or Drifting Apart? Targeting Care Work as 'Work Like No Other.'" *Canadian Journal of Women and the Law* 23, no. 1 (2011): 289.

Munn, Christopher. "Hong Kong, 1841–1870: All the Servants in Prison and Nobody to Take Care of the House." In *Masters, Servants, and Magistrates in Britain and the Empire, 1562–1955*, edited by Douglas Hay and Paul Craven, 365–401. Chapel Hill: University of North Carolina Press, 2004.

Murray, Jill. *Transnational Labour Regulation: The ILO and EC Compared*. Boston: Kluwer Law International, 2001.

Nadasen, Premilla, *Household Workers Unit: The Untold Story of African American Women Who Built a Movement*. Boston: Beacon Press, 2015.

Nedelsky, Jennifer. *Law's Relations: A Relational Theory of Self, Autonomy, and Law*. Oxford: Oxford University Press, 2011.

——. *(Part)-Time for All: Generating New Norms of Work and Care* (forthcoming).

Obasogie, Osagie K. *Blinded by Sight: Seeing Race through the Eyes of the Blind*. Stanford: Stanford University Press, 2014.

Orford, Anne. "A Jurisprudence of the Limit." In *International Law and Its Others*, edited by Anne Orford, 1–32. Cambridge: Cambridge University Press, 2006.

Pahuja, Sundhya. *Decolonising International Law: Development, Economic Growth, and the Politics of Universality*. Cambridge: Cambridge University Press, 2011.

Pape, Karin. "ILO Convention C189—A Good Start for the Protection of Domestic Workers: An Insider's View." *Progress in Development Studies* 16, no. 2 (2016): 189–202.

Parreñas, Rhacel Salazar. *Children of Global Migration: Transnational Families and Gendered Woes*. Stanford, CA: Stanford University Press, 2005.

——. *Servants of Globalization: Migration and Domestic Work*. 2nd ed. Stanford, CA: Stanford University Press, 2015.

Patterson, Orlando. *Slavery and Social Death*. Cambridge, MA: Harvard University Press, 1982.

——. "Trafficking, Gender and Slavery: Past and Present." In *The Legal Understanding of Slavery: From the Historical to the Contemporary*, edited by Jean Allain, 322–59. Oxford: Oxford University Press, 2012.

Piketty, Thomas. *Capital in the Twenty-First Century*. Cambridge, MA: Harvard University Press, 2014.

Pilarczyk, Ian C. "The Law of Servants and the Servants of Law: Enforcing Masters' Rights in Montreal, 1830–1845." *McGill Law Journal* 46 (2001): 780–836.

——. "'Too Well Used by His Master': Judicial Enforcement of Servants' Rights in Montreal, 1830–1845." *McGill Law Journal* 46 (2001): 491–529.

Pinnix, Esther Searle, Alice Jones, and James Larkin Pearson. *Sudie Holton*. North Carolina, 1939. Manuscript/Mixed Material. https://www.loc.gov/item/wpalh001881/.

Poblete, Lorena, "The Influence of the ILO Domestic Workers Convention in Argentina, Chile and Paraguay." *International Journal of Comparative Labour Law and Industrial Relations* 34, no. 2 (2018): 177–201.

Polanyi, Karl. *The Great Transformation: The Political and Economic Origins of Our Time*. Boston: Beacon Press, 2001.

Poo, Ai-jen. *The Age of Dignity: Preparing for the Elder Boom in a Changing America*. New York: New Press: 2015.

Pope, James Gray. "Contract, Race and Freedom of Labor in the Constitutional Law of 'Involuntary Servitude.'" *Yale Law Journal* 119 (2010): 1474–567.

Pope Melish, Joanne. *Disowning Slavery: Gradual Emancipation and "Race" in New England, 1780–1860*. Ithaca, NY: Cornell University Press, 1998.

Prebisch, Raul. "The Economic Development of Latin America and Its Principal Problems." Lake Success, NY: United Nations Department of Economic Affairs, 1950. http://archivo.cepal.org/pdfs/cdPrebisch/002.pdf.

Rajagopal, Balakrishnan. *International Law from Below: Development, Social Movements and Third World Resistance*. Cambridge: Cambridge University Press, 2003.

Ramirez-Machado, José Maria. "Domestic Work, Conditions of Work and Employment: A Legal Perspective." Geneva: International Labour Office, 2003. http://adapt.it/adapt-indice-a-z/wp-content/uploads/2014/09/ilo_domestic_work_2003.pdf.

Razack, Shireen. *Looking White People in the Eye: Gender, Race and Culture in Courtrooms and Classrooms*. Toronto: University of Toronto Press, 1998.

Rediker, Marcus. *Between the Devil and the Deep Blue Sea: Merchant Seamen, Pirates and the Anglo-American Maritime World, 1700–1750*. Cambridge: Cambridge University Press, 1987.

Rittich, Kerry. "Informality and Formality in the World of Work." In *The Daunting Enterprise of the Law: Essays in Honour of Harry Arthurs*, edited by Simon Archer, Daniel Drache, and Peer Zumbansen, 109–23. Montreal: McGill-Queen's University Press, 2017.

Roberts, Dorothy. *Killing the Black Body: Race, Reproduction, and the Meaning of Liberty*. New York: Vintage Books, 2014.

Roberts, Robert. *The House Servant's Directory*. Boston: Munroe and Francis, 1828.

Robinson, Cedric J. *Black Marxism: The Making of the Black Tradition*. Chapel Hill: University of North Carolina Press, 1983.

Rockman, Seth. *Scraping By: Wage Labour, Slavery, and Survival in Early Baltimore*. Baltimore, MD: John Hopkins University Press, 2009.

Rodriguez, Robyn Magalit. *Migrants for Export: How the Philippine State Brokers Labor to the World*. Minneapolis: University of Minnesota Press, 2010.

Rodríguez-Piñero, Luis. *Indigenous Peoples, Postcolonialism, and International Law: The ILO Regime (1919–1989)*. Oxford: Oxford University Press, 2006.

Rollins, Judith. "And the Last Shall Be First: The Master-Slave Dialectic in Hegel, Nietzsche and Fanon." *Human Architecture* 5, no. 3 (2007): 163–77.

——. *Between Women: Domestics and Their Employers*. Philadelphia: Temple University Press, 1985.

Romero, Mary. *Maid in the U.S.A.* New York: Routledge, 1992.

Ruggie, John G. "Taking Embedded Liberalism Global: The Corporate Connection." In *Taming Globalization: Frontiers of Governance*, edited by David Held and Mathias Koenig-Archibugi, 93–129. Cambridge: Polity Press, 2003.

Russell, Malinda. *A Domestic Cook Book: Containing a Careful Selection of Useful Receipts for the Kitchen by Malinda Russell, an Experienced Cook.* Ann Arbor, MI: William L. Clements Library, 2007. Originally published by author, 1866.

Sankaran, Kamala. "Informal Employment and the Challenges for Labour Law." In *The Idea of Labour Law,* edited by Guy Davidov and Brian Langille, 223–33. Oxford: Oxford University Press, 2011.

Sassen, Saskia. *The Global City: New York, London, Tokyo.* Princeton, NJ: Princeton University Press, 1991.

——. *Territory, Authority, Rights: From Medieval to Global Assemblages.* Princeton, NJ: Princeton University Press, 2006.

Schwenken, Helen, and Lisa-Marie Heimeshoff, eds. *Domestic Workers Count: Global Data on an Often Invisible Sector.* Kassel, Germany: Kassel University Press, 2011.

Seely, Lida. *Mrs. Seely's Cook Book: A Manual of French and American Cookery with Chapters on Domestic Servants: Their Rights and Duties and Many Other Details of Household Management.* New York: MacMillan Company, 1902.

Shaffer, Gregory, and Terrence Halliday. *Transnational Legal Orders.* Cambridge: Cambridge University Press, 2015.

Sharpless, Rebecca. *Cooking in Other Women's Kitchens: Domestic Workers in the South, 1865–1960.* Chapel Hill: University of North Carolina Press, 2010.

Sheppard, Colleen. *Inclusive Equality: The Relational Dimensions of Systemic Discrimination in Canada.* Montreal: McGill-Queen's University Press, 2010.

Silvera, Makeda. *Silenced: Talks with Working Class Caribbean Women about Their Lives and Struggles as Domestic Workers in Canada.* Toronto: Sister Vision Press, 1983.

Simpson, Leanne Betasamosake. *Dancing on Our Turtle's Back: Stories of Nishnaabeg Re-Creation, Resurgence, and a New Emergence.* Winnipeg, MB: Arbeiter Ring Press, 2011.

Simpson, William R. "Standard-Setting and Supervision: A System in Difficulty." In *Les normes internationales du travail: Un patrimonie pour l'avenir: Mélanges en l'honneur de Nicola Valticos,* edited by Jean-Claude Javillier and Bernard Gernigon, 47–73. Geneva: International Labour Office, 2004. http://www.ilo.org/wcmsp5/groups/public/—ed_norm/—normes/documents/publication/wcms_087423.pdf.

Sivan, Faina Milman. "Freedom of Association in Deliberative Spaces: The ILO Credentials Committee." In *Research Handbook on Transnational Labour Law,* edited by Adelle Blackett and Anne Trebilcock, 204–16. Cheltenham, UK: Elgar Publishing, 2015.

Smith, Gail. "*Madam and Eve*: A Caricature of Black Women's Subjectivity?" *Agenda* 12, no.31 (1996): 33–39.

Smith, Peggie R. "The Pitfalls of Home: Protecting the Health and Safety of Paid Domestic Workers." *Canadian Journal of Women and the Law* 23, no. 1 (2011): 309–39.

——. "Work Like Any Other, Work Like No Other: Establishing Decent Work for Domestic Workers." *Employee Rights and Employment Policy Journal* 51, no. 1 (2011): 57–100.

Standing, Guy. *Basic Income: A Guide for the Open-Minded*. New Haven, CT: Yale University Press, 2017.

——. *Beyond the New Paternalism: Basic Security as Equality*. London: Verso, 2002.

——. *Global Labour Flexibility: Seeking Distributive Justice*. Basingstoke, UK: Palgrave Macmillan, 1999.

Stasiulis, Daiva K., and Abigail B. Bakan. *Negotiating Citizenship: Migrant Women in Canada and the Global System*. Toronto: University of Toronto Press, 2005.

Steedman, Carolyn. *Labours Lost: Domestic Service and the Making of Modern England*. Cambridge: Cambridge University Press, 2009.

——. *Master and Servant: Love and Labour in the English Industrial Age*. Cambridge: Cambridge University Press, 2007.

Steel, Flora Annie Webster, and Grace Gardiner. *The Complete Indian Housekeeper and Cook: Giving the Duties of Mistress and Servants, the General Management of the House and Practical Recipes for Cooking in All Its Branches*. Cambridge: Cambridge University Press, 1890.

Stoler, Ann. *Carnal Knowledge and Imperial Power: Race and the Intimate in Colonial Rule*. Berkeley: University of California Press, 2002.

Supiot, Alain. *Beyond Employment: Changes in Work and the Future of Labour Law*. Oxford: Oxford University Press, 2001.

Teubner, Gunther. *Autopoietic Law: A New Approach to Law and Society*. Berlin: Walter de Gruyter, 1988.

——. *Law as an Autopoietic System*. Hoboken, NJ: Blackwell, 1993.

——. "Legal Irritants: How Unifying Law Ends up in New Divergences." In *Varieties of Capitalism: The Institutional Foundations of Comparative Advantage*, edited by Peter A. Hall and David Soskice, 417–41. Oxford: Oxford University Press, 2001.

——. "Self-Constitutionalizing TNCs? On the Linkage of 'Private' and 'Public' Corporate Codes of Conduct." *Indiana Journal of Global Legal Studies* 18, no. 2 (2011): 617–38.

Thomas, Albert. *International Social Policy*. Translated by Monica Curtis. Geneva: International Labour Office, 1948.

Thomas, Chantal. "Migrant Domestic Workers in Egypt: A Case Study of the Economic Family in Global Context." *American Journal of Comparative Law* 58, no. 4 (2010): 987–1022.

Thompson, E. P. *The Making of the English Working Class*. London: Penguin Books, 2002.

Thornton Dill, Bonnie. *Across the Boundaries of Race and Class: An Exploration of Work and Family among Black Female Domestic Servants*. New York: Garland, 1994.

Tigno, Jorge V. "At the Mercy of the Market? State-Enabled, Market Oriented Labor Migration and Women Migrants from the Philippines." *Philippine Political Science Journal* 35, no. 1 (2014): 19–36.

Tipton-Martin, Toni. "Breaking the Jemima Code: The Legacy of African American Cookbooks." *Ecotone* 10, no. 1 (2014): 116–20.

——. *The Jemima Code: Two Centuries of African American Cookbooks*. Austin: University of Texas Press, 2015.

Tomlins, Christopher L. *Freedom Bound: Law, Labour and Civic Identity in Colonizing English America, 1560–1865.* Cambridge: Cambridge University Press, 2010.

Trebilcock, Anne. "Challenges in Germany's Implementation of the ILO Decent Work for Domestic Workers Convention." *International Journal of Comparative Labour Law and Industrial Relations* 34, no. 2 (2018): 149–76.

——. "International Labour Standards and the Informal Economy." In *Les normes internationales du travail: Un patrimonie pour l'avenir: Mélanges en l'honneur de Nicola Valticos*, edited by Jean-Claude Javillier and Bernard Gernigon, 585–614. Geneva: International Labour Office, 2004. http://www.ilo.org/wcmsp5/groups/public/—ed_norm/—normes/documents/publication/wcms_087423.pdf.

——. *Towards Social Dialogue: Tripartite Cooperation in National Economic and Social Policy Making.* Geneva: International Labour Office, 1994.

——. "Using Development Approaches to Address the Challenge of the Informal Economy for Labour Law." In *Boundaries and Frontiers of Labour Law: Goals and Means in the Regulation of Work*, edited by Guy Davidov and Brian Langille, 63–86. Oxford: Hart Publishing, 2006.

Tsikata, Dzodzi. "Employment Agencies and the Regulation of Domestic Workers in Ghana: Institutionalizing Informality." *Canadian Journal of Women and the Law* 23, no.1 (2011): 213–34.

Tuck, Eve, and K. Wayne Yang. "Decolonization Is Not a Metaphor." *Decolonization* 1, no. 1 (2012): 1–40.

Turner, Mary. *The British Caribbean, 1823–1838: The Transition from Slave to Free Legal Status.* Chapel Hill: University of North Carolina Press, 2004.

Umrigar, Thrity. *The Space between Us.* New York: Harper, 2006.

United Nations Committee on Economic, Social and Cultural Rights. "The Right to Work: General Comment No. 18." February 6, 2006. https://undocs.org/E/C.12/GC/18.

United Nations Committee on the Elimination of Discrimination against Women. "General Recommendation No. 26 on Women Migrant Workers." December 5, 2008. http://www2.ohchr.org/english/bodies/cedaw/docs/GR_26_on_women_migrant_workers_en.pdf.

United Nations Committee on the Protection of the Rights of all Migrant Workers and Members of Their Families. "General Comment No. 1 on Migrant Domestic Workers."February 23, 2011. https://documents-dds-ny.un.org/doc/UNDOC/GEN/G11/411/82/PDF/G1141182.pdf?OpenElement.

——. "General Comment No. 2 on the Right of Migrant Workers in an Irregular Situation and Members of Their Families." August 28, 2013. http://www2.ohchr.org/english/bodies/cmw/docs/CMW_C_GC_2_ENG.PDF.

United Nations Development Programme. *Human Development Report 2009: Overcoming Barriers: Human Mobility and Development.* New York: Palgrave Macmillan, 2009.

United Nations General Assembly. *Global Compact for Safe, Orderly and Regular Migration.* July 30, 2018. Adopted at the Intergovernmental Conference to Adopt the Global Compact for Migration, Marrakech, Morocco, December 11, 2018. https://undocs.org/A/CONF.231/3.

United Nations Human Rights Council. "Forum on Minority Issues—Third Session of the Forum on Minority Issues." December 14–15, 2010. http://www.ohchr.org/EN/HRBodies/HRC/Minority/Pages/Session3.aspx.

Urban, Andrew. *Brokering Servitude: Migration and the Politics of Domestic Labor during the Long Nineteenth Century*. New York: New York University Press, 2017.

Vallée, Guylaine. "La contribution scientifique de Pierre Verge à l'affirmation et à la recomposition du droit and travail." In *Autonomie collective et droit du travail*, edited by Dominic Roux, 1–55. Laval, France: Presses de l'Université Laval, 2014.

VanderVelde, Lea. *Mrs. Dred Scott*. Oxford: Oxford University Press, 2009.

——. *Redemption Songs: Suing for Freedom before Dred Scott*. Oxford: Oxford University Press, 2014.

VanderVelde, Lea S. "Labor Vision of the Thirteenth Amendment." *University of Pensylvannia Law Review* 138, no. 2 (1989): 43–504.

Van Walsum, Sarah. "Regulating Migrant Domestic Work in the Netherlands: Opportunities and Pitfalls." *Canadian Journal of Women and the Law* 23, no. 1 (2011): 141–65.

Vega Ruiz, Maria Luz. "L'administration et l'inspection du travail dans le domaine du travail domestique: Les expériences de l'Amérique latine." *Canadian Journal of Women and the Law* 23, no. 1 (2011): 341–58.

Veneziani, Bruno. "The Evolution of the Contract of Employment." In *The Making of Labour Law in Europe: A Comparative Study of Nine Countries up to 1945*, edited by Bob A. Hepple, 99–128. Portland, MI: Mansell Publishing, 1986.

Verge, Pierre. "Vers une graduelle 'continentalisation' du droit du travail? Aperçu de l'impact des accords plurinationaux américains en matière de travail." *Études internationales* 35, no. 2 (2004): 287–306.

Verge, Pierre, and Guylaine Vallée. *Un droit du travail? Essai sur la spécificité du droit du travail*. Cowansville, Quebec: Éditions Yvon Blais, 1997.

Vosko, Leah F. "'Decent Work': The Shifting Role of the ILO and the Struggle for Global Social Justice." *Global Social Policy* 2, no. 1 (2002): 19–46.

——. *Managing the Margins: Gender, Citizenship, and the International Regulation of Precarious Employment*. Oxford: Oxford University Press, 2010.

——. "Out of the Shadows? The Nonbinding Multilateral Framework on Migration (2006) and Prospects for Using International Labour Regulation to Forge Global Labour Market Membership." In *The Idea of Labour Law*, edited by Guy Davidov and Brian Langille, 369–77. Oxford: Oxford University Press, 2011.

Webb, Beatrice, and Sidney Webb. *Industrial Democracy*. London: Longmans, Green, and Company, 1897.

Webber, Jeremy. "Legal Pluralism and Human Agency." *Osgoode Hall Law Journal* 44, no. 1 (2006): 167–98.

Weber, Max. *Economy and Society: An Outline of Interpretive Sociology*. Edited by Guenther Roth and Claus Wittich. Berkeley: University of California Press, 1978.

Williams, Patricia, J. *The Alchemy of Race and Rights*. Cambridge, MA: Harvard University Press, 1991.

Witt, Doris. *Black Hunger: Soul Food and America*. Minneapolis: University of Minnesota Press, 2004.

World Bank Group. *Migration and Remittances: Recent Developments and Outlook.* Migration and Development Brief 27. April 2017.

Yates, Charlotte. "Organizing Women in the Spaces between Home, Work and Community." *Relations Industrielles* 66, no. 4: (2011) 585–603.

Yeates, Nicola. "The Globalization of Nurse Migration: Policy Issues and Responses." *International Labour Review* 149, no. 4 (2010): 423–40.

Zumbansen, Peer. "Transnational Legal Pluralism." *Transnational Legal Theory* 10, no. 2 (2010): 141–89.

INDEX

Aacharya, Lila, 3
abuse
  agencies and, 125
  employers' justifications of, 62, 152
  live-in work and, 59, 123–124, 150–155
  murders and killings, 3, 162–163, 165
  sending countries' efforts to prevent,
    162–167
  See also boundarilessness
ACLI-COLF (Italian Christian Workers
    Association-Family Collaborators), 61,
    69, 229n92
Adams, Samuel and Sarah, 100–102
aesthetics/art of domestic work, 2, 78, 91,
    98, 233n197
African American workers
  in civil rights movement, 5–6
  cookbooks by, 97, 98–100, 104–108, 109,
    241n161, 241n172
  Dred Scott case, 85
  employers, relationships with, 6–7, 73
  exclusion from labor laws, 7
  "girl" in place of names of, 71
  legal conflation of race with status, 54
  as proportion of domestic workforce, 57
  Somerset case, 53, 227n29
  stereotyping of, 97, 105, 177, 239n112;
    challenges to, 106–108
African workers
  discrimination against, 47, 64
  structuring of employment for, 36, 55–56,
    142–143, 164, 228n52
agencies (employment)
  abuse by, 125
  in collective negotiations, 145
  as disadvantageous to workers, 7, 74
  fees of, 127, 245n55
  public, 126–127
  standard setting on, 125–128
agency of workers
  myth of passivity vs., 6–7, 177

protection and autonomy, 45, 146
  See also organization; resistance
All India Domestic Workers' Union, 144
Ally, Shireen, 48, 55–56, 62, 71–72, 75, 208,
    217n28, 225n51, 228n50
alternative law, 43–44. *See also* law of the
    household workplace; law of the shop;
    legal pluralism
alternative opportunities
  entrepreneurial, 104–106
  lack of, 66–67, 122
  need for, 173
Andall, Jacqueline
  on employers' control, 62, 65, 66–67
  on firings, 76–77
  on Italian legal environment, 56–57, 69
  on lack of alternative jobs, 66
  on resistance, 75
  on social security, 69
  on structural racial segregation,
    229n92
  summary of work of, 207
  on unions, 61
apartheid, 35–36, 55–56, 75, 138, 143, 177,
    209–210, 222n2
asymmetrical power relations
  collective agreements to unsettle, 147
  in law of household workplace, 11–14,
    43–44, 49, 83–85, 112–113,
    113fig, 121
  in law of servant and master, 82–85,
    227n22, 234n11
  in servant-master/mistress relationships,
    57, 83, 110–111
  in state law, 55, 134–135, 234n11
  See also servant-master/mistress
    relationships; servitude; subordination
Atleson, James, 50, 224n41
Augustine, Jean, 176–177
Aunt Jemima stereotype, 97, 105, 239n112
au pairs, 23

unfree labor, 53. *See also* slavery
UN General Assembly, 246n63
UN Human Rights Council, 253n10
uniforms, 70, 90
unions
 domestic workers' actions in, 144
 failures of, 7, 145–146, 148, 229n92
 support for laws specific to domestic
  workers, 38, 56–57
 See also specific union
United Kingdom
 colonial households, 90–96
 master and servant law in, 83–84, 227n22
 servants and slaves in the law in, 50–54,
  227n29
 wages and working time in, 116–117
United States
 civil rights movement, 5–6
 cookbooks from, 87, 88–90, 96–97,
  102–104; by African Americans, 97,
  98–100, 104–108, 109
 Dred Scott case, 85
 employment and enslavement in, 53–54
 failure to ratify, 133
 "girl" to address workers in, 71
 racial profile of domestic workers in, 57
 in standard setting process, 30, 128
 status *vs.* contract in, 50
 See also African Americans
Universal Declaration of Human Rights, 26,
 221n28
universality, 118
urbanization, 55–56
Uruguay, 25, 132

vacation pay, 8
vacations (employers'), 121
VanderVelde, Lea, 51, 52, 85
Veneziani, Bruno, 227n22
Verge, Pierre, 147
Vienna Convention on Diplomatic
 Relations, 214, 245n60
violence and killings, 3, 162–163, 165
Vosko, Leah, 117, 243n19

wages and pay
 deductions: for alleged damage, 64; for
  room and board, 63
 equal pay, 18, 27, 244n32
 gifts in lieu of, 27–28, 151, 152
 lack of (forced labor), 150–155
 lower for longer hours, 63–64
 low levels of, 63, 222n5
 minimum wages, 27, 63, 121, 156, 159,
  172
 overtime pay, 64, 116, 117
 pay periods, 89
 racialized hierarchies in, 64
 slavery and, 63
waiters, 92–93
Walsum, Sarah van, 64
Webb, Beatrice and Sidney, 6–8, 116–117,
 235n19
Weber, Max, 147
Westphalian sovereignty (state sovereignty),
 214
WIEGO (Women in Informal Employment:
 Globalizing and Organizing network),
 28–29, 214
Wilkinson, Frank, 50, 68–69
Williams, Patricia J., 112
Witbooi, Myrtle, 29–30, 132, 137–138
worker (term), 181
working hours, 90, 93, 239n82
 boundarilessness of, 61–63, 65, 101,
  150–155, 156, 238n81
 compared to other workers, 235n19
 ILO's tackling of, 116–122, 130, 172,
  230n93
"work like any other" and "work like no
 other," 19, 26, 79, 134, 172
World Bank, 211

Yacob, Halimah, 26, 30, 32, 123, 124
Yates, Charlotte, 244n32
Yeates, Nicola, 251n99

zero hours contracts, 119
Zumbansen, Peer, 44

CPSIA information can be obtained
at www.ICGtesting.com
Printed in the USA
BVHW040439280519
549332BV00042BA/544/P